What Animals Mean
in the Fiction of Modernity

'*What Animals Mean in the Fiction of Modernity* is a fresh and incisive contribution to scholarship in human–animal studies: intelligent and theoretically informed, engaging and highly readable...What *do* animals mean? The animal question is a fascinatingly important one, and Armstrong has done as much as is humanly possible to help answer it.'

Randy Malamud, *Georgia State University, USA*

What Animals Mean in the Fiction of Modernity argues that nonhuman animals, and stories about them, have always been closely bound up with the conceptual and material work of modernity.

In the first half of the book, Philip Armstrong examines the function of animals and animal representations in four classic narratives: *Robinson Crusoe*, *Gulliver's Travels*, *Frankenstein* and *Moby-Dick*. He then goes on to explore how these stories have been re-worked, in ways that reflect shifting social and environmental forces, by later novelists, including H.G. Wells, Upton Sinclair, D.H. Lawrence, Ernest Hemingway, Franz Kafka, Brigid Brophy, Bernard Malamud, Timothy Findley, Will Self, Margaret Atwood, Yann Martel and J.M. Coetzee.

What Animals Mean also introduces readers to new developments in the study of human-animal relations. It does so by attending to the significance of animals to humans, and to animals' own purposes or designs; to what animals mean to us, and to what they mean to do, and how they mean to live.

Philip Armstrong teaches at the University of Canterbury, Aotearoa, where he is Co-Director of the New Zealand Centre for Human-Animal Studies.

D1312866

What Animals Mean
in the Fiction of Modernity

Philip Armstrong

Routledge
Taylor & Francis Group

LONDON AND NEW YORK

First published 2008
by Routledge
2 Park Square, Milton Park, Abingdon, Oxon OX14 4RN

Simultaneously published in the USA and Canada
by Routledge
711 Third Avenue, New York, NY 10017, USA

Routledge is an imprint of the Taylor & Francis Group, an informa business

© 2008 Philip Armstrong

Typeset in Baskerville by
Saxon Graphics Ltd, Derby

British Library Cataloguing in Publication Data
A catalogue record for this book is available from the British Library

Library of Congress Cataloging in Publication Data
Armstrong, Philip, 1967–
What animals mean in the fiction of modernity / Philip Armstrong.
p. cm.
Includes bibliographical references and index.
1. Animals in literature. 2. English fiction—History and criticism.
3. American fiction—History and criticism. 4. Human-animal
relationships in literature. 5. Animals—Social aspects. 6. Modernism
(Literature)—Great Britain. 7. Modernism (Literature)—United
States. I. Title.
PR830.A54A76 2008
823.009362–dc22

2007036625

ISBN 10: 0–415–35838–8 (hbk)
ISBN 10: 0–415–35839–6 (pbk)
ISBN 10: 0–203–00456–6 (ebk)

ISBN 13: 978–0–415–35838–5 (hbk)
ISBN 13: 978–0–415–35839–2 (pbk)
ISBN 13: 978–0–203–00456–2 (ebk)

Contents

Acknowledgements   vi

Introduction   1

1   The Inhuman Fictions of Swift and Defoe   5

2   Gulliver, Frankenstein, Moreau   49

3   Rendering the Whale   99

4   Modernism and the Hunt for Redemption   134

5   Animal Refugees in the Ruins of Modernity   170

Notes   226
References   235
Index   249

Acknowledgements

I am very grateful to those who provided scholarly advice and influence during the writing of this book: they include Erica Fudge, Erin Mackie, Randy Malamud, Jed Meyer, Michael Moon, Peter Nicholls, Annie Potts, Tanja Schwalm, Kenneth Shapiro, Laurence Simmons and Helen Tiffin. Sincere thanks to Mandala White, Creon Upton and Sally Borrell for their meticulous work as research assistants, and to Patrick Evans, Erin Mackie, Howard McNaughton and Maureen Montgomery for their personal and institutional support as successive heads of my department and school. Acknowledgement is also due to the Marsden Fund of the Royal Society of New Zealand for financial help granted as part of the project 'Kararehe: The Animal in Culture in Aotearoa New Zealand'.

What Animals Mean in the Fiction of Modernity is fundamentally concerned with sympathy, sentiment and human–animal relationships, so my greatest debts are to those who have influenced me in these areas of thought and feeling. Profound thanks are due to my immediate family, Ian, Doff, David and Susan Armstrong, and to my friends Anthony Terry, Nichola Kriek, Hans Kriek, John O'Connor and Faith Potts. I want to acknowledge with sorrow several who passed away while I was writing this book: Justin Lalor, whose love for nature was an early influence on mine; Matthew Oswin, who I remember coolly liberating a frog from our school science class; and also Cody, Dodos, Mottie and Tui, who each taught me a thing or two about animal agency.

Most of all I am indebted to Annie Potts, without whose inspiration and influence I would never have attempted such a book, and to Lola, who kept me company during long hours of reading and writing. *What Animals Mean in the Fiction of Modernity* is dedicated to them.

Parts of this volume have appeared elsewhere. Chapter 3 draws together arguments from the following publications: '"Leviathan is a Skein of Networks": Translating Nature and Culture in *Moby-Dick*', *ELH*, 71 (2004): 1,039–63; '*Moby-Dick* and Compassion', *Society and Animals* 12, 1 (2004): 19–38; and 'What Animals Mean, in *Moby-Dick*, for Example', *Textual*

Practice 19, 1 (2005): 1–19. I am grateful to these journals for permission to republish this work here.

Finally, many thanks to Peter Zokosky for permission to reproduce his wonderful painting as the cover image.

Introduction

An animal sits at a desk, writing. A common enough scene, but seldom described that way. What does this animal writing mean? Perhaps, among other things, it means to remind us of our debt to other animals, materially and conceptually.

In studies of literature and the visual arts, in cultural history and the analysis of popular culture, the extent to which human–animal relations have been central to the mission of modernity is becoming apparent. As a resource for thought and knowledge, the generic notion of 'the animal' has provided modernity with a term against which to define its most crucial categories: 'humanity', 'culture', 'reason', and so on. Meanwhile, in material terms, the use and pursuit of actual animals has facilitated and motivated the unrelenting expansionism of modern cultures.

For many contemporary scholars the starting place for considering the relationship between modernity, animals and cultural representation is John Berger's essay 'Why Look at Animals?' (1980). From his Marxist perspective, Berger argues that the relation between human and animal was utterly reconfigured by the emergence of industrial capitalism. In particular he suggests that a profound separation between humanity and the natural world was instituted, resulting in the alienation of modern citizens from a working engagement with nature, the isolation of urban dwellers, the artificiality of contemporary relations to animals, and the degradation of the non-human world by industrial technologies. Like all large histories this account is too generalizing, partial and tendentious to be trusted without question. Subsequent work in this area has therefore worked hard to complicate and revise Berger's view of modernity in various ways.[1]

In Renaissance studies, for example, scholars have explored how the emergence of an early modern cultural and material economy, and a concomitant reinvention of the human, was already producing complex reconfigurations of received understandings of animals before the heyday of either capitalism or industrialization (Fudge 1999). Others have demonstrated that the separation from the animal, which underwrote the ascendancy of the modern subject during the Enlightenment, must be seen as both recent and in many ways extremely fragile (Thomas 1984, Bate 2000). Further studies have shown how the representation, consumption and management of animals in the nineteenth century did not always facilitate, but sometimes resisted European imperialism, scientific empiricism and capitalism, along with their more oppressive counterparts: colonial racism, slavery, indigenous dispossession and environmental depredation.[2] Reassessments and reinterpretations of the animal's place in contemporary contexts are also proliferating.

The aim of this book is to contribute to this unfolding cultural history of the human–animal relation in the context of globalizing modernity. It will seek to do so both horizontally and vertically, to explore the terrain both topographically and geologically, as it were. Thus, although it progresses from the eighteenth century to the twenty-first, *What Animals Mean* treats a relatively small number of literary texts as core samples whose examination permits a more layered analysis of human–animal relations in specific times and places than a broader survey might allow. My approach will be contextual, with a particular focus on three elements: the relationship between human–animal narratives and the social practices and conditions from which they emerge; the evidence of exchanges between human and non-human forms of agency; and the documentation of shifts in the emotional and affective engagements between humans and other animals.

By means of these three emphases I hope to go beyond reading animals as screens for the projection of human interests and meanings, which until recently was the predominant way of treating cultural representations of animals. Claude Lévi-Strauss famously declared animals 'good to think with' (1963: 89), implying that animality mediates the construction of humanity, so that animals mean whatever cultures mean by them. Scholars in the rapidly-developing field known as 'Animal Studies' or 'Human–Animal Studies', however, reject the anthropocentric assumptions of such an approach. They are interested in attending not just to what animals mean to humans, but to what they mean themselves; that is, to the ways in which animals might have significances, intentions and effects quite beyond the designs of human beings. The possibility of treating non-humans as something other than passive objects of study was anticipated in a paper by Donna Haraway that espoused the recognition of the non-human world as a 'witty agent and actor', a 'coding trickster', an active collaborator in the construction of meaning, or a rebellious obstacle to it (1991: 201). As Erica Fudge puts it, in this type of analysis, '[w]hat is at stake ultimately is our own ability to think beyond ourselves' (2002a: 22). Similarly, Steve Baker describes 'the postmodern animal', which 'does not so much set itself against meaning as operate independently of it' (2000: 82).

Of course novelists, scientists and scholars can never actually access, let alone reproduce, what other animals mean on their own terms. Humans can only represent animals' experience through the mediation of cultural encoding, which inevitably involves a reshaping according to our own intentions, attitudes and preconceptions. Hence, in seeking to go beyond the use of animals as mere mirrors for human meaning, our best hope is to locate the 'tracks' left by animals in texts, the ways cultural formations are affected by the materiality of animals and their relationships with humans (Simons 2002: 5–6, 85–7). As human–animal geographers Chris Philo and Chris Wilbert argue:

> If we concentrate solely on how animals are represented, the impression is that animals are merely passive surfaces on to which human groups inscribe imaginings and orderings of all kinds. In our view, it is also vital to give credence to the practices that are folded into the making of representations, and – at the core of the matter – to ask how animals themselves may figure in these practices. This question duly raises broader concerns about non-human agency, about the agency of animals, and the extent to which we can say that animals destabilize, transgress or even resist our human orderings, including spatial ones (2000: 5).

But to speak of 'non-human agency' immediately invites the allegation of anthropomorphism. Surely such a notion imputes to non-humans a capacity – traditionally considered unique to human beings – for conscious planning, decision-making and choice? However, as Jonathan Burt points out, mobilizing a concept of animal agency need not imply 'assumptions about what specifically constitutes animal subjectivity or interiority, nor that there is necessarily a sense that the animal wills any specific change in human beings' (2002: 31). Indeed, Philo and Wilbert turn the charge of anthropomorphism on its head, asking instead whether evidence of animal resistance in cultural texts and practices might not destabilize taken-for-granted assumptions about how agency works in the first place: 'many people (outside the West, but in it too) have started to deconstruct seemingly obvious claims about the privileged status of the human, in contradistinction to the animal, as *the* source of agency in the world' (2000: 15–16). Moreover, they argue, the assumption that agency – the capacity to effect change – necessarily requires a combination of rational thought and conscious intention depends in the first place upon an Enlightenment humanist paradigm within which these traits came to define the human as such. Hence, the allegation of anthropomorphism itself derives from an anthropocentric and ethnocentric understanding about what agency is. A reconceptualization of agency, on the other hand, might facilitate a mode of analysis that does not reduce the animal to a blank screen for the projection of human meaning, and might offer productive new ways of accounting for the material influence of the non-human animal upon humans, and *vice versa*.

The ways in which animals are understood and treated by humans must also be considered in relation to the ways we feel towards them. In documenting the potent but sometimes evanescent dispositions that link humans and animals over time, the study of fiction has a special role to play. For Raymond Williams, literature provides 'often the only fully available articulation . . . of structures of feeling which as living processes are much more widely experienced' (1977: 133). Literary texts testify to the shared emotions, moods and thoughts of people in specific historical moments and places, as they are influenced by – and as they influence – the surrounding sociocultural forces and systems. Williams introduces the phrase 'structure of feeling' to denote a 'lived' or 'practical consciousness' of meanings and values, prior to their explicit articulation, definition, classification or rationalization in fixed or official ideologies: 'it is a kind of feeling and thinking which is indeed social and material but each in an embryonic phase before it can become fully articulate and defined exchange' (130–1). In what follows, I will be concerned to identify the various structures of feeling that characterize human–animal relations during the emergence, zenith and decline of Western modernity.

In order to achieve coherence while attempting to move between a very broad cultural history and very specific examples, I have chosen familiar texts, classics in many cases, which however share two features: the inclusion of human–animal relations as significant components of their representational structures, and an engagement with the outwardly expanding, imperialist or globalizing dimension of modernity. My opening chapter examines the two most famous eighteenth-century narratives, Daniel Defoe's *Robinson Crusoe* and Jonathan Swift's *Gulliver's Travels*. The second and third chapters analyse similarly exemplary fictions from the nineteenth century by Mary Shelley, Herman Melville, and H. G. Wells. And the last two chapters survey how the human–animal narratives dealt with so far – the Robinsonnade, the Swiftian reversal, the Frankensteinian experiment and the hunt for the White Whale – influence and are reshaped by modernist and postmodern writers during the twentieth century and at the start of the twenty-first.[3]

1 The Inhuman Fictions of Swift and Defoe

Two travellers go on separate journeys. Both are marooned on alien shores, where they encounter exotic peoples and species. They have to make do with unfamiliar foods, company and clothing. They consume the animals they discover and use their skins for clothing, but also, seeking consolation for the absence of other humans, befriend them. One keeps pets, the other is kept as a pet; one uses empirical observation to master the natural world, the other is scrutinized as a natural-historical specimen; one breeds a stock of domesticated animals, the other is offered a mate to establish a breeding stock of his own kind.

Comparison between the adventures of Robinson Crusoe and Lemuel Gulliver highlights two features integral to Enlightenment modernity.[1] The first is mobility. By turning their gaze beyond Europe, towards unfamiliar lives and locations, Enlightenment thinkers developed their notions about the world and the place of humans in it. The epistemological movements of the period were inextricably entwined with material expansion: trade, navigation, cartography, colonialism, slavery. And the fictional voyages created by Defoe and Swift drew extensively upon the experiences of real-life travellers – for example those of explorer, adventurer, trader, slaver and pirate William Dampier, and of Alexander Selkirk, the marooned Scottish sailor who survived four years alone on one of the Juan Fernandez Islands (Rowse 2000: 59–60).

The second feature of Enlightenment modernity demonstrated by all these adventures is the formative role played by human–animal relations. Whether as a concept (*animality*) or as a brute reality (*actual animals*), non-humans play a constitutive role in the preoccupations of the modern enterprise: its relentless mobility (spatial, social, economic and epistemological), its development of commodity culture, its promotion of new scientific paradigms and its determination to reconceptualize the human. The animal imagery created by Defoe and Swift – Crusoe in his goatskins with his parrot and dog; Gulliver swallowing forkfuls of tiny cows, struggling in the affectionate grip of a gigantic monkey, or talking politics with well-bred horses – have enduring appeal because they embody this relationship.[2]

The Beast-Machine

> It was as a comment on *human* nature that the concept of 'animality' was devised (Thomas 1984: 41).

> It is possible to oppose man to other living things, and at the same time to organize the complex – and not always edifying – economy of relations between men and animals, only because something like an animal life has been separated within man, only because his distance and proximity to the animal have been measured and recognized first of all in the closest and most intimate place (Agamben 2004: 15–16).

As Keith Thomas concludes, the rethinking of human nature during the late seventeenth and early eighteenth centuries occurred in reference to animality as its accompanying term. In this sense modern 'man' depends upon what Giorgio Agamben refers to as 'anthropophorous' animality: the conceptual animal that produces or bears the concept of the human as such (2004: 12).

In medieval Europe the security of the division between human and animal rested upon theological and moral qualities. Christian dogma, exemplified by Augustine and Aquinas, saw human nature as a conflict between the animal passions of the mortal body and the divine aspirations of the immortal soul, and as subject to an eschatological imperative to transcend the former in favour of the latter. This version of humanity was guaranteed by a divinely created chain of being that ordered the world, material and immaterial, into a hierarchy which placed animals below humans, and angels above. Hence, while in the mortal, fallen world humanity was constituted by an animality at once beneath and internal to it, the true and immortal nature of the human was emphatically non-animal. Theology licensed, indeed demanded, the subjugation not only of the human's own animality, but also of the non-human animals over whom Adam and Eve were granted dominion (Thomas 1984: 17–30, 36–41).

Humanism, however – first emerging within Christian philosophy, but eventually arrogating the cultural dominance of its theological parent – required a reconfiguration of this bifold nature of 'man'. Over the course of the seventeenth and eighteenth centuries, the growing authority of science and philosophy gradually but inexorably shifted the distinction between the human animal and all others away from the former's unique access to divine grace and possession of an immortal soul, towards a more anthropocentric concept of mind, as characterized by the capacity for rational thought. Again, animals were integral to this movement – literally, as tools for scientific experimentation, and conceptually, as a control group against which to prove the uniqueness of human intellect and agency.

René Descartes provided the paradigm for this extreme remaking of the human via manipulation of the animal. *Cogito ergo sum*: for Descartes the ability to think is the precondition for human being, and in order to apprehend the distinctive nature of human thought, Descartes produces his infamous comparison with animals. The exceptional esteem accorded to a particular species of human intellect demands a correlative underestimation of the cognitive capacities of non-human animals, who are thus reduced to mindless automatons, indistinguishable from perfectly crafted machines. Animals 'have no intelligence at all' writes Descartes; when they act, it is merely 'nature working in them according to the disposition of their organs', just as a machine operates not of its own volition but according to the design of its maker: '[t]hus a clock, composed only of wheels and springs, can count the hours and measure the time' (1960 [1637]: 81–2). As Thomas points out, many early modern intellectuals, inspired by a new 'host of mechanical marvels – clocks, watches, moving figures and automata of every kind – [were] well prepared to believe that animals were also machines . . .' (1984: 33–4). The attractiveness of Descartes' comparison was that it caught the flavour of modernity, and in particular the preoccupation with technological and temporal advancement. More importantly, the material agenda of early modern and Enlightenment culture required this kind of absolute distinction: 'Descartes' explicit aim had been to make men "lords and possessors of nature"', and 'the most powerful argument for the Cartesian position was that it was the best possible rationalization for the way man actually treated animals' (34). Accordingly, in the century following Descartes, the definition of modern 'man' according to a strict demarcation between animals and humans, and predicated on the possession or absence of rationality, achieved a growing authority in scientific and philosophical circles (Hulme and Jordanova 1990).

Yet as Thomas also argues, the extent and manner of the adoption of the Cartesian paradigm within the larger cultural milieu must be measured with great care. In Britain, a flurry of interest in this topic was given added momentum by the publication of a popular English translation of Descartes in 1694 (Shugg 1968). But while some devout proponents of the 'new science' advanced the Cartesian model, the greater part of English writing on the topic scrutinized it sceptically and, more often than not, rejected it. The rhetorical vehicle for this debate was provided by narratives about humans and animals, especially those that carried traces of dirt and blood from material relationships between species.

Non-Apes, Non-Horses, Non-Humans

The commonest of such vehicles was the horse. According to a long-standing convention, a man on horseback represents reason reining in the passions, while the inverted form, a horse comically riding a man, signifies the overcoming of reason by the passions (Rivero, in Swift 2002 [1726]: 192). Either way, the relation between the human and the equine provided an immediately recognizable image of the bifold nature of the human as it was commonly understood: animal flesh and immortal soul; brute body and knowing, judging mind. It recurred as a syllogism commonly used in schools: '[m]an is a rational animal. No horse is rational. Only rational animals are capable of discipline' (Weiner 2000: 15). '*Homo est animal rationale*: no one could study elementary logic anywhere in the British Isles in the generation before *Gulliver* without encountering this formula', most often 'given without comment or explanation as the obviously correct formula for man's distinctive nature' (Crane 1962: 245). Such micro-narratives – man rides horse, horse rides man – often inform and give shape to philosophical abstractions, but they always owe their self-evident authority to human–animal practices. Prior to the nineteenth century, no animal was more central to the commerce of everyday European life than the horse, as a mode of transport, agricultural machine, agent of communication, weapon of war and tool of colonization. European states rode to national prosperity and global power on the back of the horse (Wintle 1994).

Gulliver's Travels deploys the inverted form of this long-established emblem. In Book 4, it is not *homo* but the equine Houyhnhnm that is *animal rationale* – 'their grand Maxim is, to cultivate *Reason*, and to be wholly governed by it' – in contrast to the hominid Yahoo, whom Gulliver portrays as the embodiment of irrational, carnal appetite (Swift 2002 [1726]: 219–23, 225). Although the reader is never actually asked to imagine a Houyhnhnm astride the back of a Yahoo, Gulliver does see an 'old Steed, who seemed to be of Quality', riding in a sledge pulled by four of his Yahoo beasts of burden (196). Swift suggests the reversal linguistically as well. 'Houyhnhnm', presumably, should be pronounced like the word 'human' (with the final consonants swapped) as if spoken by a horse. And just as the equine whinny provides a language for the Houyhnhnms' perfectly rational horse-sense, human speech transforms into the irrational vocalizations that give the Yahoos their name.

This apparently simple reversal of the conventional emblem, however, proves on examination to be fraught with complexities. Some scholars consider that Swift intends Gulliver's high estimation of Houyhnhnm society to be taken seriously, as a neo-Stoic utopia based on the rational disposition of civic virtue. Others point out that Gulliver has become, in the course of his travels, a wildly unreliable observer, whose perceptions are distorted to the point of insanity after the first three voyages. According to this perspective, when considered outside the narrator's idealized view of them, the Houyhnhnms are ascetic fascists, exemplars of a dispassionate extremism resulting from a moral code dependent on strict ratiocination.[3] I suggest that the meaning of Swift's extended portrait of equine rationality can be clarified only by placing it in context: first in relation to the preceding three parts of the *Travels*, and second within a wider cultural debate regarding the superimposed binary oppositions: reason/passion and human/animal.

Gulliver's third voyage, for example, provides the most direct satire against Descartes and other proponents of the new science, and the concomitant exaggeration of the distinction between animal body and rational mind. The most evidently Cartesian culture anywhere in the

Travels is that of Laputa, the flying island founded upon a scientific imperative to transcend the material world, whose gentry have their heads permanently 'reclined either to the Right, or the Left; one of their Eyes turned
inward, and the other directly up to the Zenith'. Preoccupied by 'intense
Speculation', obsessively contemplating the worlds of inner thought or
transcendent space, the Laputans so neglect their material conditions that
they require servants to strike them with rattles periodically to remind
them of their proximity to other people or to physical risks. Without this,
the typical Laputan is 'so wrapped up in Cogitation, that he is in manifest
danger of falling down every Precipice' (Swift 2002 [1726]: 133–4). The
subjectivity proposed by the Cartesian *cogito* here reduces the human body
to an inconvenient drag on the mind, an unfortunate material residue
capable only of precipitating a distracted intellect into physical pratfalls.

Even when the Laputans are forced to deal with any aspect of the body,
they do so according to mathematical principles. For example, diet:
Gulliver is served 'Mutton, cut into a Aequilateral Triangle, a piece of Beef
into a Rhomboides, and a Pudding into a Cycloid', resulting in an
'Indisposition that held me some Days' (Swift 2002 [1726]: 135–6). The
same problems occur with clothing: the king's tailor measures Gulliver's
'altitude' with a quadrant and 'the Dimensions and Out-Lines' of his body
with a ruler and compass, but when the clothes come they are 'very ill
made, and quite out of shape' (136). As for Laputan architecture: '[t]heir
Houses are very ill built, with Walls Bevil, without one Right Angle in any
Apartment, and this defect ariseth from the Contempt they bear to practical Geometry' (137). Laputan intellectual calculus proves imperfect in
proportion to its engagement with the material body and environment.

However the divorce between mental and bodily phenomena on Laputa
merely exaggerates Gulliver's own tendency to lapse into a kind of body
dysmorphia. Returning from Brobdingnag, his psychological sense of his
own anatomy is skewed. Having grown accustomed to the gigantic proportions of those around him, he keeps overestimating his own stature –
bending down to enter his house for fear of striking his head, stooping
below his wife's knees to embrace her, and attempting to pick up his daughter by the waist in one hand (Swift 2002 [1726]: 124–5). Similarly, coming
home from Houyhnhnmland after his long immersion in equine culture,
he speaks in a whinnying tone and trots like a horse (235, 241). In this
regard, Gulliver – 'a Person of much Curiosity and easy Belief' (151) whose
name hints at his gullible introjection of the values of the two alien cultures
he admires most – provides another instance of that disease of modern
humanity which Swift diagnoses in Laputa: the devaluation of the body at
the expense of an abstract notion of intellectual transcendence. Gulliver's
own growing contempt for human flesh is evident in his horrified depic-
tions of dermatological pathologies in Brobdingnag, and his disgusted
anatomization of the Yahoos (93–4, 98–9, 189–90).

The Yahoo–Gulliver–Houyhnhnm relation thus occurs as a culmination
of Swift's critique of the opposition and hierarchy put in place by the

Cartesian view of the relationship between reasoning mind and sensual body. But it must also be considered in the light of a related challenge that targets the Cartesian distinction between human and animal on the basis of the former's unique possession of rationality. Throughout the *Travels*, and most obviously in the fourth voyage, Swift destabilizes the privileged relationship between reason and the human that provides the crux of Descartes' formulation. He does this in two symmetrical ways: through Gulliver's portrayal of the Houyhnhnms as a species embodying virtuous reason conjoined to an indisputably non-human body, and through his attitude to the Yahoos, in whom, despite their hominid forms, Gulliver can recognize no sign of any rational or moral capacity whatsoever.[4]

A sustained inter-implication of the two anti-Cartesian conceits described above – one that mocks the supremacy of reason, and another its unique possession by humans – thus structures Gulliver's final voyage. It is within this context, I suggest, that the moral character of the Houyhnhnms must be considered, since they represent both aspects of Swift's anti-Cartesianism simultaneously. While clearly embodying the displacement of rationality from the human form, they also demonstrate its unreliability as an ultimate source of virtue. The faults apparent in Houyhnhnm society, indeed, arise from an overestimation of rationality as the basis for social division. Just as certain strains in Enlightenment thought took rationality as the measure of full humanity, thereby excluding those found wanting (women, the poor, non-Europeans), the Houyhnhnms believe that 'it is *Reason* only that maketh a Distinction of Persons', using abstract ratios and principles to regulate marriage, the production and distribution of offspring, the education of the young, and servant-master relationships (Swift 2002 [1726]: 226).[5] The same application of rationality as the measure of all things applies to the Houyhnhnms' treatment of others, most obviously the Yahoos. Given the anthropomorphism with which the latter are described, the discussion in the Houyhnhnm General Assembly of a plan to exterminate them cannot help but evoke genocidal implications – an effect not far removed from the black humour of Swift's 'Modest Proposal' (1969 [1729]), which recommended the consumption of Irish infants as a way of easing that country's poverty while at the same time answering its demand for food (Hawes 1991; Rawson 2001).

Ultimately, when placed alongside the Cartesian debates characteristic of English letters during the first part of the eighteenth century, neither Yahoos nor Houyhnhnms should be considered as portraits of *the human*, ideal or otherwise, in the sense given to that term by the Enlightenment. Neither indeed are they *animals*, according to the Enlightenment understanding of that accompanying term. They are something more like Locke's 'shape of an ass with reason', which the philosopher insists must be considered 'different from either that of man or beast . . . a species of an animal between, or distinct from both' (1997 [1689]: I, 134).[6] Furthermore, having lived so long and so gullibly with these two (non-species, Gulliver also is no longer human; neither has he become an animal, properly speaking. Instead, Gulliver's radical mental and bodily unease at the conclusion of his final voyage demonstrates the conceptual disarray that Swift perceived to be endemic to the category of the human as produced by Enlightenment thought. This 'modern man' cannot conceive of himself as a reasoning animal body like the Houyhnhnms; nor do his pretensions permit him to inhabit the world as a bare, forked animal like a Yahoo. In keeping with their satirical function, then, the Yahoos and Houyhnhnms – unlike the Cartesian beast-machine, or even Locke's rational ass – do not function to support, define, give shape to or bear the human as a concept or category. Rather they demolish, unfasten, annul, delegitimize or subvert it. Instead of being anthropophoric, then, their role is anthropoluotic.[7] The modern notion of *homo* as *animal rationale* evaporates under Swift's scorching gaze, and leaves nothing behind. No longer defined by a theological regulation of the relation between the spiritual and the animal, yet still unable to settle itself convincingly into one domain or the other, the modern category of the human fractures and dissipates even as it begins its ascent to dominance.

Animals and the Animal

In dismantling 'man', the early eighteenth-century English literary interrogation of the Enlightenment simultaneously deconstructs the crucial companion term, 'animal'. Insisting upon the ways in which different animals and varying animal practices call into doubt the magisterial opposition of these two abstract categories, Swift, Defoe and others undermine a conceptual assumption central to modernity and humanism alike.

In some of his last work, Jacques Derrida asserted that use of a general and singular concept of 'the Animal' signals the 'complicit, continued and organized involvement' of European philosophy since Descartes 'in a veritable war of the species', insofar as it attempts to confine

> within this catch-all concept, within this vast encampment of the animal, in this general singular, within the strict enclosure of this definite article ('the Animal' and not 'animals'), as in a virgin forest, a zoo, a hunting or fishing ground, a paddock or an abattoir, a space of domestication . . . *all the living things* that man does not recognize as his fellows, his neighbours, or his brothers (2002: 399–402).

Derrida indicates the constraints of the modern notion of 'the Animal' – the same limits that allow the concept to do the ideological work of defining 'Man' – by beginning the impossible task of listing all the material practices and contexts within which humans encounter different species (Fudge 2002a: 164).

The animal–human reversals of Gulliver's first two voyages demonstrate the same effect: that of a deconstructive, anthropoluotic oscillation between the singular concept of 'animality' – with its anthropophorous function in

[handwritten margin note: link / use with Goblin Market.]

defining humanity – and the multiple categories to which animals are assigned by the material practices of human societies. On first landing in Lilliput, Gulliver awakens to find he is bound and netted like some gigantic wild beast. His departure from the island is motivated by the realization that the Lilliputians, instead of seeing him as a human being, think of him as a beast of burden or a warhorse, and accordingly plan to mutilate him to keep him under control. In Brobdingnag, Gulliver's survival amongst the giant inhabitants depends entirely upon the various animal categories they apply to him, each of which invites different practices. Initially he is taken for a pest, and spared the fate of vermin not because he is recognized as human, but because he is transferred into a different category of non-human: first that of a sideshow or circus exotic, then that of a pet. In these ludicrous narratives, the singular category relied on by the Cartesian paradigm inevitably multiplies into different kinds of animal, treated according to their varying lived relationships with human beings.

The same effect occurs in *Robinson Crusoe*. Defoe's fiction puts pressure on the abstract distinction between man and animal, and the abstract concepts of rationality and language upon which this depends, by imagining their application in practical terms. As Crusoe settles into life on the island, his attitude changes from an initial wonder and fear to something much more appropriate to one of Descartes' 'lords and possessors of nature':

> It would have made a Stoick smile to have seen, me and my little Family sit down to Dinner; there was my Majesty the Prince and Lord of the whole Island; I had the Lives of all my Subjects at my absolute Command. I could hang, draw, give Liberty, and take it away, and no Rebels among all my Subjects.
>
> Then to see how like a King I din'd too all alone, attended by my Servants; Poll, as if he had been my Favourite, was the only Person permitted to talk to me. My Dog who was now grown very old and crazy, and had found no Species to multiply his Kind upon, sat always at my Right Hand, and two Cats, one on one Side the Table, and one on the other, expecting now and then a Bit from my Hand, as a Mark of special Favour (Defoe 1994 [1719]: 108).

Crusoe's establishment of dominion over the island is mediated and represented via his everyday relation to animals, just as his earlier feelings of desolation were. His assumption of 'absolute Command' echoes the kind of mastery that Descartes' followers claimed over non-human nature: authority over life and death, the right to inflict suffering and to suppress resistance. But of course Crusoe's lordship over nature is thoroughly ironized. And this self-mockery, in turn, depends upon the juxtaposition of the Cartesian human–animal relation with another, more intimate one that includes elements foreclosed by the Cartesian method: affection, anthropomorphism, sentiment, favour, sympathy. Crusoe's 'little family' represents a culture of pet-keeping that emerged as cultural compensation for the onto-logical and material separation of human from animal. According to Thomas, '[b]y 1700 all the symptoms of obsessive pet-keeping were in evidence. Pets were often fed better than the servants . . . and they became an increasingly regular feature of painted family groups' (1984: 117).

Crusoe's lordship of his island is associated with other human–animal practices as well. His mastery appears to be held by right of rationality, but he can never take it for granted. On the contrary, it must constantly be produced by the industrious application of instrumental reason.[8] '[B]y stating and squaring every thing by Reason, and by making the most rational Judgment of things, every Man may be in time Master of every mechanick Art', he asserts, going on to demonstrate how, through applied reason, he can build defences against wild animals, hunt them, domesticate them for meat and milk, and make from their hides the clothing that marks him out as human (Defoe 1994 [1719]: 51). Paradoxically, then, Defoe's narrative compromises the Cartesian exaltation of reason, which, rather than a transcendent value or *a priori* distinction between humanity and animality, is instead presented as a strenuous form of labour, the product of material practices. Hence the obsessiveness with which Crusoe manages his environment: in the absence of a practical, instrumentalist relationship between the human and the non-human worlds, reason and therefore humanity (as understood in Enlightenment terms) might simply cease to pertain. This is precisely the anxiety that attaches to the story of Crusoe's real-life avatar, Alexander Selkirk.

Goat-Men

Comparison with Defoe's most important source, the story of Alexander Selkirk's sojourn on one of the Juan Fernandez Islands, demonstrates that all the features Crusoe shares with Enlightenment man – his individualist self-sufficiency, his detached and objective mode of observation, his eye for investment, and above all his rationality – were in short supply for his real-life model. Selkirk's isolation, which lasted only a sixth of the duration of Crusoe's, demonstrates a *habitus* more akin to the animal than the human, as those terms were conceived by Enlightenment humanism. In the first-hand account provided by Dampier's commander-in-chief, Woodes Rogers, Selkirk is described upon his initial appearance as 'a Man cloth'd in Goat-Skins, who look'd wilder than the first Owners of them' (Rogers 1994 [1712]: 231).

The Juan Fernandez Islands, 34 degrees south of the equator, have a climate cold enough for frosts during winter. No wonder Selkirk first appears to his rescuers in goatskins. But Crusoe's island, situated at the mouth of the Orinoco River, lies *within nine or ten Degrees of the Equinox* (Defoe 1994 [1719]: 109). So why does Crusoe also insist on wearing heavy fur pelts at all times? He takes pride in the home-made costume – a goat-skin jacket, breeches, buskins, a belt, pouches, a hat, and even 'a great clumsy ugly . . . Umbrella' (108) – which would make him, over the ensuing centuries, an instantly recognizable cultural figure. The function of this cumbersome attire, he explains earnestly, is to protect him from the extremes of the tropical climate: 'I could not bear the heat of the Sun so well when quite naked, as with some Cloaths on' (98). All the same, the texture of his dress causes him problems: 'nothing being so hurtful in these Climates, as the Rain upon the Flesh under the Cloathes', he makes himself a 'great high shapeless Cap . . . to shoot the Rain off from running into my Neck' (108). Of course, all this clothing is made extraneous by the umbrella, which 'cast off the Rains like a Penthouse, and kept off the Sun so effectually, that I could walk out in the hottest of the Weather' (99). Yet even under its shelter Crusoe does not abandon any item from his sweltering wardrobe, preferring instead to superimpose layer upon layer of animal-derived cultural vestments between his body and the elements: umbrella over cap, over jacket, over leggings, over buskins. Even he concedes the excessiveness of this sumptuary arrangement:

> tho' it is true, that the Weather was so violent hot, that there was no need of Cloaths, yet I could not go quite naked; no, tho' I had been inclin'd to it, which I was not, nor could abide the thoughts of it, tho' I was all alone (98).

Even when otherwise protected from the sun and rain, Crusoe cannot face his own nakedness. Emphatically not: habitually garrulous and repetitive though he is, Crusoe outdoes himself here – *I could not; no; I was not; nor could abide the thoughts of it* – but without telling us why.

Contemporary attitudes suggest one reason. In Defoe's time, clothes make the man, as distinct from the animal, from whom clothes are made: '[n]akedness was bestial, for clothes, like cooking, were a distinctive human attribute' (Thomas 1984: 38–9). Hence Crusoe's first act after 'rescuing' Friday from the other 'savages' is to rescue him again from savagery, this time by clothing him (Defoe 1994 [1719]: 150). His own overdressing signifies a refusal to accede to beastliness: not just because clothes hide the flesh, which like his contemporaries he considers the animal part of a man; not just because other animals do not wear clothes; but also because the production of clothing is a practice that establishes a clear relation of dominion between human and beast. 'I saved the Skins of all the Creatures that I kill'd', he remarks, going on to describe the use of these pelts to make a complete wardrobe: cap, suit, waistcoat, breeches (98).

However one detail suggests a weakness or potential reversal of Crusoe's resistance to human–animal transgressions – his bare feet: 'Stockings and Shoes I had none', he admits ruefully (Defoe 1994 [1719]: 108). Indeed, this is the gap through which the reader first glimpses unaccommodated man. It is the 'Print of a Man's naked Foot on the Shore', famously, that provides the point at which Crusoe's complacent isolation turns to face the prospect of other human intruders. Thrown into panic by this footprint,

Crusoe takes refuge in his den. But after a jittery couple of days, he is struck by the comforting thought that this could be nothing but 'the Print of my own Foot' (115). Testing his theory, he finds to his dismay that the print is larger than his own; yet the possibility makes Crusoe for a time, in his bodily nature, interchangeable with the savages who visit his island. Bare feet, metonyms for nakedness, threaten the security of the European notion of humanity: they reveal the potentially animalistic savagery of the body, but also its vulnerability – like that of an animal also – to pursuit, capture and consumption by others.

If the naked human foot leaves the imprint of wildness, savagery, animal-ity, it is only by means of certain material cultural processes, such as the treatment of flayed animal skins to produce fur and leather for clothing and shoes, that 'humanity' is preserved and assumed. So, in Swift's satire, after describing with consternation the similarity between his face and hands and those of the Yahoos, Gulliver remarks that '[t]here was the same Resemblance between our Feet . . . which I knew very well, tho' the Horses did not, because of my Shoes and Stockings'. Indeed, the Houyhnhnms so far consider his body 'very different from that of a Yahoo, for which I was obliged to my Cloaths' (Swift 2002 [1726]: 195). While he remains clothed and shod, Gulliver can conceal his bodily resemblance to the savage Yahoos. In particular, the naked foot that would betray its affinity to the Yahoo 'hind-Paw' is hidden inside a shoe, which of course makes it look like the extremity of a civilized, cultured and rational Houyhnhnm. After the secret of Gulliver's feet is revealed, his Houyhnhnm master remarks that '[h]e knew not what could be the Use of those several Clefts and Divisions in my Feet behind, that these were too soft to bear the Hardness and Sharpness of Stones without a Covering made from the Skin of some other Brute' (205). Despite the Houyhnhnms' discovery of his disguise, and their criticism of the self-shame involved in hiding the natural body, Gulliver (like Crusoe) cannot overcome his unwillingness to expose his animal-shaped body. This leads him to one of the most vertiginously ironic moments in the *Travels*: 'I considered that my Cloaths and Shoes would soon wear out, which already were in a declining Condition, and must be supplied by some Contrivance from the Hides of Yahoos or other Brutes' (200). Although eventually he finds other animals with softer pelts to make into clothing, he does have recourse to Yahoo leather for – what else? – his shoes (232–3). He uses the skins of hominid beings to conceal his own hominid form; he covers his limbs with the pelts of Yahoos to hide his own pelt's similarity to theirs. This logic works only because the practice of clothing creates a human–animal distinction: the animal is by definition what gets made into clothing, and the human is the one who wears it.

Yet clothing can be a supple and two-sided signifier. For Crusoe his layers of pelts mark him as a human, and a civilized one, but from the other side of the beach, encountering Crusoe's forerunner in his goatskins, Rogers' impression is of a wild goatiness. As for Selkirk's feet, after four years of chasing goats unshod, they became as hardened as the hooves of the goats he preyed on, 'and it was some time before he could wear Shoes after we found him; for not being us'd to any so long, his Feet swell'd when he came first to wear' em again' (Rogers 1994 [1712]: 233). In Swift's satirically reversed world, hooves might be evidence of reason rather than brutality, of equine cultivation, but goats are not Houyhnhnms, and within the harsh realities of British maritime enterprise, Selkirk's horny soles convey an animalistic ferity.[9]

There are other distinctions between Crusoe and his real-life model, which also depend upon their divergent relations to specific kinds of animal, as these are shaped by different practices. Whereas Defoe's hero continues to hunt with his gun throughout his time on the island, having employed his accountant's prudence to conserve his powder, Selkirk squanders his firepower and quickly degenerates from a human hunter into a wild predator. In the process he acquires such speed and agility that his rescuers are astonished to see him outstrip their dogs in pursuit of prey. And famously, Rogers also describes how Selkirk found a remedy for his solitude by singing and dancing with his goats and cats (1994 [1712]: 233). One way of understanding this exchange is to imagine Selkirk teaching his domestic animals to sing and dance like an eighteenth-century Scotsman; the other – which seems more likely – is to envisage a further instance of Selkirk's ferity: a dispersal of rational, individual humanity into the corporeal intensities of the herd, something akin to the assemblage described by Deleuze and Guattari as becoming-animal, a movement 'from the individuated animal to the pack or to a collective multiplicity' (cited in Baker 2000: 117). Crusoe, by contrast, conscientiously maintains the boundaries established by his culture, for example by attempting to replicate the structure of the bourgeois family, the social mechanism by which modern individualist identity is produced. Nevertheless, in describing his animal companions as both family members and subjects, he keeps them subservient and distanced, deliberately ironizing his own indulgent anthropomorphisms. As long as they remain in their place, within this paradigm of familial subjection, animal companions preserve rather than threaten the humanist self.

More than anything else, though, the difference in the degree of humanity or animality represented by Selkirk's and Crusoe's respective responses to the same circumstances is demonstrated by their relation to language. 'I have no Soul to speak to, or relieve me', complains Crusoe (Defoe 1994 [1719]: 50). Prior to the arrival of Friday – that is, for the first twenty-five years – he comes up with a variety of solutions, talking incessantly to God and his conscience in his prayers and moral debates, to himself and his reader in his journal, and of course to his parrot as they repeat to each other, with plaintive sympathy, the same phrases, over and over. And the instant he acquires another human companion, Crusoe begins teaching him English, starting with a name derived from the calendar he uses to bind himself into the rhythm of English social and economic life (149). For Selkirk, on the contrary, the supposedly distinctive human capacity for speech deteriorated severely in little more than four years alone. 'At his first coming on board us', writes Woodes Rogers, 'he had so much forgot his Language for want of Use, that we could scarce understand him, for he seem'd to speak his words by halves' (1994 [1712]: 234). From an Enlightenment perspective, the rapidity of Selkirk's loss of humanity is alarming; consequently, Rogers' eyewitness testimony was rapidly transformed into a parable extolling the triumph of humanist rationality over brute adversity. Only a year later, Richard Steele wrote a piece about Selkirk in *The Englishman*, in which he asserted that 'by the Force of Reason, and frequent reading of the Scriptures, and turning his Thoughts upon the Study of Navigation, after the Space of eighteen Months, he grew thoroughly reconciled to his Condition'. In Steele's account, all references to Selkirk's wild appearance, his animal agility and speed, his wild hairiness and his hooves are replaced with detailed descriptions of his farming practices and cultivated domestic pursuits. And of course any suggestion of more intimate bestial antics – singing, dancing or otherwise – are entirely removed. So too is the suggestion that Selkirk lost his linguistic ability: on the contrary, Steele emphasizes the castaway's regular 'Exercises of Devotion', which he performed aloud, in order to keep up the Faculties of Speech' (Steele 1994 [1713]: 236–7).

Dogs, Parrots and a Talking Splacknuck

Crusoe is clearly modelled upon this refashioned Selkirk, who embodies the human as *animal rationale*, but Defoe's attitude to this Enlightenment ideal is not without ambivalence. Long before publishing *Robinson Crusoe*, he took issue with the aspect of the Cartesian doctrine that denied any capacity for thought, judgement, or decision-making to non-human animals. In his *Review* of 27 March 1705, Defoe responds to the question of '[w]hether a Dog may not properly be said to THINK on Things past and to come'. He adduces a series of situations in which dogs assemble data, form judgements, and act according to a choice made: deciding at a crossroads which way a quarry has gone; coming across more food than they can eat at once and so hiding some for later; finding their way home from a distance of twenty or thirty miles; returning over land despite having made the outward journey by water; recognizing their own names; distinguishing sounds of pleasure from anger; and assisting their masters in the case of physical threat. To those who characterize all these achievements as 'instinct', Defoe replies, '[i]f this be not Thinking . . . it performs all the Parts of Thinking, that a Brute stands in need of', and 'if Instinct performs the Office of Thinking, it is Thinking in its Degree, and the Difference of the Name has no manner of Effect' (Defoe 1705). The dog, as the animal that perhaps more than any other runs to and fro between the human and animal worlds, simultaneously marking and crossing the boundary between them, here provides Defoe's challenge to the separation of human rationality from brute mechanical instinct.

In putting forward this kind of challenge to Cartesianism, Defoe and Swift were not alone. Indeed, according to Shugg, 'all [English] poets, essayists and journalists rejected the doctrine of the beast-machine' (1968: 292). Some, like Addison and Shaftesbury, agreed with Descartes that animals were not capable of reason, but insisted they must not be denied a capacity for sensation and feeling. A greater number, however, conceded to animals 'a degree of reason', and often took dogs as their example, as Defoe does (Shugg 1968: 289). Worrying away at this preoccupation of their age, Swift and Defoe both identify language as a crucial bone of contention in the Enlightenment attempt to distinguish between humans and animals on the basis of rationality. Recalling his own dog fondly, Crusoe remarks that he 'only wanted to have him talk to me, but that would not do' (Defoe 1994 [1719]: 48). For Descartes, meaningful speech provided the key indicator of the possession of rationality, and thereby of humanity. In the same chapter of the *Discourse on Method* that describes the beast-machine, Descartes declares that no animal is able to speak. Although 'magpies and parrots can utter words', they cannot 'speak, as we speak, that is to say, by showing that their words express their thoughts'. He concludes that 'this does not only show that animals have less reason than men; it shows that they have none at all' (1960 [1637]: 80–1).

Following Descartes, English philosophers (for example John Locke) and natural historians (for example John Ray) and scientists (for example Edward Tyson) would agree in defining language as a distinguishing marker of human reason (Thomas 1984: 32; Wiseman 1999: 221). Crusoe's repeated lament that he has 'no Soul to Speak to' (Defoe 1994 [1719]: 50) is therefore a shorthand for separation from other humans. However, the distinction between garrulous humans and dumb animals – the latter of course including those that only seem to speak, or to mimic speech – becomes far less clear as Crusoe's narrative proceeds. For Crusoe, as for a long list of precursors, this ambiguity attaches most vividly to the parrot.

After some effort, he succeeds in catching a young parrot, which after some years learned 'to call me by my Name very familiarly: But the Accident that follow'd tho' it be a Trifle, will be very diverting in its Place' (80). Both a familiar and a family member, the parrot mimics the presence of another 'soul', that is, a proper linguistic other, a reasoning and speaking human companion. As such, he seems at first no more than a beast-machine, like Descartes' parrots and magpies – a kind of organic recording device reproducing the sound of speech without the reasoning thought that (supposedly) accompanies it in humans. To this extent the parrot merely repeats the function of Crusoe's other archives – his balance-sheet, his journal – in providing him with the opportunity for a dialogue with an imagined other, presenting himself back to himself. The bird's name suggests this structural function: 'Poll' had been the default name for pet parrots for at least a century prior to Defoe's text.

Yet even as he introduces this most self-affirming of animal companions, Crusoe foreshadows the 'accident' through which this reassurance will be shattered – at least momentarily – by the same characteristic that produces it: the parrot's ability to utter his name. One day, far from his usual residence which he shares with his bird and other domestic companions, Crusoe is rudely startled out of his self-assurance:

> I was wak'd out of my Sleep by a Voice calling me by my Name several times, Robin, Robin, Robin Crusoe, poor Robin Crusoe, where are you Robin Crusoe? Where are you? Where have you been?
>
> I was so dead asleep at first . . . that I did not wake thoroughly, but dozing between sleeping and waking, thought I dream'd that some Body spoke to me: But as the Voice continu'd to repeat Robin Crusoe, Robin Crusoe, at last I began to wake more perfectly, and was at first dreadfully frighted, and started up in the utmost Consternation: But no sooner were my Eyes open, than I saw my Poll sitting on the Top of the Hedge; and immediately knew that it was he that spoke to me; for just in such bemoaning Language I had used to talk to him, and teach him; and he had learn'd it so perfectly, that he would sit upon my Finger, and lay his Bill close to my Face, and cry, *Poor* Robin Crusoe, *Where are you? Where have you been? How come you here?* (Defoe 1994 [1719]: 104).

Uncannily, Crusoe hears his own sense of his isolation and dislocation articulated elsewhere, in the voice of another. His organic recording device, his avian ventriloquist's dummy, has awoken eerily to a life of its own. The homely phrases become *unheimlich* – their familiar content returning in unfamiliar form – because they are simultaneously out of their usual context and yet perfectly appropriate to their new one, removed from the domestic sphere where the parrot belongs as one of Crusoe's house pets, yet disturbingly pertinent to the place they are spoken: Crusoe's home-away-from-home on the other side of the island. 'I was amazed how the Creature got thither, and then, how he should just keep about the Place, and no where else' (104). Indeed the questions '*Where are you?*' and '*How come you here?*' betray the unhomely aspect endemic even to Crusoe's more habitual home-base, echoing the castaway's underlying sense of displacement.

The more manifest fear this incident provokes is of course the possibility that the voice speaking is that of a human intruder. This effect is related to the question of place as well. The parrot's mimicry of another human, by drawing attention to Crusoe's dislocation from the circuit of European commerce, his placement beyond the reach of those social and ideological transactions within which modernity understood the human to exist, calls into question his occupation of that category. The widespread contemporary doubt regarding whether peoples located beyond the geopolitical reach of European civility were actually or fully human reappears with an ironic twist. Poll, notably, calls Crusoe by a diminutive name, a 'pet' name, Robin – indeed, the name of another bird, although one belonging to a much more homely species (to an Englishman) than its own. The comforting humanization of the animal and the discomfiting animalization of the human are here chiasmatically intertwined.

Crusoe's alarm has often been compared with Locke's well-known discussion of language, in which the parrot fulfils, initially, the same function that it does for Descartes. Locke distinguishes the parrot's ability to make 'articulate sounds' from language proper, which involves 'signs of internal conceptions': 'for parrots, and several other birds, will be taught to make articulate sounds distinct enough, which yet by no means are capable of language' (Locke 1997 [1689]: I, 427). However as Laura Brown argues, Locke's suggestion 'that language is a means of defining man', as it was for Descartes, is qualified by an anecdote recounted earlier in the essay. The story centres upon a parrot in Brazil, which 'spoke, and asked, and answered common Questions like a reasonable Creature', engaging in a dialogue that suggests understanding of the words rather than mere mimicry (Locke 1997 [1689]: I, 331). If such a sagacious bird can be imagined without being mistaken for a human, Locke suggests, there must be something other than rationality or language that distinguishes the human from other animals: the ingredient missing from this otherwise perfectly human animal is of course the human form (Brown 2001: 245–50). 'For I presume it is not the idea of a thinking or rational being alone that makes the idea of a man in most people's sense', writes Locke, 'but of a body, so and so shaped, joined to it' (1997 [1689]: I, 333). What constitutes the human, therefore, is the unique *combination* of hominoid body – which apes have, but parrots don't – and the capacity for reason and its expression in language – which a parrot might have, but which apes (supposedly) never do. Locke thus reverses Descartes' method – the separation of rationality from the body, the abandonment of the latter to the realm of animality and the location of humanity in the former – by welding body and mind back together. What makes Crusoe's experience especially disturbing is the extended dislocation of these two elements. Even after seeing the parrot he remains uncertain about the presence or absence of something like the human – that is, about the relation between bodily presence and speaking mind: 'even though I knew it was the Parrot, and that indeed it could be no Body else, it was a good while before I could compose my self'. In time, of course, Crusoe does pull himself together: 'as I was well satisfied it could be no Body but honest Poll, I got it over', he says, taking a deep breath, calling the parrot to his hand and walking home with it (Defoe 1994 [1719]: 104).

Swift, typically, dwells longer upon such moments. Gulliver's fourth voyage is the satirist's most extended disruption of the relationship between the human body and language as a marker of rational thought. From the Houyhnhnm point of view, Gulliver's ability to speak signifies only a partial and subordinate rationality, precisely because it is inappropriately separated from its natural – that is, equine – bodily form: 'they looked upon it as a Prodigy that a brute Animal should discover such Marks of a rational Creature' (Swift 2002 [1726]: 198). While in Houyhnhnmland

Gulliver can never be anything other than the equivalent of a trained parrot, momentarily surprising as Crusoe's or Locke's, but ultimately just an anomalous, pseudo-rational beast. Similarly, amongst the giants of Brobdingnag, Gulliver is never considered anything more than a kind of exotic pet, something like a monkey–parakeet hybrid, 'a strange Animal . . . about the bigness of a Splacknuck', which 'seemed to speak in a little Language of its own, had already learned several Words of theirs, went erect upon two Legs, was tame and gentle, would come when it was called, do whatever it was bid' (80).

Even for Crusoe – despite his determined attempts to embody modern values and preserve his own humanity – the 'accident' with the parrot is not the only moment at which he slips, albeit momentarily, into a kind of animal metamorphosis. Exploring a cave, Crusoe hears 'a very loud Sigh, like that of a Man in some Pain, and it was follow'd by a broken Noise, *as if* of Words half express'd'. Stepping forward with his torch, he sees 'lying on the Ground a most monstrous frightful old He-goat, just making his Will, as we say, and gasping for Life, and dying indeed of meer old Age' (Defoe 1994 [1719]: 129). While it is typical of Crusoe (and Defoe) to imagine a dying animal spending his last moments fussing over disposal of assets, the old billy-goat's 'words half-expressed' are much closer to Selkirk's aphasia, when after his rescue 'he seem'd to speak his words by halves' (Rogers 1994 [1712]: 234). Crusoe's perception of this animal thus combines anthropomorphic and zoomorphic projections of his own state, that of a London merchant hybridized with a Selkirkian goat-man. In turn, a few pages later, he borrows back the attributes of this animal to describe himself. Reviewing his twenty-third year of residence on the island, Crusoe remarks that he is 'so natural-iz'd to the Place' that, if he could be free of the threat of intrusion by 'Savages', he 'could have been content to have capitulated for spending the rest of my Time there, even to the last moment, till I had laid me down and dy'd, like the old Goat in the Cave' (Defoe 1994 [1719]: 130). At this point the only thing that distinguishes Crusoe from this animal is the possibility of a re-emergence into human society, that is, the threat of intrusion by 'savages'.

This intrusion is of course just what the startling episodes with the parrot and the goat foreshadow, inasmuch as both begin with the mistaken appre-hension of human voices. It is midway between these two incidents that Crusoe stumbles upon a human footprint on the beach, and feels the same shock produced by hearing his name unexpectedly pronounced. Looking behind him as he flees 'like one pursued', Crusoe rushes home to his 'Castle, for so I think I call'd it ever after this' (Defoe 1994 [1719]: 112). Faced with the imprint of another human body, Crusoe remains 'perfectly confus'd and out of my self' – just as it took him 'a good while to compose my Self' after his fright with the parrot. In these three moments of alarm – the parrot's speech, the man's footprint, the goat's voice – Crusoe's transi-tion to temporary animality provides a refuge from a human subjectivity that appears in the form of a threat. Where the companionship of his parrot has avianized Crusoe ('Poor Robin'), what shocks him is a sudden interpellation – a summoning through language – back into a social form of human subjectivity. Similarly, Crusoe's alarm at the prospect of meeting another human in the depths of a cave turns to relief and sentimental identification with a dying animal: a page or two later he imagines himself in the place of the old goat. And responding to the sight of the footprint, which forebodes another human presence on the island, Crusoe retreats strenuously from the field of human social engagements, backing nervously into the den of his animality: '[n]ever frighted Hare fled to Cover, or Fox to Earth, with more Terror of Mind than I to this Retreat' (112).

This last simile evokes not the hunting of prey by another animal, but by humans, as members of the species (along with dogs) most likely to pursue both hares and foxes with equal enthusiasm. Thus Crusoe is not primarily scared of encountering humans who act like animals, but of being encountered and treated by other humans as though he were an animal himself. His bestial state remains a source of security and contentment only in the absence of (other) humans. Hence, to the extent that cannibalism and animality are associated, it is the consumed, rather than the consumer, who becomes animalized; not as predator but as prey, and not by acting like an animal but by being treated as one.[10] Crusoe fears

> the worst kind of Destruction, *viz.*, That of falling into the Hands of Cannibals, and Savages, who would have seiz'd on me with the same View, as I did of a Goat, or a Turtle; and have thought it no more a Crime to kill and devour me, than I did of a Pidgeon, or a Curlieu (Defoe 1994 [1719]: 142).

Throughout his time on the island, Crusoe's rhetorical and practical relations to various animals results in intimate, recurrent identifications of and with his own animality. As manifestations of his naturalization on the island, these moments express or provide comfort. But they become immediately anxiogenic with the entrance of another human party, real or imagined. Crusoe's animality, at least on his island, worries him only when it exposes him as a potential target of human practices of dominion over the non-human environment – the same modes of consumption and exploitation that he enacts over animals himself. In other words, Crusoe happily thinks of himself as an old goat, or converses with his birds like another bird, until the anticipated entrance of other humans reminds him of the vulnerability, which he shares with these other species, to being hunted, captured, farmed or devoured.

Brutes in Human Shape

It is striking that Crusoe should represent himself, rather than his putative attackers, in animalistic terms, considering the well-known European tendency to attribute an inferior animality to non-European humans, especially during the period of imperialist modernity.[11] In contrast to this convention, rather than envisaging 'savage' humans as animals, Crusoe typically refers to them as 'inhuman'.[12] As John Simons points out, for writers like Swift and Defoe, the notion of *inhumanity* operates as a third term generated by the human–animal distinction (2002: 125–7).

Travelling down the coast of Africa, Crusoe describes his approach to 'the truly Barbarian Coast . . . where we could ne'er once go on shoar but we should be devour'd by savage Beasts, or more merciless Savages of humane kind' (Defoe 1994 [1719]: 19). Here, human and animal savagery can be distinguished precisely because the former is 'more merciless'. Similarly, after arriving on the island, Crusoe's industry is strongly motivated by his constant anxiety that he might 'fall into the Hands of Savages' who again might be 'far worse than the Lions and Tigers of Africa . . . for I had heard that the People of the Carribean Coast were canibals, or Man-eaters' (91). Discovering evidence of cannibal feasts on the far side of the island, Crusoe refers to 'Inhumanity . . . something so much below, even Brutality itself, as to devour its own Kind' (142–3).[13] In Defoe's text, then, the notion of inhumanity supports the definition of the human, but in a rather unreliable way.

Conventionally, the term *inhuman* signifies a mode of behaviour that represents the negative of the Enlightenment paradigm of the human: brutal, primitive, ruthless, cruel and excessive as opposed to civil, advanced, just, compassionate and decorous. In the version of history that underwrites the imperial mission, this kind of inhumanity constitutes a pre-modern phase that humans occupy before they are trained out of it, which is what Crusoe aims to do with Friday. Inevitably, however, along with the imperative to progress beyond such inhumanity comes an anxiety about the potential for regression. It is for this reason that Crusoe checks his initial desire to massacre the cannibal visitors to his island, which upon reflection he concludes would be 'a meer Butchery, a bloody and unnatural Piece of Cruelty' that would only represent a regression to past 'Barbarities' (124–55). He reaffirms his own enlightened humanity in contrast to their benighted inhumanity by reminding himself that he must maintain the very distinction that they transgress, namely between the treatment of humans and of animals: they 'think it no more a Crime to kill a Captive taken in War, than we do to kill an Ox; nor to eat humane Flesh, than we do to eat Mutton' (124).

Elsewhere, however, Defoe identifies another kind of brutality, typical of contemporary Europeans and even worse than the vice of inhumanity found among non-Europeans, past Europeans, or regressed Europeans. A few years after the publication of *Crusoe*, Defoe was inspired by the visit to England of 'Peter, the wild boy' – allegedly discovered 'naked, inarticulate, and brutish' near Hamelin in 1724 – to compose a lengthy satirical treatise, in which he remarked:

> to act as a Man, and to have no Pride, no Ambition, no Avarice, no Rancour or Malice, no ungovern'd Passions, no unbounded Desires, how infinitely more happy is he than Thousands of his more inform'd

and better-taught Fellow Brutes in human Shape, who are every Day raging with Envy, gnawing their own Flesh, that they are not rich, great, and cloath'd with Honours and Places as such-and-such, studying to supplant, suppress, remove, and displace those above them, and even to slander, accuse, murder, and destroy them to get into their Places? Had Nature been beneficent to him, in bestowing something more upon him in other ways, and yet kept his Soul lock'd up as to these Things, how had he been the happiest of all the Race of Rationals in the World? (cited in Novak 1972: 197).

The reference to 'the Race of Rationals', in the context of this diatribe, is as heavily freighted with misanthropy as anything in Swift, following as it does a whole series of bestial appetites, including an auto-cannibalistic appetite for 'gnawing their own flesh', ascribed to Europe's 'more inform'd and better-taught Fellow Brutes in Human Shape'. In this combination of animal and human attributes – ungoverned brutality intermixed with educated and knowing rationality – Defoe identifies a disposition neither primitive nor atavistic, but modern and specifically European.

Hence, although 'the idea that man is worse than beasts in uniquely human ways' has a long history in Western and classical writing (Rawson 2001: 14), it becomes significantly reconfigured with the advent of modernity. In the *Travels* Gulliver himself displays the kind of savagery that results from an excessive faith in rationality, most obviously in his trigger-happy enthusiasm for modern armaments. Sardonically echoing Crusoe's obsession with hoarding ammunition, Swift includes a firepower allusion in each part of the *Travels*. In Lilliput Gulliver fires his pistol in the air to demonstrate its use, at which '[h]undreds fell down as if they had been struck dead'; at the Grand Academy of Lagado he encounters a projector 'at work to calcine Ice into Gun-Powder'; in Brobdingnag he describes the military use of explosives as evidence of the genius of his species, and offers to reveal to the king the secret of its manufacture (Swift 2002 [1726]: 30, 112–13, 152). To Gulliver's surprise the king reacts with disgusted amazement that 'so impotent and grovelling an Insect as I (these were his Expressions) could entertain such inhuman Ideas, and in so familiar a manner as to appear wholly unmoved at all the Scenes of Blood and Desolation' (112).[14] The Brobdingnagian sovereign here identifies, in Gulliver's cheerful advocacy of mass slaughter, a form of inhumanity which, rather than being associated with the non-European or the pre-modern, is located at the very heart of modern European polity itself.

Missing the point, Gulliver dismisses the Brobdingnagians as 'very defective' in learning, because of their insistence that discoveries must lead to improvements in society: 'as to Ideas, Entities, Abstractions and Transcendentals, I could never drive the Least Conception into their Heads' (Swift 2002 [1726]: 113). He shares the same trait that he observes later in the citizens of Laputa and Lagado: an overdeveloped capacity for rational instrumentalism, inhumanly divorced from comprehension of its material consequences. Nor does he learn the lesson of his exposure to absurd abstractionism on his third voyage, since he later repeats his enthusiastic account of modern warfare to his Houyhnhnm master, concluding with a description of the 'Valor of my own dear Countrymen' in blowing up 'a Hundred Enemies at once in a Siege' so that 'the dead Bodies come down in pieces from the Clouds, to the great Diversion of the Spectators'. The Houyhnhnm master's response, once again, distinguishes between animal brutality and the kind of inhumanity resulting from rationality. Whereas the Yahoos of his own country can no more be blamed for their 'odious Qualities' than a bird of prey for its cruelty, he suggests that 'when a Creature pretending to Reason, could be capable of such Enormities . . . the Corruption of that Faculty might be worse than Brutality itself' (Swift 2002 [1726]: 209). Similarly, the Houyhnhnm Assembly decides Gulliver is more dangerous than ordinary Yahoos because he has 'some Rudiments of Reason, added to the natural Pravity of those Animals' (235).

Typically, though, the charge of rational depravity is no sooner made by the Houyhnhnms than Swift's double-edged satire turns it back on them. At their General Assembly, the virtuous equines make plans for their hominid neighbours that demonstrate the same (modern and human) propensity for detached, reasoned, calculated ruthlessness which they have just diagnosed in Gulliver. They debate whether and by what means 'the Yahoos should be exterminated from the face of the Earth' (Swift 2002 [1726]: 228). For Swift's contemporaries, the Houyhnhnms' calm appraisal of various modes of genocide – particularly the 'Expedient' proposal to borrow the European custom of castrating horses and apply it to 'the younger Yahoos here, which, besides rendring them tractable and fitter for Use, would in an Age put an end to the whole Species without destroying Life' (229–30) – would immediately have recalled current debates in England about eradicating the Irish, and more specifically, a statute proposed in 1719 that would have allowed their castration (Rawson 2001: 230).

In Defoe and Swift, then, two notions of inhumanity are at work. According to orthodox Enlightenment humanism, the inhuman, defined as any form of behaviour more brutal and merciless than that of predatory animals, is associated with non-European, pre-modern human populations. This 'atavistic' inhumanity provides, along with animality, a negative term against which a modern form of humanity can be defined. Conversely, critical interrogations of Enlightenment humanism – as represented by certain tendencies in Defoe's writing, and by the dominant tenor of Swift's – evoke an alternative, instrumentalist mode of inhumanity. While this second form of moral degradation is also considered worse than animalistic, it is presented not as a primitive phenomenon but as a disposition arising from the very kinds of rationalistic paradigms and experimental technologies privileged by modernity.

Gulliver and Crusoe, of course, remain oblivious to this distinction. Hence, for instance, Gulliver invokes a comparison between 'lower' (Yahoo) and 'higher' (Houyhnhnm) forms of polity in his critique of the establishment of a '*modern* Colony' at the end of his account. European imperialism begins with the actions of a 'Crew of Pyrates' who rob, plunder, murder and enslave the 'harmless People' of a new colony, followed by official annexation and 'a free Licence given to all Acts of Inhumanity' (Swift 2002 [1726]: 248). The disposition of these butcher-pirate-colonists echoes that of the Yahoos, who prefer 'what they could get by Rapine or Stealth at a greater distance' over 'much better Food provided for them at home' (Swift 2002 [1726]: 221; Aravamudan 1999: 138). Both groups exemplify the atavistic form of inhumanity – from which, however, Gulliver emphatically excludes the British nation, claiming his own countrymen to be 'an Example to the whole World for their Wisdom, Care and Justice in Planting Colonies' (248). The British, then, embody the Houyhnhnm virtues. But Gulliver's faith in this distinction is undercut for Swift's readers by an implied reference to the contemporary governance of Ireland (Rawson 2001: 22–3), and to other contemporary features of Britain's international relations, such as its monopoly over the Spanish-American Atlantic slave trade (Hawes 1991: 211; McInelly 2003: 20). For Swift, then, the Enlightenment principles of rationality and humaneness are hypocrisies, maintained only by systematic denial of the relationship between the atavistic or primitive manifestations of inhumanity and its civilized, modern expressions – the latter exemplified by the colonial systems designed to exploit and control human and non-human populations alike.

Just as these different notions of inhumanity arise from the human–animal relation, both are associated with unconstrained appetite, often in the form of cannibalism. For Crusoe, cannibalism invokes the horror of an atavistic inhumanity that would treat humans as animals to be hunted, killed and eaten. At the broader cultural level, however, both Defoe's and Swift's texts also use cannibalism as an image of exorbitant appetite, associated with the instrumentalism peculiar to European modernity. Both narratives reflect the cost that Europe's rapidly expanding consumer culture was beginning to impose upon the rest of the world. There is something excessive in Crusoe's cultivation of an entire island biosystem to provide solely for himself, in ways that include more luxury items as his mastery of his environment improves. And as Carol Houlihan Flynn points out, Gulliver's habits of consumption during his travels are more than extravagant (1990: 97). The citizens of Lilliput are required to 'deliver in every Morning six Beeves, forty Sheep, and other Victuals for my Sustenance'; his food is prepared by 300 cooks each day, and served by twenty waiters; '[t]heir Geese and Turkeys I usually eat at a Mouthful . . . [and of] their smaller Fowl I could take up twenty or thirty at the end of my Knife' (Swift 2002 [1726]: 27, 53). No wonder the Lilliputian court fears that he will cause a famine (20, 40). Even Gulliver's departure from Blefuscu proves expensive: his boat is greased with 'the Tallow of three hundred Cows', and supplied with 'the Carcasses of an hundred Oxen, and three hundred Sheep, with Bread and Drink proportionable, and as much Meat ready dressed as four hundred Cooks could provide' (64). In this context, his regretful aside that he would 'gladly have taken a Dozen of the Natives' had this not been 'a thing the Emperor would by no means permit' takes on a similarly voracious tone, recalling his earlier threat to eat one of the Lilliputians who shoots at him (25).

It is in the relation between over-consumption and poverty or famine that cannibalism emerges most vividly as a figuration of the exploitative economic relation between European imperial powers and their colonies, as in 'A Modest Proposal'. For Flynn, the many allusions to cannibalism and appetite in *Crusoe* and *Gulliver* demonstrate the extent to which 'England depended upon its colonized bodies to feed the "necessary" needs that resulted from its expansion' (1990: 150). It is in this sense that Gulliver, in conversation with his Houyhnhnm master, represents the global network of European mercantile capitalism as nothing other than a support for the luxurious tastes of the upper classes: 'I assured him, that this whole Globe of Earth must be at least three times gone round, before one of our better Female Yahoos could get her Breakfast, or a Cup to put it in' (Swift 2002 [1726]: 212–13). Locating cannibal appetite within rather than outside Europe, Swift once again portrays modernity as an advanced form of inhumanity, rather than a departure from it.

Five Cows, Some Sheep and Some Hogs

In the fictions of Defoe and Swift, both animality and inhumanity emerge as concepts disruptive to the protagonist's secure claim to humanity. Crusoe comes to think of himself as an animal, and fears acting inhumanly; Gulliver is treated as an animal, and thought inhuman by those he meets. But whereas Gulliver ends up estranged from all three categories, Crusoe makes his way back to identification with the specific form of humanity characteristic of Enlightenment modernity. Although his fear of intruders makes him feel like a hunted beast, once other humans actually appear in the narrative, he emerges from his identification with animality to reassert himself as a modern subject by means of the unequivocal separation from, and dominion over, non-humans and non-Europeans alike. And this can only occur because he has maintained the cultural and economic scaffolding of modernity's human–animal practices: an agricultural system based on capitalist principles; the facilitation of hunting and slaughter by gunpowder; participation in the wider circuit of mercantile exchange in animal products; and a relentless infrastructural forward momentum in the harvesting and processing of animal resources.

Each of these elements displays the defining quality of the modern, that is, mobility: temporally, the assumption that history advances from a lesser past to a greater present and an improved future; spatially, the commitment to scientific, mercantile and imperialist expansion. In their initial desire for travel, their fascination with innovation, their entrepreneurial acumen and their faith in the conjunction between technological and moral advancement, Crusoe and Gulliver are both embodiments of the modern disposition. Indeed it is Gulliver's blindness to the complacencies of this disposition that makes him a perfect target for Swift's satire. Hence, for example, when the King of Brobdingnag rejects his offer of the means to perpetrate mass slaughter on any who oppose him, Gulliver can only deplore the '*Narrowness of Thinking*' that holds the giant nation back (Swift 2002 [1726]: 111). It is only at the end of the *Travels*, as a result of his identification with the anti-progressive Houyhnhnms, that Gulliver renounces modernity and returns to life in a stable with his horses. This coda is a droll reversal of the historical process of separation between farmers and animals that marked the rise of the modern agricultural system: namely the move away, during the sixteenth and seventeenth centuries, from the pre-modern long-house in which humans and cattle had slept under the same roof (Thomas 1984: 40, 95).

In Defoe's narrative, however, progress and expansionism continue to be presented in a positive light, despite significant moments of ambiguity. Crusoe's reverence for modern commodity production is emblematized in his extended description of making bread. Beginning from the 'meer State of Nature', he has to reinvent each piece of equipment and each specialized form of labour that he would rely on at home, from ploughing to baking (Defoe 1994 [1719]: 86–7). In the same way he details his painstaking, step-by-step reconstruction of a modern agricultural economy based on animal capital. Unlike his precursor Selkirk, Crusoe is thrifty with his gunpowder, dividing it into numerous small caches like a speculator diversifying his portfolio. And this investor acumen provides the motivation and means to build up a herd of farmed animals. As his supplies of powder dwindle, Crusoe wonders how he will be able to kill goats without it. He does not consider the type of metamorphosis reputedly undergone by Selkirk, into the bodily form of a predator. Instead, 'I set my self to study some Art to trap and snare the Goats, to see whether I could not catch some of them alive, and particularly I wanted a She-goat great with young' (Defoe 1994 [1719]: 105). A series of painstaking attempts – the hunting of goats with his dog, the treating and fostering of injured animals, the setting of snares – demonstrates Crusoe's penchant for applied, experimental progressivism (56, 81–2). Eventually he acquires the elements of a future breeding stock, one male and two female kids, and sets about developing, stage by stage, the infrastructure needed to support this embryonic primary industry: the construction of a secure hedge around a piece of land, the establishment of a stock-feeding regime, the first season's breeding, the fencing of 'five several Pieces of Ground to feed them in, with little Pens to drive them into, to take them as I wanted, and Gates out of one Piece of Ground into another', and eventually the commencement of dairying (first milk, then butter, then cheese) as a secondary venture (105–7).

As Robert Marzec has argued, Crusoe enacts in microcosm one of the fundamental economic, social and environmental processes underlying Britain's transition to modernity: that of enclosure. Involving 'the meticulous measurement of a piece of land, followed by the surrounding of that land with barriers designed to close off the free passage of people and animals' (2002: 138), enclosure prepared the ground for an intensively managed agricultural system that would find its logical conclusion in the feed-lotting of the twentieth century. With this reorganization of human–animal space came the dislocation of large portions of the human populace, a reconstitution of the rural labour force and a displacement of the traditional peasantry, many of whom moved to the cities and became the urban working class or unemployed poor (139). Moreover enclosure provided a paradigm which, with the emergence of British imperialism, 'could readily be transplanted to distant territories' both as a material 'apparatus' and a 'structure of feeling', thereby giving ideological, social and economic form to colonial plantation agriculture (131). Defoe himself, in his *Tour Through the Whole Island of Great Britain*, expresses a strong advocacy of enclosure as a 'radically new mode of enlightened (imperial) existence' (Marzec 2002: 130).

In accordance with this attitude, Crusoe's second thought in the event of danger – following immediately on his first, which is for his own survival – is for the security of his agricultural property. Discovering his island is visited by cannibals, he imagines they will return 'in greater Numbers, and devour me', before worrying 'that if it should happen so that they should not find me, yet they would find my Enclosure, destroy all my Corn, carry away all my Flock of tame Goats, and I should perish at last for meer Want' (Defoe 1994 [1719]: 113). Indeed, Crusoe's commitment to his investments eventually outweighs his (prodigious) desire for self-preservation. During this attack of fright, which afflicts him for several days, the thought that forces him to leave his fortification is the need to attend to his flock (115). And when he calms down sufficiently to plan more secure defences – for himself and his animal capital – he repeats the strategy he used to husband his gunpowder, deciding that 'the most rational Design' would be

> to enclose two or three little Bits of Land, remote from one another and as much conceal'd as I could, where I might keep about half a Dozen young Goats in each Place: So that if any Disaster happen'd to the Flock in general, I might be able to raise them again with little Trouble and Time (118).

Later, once the island's human population has been augmented by Friday and some other castaways, Crusoe subcontracts management of his stock portfolio to these settlers before he departs: 'I gave them a Description of the Way I manag'd the Goats, and Directions to milk and fatten them, and to make both Butter and Cheese' (199). This enables him on his eventual return to subdivide the island amongst his tenants, although of course 'reserv[ing] to myself the Property of the whole' (220). He is now well-placed to integrate his new colony into the commercial trading networks of the circum-Atlantic economy: 'I sent them also from the Brasils five Cows, three of them being big with Calf, some Sheep, and some Hogs, which, when I came again, were considerably encreas'd' (220). Crusoe concludes his parable of colonial economic enclosure by introducing further stock, just as the acclimatization societies in Australasia and the Americas would do a century later (Ritvo 1987: 232–42). In so doing, Crusoe completes his single-handed progression through the stages of those conjectural histories of social evolution produced during the Enlightenment which trace human progress from vulnerability to wild beasts and natural disaster, to the establishment of agriculture by means of sequential enclosure, and the concomitant development of a complex economic and social infrastructure.[15]

It is clear, however, that Crusoe's ability to move from primitivism to modernity in little more than two decades depends not merely upon his entrepreneurial acumen, but also upon his firepower. The first time he discharges his firearm on the island, Crusoe imagines that 'it was the first Gun that had been fir'd there since the Creation of the World'. Although he brings down nothing but the flesh of a 'Great Bird' which is 'Carrion and fit for nothing' (Defoe 1994 [1719]: 40), what matters most are the rhetorical echoes of this inaugural report. The weapon is being deployed not merely as a hunting tool but as an instrument of discovery: it is to the colonial terrain what the scalpel is to the scientist's table. Crusoe surveys his domain down the barrel of a gun, in the same way that eighteenth- and nineteenth-century natural historians collected specimens. In his first few weeks on the island he goes out 'once at least every Day with my Gun' not just to hunt for food but also 'to divert my self' and 'to acquaint my self with what the Island produc'd' (46). The report of the gun announces the commencement of the new terrain's transition to modernity, and the introduction of the technological instrument by which this will be achieved.

Enlightened expansionism requires that Crusoe's advancement demonstrates a concomitant improvement of non-European peoples as well as territories. Because it conjoins symbolic and material dominion, the gun proves indispensable to Crusoe's repeated enactment of one of the central fantasies of Enlightenment historiography: the facilitation of the non-European's progression from helpless savagery to engagement in the modern economy. The first instance is provided by Crusoe's landfall on the African coast with Xury – first his fellow-slave, then his friend and servant, and ultimately his ex-slave. The two runaways are in constant fear of the wild beasts they see upon shore, but Crusoe deals with this according to what will become a familiar two-act theatre of cultural superiority. First, he shoots an animal. This immediately establishes his dominion over the non-human world, while displaying his power to awestruck non-European observers. When he shoots a lion this witness is Xury; a few weeks later he kills a leopard for an admiring audience of local Africans: '[i]t is impossible to express the Astonishment of these poor Creatures at the Noise and Fire of my Gun; some of them were even ready to dye for Fear, and fell down as Dead with the very Terror' (Defoe 1994 [1719]: 22, 24). The second act involves teaching the non-European to use a gun as the agent of the European master. Thus, having first wounded the lion, Crusoe instructs

Xury to go ashore and finish it off (22). This demonstrates the moderniza-
tion of the non-European, who gratefully gains (subordinate) access to the
benefits of European technological progress. An optional coda to this two-
part performance entails the extraction of profit. Crusoe is at first disap-
pointed with the lion's death, since he can see no return on his investment
of powder and shot (22); on reflection, however, he decides to take the
animal's skin, which he later sells for forty ducats (25). The leopard gives an
even better return: not only does Crusoe collect another skin to sell later
on, but by donating the animal's flesh to the local people he wins both their
gratitude and their gifts of water, vegetable roots and corn (24).

The same theatre of European polity and commerce is performed during
Crusoe's more extended relationship with Friday. Crusoe's intervention in
Friday's flight from his captors rehearses the Englishman's superior
ordnance, which results in the stock imperial fantasy of a non-European
savage making voluntary obeisance to European power. Crusoe's naked foot,
associated earlier in the text with his own vulnerability to predatory invasion,
is seized by Friday and placed on his head in a pageant of welcome submission to the redemptive intervention of just European force (Defoe 1994
[1719]: 147). As usual in such scenes, an attitude of cargo-cult devotion – or
what Rawson calls 'gunpowder magic' (2001: 66) – is imputed to the non-
European: ignorant admiration and awe in the face of technological modernity. Nor is Friday's reaction different the next time he witnesses a firearm in
use. On this occasion, Crusoe's intention is explicitly to advance his new
subject's rapid evolution through the same developmental sequence – from
primitivism to modernity – marked out by his own tenure on the island. In
order to 'bring Friday off from his horrid way of feeding, and from the
Relish of a Cannibal's Stomach', Crusoe resolves to 'let him taste other Flesh;
so I took him out with me one Morning to the Woods':

> I saw a She Goat lying down in the Shade, and two young Kids sitting
> by her. I catch'd hold of Friday, Hold, says I, stand still; and made
> Signs to him not to stir, immediately presented my Piece, shot and
> kill'd one of the Kids. The poor Creature . . . did not know, or could
> imagine how it was done, was sensibly surpriz'd, trembled, and shook,
> and look'd so amaz'd, that I thought he would have sunk down. He
> did not see the Kid I shot at, or perceive I had kill'd it, but ripp'd up
> his Wastcoat to feel if he was not wounded (152).

As Flynn argues, the semantic transfer between Friday and the slaughtered
kid – the phrase 'poor Creature' at first seems to refer to the latter –
mirrors Friday's own confusion about who has been the victim of Crusoe's
weapon (1990: 156). In Crusoe's view, for Friday the boundary between
human and animal remains unclear, a perception confirmed by his continued tendency to regard other people as meat. In this sense, Friday becomes
the negative of Crusoe's own animal identifications, which must now be
superseded. Crusoe's aim is to allow Friday access to a form of enlightened

humanity defined by its separation from and dominion over animality, thereby inviting him into the economic structure of modernity. This requires a lesson in what it means to be human – undertaken, inevitably, in relation to the animal. In the process, of course, Crusoe simultaneously reasserts his own position within the modern category of the human. The forms of human–animal intimacy and identification he relied upon prior to Friday's arrival now disappear entirely from the narrative.

Friday's successful apprenticeship is displayed in the final pages of the novel. Upon returning to Europe, Crusoe travels with his man through the Pyrenees in an adventure that echoes his adventures with Xury prior to his arrival on the island. Thus, during the attack by wolves, Friday plays the role of Crusoe's agent in the second act of the theatre of dominion. And as the consummation of this process Friday kills a bear, stepping up to the animal and placing his gun directly against its head before firing – just as Xury did with the lion during Crusoe's first trial of his system of gun-barrel husbandry (Defoe 1994 [1719]: 22, 214).

Colonizing Animals

Read as a parable of modernity, *Robinson Crusoe* seems to celebrate and naturalize the programme of advancement promulgated by its restless hero. Yet the text is pervaded by hints of the elements repressed in order for this celebration to ring true. Such moments betray the ways in which the cultivation of a capitalist economy and infrastructure, far from being spontaneous and self-sufficient, can occur only because Crusoe is never at any point beyond the circuit of mercantile capitalism and colonial improvement. Crusoe reproduces capitalist modernity not because it is the most natural, the best or the only way he can survive, but because it has already transformed his environment in ways that neither he nor Defoe recognize.

Ian Watt argues that Crusoe's rise from desolate subsistence to wealth, while appearing to typify the career of the self-made man, actually depends upon certain favourable preconditions – the lucky provision of a stock of primary materials and tools produced by the labour of others, for example – which are overlooked or underemphasized when Defoe's tale is trans-formed into capitalist myth (1972). Even Crusoe admits that, had he 'got nothing out of the Ship', he could only have lived 'like a meer Savage'. Under such circumstances, even if he could succeed in killing a goat or bird, he would have had 'no way to flea or open them, or part the Flesh from the Skin, and the Bowels, or to cut it up; but must gnaw it with my Teeth, and pull it with my Claws like a Beast' (Defoe 1994 [1719]: 95). Crusoe's fantasies about his own transformation to beastliness make it clear that not only his immediate survival, but also his maintenance of modern humanity, as defined against both animality and savagery, depend upon items salvaged from the European commercial and ideological economy. With a kind of indulgent horror, he envisages his life without these advantages, evoking the same mode of predatory animality that Rogers and his men witnessed in the person of Alexander Selkirk.

However, Crusoe's debt to a pre-existent modern asset-base also takes less explicit forms, invisible not just to him but to subsequent readers of the text. Once he uses up his supplies from the shipwreck, their home-made replacements – goatskin clothes, tallow fuel and a goats'-meat diet – are supposed to convince the reader that by hard work, resourcefulness and self-sufficiency (in short by embodying the ideal capitalist disposition) Crusoe has dispensed with reliance upon goods imported from Europe in favour of those produced locally. However this moral can only be maintained in ignorance of the historical provenance of those skins, that meat, that fuel. Crusoe does not speculate on the origins of the goat population he discovers in his new home. But in fact these goats can only come from the Juan Fernandez Islands: that is to say, when Defoe transports Selkirk's story from the Pacific to the Atlantic, he takes with him the goats found by the Scotsman on his island, recognizing them as integral to the tale. But goats are no more endemic to Juan Fernandez than they would be to Crusoe's island. The only reason Selkirk, and consequently Crusoe, can depend on these animals for food, clothing, fuel and company is because throughout the sixteenth and seventeenth centuries, European sailors routinely seeded mid-oceanic islands with hardy mammal stock, thereby providing a self-reproducing resource for subsequent voyagers. Sheep, cattle, goats and rabbits were all deliberately established on the mid-Atlantic islands in this way as provisions for journeys down the African coast or to the Americas (Crosby 1986). The goats of Juan Fernandez were introduced by Spanish mariners who recognized the need for a pit-stop upon entering the Pacific (Souhami 2001). Such populations were a vital element in transglobal transportation and trade networks; they comprised fuelling-stations along the routes followed by the agents of European slavery, colonialism and mercantile capitalism. In this context, Crusoe's declaration that his initial gunshot is the first ever heard on 'his' island must be seen as a fantasy of modern capitalist improvement *ex nihilo*.[16]

Seeding islands with livestock, however, represented only the first engagement of a much larger ecology-processing machine. The dream of a civilizing mission, which offered a motive and alibi for European imperialism by promising enlightened cultivation of benighted races, was accompanied by an equivalent biological mission, which foresaw the domestication and improvement of wild terrains through the importation of European life-forms necessary to the reproduction of a colonial economy and social system (Crosby 1986; Morton and Smith 1999). Donna Haraway considers this 'intensified transportation of seeds and genes' the defining feature of modernity, a process exemplified by 'the invention of the first great industrial system – plantation agriculture' (Haraway and Goodeve 2000: 88). In their voyages of discovery, trade, and settlement, Europeans invariably brought with them 'a scaled-down, simplified version of the biota of Western Europe', writes Crosby (1986: 88). This 'grunting, lowing, neighing, crowing, chirping, snarling, buzzing, self-replicating and world-altering avalanche' was crucial to the success or failure of various colonial investments. Success depended upon a cooperation between human and animal colonists which altered the host terrain, sculpting it into an ecological shape that fitted the economic and social habitats that the settlers brought from home: '[b]ecause these animals are self-replicators, the efficiency and speed with which they can alter environments, even continental environments, are superior to those of any machine we have thus far devised' (173).

Yet this organic, imperial combine-harvester also produced effects quite different from those envisaged or intended. For livestock animals were not the only animal species with which Europeans seeded new environments. Deliberately or inadvertently, visiting ships and mariners also introduced a menagerie of other species, some of which prospered because they were removed from the predators, parasites or diseases that might limit their populations at home. Rats, for example, soon reached plague proportions after their introduction to Peru following the arrival of Pizarro; they did the same in Jamestown, Virginia, in 1609, only two years after the foundation of the colony, and in Sydney in 1790 (Crosby 1986: 190–2). Similarly, during his first months on Juan Fernandez, Alexander Selkirk found himself 'much pester'd with Cats and Rats, that had bred in great numbers from some of each Species which had got ashore from Ships that put in there to wood and water' (Rogers 1994 [1712]: 233).

While colonists are unequivocal in seeing some of these species as vermin, others provoke a more ambivalent response. Selkirk's 'pestering' cats, for example, eventually provide the solution to his rat problem once he tames them by feeding them goats' flesh. Thus both goats and cats become his domestics and later, as we know, his song-and-dance partners. Yet the boundaries between the three major categories constitutive of the European economic and social animal taxonomy – the farmed animal, the pet and the pest – prove unstable and liable to feralization. This is true both for Selkirk, at least in Rogers' version of his adventures, and for Crusoe. The first living being Crusoe encounters face-to-face on his island is a 'Creature like a wild Cat', whom he finds sitting on one of the chests he salvages from the wreck on his return to home base. Appearing at such a moment, and in such a manner, the cat seems to represent an embodiment of whatever indigenous life may greet him on the island, and the encounter therefore encodes and anticipates much of his current and future struggle with his new life. As he approaches, the cat

> ran away a little Distance, and then stood still; she sat very compos'd, and unconcern'd, and look'd full in my Face, as if she had a Mind to be acquainted with me, I presented my Gun at her, but as she did not understand it, she was perfectly unconcern'd at it, nor did she offer to stir away; upon which I toss'd her a Bit of Bisket, tho' by the Way I was not very free of it, for my Store was not great: However, I spar'd her a Bit, I say, and she went to it, smell'd of it, and ate it, and look'd (as

pleas'd) for more, but I thanked her, and could spare no more; so she march'd off (Defoe 1994 [1719]: 41).

The gaze that this animal directs at Crusoe seems to express the attributes of agency and mental intentionality that a Cartesian would reserve for humans. As the encounter goes on, Crusoe's amused tone projects on to this 'wild' creature all those characteristics commonly associated with cats: composure, nonchalance in the face of human authority, and a qualified affability that serves and is limited by self-interest. Cats, of course, retain a greater degree of agency over their own lives than dogs, or indeed any other domesticated species. Indeed the cat's infrangible autonomy locates it insistently on the boundary between tame and wild, domestic and feral. As Buffon put it, 'the cat may be said to be only half domestic; he forms the shade between the real wild and real domestic animals' (cited in Ritvo 1998: 40).

Such, at least, is the case with Crusoe's cats. He gives the two cats rescued from the shipwreck pride of place at his table (Defoe 1994 [1719]: 48), as part of his 'little family'. But the problematic nature of the species is evidenced soon after:

> In this Season I was much surpriz'd with the Increase of my Family; I had been concern'd for the Loss of one of my Cats, who run away from me, or as I thought had been dead, and I heard no more Tale or Tidings of her, till to my Astonishment she came Home about the End of August, with three Kittens; this was the more strange to me, because tho' I had kill'd a wild Cat, as I call'd it, with my Gun; yet I thought it was a quite differing Kind from our European Cats; yet the young Cats were of the same Kind of House breed like the old one; and both my Cats being Females, I thought it very strange: But from these three Cats, I afterwards came to be so pester'd with Cats, that I was forc'd to kill them like Vermine, or wild Beasts, and to drive them from my House as much as possible (75).

The interbreeding between the ship's cats and the wild animals suggests their common origins as accidental or deliberate settlers from visiting European ships, and anticipates the detrimental environmental impacts of European bio-colonialism. But it also emphasizes the nature of the cat as a trespasser crossing the boundary between pet and pest. As long as the animal belongs in the former category its apparent self-sufficiency can be accepted, and anthropomorphically enjoyed, as a limited and trivialized form of agency. But once the animal becomes a pest – once it joins the category of those species competing with humans for resources, or threatening damage to human agricultural or domestic spatial arrangements – agency is reconfigured as ferity. It is for this reason that Nigel Clark describes the feral as 'the unintentional or uncanny' element that inevitably accompanies the 'ordering and improving project' of 'enlightened' modernisation' (1999: 140).

Swift, typically, finds animal resistance a fit vehicle for his satirical reversals. The Houyhnhnms' treatment of the Yahoos as beasts of burden inverts
the conventional emblem of the horse-rider as a representation of the
agency of rational thought over the carefully constrained but potentially
wayward intentionalities of the body and the passions. But the
Houyhnhnm–Yahoo relation also reverses the material practices by which
modernity organizes interactions between human and animal forms of
agency. The domestication of the horse – replayed with each animal in the
rituals of castration, breaking and bridling – embodies the economically
essential processes by which animals' agencies are harnessed in the service
of human commerce, transport and industry. These processes are sardon-
ically overturned when Gulliver's description of the treatment of English
horses to his Houyhnhnm master is undercut by the sight of an 'old steed'
riding a sledge pulled by Yahoos (Swift 2002 [1726]: 196, 203–4). Similarly,
the harnessing of equine agency in the service of European military expansion is turned around as Gulliver contemplates the likely outcome of any
attempt to invade the island of the Houyhnhnms. He invites the reader to
'[i]magine Twenty thousand of them breaking into the midst of an
European Army, confounding the Ranks, overturning the Carriages,
battering the Warriors Faces into Mummy, by terrible Yerks from their
hinder Hoofs'; conversely, he wishes the Houyhnhnms would 'send a sufficient Number of their Inhabitants for civilizing Europe' (247).

Meanwhile, according to the Houyhnhnms' perspective, Yahoos
display all the attributes of vermin: dangerous aggressiveness, uncontrolled reproduction, liability to host infectious diseases and a pestiferous
interference in the everyday transactions of agricultural commerce.
Hence the motion put to the Houyhnhnm General Assembly regarding
their extermination. Arguing in favour of this proposal, one member of
the assembly describes the Yahoos as 'the most filthy, noisome, and
deformed Animal which Nature ever produced, . . . the most restive and
indocible, mischievous and malicious'. He goes on to assert that '[t]hey
would privately suck the Teats of the Houyhnhnms Cows, kill and devour
their Cats, trample down their Oats and Grass, if they were not continually watched, and commit a thousand other Extravagancies' (Swift 2002
[1726]: 228). These are all feral behaviours – that is, they represent an
animal agency inimical to agricultural and domestic order. Indeed, the
origin of the Yahoo presence in Houyhnhnmland is presented not as a
colonial invasion by a race of human aggressors, but as the feral outbreak
of an introduced species:

> the Two Yahoos said to be first seen among them had been driven
> thither over the Sea; that coming to Land, and being forsaken by their
> Companions, they returned to the Mountains, and degenerating by
> degrees, became in process of time, much more savage than those of
> their own Species in the Country from whence these two Originals
> came (229).

The Yahoos, in this account, are members of an introduced species which, domesticated in its home country, has lapsed into ferity upon release into a new environment – exactly the fate of the goats, pigs, cats, rabbits and other species brought to islands and continents by Europeans in the interests of imperial and mercantile expansion. And just as Defoe's tame cats demonstrate the European provenance of his islands' feral cats, Gulliver's evident consanguinity with the Yahoos gives weight to the theory that they are colonists. His Houyhnhnm master testifies that 'when he saw me without my Covering, I was an exact Yahoo in every Part, only of a whiter Colour, less hairy, and with shorter Claws' (229); the differences between Gulliver and the other Yahoos are superficial, and presumably subject to the same process of transformation that turned Alexander Selkirk within four years into a sunburned, shaggy, hoofed goat-man. By the end of the book Gulliver accepts this account of the Yahoos' origins: indeed he concludes that their ancestors 'may have been English, which indeed I was apt to suspect from the Lineaments of their Posterity's Countenances, although very much defaced' (249).

Swift leaves his reader with this topsy-turvy animal–human relation still in place, of course. Gulliver returns to England and dedicates himself to rendering 'docible' his own family of Yahoos, even admitting the possibility of domesticating a neighbour despite 'the Apprehensions I am yet under of his Teeth or his Claws' (Swift 2002 [1726]: 249). Nevertheless he prefers the company of his two horses, whom he exempts from the human practices designed to tame them: they are '[s]trangers to Bridle or Saddle', and uncastrated (244). Meanwhile, with perfect symmetry, castration is precisely the measure to be taken against the feral Yahoos in Houyhnhnmland – a practice also introduced from England, unintentionally, by Gulliver himself (229–30).

Poor Creatures

The interrogation of Enlightenment ideas about humanity and inhumanity produced a powerful structure of feeling associated with terms such as sympathy, compassion, sensibility, sentiment and kindness. As a challenge to modernity's valorization of dispassionate rationalism, this disposition became a defining feature of the literary culture of the time. As Jonathan Lamb puts it, 'sympathy' was taken during the Enlightenment to involve 'the measure of the "kindness"' at work in the engagement between human sensibility and the experience of an object or animal; 'the degree to which the feelings of different creatures might be communicated and shared' (2001: 133). The more overt emotionalism of later literary production had its roots in the early part of the eighteenth century and the latter half of the seventeenth, amongst divines and philosophers who taught that 'man's innate instincts were kindly and that it was unnatural to take pleasure in cruelty' (Thomas 1984: 175).[17]

Two things are notable about the formulation of this disposition. First – like the conceptualization of humanity, inhumanity, rationality and other terms fundamental to Enlightenment modernity – the culture of sensibility cannot be understood without reference to human–animal interactions. Hence, for example, the recognition of animal suffering, like instances of animal agency or ferity, provided a means to disrupt the instrumentalist paradigm that united Cartesian philosophy, new scientific practice, capitalist economics, and colonial dominion over populations and terrains. Second, early eighteenth-century manifestations of sympathetic engagement between humans and other animals proved to be remarkably varied. They ranged from the comfortable, transient and rather shallow affect that would nowadays be associated with the term 'sentimental', to moments that were anything but complacent, trivial, reassuring or benevolent. Lamb has gone on to argue more recently that the modes of sympathy emerging in the eighteenth century can be grouped into four categories: emotional affinity based on observation of shared physiological traits; consideration of rights and duties owed to others thus recognized as similar; 'the more oblique degree of resemblance' prompted by imaginative or figurative representation; and finally and most radically, 'the obliteration of all differences in a species of sympathy that proclaims the identity of the subject and the object' (2006: 171).

In *Robinson Crusoe*, the hero's engagements with animals provide ample occasions for the establishment of dominion over non-European and non-human nature, but at the same time, confidence in his right to sovereignty is repeatedly undercut by instances of sympathy of a kind consistent with the first two of Lamb's categories: the recognition of physiological affinity to other animals, resulting in the uneasy intimation that rights and duties may be owed to them. In this regard, Crusoe anticipates the kind of imaginatively incarnated structure of feeling that becomes central to the novel of sensibility later in the century: his characterization is finely balanced between the competing dispositions typical of his class (and of his creator). This is apparent during Crusoe's display of firepower for the edification of Friday. Loading his gun after killing a young goat, he prepares to shoot again, this time at the 'great Fowl like a Hawk' he sees land within range. But he finds he has made a mistake: the bird 'was indeed a Parrot, tho' I thought it had been a Hawk' (Defoe 1994 [1719]: 153). This awkward self-correction emphasizes that the bird he deliberately shoots belongs to the same species that stood in for human companionship prior to Friday's appearance. In dealing with a game bird, wild animal or predator, Crusoe need not indulge in sympathetic identification: hawks can be shot with equanimity. But affinity with the parrot has been a primary technique for preserving his sense of self during his isolation. Flynn describes the resulting narrative ambivalence as follows:

> when Friday runs to fetch the parrot, we learn that the 'Parrot not being quite dead, was flutter'd away a good way off from the Place where she fell'. Pronouns tell. 'She' fell. Verbs tell more. 'Flutter' suggests a nervous presence, a tremulous emotion sympathetic in its neurological connections. Crusoe himself experienced 'fluttering

thoughts' after viewing his primal footprint on his deserted shore. Insistent upon computing the cost of living, Defoe makes his readers know the creatures they consume: the idle kid sitting next to its mother in the shade, the sentient parrot picked out of the tree, beings sacrificed to make safer the idea of civilization (Flynn 1990: 156–7).

Flynn's assessment of the conflict between detached instrumentalism and compassionate sympathy makes it easier to understand another psittacine oddity in the narrative. Well before this scene, Crusoe has speculated that his first companion, Poll, may still be living on the island after his own return to England (Defoe 1994 [1719]: 130–1). But later he mentions taking a parrot with him when he leaves the island, as one of the 'reliques' of his sojourn (200). This of course may be one of Poll's successors – Crusoe tells us he 'had two more Parrots which talk'd pretty well, and would all call Robin Crusoe; but none like my first; nor indeed did I take the Pains with any of them that I had done with him' (131). But in that case, why does he not take the first Poll with him when he goes? The bird he does take completes the transition from interlocutor to souvenir, from companion animal to pet, and thus belongs in the same category as Gulliver's collection of 'reliques' from his travels (which includes a herd of Lilliputian cattle, some wasp stings from Brobdingnag, and some Yahoo skins) – not to mention the real-life animal commodities (including a great many parrots) transported between Europe and its colonies throughout the eighteenth century. By contrast, in his unexplained fantasy of Poll's continued existence on the island after his own departure, Crusoe envisages a life for his erstwhile companion outside of this economy.

Two conflicting tendencies are operating here – commodification of the animal on one hand, and a heightening of the potential for sympathetic identification between human and non-human on the other – which are both closely associated with a newly important category of human–animal relations during the eighteenth century: pet-keeping. Thomas agrees with Berger that modern trends in pet-keeping emerged contemporaneously with, and as expressions of, the rise of capitalism and the ascendancy of the bourgeois nuclear family (Thomas 1984: 119; citing Berger 1980). It was during the sixteenth and seventeenth centuries that companion animals, often belonging to species specially bred or imported as part of a distinct commercial enterprise, 'established themselves as a normal feature of the middle-class household, especially in the towns' (Thomas 1984: 110). This intensification of relationships between certain animal species and an increasingly powerful class provided a vigorous source of everyday resistance to the rationalized separation between human and animal proposed by Cartesian philosophy. Pet-keeping, writes Thomas,

> encouraged the middle classes to form optimistic conclusions about animal intelligence; it gave rise to innumerable anecdotes about animal sagacity; it stimulated the notion that animals could have character and

individual personality; and it created the psychological foundation for the view that some animals at least were entitled to moral consideration (119).

Crusoe's descriptions of his parrots clearly evince this attribution of 'character and individual personality' to animals. Unsurprisingly, so do his accounts of his dogs. The first of these animals 'jump'd out of the Ship of himself, and swam on Shore to me the Day after I went on Shore with my first Cargo, and was a trusty Servant to me many Years'. Only lack of speech prevents this dog from being a perfect companion: 'I wanted nothing that he could fetch me, nor any Company that he could make up to me, I only wanted to have him talk to me, but that would not do' (Defoe 1994 [1719]: 48). Even when he is no more use as a hunting assistant, after he has 'grown very old and crazy', this animal still sits at the 'Right Hand' of his master at the dinner table, until he dies after sixteen years on the island (108, 131). Several years later he is succeeded by a second dog, who joins Crusoe in the same way: a vessel is wrecked on the shore with no human survivors, but 'a Dog appear'd upon her, who seeing me coming, yelp'd, and cry'd; and as soon as I call'd him, jump'd into the sea, to come to me, and I took him into the Boat' (138). These two canines provide the strongest and most enduring sympathetic identification between the human and non-human because they offer the most vivid mirrors for the emotions and experiences of their human companion. Like Crusoe they are travellers, shipwreck survivors and castaways; like him their immediate needs are for food, shelter and companionship. Prior to the arrival of Friday, moreover, these two animals are the only living beings who share Crusoe's own status as isolates, devoid of the company of their own kind – in contrast to the parrots and goats, who belong on the island, or the ship's cats, who interbreed with the resident population. And of course, through their vocalizations and body language, Crusoe's canine companions demonstrate their willing participation in that relationship of intimate communication and trust which pertains, proverbially, between man and dog.

Crusoe's emotional bond with his dogs, of course, does not disrupt his narrative or ideological claim to either individualism or mastery of nature. The readiness of canine subalternity means that a man with a gun and a dog is still – indeed more than a man without either – an emblem of human power and self-sufficiency. However, as his mistake with the hawk-like parrot demonstrates, Crusoe displays the same tendency for sympathetic identification in other cases where the result is potentially more unsettling, since it involves either an inconvenient moral obstacle to the killing of an animal, or a moral regret consequent upon doing so. Such feelings recur in Crusoe's relation to the island's goats. His first hunting expedition introduces the quandary of how to represent a species that is capable of providing prey for hunting, stock animals and companionship all at once, thereby blurring the boundaries between the different kinds of moral consideration proper to each category:

[t]he first shot I made among these Creatures, I kill'd a She-Goat which had a little Kid by her when she gave Suck to, which grieved me heartily; but when the Old one fell the Kid stood stock still by her till I came and took her up, and not only so, but when I carry'd the Old one with me upon my Shoulders, the Kid follow'd me quite to my Enclosure, upon which I laid down the Dam, and took the Kid in my Arms, and carry'd it over my Pale, in hopes to have bred it up tame, but it would not eat, so I was forc'd to kill it and eat it myself (Defoe 1994 [1719]: 46).

Of course it is the young animal that provokes the most immediate compassion, perhaps because its mother's nursing constitutes a reminder of mammalian kinship, or because of a projection on to the animal of a structure of family relations derived from humans. Either way, the 'forc'd' termination of this relationship grieves Crusoe heartily – a strong statement of compassion from one so rational, and in such dire need. Some time later he acquires another kid after it is seized by his dog. He encloses it in his 'Bower' in the centre of the island, and then returns home. After a week, however, 'I began to think of the poor Kid, which I had penn'd in within my little Circle, and resolv'd to go and fetch it Home, or give it some Food'. On reaching the place, he finds that

> it was so tame with being hungry, that I had no need to have ty'd it; for it follow'd me like a Dog; and as I continually fed it, the Creature became so loving, so gentle, and so fond, that it became from that Time one of my Domesticks also, and would never leave me afterwards (81–2).

Comparison with a dog suggests the strength of the sympathetic bond established between this animal and Crusoe, so that, despite his subsequent failure to acquire a he-goat to mate with her, he 'could never find it my Heart to kill her, till she dy'd at last of meer Age' (105). In the course of her lifetime this goat crosses from prey to domestic stock to companion animal. Correspondingly, Crusoe's relation to her forms another compressed history of human progress: from hunter to farmer to (frustrated) stock breeder to pet-keeper.

The uneasiness associated with this process signifies a transition from one dominant mode of human–animal relations to another. In its maturity, modernity depends upon clear demarcations between various categories of human–animal relationship, geographically as well as emotionally. The very different dispositions appropriate to the treatment of the pet and the stock animal, for example, are usually kept from a potentially confusing proximity by urbanization. By contrast, as John Berger points out, in pre-industrial cultures a number of diverse interactions between humans and animals were integrated both spatially and affectively, producing a disposition whereby the 'peasant becomes fond of his pig and is glad to salt away its pork. What is significant, and so difficult for the urban stranger to understand, is that the two statements in this sentence are connected by an *and* and not by a *but*' (Berger 1980: 5). Berger considers that the intimacy and authenticity of this relation have been swept away by modernity, and especially by science, capitalism and industrialization, all of which corral human–animal relations into different and discrete compartments. The emergence of this modern attitude can be seen in a partial and incipient form in Crusoe's tenuous distinction between wild goats for hunting, domestic goats for eating, and goats he cannot find it in his heart to kill.

Crusoe's sympathetic tendencies are repeated more obviously in his two most strikingly ambivalent human relationships, namely with Friday and his precursor, Xury. Here, as with his non-human animals, Crusoe's moments of compassionate benevolence remain entirely qualified or compromised by the larger pursuit of self-interested enterprise. Nowhere is this more evident than in his negotiations with the captain who rescues him and Xury during the first part of his narrative:

> he offer'd me also 60 Pieces of Eight for my Boy Xury, which I was loath to take, not that I was not willing to let the Captain have him, but I was very loath to sell the poor Boy's Liberty, who had assisted me so faithfully in procuring my own. However when I let him know my Reason, he own'd it to be just, and offer'd me this Medium, that he would give the Boy an Obligation to set him free in ten Years, if he turn'd Christian; upon this, and Xury saying he was willing to go to him, I let the Captain have him (Defoe 1994 [1719]: 26).

The friendship and loyalty of the young man do not prevent Crusoe selling him into slavery to the first person who makes an offer, although they do shape the way the deal is conceived: the owner is to behave humanely; the slave is to demonstrate a willing submission to service. This paradigm of course is worked out first – or simultaneously – in the context of animal husbandry, as are other aspects of slave ownership. English travellers noted that the Portuguese marked slaves 'as we do sheep, with a hot iron', and observed potential buyers inspecting them 'as we handle beasts, to know their fatness and strength'. Meanwhile in England, slaves were given the same names as dogs and horses, while eighteenth-century advertisements offered 'silver padlocks for blacks or dogs', or rewards for runaway slaves known by the collars around their necks (Thomas 1984: 44–5). Thus, at the very best, slaves could expect only that partial and conditional sympathy granted to the domestic animals with whom they were routinely associated.

The last section of Crusoe's narrative exemplifies even more blatantly the regulation of compassionate and dispassionate affect that will permeate the modern attitude to the non-human and the non-European human alike. Mirroring Crusoe's adventures with Xury in the first section of the text, the final pages recount his travels through Europe in the company of Friday after their departure from the island. The climax is a fight with ravaging wolves in the Pyrenees, followed by the bathetic slaughter of a wild bear by Friday. The latter has been variously described in the text as Crusoe's willing slave, his servant, his companion, his friend, and – most commonly and with an ambiguity that has since become idiomatic – his 'man'. By this point, Friday demonstrates how well he has learned the lessons of Crusoe's gun-barrel husbandry. He uses his pistol to save the life of the party's guide from wolves, and then to slaughter a bear for the entertainment of his master and companions. Nowhere in this narrative, however, is there evidence of the compassionate attitude towards animals that emerged so frequently in Crusoe's description of his life on the island. On the contrary, Friday's baiting, tormenting and execution of the bear is recounted in approving and amused detail. The entire incident is also explicitly gratu-itous since, according to Crusoe, a bear seldom initiates an attack: '[o]n the contrary, if you meet him in the Woods, if you don't meddle with him, he won't meddle with you; but then you must take Care to be very Civil to him, and give him the Road; for he is a very nice Gentleman, he won't go a Step out of his Way for a Prince'. However, the least interference with a bear – even throwing at him 'a bit of a Stick, as big as your Finger' – will be taken as 'an Affront', and the animal will set 'all his other Business aside to pursue his Revenge'. Faced by a lack of immediate hostile intention on the part of the animal, Friday throws a stone at him 'purely to make the Bear follow him, and show us some Laugh as he call'd it' (Defoe 1994 [1719]: 211). Considering the range of sensitivities that characterizes Crusoe's prior engagement with animals, and the humorously anthropomorphic repre-sentation of the bear, it seems remarkable that no compassionate sympathy is accorded to this animal at all.

In fact, the emergence of a new kind of sympathy for the suffering of animals during Defoe's lifetime was most often confined to certain species. Bear-baiting, although banned during the Civil War and Interregnum, was legal again from 1660 until 1835 (Thomas 1984: 149, 158), and Friday's circus act with the bear clearly owes a good deal to this kind of cultural practice. This is because the relatively new urban sensibility of compassion pertained, in its orthodox form, mainly to domesticated animals. That is to say, anthropomorphic identification with the non-human would mainly be deployed to invite measured sympathy for animals belonging to species already enlisted into human agricultural, commercial or family life. Other species were likely to find themselves classed as vermin, for example: 'animals harmful to human interests and therefore "necessary to be hunted", as one seventeenth-century manual of venery put it' (Ritvo 1998: 38–9). Eligibility for human sympathy was thus distributed according to the pragmatic categorization of animals' usefulness to humans. As late as 1772, a writer on human and animal physiologies wrote that: 'all Animals, except ourselves . . . are strangers to pain and sickness', but added that '[w]e speak of wild animals only. Those that are tame . . . partake of our miseries' (cited in Ritvo 1998: 40). Perhaps surprisingly, then, the Cartesian denial of animals' capacity for feeling was resisted longest in relation to those species most widely exploited for human benefit, since it was believed that their 'cooperation' with human designs was less 'a human accomplishment' than 'an innate, divinely inculcated propensity "to submit . . . cheerfully and willingly"' (Ritvo 1998: 40). Defoe expressed his own assent to this viewpoint in his *Review*, asserting that the best proof of a divine plan is the 'subjection . . . to the dominion of man' of 'the useful part of the creatures', which are thus 'tame, docible, tractable, and submissive, while the less needful part are left wild and at war with us'. Without this docility, 'how useless would they be to mankind, and with what difficulties should we live; what a turn would it give to trade, what a universal stop to all manner of commerce!' (Defoe 1951 [1713]: 108).

According to this principle, then, Crusoe's attitude is consistent throughout the various sections of his narrative. House cats are entitled to (limited) moral consideration, but feral cats on the island and big cats in Africa are not; dogs are, but not wolves; goats, but not bears; parrots but not hawks. The activation of compassionate identification is incommensurate with the kinds of non-human agency that challenge or escape the modern dispensation: hence the vilification of wild or feral animals. Crusoe's humorously anthropomorphic description of the bear, then, is designed not to evoke sympathetic identification, but to trivialize the kinds of wild agency – exemplified by the bear's refusal to accommodate his behaviour to the presence of humans, and the insistence of his hostility once his own affairs are disrupted – which came to seem intolerable, and were progressively marginalized, as a consequence of modernity.

Of course, as the comic pairing of Friday and the bear suggests, this moral eschatology – dividing the goats from the bears, as it were, assigning some species to the light of moral consideration and others to the outer darkness of moral ineligibility – had everything to do with the categorizations applied to non-European humans. Sympathy occurs between Crusoe and the savages encountered on the shores of Africa only insofar as the latter enter into the domain of human commerce, and become trading partners. Similarly, Crusoe's companions, Xury and Friday, are presented as sympathetic characters according to their amenability to domestication as servants and slaves. It is in Friday's circus act with the bear that he attains, to the fullest extent possible, a secondary subjectivity that depends upon the subordination of his agency to Crusoe's authority. He is Crusoe's subaltern, his 'man', a creature of his will. 'His very Affections were ty'd to me, like those of a Child to a Father', remarks Crusoe (Defoe 1994 [1719]: 151), but considering the latter's poor relationship with his own father, another kind of affectionate bond provides a more vivid precursor: that of dog and master. Indeed, the attributes ascribed to Friday are identical to those of Crusoe's canine familiars: willing and loyal subalternity expressed as an enthusiastic and slightly comical affability.[18]

Despite its disruptive potential, then, Crusoe's compassionate sensibility is ultimately contained by the demands of the modern enterprise. The genre of satire, on the other hand, allows Swift far greater license to indulge the more radical dimensions of sympathetic identification. Predominantly this involves repeatedly subjecting his protagonist to the practices endured by animals, thereby describing the experience of such treatment from the inside. For the Lilliputians, for instance, Gulliver remains an 'indocible' animal. He proves impervious to house-training – a fact copiously demonstrated when he extinguishes a fire in the royal apartments by urination – and is too unpredictable and powerful to be considered a domestic animal. They consider taming him by means of starvation (just as Crusoe domesticates goats), or by putting out his eyes, according to 'the common practice of blinding some kind of Fowl' (Swift 2002 [1726]: 59). At this point Gulliver decides to escape, but his second voyage finds him subjected to even more practices associated with the management of non-human animals. In Brobdingnag he becomes in rapid succession a pest, a circus animal and an object of taxonomic study. Most often, his gigantic keepers treat him as a pet, as do the other animals inhabiting their homes and gardens. He finds himself initiated into the pet's-eye view of the household – a world of table-tops, overgrown gardens and building-sized cages – and forced to compete with the other animals that inhabit this same environment: the cat occupying its mistress' lap while Gulliver is on the dinner table, the dogs entering soon afterwards, the rats climbing on to the bed in his mistress' chamber, the gardener's spaniel seizing him in its mouth, and the tame monkey kidnapping him (76, 78, 97, 101–3).

In the farming household where he first lives, Gulliver discovers that the status of a 'pet' is not a stable one. According to Berger, prior to the eighteenth century the term 'pet' usually applied to a lamb raised by hand prior to slaughter (1980: 12), something the farmer's daughter Glumdalclitch understands, for she claims that 'her Papa and Mamma had promised' that she could keep Gulliver, 'but now she found they meant to serve her as they did last Year, when they pretended to give her a Lamb, and yet, as soon as it was fat, sold it to a Butcher' (Swift 2002 [1726]: 81). Glumdalclitch's suspicion of her parents' intentions demonstrates that the emergence of pet-keeping as a category of animal practice, and especially the firm distinction between pets and animals destined for ultimate slaughter and consumption, depended upon urbanization and the ensuing distance from agricultural processes. Being a pet guarantees immunity from consumption only in the city, as Gulliver finds when he reaches the capital of Brobdingnag.

It is Gulliver's experience as a circus animal that provides the most extended opportunity for sympathetic identification with an object of commercial exploitation. Glumdalclitch's father advertises his possession of this odd beast, who 'in every part of the Body resembling an human Creature, could speak several Words, and perform an hundred diverting Tricks' (Swift 2002 [1726]: 81–2). He assumes the role of the cruel circus impresario or slave owner:

> the more my Master got by me, the more unsatiable he grew. I had quite lost my Stomach, and was almost reduced to a Skeleton. The

Farmer observed it, and concluding I soon must dye, resolved to make as good a Hand of me as he could (84).

As Gulliver tells the Queen of Brobdingnag, this life is 'laborious enough to kill an Animal of ten times my Strength . . . my Health was much impaired by the continual drudgery of entertaining the Rabble every hour of the Day' (85). The implications of identification with an animal exhibit are heightened for Swift's contemporaries by the fact that some categories of humans were also subject to this particular mode of commercial enterprise. Perhaps the most famous of early modern arguments for sympathy with human otherness, Montaigne's 'Des Cannibales' derives from his contact with Brazilian Indians on display in Europe at the time (Hawes 1991: 190–91). Similarly 'dwarfs' and 'pigmies' were also often put on display – a fact ironically implied by Gulliver's rivalry with the Queen of Brobdingnag's dwarf (Swift 2002 [1726]: 90).

Gulliver's experience in Brobdingnag gives a speaking voice to the sideshow animal and the pet. In this respect, the *Travels* engages with the eighteenth-century genre sometimes called the 'novel of circulation' or the 'it-narrative'; stories told from the point of view of some everyday commodity, such as a coin, goose-quill, pin, sofa, reading desk, mirror, old shoe, smock, wig, watch, ring, umbrella, cane, sedan or stagecoach (Flint 1998: 214–15). The vicissitudes of such object-protagonists provided ample scope for the satirical exposure of human vanities and venalities, and the disempowering effects of early commodity capitalism. Since Gulliver is sometimes the human dealer in commodities and sometimes a commodity himself, his experience of human–animal transactions is particularly ironic. Thus after taking home miniature cattle from Lilliput and contemplating collecting some specimens of the people themselves, Gulliver is treated as an animal or anthropological commodity in Brobdingnag, and forced indignantly to reject the King of Brobdingnag's offer of a mate with whom he might establish a breeding stock of his own kind (Swift 2002 [1726]: 116).

The eighteenth-century it-narratives' insistent denigration and diminution of the human implies a theory of sympathy quite different from the calculated and conditional kindliness demonstrated by Crusoe. As Lamb describes it, this alternative form of sympathy is characterized by discomfort, unease and even revulsion: it is 'a perverse outcome of a defensive or hostile relation between species and things'. As in *Gulliver's Travels*, 'when they find their voices, things and creatures use them not to admire and claim association with human beings but to report matters that humiliate and disgrace them, such as their avarice, delusion, cruelty, ugliness, and mortality'. Sympathy, then, is revealed by the it-narrative to be capable of producing hostile and antagonistic affects alongside or even at the expense of benevolent ones. Moreover inter-species sympathy can be the outcome, not of moral virtue on the part of the one sympathizing, but of a radical disgust for humankind itself: 'humans may be propelled towards another kind not for sentimental pleasure but as a refuge from loneliness or self-loathing' (Lamb 2001: 134).

The most complex and powerful instance of trans-specific sympathy in *Gulliver's Travels* occurs in just this way, when Gulliver describes to the Houyhnhnms how horses are treated in England. Admitting that these 'were the most generous and comely Animal we had', he assures his listeners that 'when they belonged to Persons of Quality, employed in Travelling, Racing, or drawing Chariots, they were treated with much Kindness and Care'. At least, that is, he adds rather less tactfully, until

> they fell into Diseases, or became foundred in the Feet; and then they were sold, and used to all kind of Drudgery till they died; after which their Skins were stripped and sold for what they were worth, and their Bodies left to be devoured by Dogs and Birds of Prey. But the common Race of Horses had not so good Fortune, being kept by Farmers and Carriers and other mean People, who put them to greater Labour, and fed them worse. I described as well as I could, our way of Riding, the shape and use of a Bridle, a Saddle, a Spur, and a Whip, of Harness and Wheels (Swift 2002 [1726]: 203).

When his Houyhnhnm master asks indignantly how horses could put up with such treatment, Gulliver goes on to explain that they are broken in at a young age, 'employed for Carriages' if they prove 'intolerably vicious', 'severely beaten while they were young, for any mischievous Tricks', and if male, 'castrated about two Years after their Birth, to take down their Spirits, and make them more tame and gentle' (204).

The structure of sympathetic identification at work here is vertiginous (Wintle 1994). Unlike other parts of the narrative, Gulliver's description does not evoke his own experience of disgrace or cruelty, either as an animal or an object; rather, it recounts – for the edification of a horse-like interlocutor – the humiliations undergone by horses at the hands of Gulliver's own species. The various identifications available include the reader's imagination of the life of a horse in eighteenth-century London; Gulliver's desire to be a Houyhnhnm; the Houyhnhnm master's recognition of an affinity with English horses; and everyone's growing suspicion of kinship between the Yahoos and human beings, and in particular, Gulliver himself. In this way, the conventions of narrative are folded back upon themselves in a way that leaves in disarray all those distinctions that sympathy seeks to cross – between subject and object, human and animal, owner and commodity. Moreover these identifications become increasingly uncomfortable as their logic is pursued. The Houyhnhnm master responds to these revelations with a long diatribe detailing the physical and aesthetic, mental and moral faults of Gulliver's species. The latter's own acceptance of this misanthropy leads him to that form of inter-species sympathy resulting from 'self-loathing' or 'disgrace', as Lamb would put it, which is expressed by his rejection, on returning to England, of the company of his family in favour of life in a stable.

Both Defoe and Swift, then, register the growing impact of sympathy as a locus for the literary and philosophical interrogation of modernity. But they also demonstrate the wide variation in types of sympathetic identification that could be evoked, and the extraordinary range of effects that could result. Indeed, their narratives could hardly reach more different conclusions. Crusoe's last few adventures celebrate his triumph over the potentially disruptive effects of sympathy and non-human agency, while the final turn of Swift's satire entails a complete, and completely disruptive, identification between human and animal.

2   Gulliver, Frankenstein, Moreau

Gulliver's Laboratory

In their fictions of modernity, Defoe and Swift demonstrate that the shift in human–animal relations occurring in Europe in the eighteenth century was, although radical, anything but uniform. Rather it was unstable, contested, and accompanied by doubt and anxiety, both ethical and epistemological; it was, in every sense of the word, experimental. Indeed, experimentalism provided the characteristic *modus operandi* of Enlightenment modernity, and 'the animal' its paradigmatic object, insofar as the latter offered both a conceptual category against which the Cartesian *cogito* could define itself, and the biological raw material to which cogitation could be applied. In the laboratory, on the farm, in cities, on ships, in the wild, throughout the colonies, the development and testing of novel ways to manage the relationship between human and non-human life became the defining labour of modernity.

Animals on the Slide

Gulliver's career embodies the rise of scientific experimentalism in England. Clues in the text suggest that his birth date is 1660, the year of the founding of the Royal Society, Britain's pre-eminent institution for promulgation of the new sciences (Jaffe 2005). As a young man he studies at Emmanuel College in Cambridge, an institution strongly associated with the new science; goes on to a surgical apprenticeship in London; learns 'Navigation, and other Parts of the Mathematicks, useful to those who intend to travel'; and undertakes higher education in 'Physick' at the University of Leiden, noted throughout Europe at the time for its medical faculties (Swift 2002 [1726]: 15). Having established Gulliver's scientific credentials, Swift uses his voice to parody the kind of documentary observation, heavy with material detail and ignorant of its own stylistic propensities, that characterized both discovery narratives and the proceedings of scientific assemblies. The Royal Society 'gave instructions to its members and to travellers with regard to how they should record their visual and verbal observations' (Wagner 1995: 66; Phiddian 1998: 51). Accordingly, describing his encounter with the flying island of Laputa, Gulliver draws on astronomy, physics and optics to produce calculations of the height, velocity, mass and other features of the 'vast Opake Body' that intervenes between him and the sun. He also deploys a 'Pocket-Perspective' or telescope to examine it more closely (Swift 2002 [1726]: 132). The rhetoric in this passage exemplifies the titular conceit of the Enlightenment, namely 'that vision was queen among the senses, with observation at the heart of the acquisition of solid knowledge of the world' (Hulme and Jordanova 1990: 3–4). At the same time, Swift shows his observant narrator experiencing the most exorbitant fluctuations in his own ability for reliable measurement and judgement.

Scholars have suggested that Gulliver's first two voyages may be read as complementary applications of the visual distortions produced by the relatively new technologies of the microscope and telescope. Magnification, as used in the life sciences, operates as a man-making apparatus. Like Descartes' beast-machine, it constructs a division and distance between human subjectivity, the source of the empirical gaze, and the body of nature (planetary, terrestrial, animal or human) as the object of scrutiny. In *Gulliver*, however, the magnifying perspective is liable to inversion. 'Gulliver studies the Lilliputians as the *virtuosi* studied ant-hills, bee-hives, "Eels in Vinegar", blades of grass swarming with life', writes Marjorie Nicolson. Conversely, '[a]s the Lilliputians to Gulliver, so Gulliver to the Brobdingnagians; as he to them, so the Giants to him. All depends upon who holds the glass, and which lens is used' (1956: 197–8). Swift's reversals of perspective demonstrate the ambivalence that attended Enlightenment experiments in assisted observation. On one hand such methods, by enabling new discoveries and the testing of hypotheses about nature, reinforced the authority of the new science and belief in rational human endeavour. On the other hand they challenged the 'anthropocentric illusion' by revealing hitherto unsuspected ecologies of minute life-forms in water drops and on fragments of human skin (Thomas 1984: 168). Combined with natural historical investigations of the new worlds accessed as a result of colonial and commercial travel, and the ongoing astronomical identification of new planets, such discoveries tended to unsettle received biblical and scholastic confidence in the completeness of the human senses (Patey 1991: 838, note 39).

Gulliver's perspective reduces the hominid Lilliputians to the swarming animalcula that fascinated the virtuosi of the Royal Academy, but when he turns his magnifying gaze upon the Brobdingnagians, he finds the human form anatomized as animal matter of the grossest kind. He observes 'a Woman with a Cancer in her Breast, swelled to a monstrous size, full of Holes, in two or three of which I could have easily crept', as well as 'a fellow with a Wen in his Neck, larger than five Woolpacks' (Swift 2002 [1726]: 93–4). But most 'hateful' of all are the gigantic lice, magnified versions of those that infested the eighteenth-century European body. 'I could see distinctly', Gulliver reports, 'the Limbs of these Vermin with my naked Eye, much better than those of a European Louse through a Microscope, and their Snouts with which they rooted like Swine'. True to his vocation, he adds, 'I should have been curious enough to dissect one of them, if I had proper Instruments (which I unluckily left behind me in the Ship) although indeed the Sight was so nauseous, that it perfectly turned my Stomach' (94). In the first decades of the eighteenth century 'natural history had become a highly fashionable affair'; indeed the achievements of experts in this area were often rendered possible by the activity of amateurs (Thomas 1984: 281–3). During the 1720s Culpepper microscopes marketed to amateurs came with 'a set of four ivory slides of prepared specimens: Gulliver's most memorable images of magnified nature – hair, a bit of human skin, and a louse – appeared together on just one of these slides' (Oakleaf 1983: 169).

However Gulliver's account undermines the philosophical basis upon which this newly popular and authoritative mode of seeing depended. He can neither prevent nor deny his bodily reaction to what he sees; his nausea disrupts the supposedly disembodied attitude required of the scientific observer. Moreover the position from which Gulliver makes his observation, inside a box carried by his Brobdingnagian hosts through the streets of their capital, makes a mockery of the Enlightenment ideal of the transcendent, objective spectator. Unstable and radically contingent, Gulliver's viewpoint allows him no mastery of the field of vision, and no agency over the perspective attained. Indeed, by the time he leaves Brobdingnag Gulliver's sense of perspective is so scrambled he cannot accurately measure his own stature, nor that of the English mariners who rescue him – they appear to him like 'so many Pigmies' (Swift 2002 [1726]: 120) – nor that of his family at home.

Gulliver's perceptual vicissitudes satirize the reliance of empirical science upon rigid conventions of observation: the adoption of a point of view that disavows its own particularity and artifice; the employment of mediating technology in a way that disregards its capacity to distort; and the establishment of a distance between subject and object that denies the latter's capacity to transgress that separation, or to produce effects in the former. Swift's satirical perspectives call into doubt 'the very possibility of a detached point of view', questioning 'how one "can be both an object in the world and a subject constituting that world"' (Fox 1995: 14). They do so especially by means of a reversal that transforms the spectator into the object of other gazes. For example, Gulliver is subjected to microscopic scrutiny by 'three great Scholars' of Brobdingnag, who, 'after they had a while examined my Shape with much Nicety, were of different Opinions concerning me'. One suggests Gulliver 'might be an Embrio, or abortive Birth', a theory disproved by the evidence of bristles on his chin, 'plainly discovered through a Magnifying-Glass'. Nor can he be a dwarf, since his 'Littleness was beyond all degrees of Comparison; for, the Queen's favourite Dwarf, the smallest ever known in that Kingdom, was near thirty Foot high'. Eventually these giant virtuosi conclude that he is '*Relplum Scalcath*, which is interpreted literally, *Lusus Naturae*; a Determination exactly agreeable to all the Modern Philosophy of Europe, whose Professors . . . have invented this wonderful Solution of all Difficulties to the unspeakable Advancement of human Knowledge' (Swift 2002 [1726]: 86–7). Finding himself at the sharp end of an intrusive empirical scrutiny, Gulliver experiences first-hand the limitations of the new scientific method of observation which, turning upon the human subject, can only arrive at contradictory findings and a meaningless conclusion.

This inspection, moreover, occurs as the culmination of Gulliver's exposure to another kind of observation. He has been shown all around the country 'for Money as a publick Spectacle to the meanest of the People' by the mercenary farmer in whose harvest he was first discovered (Swift 2002 [1726]: 80–4). Reflecting the practice, common enough in Swift's time, of showing exotic or monstrous animals and peoples, this narrative implies that the new science, despite its pretensions to higher learning, was not always distinguishable from popular forms of curiosity or devoid of sordid economic motivations. 'In the winter of 1711–12, while Swift still lived in London', writes Hawes, a 'midget' and his pregnant wife from the West Indies were displayed 'at Charing Cross by a showman who exulted in print about the prospect of "breeding" them', while other 'popular spectacles of the period included . . . a rope-dancing monkey, a trained marmoset, a baboon, and a "wonderful Femal[e] Creature having a head like a Hog"' (1991: 190–91). Such exhibitions were the public face of the complicity between natural history and global commerce.

Maritime expansion – driven by trade, the race for colonial territory and the establishment of spheres of influence – provided natural historians with access to new ecosystems and species. At the same time, the observations made and specimens collected by ships' natural philosophers (like Gulliver) identified new resource areas for potential exploitation, while providing an apparently higher epistemological purpose – an 'anti-conquest narrative' – as an alibi and justification for colonial intrusion (Pratt 1992: 15–35). Gulliver himself is an avaricious collector of scientific curiosities wherever he goes, and carefully preserves organic specimens from Brobdingnag: a comb made of stumps from the King's beard, a fingernail paring and some hair from the Queen, a corn from a 'Maid of Honor's Toe', a 'Footman's Tooth', and 'Four Wasp Stings, like Joyners Tacks' (Swift 2002 [1726]: 64, 122, 224). After showing these last-mentioned items 'with some other Curiosities in several parts of Europe', Gulliver donates three of them to Gresham College, home of the Royal Society, keeping the fourth for himself (92).

Animals in Tables

The style of observation to which Gulliver is subjected by the virtuosi of Brobdingnag belongs to a branch of the new science that in Swift's time was regarded as especially prestigious: taxonomy. Natural historical inquiry during the seventeenth and eighteenth centuries was dominated by the task of classifying an ever-expanding world of living things. The great taxonomers of the time – John Ray, Louis de Buffon and Carl von Linné (Linnaeus) – produced massive treatises that organized non-human nature into complex systems. Their disciples travelled the world, as Gulliver does, on voyages of discovery and trade, collecting new specimens that extended the span of their taxonomic systems and strengthened Europe's epistemological grip on the natural world.

For Englishman John Ray, the leading taxonomist prior to Buffon and Linnaeus, the categorization of species' relationships depended on detailed scrutiny of the feet and the mouth as indicators respectively of the organism's locomotive and nutritional relationship to its environment. This is the procedure followed by the scholars of Brobdingnag:

> [t]hey all agreed that I could not be produced according to the regular Laws of Nature, because I was not framed with a Capacity of preserving my Life, either by Swiftness, or climbing of Trees, or digging Holes in the Earth. They observed by my Teeth, which they viewed with great Exactness, that I was a carnivorous Animal; yet most Quadrupeds being an Overmatch for me, and Field-Mice, with some others, too nimble, they could not imagine how I should be able to support my self, unless I fed upon Snails and other Insects, which they offered by many learned Arguments to evince that I could not possibly do (Swift 2002 [1726]: 86).

That such dedicated application of the methods of contemporary taxonomy serve, in this case, only to produce contradictory conclusions illustrates the impossibility of a disinterested perspective that excludes subjectivism, and the refusal of biological diversity to be held within firm epistemological boundaries. Non-arboreal and non-subterranean, but poorly suited for a terrestrial habitat, carnivorous but incapable of predation, Gulliver displays anomalous locomotive and nutritive features that demand a new category, *Relplum Scalcath* or *Lusus Naturae*, which is at once so compendious and so vacuous that it renders nonsensical the laws of the system that produces it.

The same form of examination is employed, reversed and satirized when Gulliver arrives in Houyhnhnmland. His first encounter with a Yahoo focuses closely on the 'distorted . . . Visage' and 'lifted . . . Fore-paw' of the creature (Swift 2002 [1726]: 190). As Wintle points out, Gulliver's immediate application of Ray's taxonomic method – classification by foot and by tooth – precludes 'the possibility that the limb is held out as a gesture with (cultural) meaning' or that the facial expression is 'communicative: a smile or a laugh'. At the same time, '[t]he creature's utterance is construed simply as "roaring", and so as empty, without human meaning or Cartesian rationality' (1994: 8).[1] Along with the perceptual limitations imposed by his taxonomic perspective, Gulliver's immediate and 'strong . . . Antipathy' to the Yahoos once more reveals the kind of affect disavowed by empirical acts of scrutiny (Swift 2002 [1726]: 190). Gulliver seems incapable of excluding subjective response from his attempt at dispassionate observation. Nor can he escape the return scrutiny on himself, for of course his aversion to the Yahoos gains its passion from the yet-unadmitted suspicion that he is one himself.

This return of the taxonomic gaze upon the scientific observer is repeated in his initial meeting with some Houyhnhnms, who examine Gulliver's face, hands and feet, 'using various Gestures, not unlike those of a [natural] Philosopher, when he would attempt to solve some new and difficult Phaenomenon' (Swift 2002 [1726]: 191). Indeed this examination is 'so orderly and rational, so acute and judicious' that Gulliver concludes these must be human beings in the shape of horses (191). Here the rituals of scientific observation have a man-making power capable of overriding the otherwise determinate factor of the observers' equine anatomy. It requires only Gulliver's identification with the perspective of the Houyhnhnms to complete the sardonic dissolution of the orthodox association between rationality, humanity and the methods of the new science, along with the human–animal distinction that depends on it. Before long, he comes to think of his family, friends, countrymen, and the 'Human Race in general' as mere 'Yahoos in Shape and Disposition', and upon observing his reflection in water, he turns away 'in Horror and Detestation of myself'. Meanwhile, '[b]y conversing with the Houyhnhnms, and looking upon them with Delight, I fell to imitate their Gate and Gesture', so that after his return to England he is told 'that *I trot like a Horse*; which . . . I take for a great Compliment: Neither shall I disown, that in Speaking I am apt to fall into the Voice and manner of the Houyhnhnms ' (234–5).

Yet such scepticism in regard to the place and nature of 'man' was not merely external or opposed to Enlightenment science. In some ways Swift merely exaggerates an anti-anthropocentrism produced by the very methods used by the new scientists to study animal life. Just as Gulliver is radically disconcerted when he turns his taxonomic eye on his own kind or his own reflection, finding nothing that resembles his idea of the human, eighteenth-century natural history was often baffled when it concentrated its observing gaze in the direction of 'man' as a species, and attempted to define categorically the nature of the human. More particularly, Gulliver's confusion as a result of his encounter with the hominoid Yahoos parallels 'the turmoil into which European thought was thrown by the discovery of the great apes of Africa and South-east Asia' (Thomas 1984: 129). In John Ray's taxonomy of 1694, the problem of categorizing human beings was evaded by omitting them altogether, thereby granting to 'man' a place beyond the world of nature (Sloan 1995: 121). However, the anatomical dissection in 1699 of 'an orang-outang, pygmie or wild man of the woods [in fact a chimpanzee]', performed and documented by Edward Tyson, placed the relation between humans and the great apes at centre stage. Susan Wiseman suggests that, as 'one of the acknowledged founders of comparative anatomy', Tyson might be expected to identify the ape 'very firmly as animal rather than human' (1999: 219). But in fact Tyson's account suggests a widening breach in both the Christian and the Cartesian attempts to maintain a border between human and beast. 'The Animal of which I have given the Anatomy, coming nearest to Mankind; seems the nexus of the Animal and the Rational', Tyson wrote, adding that 'in truth Man is part a Brute, part an Angel; and is that Link in the Creation, that joyns them both together' (cited in Wiseman 1999: 220–1). The image accompanying Tyson's text, although it emphasizes the animality of the chimpanzee, also grants it a disquietingly human stature and the capacity for tool-use: the living ape is pictured walking upright, with the aid of a stick (221).

By the time Linnaeus developed the first version of his *Systema Naturae* in 1735, humans were clearly identified as part of the natural world, although their exact position remained ambivalent. Linnaeus' classification of the *anthropomorpha* 'includes Homo (specifying distinction: reason), with varietal distinctions sapiens europaeus albus, s. americanus rubescens, s. asiaticus fuscus, s. africanus niger' (Sloan 1995: 122).[2] This concession to subspecific difference implies a flexible ratio of rational to bestial qualities amongst variants included in the category: 'if reason was to be the only defining mark separating man from animal, this was, for Linnaeus, a graduated reason, in which one could follow a clear line of descent within the human species' (123–6). It was also a capacity Linnaeus refused to deny the great apes, thereby contradicting the basis of the Cartesian distinction between human and animal: 'surely Descartes never saw an ape', he remarks in a note to the *Systema Naturae*, commenting elsewhere that from the point of view of comparative anatomy, he 'hardly knows a single distinguishing mark which separates man from the apes, save for the fact that the latter have an empty space between their canines and their other teeth' (cited in Agamben 2004: 23–4). Perhaps because of this scepticism, the author of the *Systema Naturae* 'does not record – as he does with the other species – any specific identifying characteristic next to the generic name *Homo*, only the old philosophical adage: *nosce te impsum* [know yourself]'. In this sense, '*Homo sapiens*, then, is neither a clearly defined species nor a substance; it is, rather, a machine or device for producing the recognition of the human'. The organism so named 'has no specific identity other than the *ability* to recognize [it]self'; it is '*the animal that must recognize itself as human to be human*'; moreover this recognition depends on animal otherness, for *Homo* 'must recognize [it]self in a non-man in order to be human' (Agamben 2004: 25–7).

Taking into account the epistemological alarm caused by the great apes as they swung across the human–animal boundaries erected by eighteenth-century taxonomists, it becomes evident that the most brutal indignities against Gulliver's humanity come from the confusion of this boundary between wild anthropomorph and human. The more the Yahoos see of Gulliver, the more certainly they recognize him as one of their own. 'I have reason to believe they had some Imagination that I was of their own Species', admits Gulliver reluctantly, 'which I often assisted myself, by stripping up my Sleeves, and shewing my naked Arms and Breast in their sight'. His unintended display of consanguinity produces an immediate response: they 'imitate my Actions after the manner of Monkeys, but ever with great signs of Hatred, as a tame Jack-Daw with Cap and Stockings, is always persecuted by the wild ones, when he happens to be got among them' (Swift 2002 [1726]: 223–4). In this simile the tame jackdaw is Gulliver himself. His rhetoric demonstrates an impending surrender to the idea that he shares the Yahoos' animality. Their hostile aping of Gulliver does not humanize them; rather it transforms him into a tame bird rendered both ridiculous and unnatural by its humanization. Like Crusoe's parrot, the tame jackdaw appropriates and makes strange the conventional signs of human uniqueness: speech in Crusoe's case, clothing in Gulliver's. As the Yahoos ape the jackdaw's mimicry, any possibility of an authentic and original human distinctiveness recedes into an endlessly repeating exchange of reflections, a sideshow version of Linnaeus' *Homo sapiens*, which Agamben calls 'an optical machine constructed of a series of mirrors in which man, looking at himself, sees his own image always already deformed in the features of an ape' (2004: 27).

Eventually, reluctantly, Gulliver concedes that he and the Yahoos are conspecifics, as a result of his harassment by a young female Yahoo who sees him bathing naked in a stream and leaps after him, 'enflamed by desire'. 'She embraced me after a most fulsome manner', Gulliver recalls stuffily. His 'Mortification' has less to do with sexual embarrassment or fright than the lethal effect of this incident upon his already weakened sense of the biological difference between himself and the Yahoos: 'I could no longer deny, that I was a real Yahoo, in every Limb and Feature, since the Females had a natural Propensity to me as one of their own Species' (Swift 2002 [1726]: 225). It was an article of faith among natural historians that animals possess an innate tendency to recognize their own species, especially in the context of mating (Ritvo 1998: 88–9). At the same time, this scene of unrequited lust shows another transgression, in the most carnal form, of the necessary structural distance between observing subject and object of taxonomic scrutiny. Distinctions based on an abstract system of comparison and documentation, organized from a position of transcendent visual assessment, have been replaced by a tactile, corporeal embrace that seeks to engage organs of a more intimate nature than the eyes. The detached aura of scientific observation has been dispersed by the female Yahoo's flaming desire, which receives a faint, vain and disgraceful response in the form of Gulliver's aside that his would-be paramour's '[c]ountenance did not make an Appearance altogether so hideous as the rest of her Kind' (225).

This category mistake by the young Yahoo female, which Gulliver fears is no mistake at all, echoes an earlier and even greater indignity when he is kidnapped by a gigantic pet monkey in Brobdingnag.[3] Having seized Gulliver from his chamber, the monkey 'took me up in his right fore-foot and held me as a Nurse does a Child she is going to suckle'. Again, this episode transgresses the fragile taxonomic boundary between humans and other hominoid animals: 'I have good reason to believe that he took me for a young one of his own Species' (Swift 2002 [1726]: 101). And again it does so by reference to the most intimate of bodily engagements: Gulliver describes the animal 'holding me like a Baby in one of his fore-paws, and feeding me with the other, by cramming into my Mouth some Victuals he had squeezed out of the Bag on one side of his Chaps' (102). The proximity of the relation between humans and other primates, as represented by their shared anatomical features and diets, is shoved down Gulliver's throat. Here and throughout the *Travels*, Swift sardon-ically anticipates the intensity that informs encounters between humans and other anthropomorphic beings – Frankenstein's Creature, Moreau's Beast Folk, and after them a host of science fiction beasts, monsters and aliens, not to mention apes and monkeys – when the assumptions of modernity turn back on its heroes.

Animals on the Table

The taxonomic satires of *Gulliver's Travels* emphasize the messy materiality of human–animal encounters, contradicting the Enlightenment ideal of transcendent observation. The same is true of Swift's representation of that other quintessential site for the exhibition of new scientific experimental-ism: the laboratory. Of course it was on the tables of the virtuosi that the Cartesian notion of the beast-machine was most faithfully applied. Descartes' more literal-minded followers went so far as to assert that '[a]nimal howls and writhings were merely external reflexes, unconnected with any inner sensation' (Thomas 1984: 33). In so doing they exemplified the instrumentalism of the new science, its perception of the world as a system of physical relations and reactions which could be understood only by investigators willing to disregard ruthlessly any effect or affect that was empirically unprovable, inhibiting to the scientific method being deployed, or irrelevant to the hypothesis being tested.

This mechanistic epistemology is satirized in Gulliver's visit to the Grand Academy in Lagado, Swift's version of the Royal Society (Nicolson 1956: 135). Despite the hyper-Cartesianism of the resident virtuosi, Gulliver perceives their experiments as a series of emphatically carnal engagements with animal matter, including that associated with the human animal. His first encounter is with a 'most Ancient Student of the Academy', whose body is 'dawbed with Filth' from his attempts to 'reduce human Excrement to its original Food' (Swift 2002 [1726]: 152). The old man's obliviousness to his own and his surroundings' shittiness matches the disembodied abstraction affected by the Laputan gentry and implied by Cartesian rationalism. Gulliver, though, can't help but notice the extent to which science becomes inextricably involved with its objects of inquiry, especially when he is subjected by this researcher to 'a very close Embrace, (a Compliment I could well have excused)' (152).

The same contamination of observing subject by observed animal matter, and *vice versa*, recurs during an even more intrusive procedure, which Gulliver witnesses performed on a live animal:

I was complaining of a small Fit of the Cholick, upon which my Conductor led me into a Room, where a great Physician resided, who was famous for curing that Disease by contrary Operations from the same Instrument. He had a large pair of Bellows with a long slender Muzzle of Ivory. This he conveyed eight Inches up the Anus, and drawing in the Wind, he affirmed he could make the Guts as lank as a dried Bladder. But when the Disease was more stubborn and violent, he let in the Muzzle while the Bellows were full of Wind, which he discharged into the Body of the Patient, then withdrew the Instrument to replenish it, clapping his Thumb strongly against the Orifice of the Fundament; and this being repeated three or four times, the adventitious Wind would rush out, bringing the noxious along with it (like Water put into a Pump) and the Patient recover. I saw him try both Experiments upon a Dog, but could not discern any Effect from the former. After the latter, the Animal was ready to burst, and made so violent a Discharge, as was very offensive to me and my Companions. The Dog died on the Spot, and we left the Doctor endeavouring to recover him by the same Operation (Swift 2002 [1726]: 153–4).

This incident echoes an experiment made infamous in Shadwell's satirical play *The Virtuoso* (1676), namely Robert Hooke's vivisection of a dog, reported in Sprat's *History of the Royal Society* as follows:

[i]n prosecution of some Inquiries into the Nature of Respiration in several Animals; A Dog was dissected, and by means of a pair of bellows, and a certain Pipe thrust into the Wind-pipe of the Creature, the heart continued beating for a very long while after all the Thorax and Belly had been open'd (1959 [1667]: 232).

Sprat's tone of detachment precludes mention of any signs of distress in the animal, or of its consequent death: all that pertains is the data with which the manipulation is concerned.[4] Gulliver's observation of the corresponding procedure deploys the same clinical tone but includes carnal details – the smell of the 'discharge', the distortion of the animal's body and its death – that invite other-than-rational responses (laughter, disgust, dismay). Swift's reversal of Hooke's original experiment (the Lagadan manipulation occurs via the anus rather than the trachea) produces a scatological result that once again renders absurd the sterile abstraction implied by Sprat's bloodless prose. At the same time, since this experimental 'cure' is shown to Gulliver in response to his own intestinal troubles, part of the sardonic humour of the passage depends upon his, and the reader's, anticipation of his potential subjection to this same treatment. Swift thereby combines a pastiche of the Cartesians' infamous disregard for animal suffering with a disruptive identification between the unfortunate animal and its observer. Satirically speaking, in this scene as in the other 'apartments' of the Grand Academy, the human becomes just another animal on the table.

The experiments of the Lagadan Academy of Projectors also parody 'the speculative financial projects which were floated in large numbers in the six years before 1720, when the greatest of them, the South Sea Bubble . . . burst', especially considering that in Swift's time, the word 'projector' was used for those who engaged in scientific and in entrepreneurial experiments alike (Hodgart 2000: 79).[5] The conjunction of intellectual and economic interest is also indicated by the notion of 'speculation'. Foremost amongst the 'Advancers of speculative Learning' is 'the universal Artist' who is attempting, 'by a certain Composition of Gums, Minerals, and Vegetables outwardly applied, to prevent the Growth of Wool upon young Lambs; and he hoped in a reasonable time to propagate the Breed of naked Sheep all over the Kingdom' (Swift 2002 [1726]: 154). Swift's twenty-first-century readers are more than familiar with the extravagancies practised by science on animal subjects – chemical and surgical experimentation, selective breeding, xenotransplantation, hormonal manipulation, cloning, genetic engineering – which have often resulted in outcomes no less bizarre than those described by Gulliver.[6] They are also aware of the complicity between commerce and animal science in the production of cosmetics, drugs, food, clothing and other commodities. Hence, although to Swift's first readers the projectors of Lagado might have seemed deluded in their attempts to capitalize on their experiments, subsequent history shows that the conjunction between science and commerce has been both formative and highly profitable. 'The Royal Society', writes Thomas, 'encouraged the study of animals with a view to determining 'whether they may be of any advantage to mankind, as food or physic; and whether those or any other uses of them can be further improved' (1984: 27). As a result the selective breeding of livestock was conducted along increasingly scientific principles from the late seventeenth century onwards.[7] Such manipulation of genetic stock 'was effected for other forms of consumption' too: 'horse breeding for hauling as well as hunting, homing pigeons' and, of course, the production of a range of pets from dogs to goldfish (Barker-Benfield 1992: 232).

The cooperation between commercial and scientific animal practices also benefited from colonial and mercantile expansionism. As early as the mid-seventeenth century, the suggestion was made 'that more exotic animals could be introduced into English agriculture: if turkeys, then why not elephants, buffaloes or mules?' (Thomas 1984: 27–8); while a century later, Christopher Smart would pray for 'the introduction of new creatures into this island . . . for the ostriches of Salisbury Plain, the beavers of the Medway and silver fish of Thames' (cited in Thomas 1984: 28). This attitude lies behind another of the Lagadan schemes. Gulliver describes 'a Projector, who had found a Device of Plowing the Ground with Hogs, to save the Charges of Plows, Cattle, and Labour'. Here, Swift extrapolates from a paper in the Royal Society's *Transactions* entitled 'The Culture of Tobacco in Zeylan', which described the Ceylonese use of herds of water-buffalo to fertilize newly sown fields (Nicolson 1956: 148–9). Like Crusoe's goats, the plough-hogs of Lagado exist only because of an expanding network of exchange, whereby animal practices, bodies and species became transplanted from metropolitan centres to colonial locations and *vice versa*, as part of the restless experimentalism of ecological and economic globalization.

While Gulliver seems less than enthusiastic about some of the Lagadan projects, he declares himself 'highly pleased' with the plough-hog scheme, presumably because he considers it the most promising in economic terms. After all, the reason he is taken to visit the Grand Academy in the first place is because 'I had my self been a sort of a Projector in my younger Days' (Swift 2002 [1726]: 151). And indeed, throughout the *Travels* his interest in exotic life-forms combines the intellectual ambition evinced by the scientists of the Grand Academy with an eye for the investment opportunities afforded by exotic animal stock. When during his sojourn in Houyhnhnmland he attempts to capture an infant Yahoo – which 'fell a squalling, and scratching, and biting with such Violence, that I was forced to let it go' (224) – it remains unclear whether his intentions in collecting this 'little Imp' are primarily ethnographic, taxonomic or commercial. Had the three-year-old Yahoo proven more tractable, it presumably would have joined the Lilliputian live-stock, 'six Cows and two Bulls alive, with as many Yews and Rams', which Gulliver takes with him at the end of his first voyage, 'intending to carry them to my own Country, and propagate the Breed' (64). Despite the loss of one of these minuscule sheep to a ship's rat, Gulliver (in terms that recall Crusoe at his most calculating) notes that, during

> [t]he short time I continued in England, I made a considerable Profit by shewing my Cattle to many Persons of Quality, and others: and before I began my second Voyage, I sold them for six hundred Pounds. Since my last return, I find the Breed is considerably increased, especially the Sheep; which I hope will prove much to the Advantage of the Woollen Manufacture, by the Fineness of the Fleeces (66).

Colonial expansion, economic profit, prurient curiosity, intellectual ambition: these are the motives that Swift finds at work behind the modern façade of rational and objective experimentalism.

In criticizing such exploitative tendencies, even though his sardonic temperament precludes any overt appeal to a compassionate sensibility, Swift contributes to the same sympathetic reaction against Enlightenment instrumentalism that became a defining feature of eighteenth-century literary culture. Thomas comments that 'in keeping with the new emphasis upon sensation', writers increasingly challenged 'some forms of cruelty which had passed without much comment in earlier periods. Vivisection, which Isaac Barrow in 1654 had described as 'innocent' and 'easily excusable', was castigated a century later by Dr Johnson' (1984: 177–8). Similarly, 'methods of meat production also came under attack' – a point Thomas demonstrates by citing Defoe's *Compleat English Tradesman*:

[w]hat Rapes are committed upon nature in the production of Animals as well as Plants? making Ewes bring Lambs all the Winter, fatting Calves to a monstrous size, using cruelties and contrary diets to the poor Brute, to whiten its Flesh for the Palates of the Ladies, and to gorge the dainty Stomachs of those that lay up their felicity in Eating fine, as they call it? (Defoe 1969 [1727]: II, II, 107)

Although Defoe admits '[i]t is not my business here to write a Satyr upon Luxury', his rhetoric here is not inconsistent with parts of *Gulliver's Travels*. Moreover he concludes his treatise with a call for restraint in the kinds of experimentalism produced by rampant consumer culture. If English tastes were 'a little more modest . . . a little less Curious, less Extravagant, less Exotick, and abated a little of their Excesses', then '[t]rade need not be destroy'd tho' Vice were mortally wounded, much less need we be oblig'd to encourage Flaming Luxury for fear of discouraging our Commerce, lessening our Revenue, or starving our Poor' (II, II, 173–4). Here, as in *Robinson Crusoe*, Defoe evokes a capacity for sympathetic identification which, although it stops short at limiting trade and profit, proposes a humane regulation of the means by which animals may be transformed into consumable commodities.

Swift's fiction demonstrates more extreme versions of the two competing structures of feeling at work in the eighteenth century, namely the intellectual detachment of projectors (both scientific and capitalist) satirized in the academicians of Lagado and their aristocratic patrons on Laputa, and the exorbitant sympathetic identification embodied by Gulliver, who experiences being treated as an animal and eventually aligns himself so completely with the virtues of an equine species that he can no longer bear the company of humans. Typically, Swift encourages admiration of neither disposition, instead showing modernity as a woeful separation and confusion of such oppositions, of which 'modern man' is the chaotic and risible by-product. It is a marker of how vividly *Gulliver's Travels* diagnoses the condition of the modern human animal that, throughout the ensuing three centuries, fantastic narratives have continued to demonstrate the durability of this tension between science and sensibility. Among these, of course, is Mary Shelley's *Frankenstein*, which takes up Swift's concerns in a story so animated that it continues to shape debates about scientific and humane world views today.

Frankenstein's Workshop

Few novels have entered into everyday cultural parlance as rapidly and durably as *Frankenstein*. By 1824, a few years after its publication, the expression 'Frankenstein's monster' had become a convenient tag for any kind of political or cultural innovation that threatened to 'turn and destroy' its creator (St Clair 2000: 55). In the domain of science – or more precisely, popular ideas and anxieties about science – this cliché still retains force despite two centuries of frequent use.[8] But Shelley's text demonstrates a far more complex figuration of nineteenth-century science and its counter-discourses than is signified by this summary version. Like Gulliver before them, Victor Frankenstein and his Creature are especially significant figures for the cultural-historical analysis of human–non-human relationships, as these shaped and were shaped by the ongoing modern dialogue between science and sensibility.

A Herd of Projectors

Frankenstein comprises three concentric narratives. The innermost is that of the Creature, whose autobiography is framed within that of his creator, Victor Frankenstein, who tells his story to the arctic explorer Robert Walton aboard the latter's ship. The outermost narrative is Walton's, transcribed in letters to his sister Margaret in England. The first-person speakers of each account – the Creature, Frankenstein and Walton – are thereby sutured together, inviting comparison between them. Each is male, and each embarks on a quest that – like those of Crusoe and Gulliver – results in extreme social and geographical isolation. Each mourns his separation from affective engagement with others, and attempts its redress by evoking a sympathetic understanding between speaker and audience. The narrative is thus permeated and shaped by the dialectic between, on the one hand, an Enlightenment model of strict separation between scientific subject and experimental object, and on the other, the paradigm of sympathetic identification that Romanticism inherits from the eighteenth-century culture of sensibility.

Like Crusoe and Gulliver, Shelley's three narrators embody the restless mobility typical of modern heroes. Walton is driven by the search for magnetic north and an Arctic passage from the Atlantic to the Pacific (Shelley 1996 [1818]: 7–8) – goals that conjoin scientific, commercial and imperialist interests, since their achievement would facilitate navigational accuracy and cut down voyaging time, thereby yielding opportunities for further trade and colonization to the sponsoring nation (Bate 2000: 49). Frankenstein's physiological discoveries, which equate to Walton's geographical ones, are driven by 'a resistless, and almost frantic impulse [that] urged me forward' (32), while in his final pursuit of the Creature across nations and continents he follows 'the mechanical impulse of some power of which I was unconscious' (142).

The geographical distance travelled by both men embodies their emotional separation from all the matrices of social life and from affective bonds with their own 'species'. Walton yearns for 'the company of a man who could sympathize with me' (Shelley 1996 [1818]: 10). He recognizes a potential 'brother' in Victor, but the latter spurns this friendship, insisting that his experiences have removed him as far from any capacity for emotional engagement as they have from his hometown. Indeed Frankenstein's progress – which begins with his enjoyment of a 'happy', 'indulgent' and 'amiable' family life (20), and concludes with his solitary

stranding on an ice-floe – has been understood as Mary Shelley's unflattering portrait of a disposition that gained dominance during the first decades
of the nineteenth century: that of 'remodelled Romantic genius, the master
of nature operating alone, rather than in a society of equals', recklessly
pursuing his own career in a way that was 'cut off from the social networks
that would preserve his humanity and discipline his research' (Fulford *et al.*
2004: 196–7). Frankenstein's obsessional researches cause him to neglect
his friends and family and postpone his marriage to Elizabeth, and eventually result in the deaths of every one of his intimates. As he tells Walton, '[i]f
the study to which you apply yourself has a tendency to weaken your affections' then it 'is certainly unlawful, that is to say, not befitting the human
mind' (Shelley 1996 [1818]: 33). But in fact, the most destructive failure in
Frankenstein's affections is surely the refusal of parental responsibility
towards his creature. Although Victor anticipates that '[n]o father could
claim the gratitude of his child so completely as I should deserve [his]',
these paternal emotions are promptly extinguished the moment his
offspring comes to life (32–5). As the Creature himself puts it: '[u]nfeeling,
heartless creator! You had endowed me with perceptions and passions, and
then cast me abroad an object for the scorn and horror of mankind' (94).
Many scholars find it impossible to dismiss the validity of this accusation,
and some find in it the key to the novel, which they read alongside Shelley's
castigation of Rousseau, in an essay written some years later, for that
philosopher's infamous abandonment of his own children. 'Our first duty is
to render those to whom we give birth, wise, virtuous, and happy, as far as
in us lies', she wrote, a criticism with evident applicability to Shelley's
famous flawed hero (cited in O'Rourke 1989: 547; see also Marshall 1988:
188–9).

   In this respect, Shelley again echoes the reservations of Swift, who saw in
the new science the same irresponsible isolationism and instrumentalism
that licenses Victor first to experiment with nature, and then fatally to
reject the product of his experiment. Moreover Frankenstein's fascination
with science is presented in the same Cartesian terms that Swift parodies,
insofar as it entails a quest for power over nature, both human and non-
human. Victor is won over to modern science by the rhetoric of M.
Waldman, who persuades him that although '[t]he modern masters
promise very little', they 'have indeed performed miracles'. Their 'hands
seem only made to dabble in dirt, and their eyes to pour over the microscope or crucible', but by so doing they 'penetrate into the recesses of
nature, and shew how she works in her hiding places', discovering 'how the
blood circulates, and the nature of the air we breathe', and acquiring 'new
and almost unlimited powers' (Shelley 1996 [1818]: 27–8). Waldman's
imagery anticipates Victor's own 'secret toil, as I dabbled among the unhal-
lowed damps of the grave' (32), but it also recalls Swift's Lagadan virtuoso,
covered in the shit he is trying to refine into food. His evocation of penetra-
tion of nature's hidden workings and his mention of experiments in circu-
latory and respiratory medicine recall Hooke's dog experiment and the

procedures of Harvey and Boyle, and also foreshadow Victor's dissections and vivisections. More broadly, M. Waldman's rhetoric echoes that of Francis Bacon, the founder of the British new scientific tradition, a man described by Voltaire as the 'father of experimental philosophy' (cited in Horkheimer and Adorno 1973: 3). A decade before Descartes' *Discourse on Method*, Bacon's *New Atlantis* imagined an experimental 'Foundation', Solomon's House, dedicated to 'the knowledge of Causes, and secret motions of things; and the enlarging of the bounds of Human Empire, to the effecting of all things possible' (Bacon 1942 [1627]: 288).[9] Accordingly, hubristically, Frankenstein thinks himself as far removed from his more mundane colleagues as the human experimenter is from animals. 'When I reflected on the work I had completed', he tells Walton, 'I could not rank myself with the herd of common projectors' (Shelley 1996 [1818]: 147).

A Filthy Mass that Moved and Talked

Both Walton's narrative and Frankenstein's within it show the separation of the hero of modernity from affective sympathy as a result of his quest for scientific advancement. In contrast, the third narrative embedded within these two, the account the Creature gives of his life to his creator, represents a concerted attempt to elicit sympathy from his creator: '[h]ow can I move thee? Will no entreaties cause thee to turn a favourable eye upon thy creature, who implores thy goodness and compassion?' (Shelley 1996 [1818]: 66).

Eighteenth-century literary responses to modernity, as discussed in the preceding chapter, produced an intense focus upon sympathy and related concepts such as sensation, sentiment and sensibility. These dispositions were bequeathed to Romanticism. As David Marshall remarks, 'since we cannot know the experience or sentiments of another', Romantic sympathy posed an epistemological problem to which narrative offered a solution: the imaginative inhabitation of another's 'place and person' (1988: 3, 5). It is this technique that the Creature deploys in his attempt to incite the sympathy of Frankenstein. He presents his life from the outset in terms of bodily feeling and emotional affect: '[a] strange multiplicity of sensations seized me, and I saw, felt, heard, and smelt, at the same time; and it was, indeed, a long time before I learned to distinguish between the operations of my various senses' (Shelley 1996 [1818]: 68). Borrowing from Rousseau, Shelley presents the Creature's career as the development of sensibility, that is, the ability to comprehend and articulate sensations.[10] This process is necessarily conducted in dialogue with the natural environment: the moon, a stream, trees, and then animal life: 'I was delighted when I first discovered that a pleasant sound, which often saluted my ears, proceeded from the throats of the little winged animals who had often intercepted the light from my eyes'. The Creature's desire to imitate birdsong represents his first attempt at sympathetic identification with another living being: 'I tried to imitate the pleasant songs of the birds, but was unable'.

Subsequently, his closer attentiveness to their voices shows his developing understanding: 'I found that the sparrow uttered none but harsh notes, whilst those of the blackbird and thrush were sweet and enticing' (68–9). This association between birdsong and emotional expression recurs when the Creature watches the De Laceys and so observes for the first time the interchange of human sympathies. The old man plays a musical instrument and sings for his granddaughter, producing 'sounds, sweeter than the voice of the thrush or the nightingale' which 'drew tears from the eyes of his amiable companion' (72).

It is from the De Laceys, too, that the Creature learns an even more radical mode of sympathy, an identification so powerful that the interests of the other are given priority over those of the self. He notices that despite their lack of food, 'the two younger cottagers . . . placed food before the old man, when they reserved none for themselves. This trait of kindness moved me sensibly' (Shelley 1996 [1818]: 74). As a result the Creature stops stealing their food, and starts assisting them secretly in their labours. Envying the daily 'interchanging . . . [of] looks of affection and kindness' he observes among the De Laceys, he decides to reveal himself to them, daring 'to fancy amiable and lovely creatures sympathizing with my feelings and cheering my gloom' (74, 88). This fantasy ends, inevitably, in disappointment. The young De Laceys share Frankenstein's disgusted reaction to the Creature's appearance – 'Who can describe their horror and consternation on beholding me?' (91) – and so do all other humans he meets after he flees in despair, including the 'rustic' who shoots him after the Creature rescues his lover from drowning (95) and, fatally, Frankenstein's little brother William:

> [a]s soon as he beheld my form, he placed his hands before his eyes, and uttered a shrill scream: I drew his hand forcibly from his face, and said, 'Child, what is the meaning of this? I do not intend to hurt you; listen to me'.
> He struggled violently; 'Let me go', he cried; 'monster! ugly wretch!' . . . The child still struggled, and loaded me with epithets which carried despair to my heart: I grasped his throat to silence him, and in a moment he lay dead at my feet (96–7).

The Creature's visible difference from all the human beings he encounters prevents their sympathizing with him. It is only the old man De Lacey whose blindness prevents such a rejection and allows a transient moment of sympathy to occur: 'I am blind, and cannot judge of your countenance, but there is something in your words which persuades me that you are sincere' (91). Learning this lesson well, the Creature attempts to incite Frankenstein's sympathy unhindered by the appearance of radical difference between them. 'Begone!', cries Victor, 'relieve me of the sight of your tested form'; in response the Creature puts his hands over his creator's eyes and replies, 'thus I take from thee a sight which you abhor. Still thou canst listen to me, and grant me thy compassion' (67). And indeed, such is the power of the Creature's narrative to incite the kind of imaginative sympathy upon which Romanticism placed such weight that it virtually overrides visual prejudice. 'His words had a strange effect upon me', admits Victor:

> I compassionated him, and sometimes felt a wish to console him; but when I looked upon him, when I saw the filthy mass that moved and talked, my heart sickened, and my feelings were altered to those of horror and hatred (99).

Two dispositions are critiqued here, each embodied in the person of Frankenstein. The first, of course, is that of Enlightenment science, in particular its privileging of visual perception over any other sense and its artificial separation of observation from affect. The second is a particular form of sympathy. Although Walton portrays him as a paragon of sensibility (Shelley 1996 [1818]: 15–16), Frankenstein's reaction to the Creature exemplifies a distinction between visual and affective sympathy. In this respect Shelley challenges a disposition characteristic of the Romantic movement itself, portraying Frankenstein's appreciation for 'the beauties of nature' (16) as not merely inadequate but actually inimical to the achievement of affective sympathy. Walton rhapsodizes his new companion's typically Romantic appreciation for '[t]he starry sky, the sea and every sight afforded by these wonderful regions', which so affect him that 'when he has retired into himself, he will be like a celestial spirit, that has a halo around him, within whose circle no grief or folly ventures' (16). If there seems something awry in a sensibility so refined it can exclude the emotional impact of the recent annihilation of six close family and friends, it is because Shelley is mounting the same critique that Swift expresses by ridiculing the star-and-navel-gazing Laputans. The transcendentalism of the modern gaze – its upwardness and inwardness – results in a distancing from other, more material forms of sensibility.[11]

With his hard-won appreciation of the optical prejudices of the time, the Creature specifies the need for visual compatibility when he begs Frankenstein to 'create a female for me, with whom I can live in the interchange of those sympathies necessary for my being': this being has to be 'as deformed and horrible as myself', a companion with 'the same defects', who therefore 'would not deny herself to me' (Shelley 1996 [1818]: 97–8). But even this final effort to achieve a relationship of benevolent sympathy will be denied him once again by a judgement made on visual terms. Frankenstein is hard at work creating a spouse for the Creature when he appears at the laboratory window: '[a]s I looked on him, his countenance expressed the utmost extent of malice and treachery', recalls Frankenstein. It is the Creature's looks, then, that persuade Victor it would be 'madness' to create 'another like him', so that he immediately tears to pieces 'the thing on which I was engaged' (115).

The Meanest Animal

The manufacture of the female creature brings into focus the issue of species, which the novel relates crucially to the issue of sympathy. Whether or not sympathy is due to the Creature turns on the issue of sameness or difference, or more specifically, whether or not he can be considered a member of the human species (Caldwell 1999; McLane 2000). In each of his encounters with human beings, Frankenstein's Creature faces the radical lack of sympathy that results from his ambiguous place in the taxonomic scheme. For Marshall, the central question in the novel is 'whether Frankenstein and the monster are of the same species: whether they can regard each other as fellow creatures' (1988: 198). From the outset, Victor's own views on this issue are contradictory. Having decided to 'give life to an animal as complex and wonderful as man', he begins 'the creation of a human being', while at the same time anticipating the origin of 'a new species' (Shelley 1996 [1818]: 31–2). Subsequently he refers to the product of this ambition as 'creature', 'corpse', 'spectre', 'daemon', 'wretch', 'vampire', 'being', 'animal', 'fiend', 'figure of a man', 'devil', 'vile insect', 'monster' and 'villain' (34, 35, 37, 48, 49, 60, 65, 116) – although in his final assessment he cannot resist praising himself for the creation of 'a sensitive and rational animal' (147). Each of the terms he uses for the creature is capable of being applied also to human beings in Shelley's time.[12]

No definitive answer to the question of the Creature's species is permitted by the text, with the result that definitions of the human itself, whether based on sympathy or biology, are also placed under erasure. From the perspective of the Creature, it is Frankenstein who proves inhuman, failing to display the affections proper to humanity by repeatedly rejecting his offspring. Conversely, from Victor's point of view, his refusal of the claims of the Creature is precisely what returns him to the path of human virtue – most evidently when, after imagining the consequences of his creation of a companion creature, he chooses to privilege the interests of his own kind. 'My duties towards the beings of my own species had greater claims to my attention', he asserts, a view which persuades him that he 'did right in refusing . . . to create a companion for the first creature' (Shelley 1996 [1818]: 151). Nonetheless, the confidence Victor shows at this point about the species distinction is anything but stable. Certainly, he and the Creature appear to concur that they belong to different species when deciding that Victor would create a female, a companion 'of the same species' (97), and Frankenstein repeats this assertion upon revoking his promise to do so (114). Yet at the same time, the Creature's claim to the right of companionship rests on his guarantee that this will make him – after he and his partner migrate to the 'vast wilds' of South America – 'peaceful and human' (99). In response, Victor doubts that two beings 'who long for the love and sympathy of man' can be socially content in 'those wilds where the beasts of the field will be your only companions' (99). The

Creature suggests that spatial separation from *Homo sapiens* can make him become human; Victor fears the Creature is already too human to endure such exile. It is this scepticism – about whether creatures so humanoid could permanently forgo proximity to humans – that underwrites his decision to abort the female creature (Marshall 1988: 198; McLane 2000: 100–101). These vacillations on the theme of humanity and inhumanity play an anthropoluotic role similar to that performed by the great apes in Swift's time. Attempting to create another being in his own image, and then seeking to destroy that creation, Frankenstein constructs a version of the 'optical machine' described by Agamben in his discussion of Linnaeus (2004: 27) – a 'series of mirrors' in which he sees his own idea of the human, always already deformed in the features of his monster.

It may be, however, that Frankenstein underestimates the significance of companionship with 'beasts of the field'. The second way *Frankenstein* strains and challenges what McLane calls the 'mutual implication of the discourse of sympathy and the construction of human being' is by hinting at alternative modes of sympathy to those pertaining among humans (2000: 101). While mainstream humanist theories of sensibility drew the boundaries of human nature according to the inclusion or exclusion of various subjects from the circle of those eligible for sympathetic identification, there also existed an alternative tradition, which understood sympathy as an extreme form of affect that not only crossed the species border but threatened to eradicate it. Ashton Nichols traces this extra-humanist notion of sympathy via the natural historical tradition represented by Erasmus Darwin, whose *Zoonomia* (1803) portrays humans, animals and even plants as 'connected by the possibility of sensation', and gives the mimosa, whose leaves respond to touch, as an example (Nichols 2001: para. 6, para. 12). The influence of the earlier Darwin on the Shelleys was considerable, and apparent (for example) in Percy's poetic depiction of the sensitive plant as 'trembl[ing] and pant[ing] with bliss' (cited in Nichols 2001: para 12), a line that goes beyond the evocation of a merely metaphorical relationship, suggesting instead that 'an emotion like pleasure can organically link humans with the non-human world' (para 12). In *Frankenstein*, it is this organic theory of sensation that underlies the Creature's 'delight' in his initial response to the voices of birds, and his sympathetic attempts to imitate and thereby identify with them across the species barrier (Shelley 1996 [1818]: 69). In fact, traces of radical inter-specific sympathy permeate Shelley's novel. Perhaps the most gratuitous example is that of the ship's master, whom Walton describes at the outset as 'a person of an excellent disposition', who is 'remarkable' for his 'gentleness, and the mildness of his discipline. He is, indeed, of so amiable a nature, that he will not hunt (a favourite, and almost the only amusement here), because he cannot endure to spill blood' (10–11). The implausible ascription of such a tender disposition to the master of an Arctic-bound vessel in the late eighteenth century appears designed (since this character is never mentioned again) solely to exemplify a sensibility that Shelley wants to pose as an alternative to another kind of masculinity represented by the lieutenant, 'a man of wonderful courage and enterprise' and 'madly desirous of glory', whom Walton first meets aboard a whale vessel (10). The contrast between the febrile ambition of the whaleman and the benign clemency of the master is expressed in terms of their opposed attitudes to hunting. It also alerts us to the recurrence of references to the suffering of non-human animals in the novel; these, although not numerous, bear critically upon the questions raised above.

A few scholars have mentioned Frankenstein's engagement in vivisection, as indicated by his admission that one of the 'horrors of my secret toil' involves 'tortur[ing] the living animal to animate the lifeless clay'.[13] When he adds that he 'seemed to have lost all soul or sensation but for this one pursuit', Victor associates vivisection with a marked deterioration in his sensibility (Shelley 1996 [1818]: 32). Later, moreover, he bears witness to an imaginative reversal of his own scientific instrumentalism: 'sometimes a kind of insanity possessed me', he recalls, in which 'I saw continually about me a multitude of filthy animals inflicting on me incessant torture, that often extorted screams and bitter groans' (Shelley 1996 [1818]: 101). Worthy of Swift or (as I will argue below) of H. G. Wells, this inverted vivisection fantasy occurs immediately following the termination of the Creature's autobiographical account. It thus constitutes the scientist's imaginative identification with the animal sensations and suffering voiced by his experimental subject.

In contrast to Victor's instrumentalism, the Creature embodies a fundamental compassion for non-human species. 'My food is not that of man', he tells Frankenstein; 'I do not destroy the lamb and the kid, to glut my appetite; acorns and berries afford me sufficient nourishment. My companion will be of the same nature as myself, and will be content with the same fare'. Describing the herbivorous life he and his spouse will share, he asserts that '[t]he picture I present to you is peaceful and human' (Shelley 1996 [1818]: 99). The Creature here associates the 'human', as a quality of being – a usage which here comes very close to the contemporary notion of the 'humane' – with unwillingness to cause suffering to other creatures. Considering the Shelleys' advocacy, as part of their commitment to radical politics, of both vegetarianism and concern for animal suffering, the Creature's diet suggests an authorial invitation for readers to sympathize with his point of view.[14] It also lends credibility to his claims that – unlike Frankenstein himself – he never loses his intrinsic sensitive bond with other living beings, and that only the repeated rejection of his benign overtures drives him to revenge (66, 86, 96, 98). Indeed, there is nothing in the text to suggest a general disposition towards mayhem, or even that the Creature's violence extends beyond Frankenstein's immediate circle. 'My heart was fashioned to be susceptible of love and sympathy', he insists, 'and when wrenched by misery to vice and hatred, it did not endure the violence of the change without torture, such as you cannot even imagine' (153). Thwarted in his original desire for the exchange of benevolent sympathy with other living beings and especially Frankenstein, the Creature turns to a darker form of identification indicated by the reference to 'torture'. In a moment of exultation following his first murder, that of Victor's little brother William, the Creature identifies with his creator's experiments in the infliction of suffering: 'I too can create desolation', he reflects, vowing to 'torment' his enemy by the infliction of this and 'a thousand other miseries' (97). At the same time, in deciding to persecute Frankenstein, 'the author at once of my existence and of its unspeakable torments', the creature realizes 'that I was preparing for myself a deadly torture' (153). His self- and other-tormenting experiments allow him to meet – or at least to mirror – the dangerously reversible vivisections of his maker. Hence, the only time the Creature does kill a non-human animal, when he leaves a hare for Frankenstein's meal, he does so as a taunting act of identification with the carnivorous hunter who pursues him (142), and who flogs his sled-dogs to death in the process (144).

Echoing Swift again, Shelley's novel identifies a brutality beyond the reach of any other species as the most reliable marker of difference between humans and other animals. When the Creature, in his natural state of Rousseaean innocence, eavesdrops on the De Laceys' readings in European history he learns that humanity, in its ability 'to be base and vicious, as many [men] on record have been', can embody 'a condition more abject than that of the blind mole or harmless worm' (Shelley 1996 [1818]: 80). It is this form of non-animality that the Creature ultimately recognizes, regretfully, in himself: 'I was nourished with high thoughts of honour and devotion. But now vice has degraded me beyond the meanest animal' (154). Like Swift's Yahoos and Houyhnhnms, and indeed his Europeans, Shelley's creature comes closest to being human – or most unlike an animal – when he demonstrates his capacity for inhumanity.

Brother-Emmets and Sister-Worms

Mary Shelley creates her monster as an experiment in sympathy, a way of assessing the promises and limits of contemporary philosophies of sensation and sensibility. In its finale the novel evokes an extravagant form of sympathy that knows no boundaries, or dissolves all boundaries. Witnessing the death of his maker, the Creature turns (or returns) to the most radical form of sympathy: the organic interconnectedness envisioned by Erasmus Darwin. During the first days of his life, the Creature tells Walton, 'when I felt the cheering warmth of summer and heard the rustling of the leaves and the chirping of the birds, and these were all to me, I should have wept to die; now it is my only consolation' (Shelley 1996 [1818]: 155). The same organic sympathies that first linked him to living nature will now provide his reunion with it, as the particles of his being mix with those of the larger environment. 'I shall ascend my funeral pile triumphantly and exult in the agony of the torturing flames. The light of that conflagration will fade away; my ashes will be swept into the sea by the winds' (156). The torture of the operating table, where his physical organs were first stitched together and shocked into life, will be matched by the flames that dissolve his body into the elements whence it came. By undoing his creator's experiment, the Creature evokes the possibility of a different, emphatically non-human and non-humanist state of being, free from the shackles of rational consciousness: '[m]y spirit will sleep in peace; or if it thinks, it will not surely think thus' (156). Consoling as the Creature finds this mode of thought, or rather unthinking, such threats to the stable borders separating self and other – and particularly to the boundaries used to distinguish the human species from any other – were more likely to evoke anxiety (Marshall 1988; McLane 2000). Moreover these same notions – of the dissolution of individual organisms and of species – lie at the heart of Frankenstein's initial creative act, and account for much of the aura of uncanniness and horror that surrounds it.

Like many Romantics, the Shelleys engaged avidly with the natural-historical and physiological discourses of their time, which thus shape the portrayal of Frankenstein's science. Marilyn Butler has shown that one such direct influence was 'the celebrated, publicly-staged debate of 1814–19 between the two professors at London's Royal College of Surgeons on the origins and nature of life, now known as the vitalist debate' (1996: 304). This exchange began with a lecture by John Abernathy, who proposed that scientific concentration upon matter alone could not explain the nature of life. Rather, he suggested, the difference between living and dead matter must lie in a mysterious 'superadded' element, a 'subtile, mobile, invisible substance', which he compared both to the soul and to electricity (cited in Butler 1996: 304). On the contrary, replied his colleague William Lawrence, insisting that 'the motion proper to living bodies, or in one word, life' cannot be understood as a property separate from organic matter. Rather, scientific observation shows that all organisms 'have participated in the existence of other living beings', that 'living bodies in the moment of their formation . . . when matter may be supposed to receive the stamp of life' draw their animation from the matter of other living bodies (cited in Butler 1996: 306). In short Lawrence, the materialist, 'sees no means of abstracting the animating power from the animal' (Butler 1996: 306).

Taking into account the Shelleys' association with Lawrence (who was Percy's physician), Butler argues that Mary presents Frankenstein as a 'blundering experimenter, still working with superseded notions' that are associated with the position taken by Abernathy: for example, the latter's comparison of the 'superadded life-element' to electricity is recalled when Frankenstein uses 'a machine, reminiscent of a battery, to impart the spark of life' (Butler 1996: 307). This reading has achieved wide acceptance, and its emphasis on the electrical 'instruments of life' used by Frankenstein to infuse the 'spark of being' (Shelley 1996 [1818]: 34) has been augmented by studies of the Shelleys' fascination with contemporary technological innovations, and in particular the work of Luigi Galvini, Giovanni Volta and Humphrey Davy on electrical currents and battery technology (Fulford *et al.* 2004: 179–97). More broadly, such analyses read Frankenstein's

Creature as an embodiment of the social, economic and environmental implications of industrialization (Montag 2000). Indeed some see the Creature as a radically technological artefact, created in a 'one-man factory' using industrial principles that represent an absolute departure from organic nature. 'As a purely technical product the Frankenstein monster is radically non-natural', writes Hansen (1997: 584).

While industrialization and electrical experimentation are clearly important dimensions of *Frankenstein*'s context, scholars who focus on them attend less to the novel itself than to the machinic metaphors that infuse Mary Shelley's accounts of its inception. In her introduction to the 1831 revised edition she recounts conversations between Byron and Shelley in 1816 regarding the 'principle of life . . . Perhaps a corpse would be reanimated; galvanism had given token of such things; perhaps the component parts of a creature might be manufactured, brought together, and endued with vital warmth' (Shelley 1996 [1831]: 171–2). This vivid discussion keeps Mary from sleep at night: 'I saw the hideous phantasm of a man stretched out, and then, on the working of some powerful engine, show signs of life' (172). Certainly the vocabulary of industrial culture dominates this account, but in contrast, and not surprisingly, given the pace of technological development within the thirteen years that separate this introduction from the original form of the tale, such language is much less apparent in the 1818 first edition.

To counterbalance the emphasis on technological aspects of the novel, I suggest that its original version actually emphasizes another mode of creation, which Butler misrepresents when she writes that 'Frankenstein's other procedures are made unpleasantly anti-life, recalling Lawrence's unfavourable comparison of inorganic with organic methods' (Butler 1996: 307). In fact, the principle of life is represented in the novel in very explicitly organic terms that feature alongside and indeed dominate the far slighter evidence of machinic or technological rhetoric. That scholars have focused on the evidence of industrial modes of production, and neglected the emphasis on organicist theories of generation – or dismissed them, as Butler does, as gothic unpleasantness – is attributable to the subsequent dominance of techno-culture, and an accompanying underestimation of the early nineteenth-century fascination with organic life and death and their interconnection.

Frankenstein's description of the actual moment at which he discovers the 'principle of life' has nothing to do with electricity or technology, but everything to do with natural organic processes. His discovery comes from days and nights spent in churchyards, vaults and charnel-houses, where the study of 'bodies deprived of life, which, from being the seat of beauty and strength, had become food for the worm' allows him 'to examine the cause and progress of . . . decay':

> I saw how the fine form of man was degraded and wasted; I beheld the corruption of death succeed to the blooming cheek of life; I saw how the worm inherited the wonders of the eye and brain. I paused, exam-

ining and analyzing all the minutiae of causation, as exemplified in the change from life to death, and death to life, until from the midst of this darkness a sudden light broke in upon me – a light so brilliant and wondrous, yet so simple…. After days and nights of incredible labour and fatigue, I succeeded in discovering the cause of generation and life; nay, more, I became myself capable of bestowing animation upon lifeless matter (Shelley 1996 [1818]: 30).

The answer is a simple one, says Frankenstein: he discovers the 'cause of generation and life' by observing the progress of decay. And what he finds relates intimately to other manifestations in the novel of a radical challenge to the rigidity of species boundaries. The phrases 'from life to death, and death to life' in the passage above can only refer to the change from human life to human death, and from human death to non-human animal life – that of the worm and the other living creatures generated in and nourished by the decay of the corpse. The means of 'bestowing animation upon lifeless matter' deduced by Frankenstein from his observations therefore depends on a kind of suspension of the firm species barriers that separate human from other animal life. In its origin – and this is surely part of its horror – Frankenstein's theory of animation involves recognition that in its vital and material substrate, the human is not clearly separable from the animal. This is the 'secret' that Victor refuses to reveal to Walton (31), but which the text smuggles to the reader.

This suspension of the boundary that supposedly circumscribes the human species is crucial not only to Victor's discovery of the vital principle, but also to its practical application, as indicated by his use of non-human material alongside human remains to constitute his creature. As well as collecting 'bones from charnel houses', Frankenstein admits that '[t]he dissecting room and the slaughterhouse furnished many of my materials; and often did my human nature turn with loathing from my occupation' (Shelley 1996 [1818]: 32). Here, too, is some explanation of the peculiar horror generated by the Creature. Victor and the other characters in the novel react with loathing both to his material hybridity – that of a body comprising human matter conjoined with that of other animals – and to his display of the processes of decay by which human life dissolves and transmutes into non-human life. He looks, in short, like a decaying corpse, with 'dun white [eye]sockets', 'shriveled complexion', 'straight black lips' and flesh 'in colour and apparent texture like that of a mummy' (34, 152). No wonder that the first sight of his Creature living inspires Victor to dream of his mother's corpse, upon whose shroud he sees 'the grave-worms crawling' (34).

Shelley thus offers not just a Lawrencian critique of Abernathian theories of the generation of life but an alternative model, which is Darwinian – that is to say, one that draws heavily on the Romantic proto-evolutionism of Erasmus Darwin. For of course, Charles Darwin was not the originator of the notion of species mutability through evolution most closely associated with his name; his grandfather and other contemporary naturalists had their own theories on the topic (Nichols 1997). Moreover the earlier Darwin's examples of the mutability of species include the same kinds of organic transmigration of living matter – from decaying bodies to newly generating ones – which are revealed to Frankenstein when he works the graveyard shift. In his essay on the 'Spontaneous Vitality of Microscopic Animals', Darwin senior concluded that 'the most simple animals and vegetables may be produced by the congress of the parts of decomposing organic matter' (1978 [1803]: 8). In *The Temple of Nature*, the long poetic treatise that this essay accompanies, he expands this idea in lyrical terms. 'Hence when a Monarch or a mushroom dies', he writes – the alliteration implying the radically democratic nature of his view of living matter, the protean vital stuff that inhabits all species – 'Awhile extinct the organic matter lies, / But, as a few short hours or years revolve; / Alchemic powers the changing mass dissolve'. Evoking various instances of organic decay – the 'festering carnage' left on a battlefield, or after famine, plague or earthquake have decimated populations – Darwin insists that all these 'Wrecks of Death' are also sites for generation of new life: rotting corpses are 'but a change of forms'. 'Emerging matter from the grave returns, / Feels new desires, with new sensations burns . . . / With ceaseless change, how restless atoms pass, / From life to life, a transmigrating mass'. Moreover, he argues that this organic sympathy between all living matter should properly lead to affective sympathy – the very disposition that Frankenstein and all other characters in Shelley's novel deny to the Creature. Since, Darwin suggests, 'the same organs' which one day 'compose' a plant or flower might tomorrow be seen in human faces, it follows not only that 'man should ever be the friend of man' but that he also '[s]hould eye with tenderness all living forms, / His brother-emmets, and his sister-worms' (160–3). The same worms, one presumes, that might soon, in their turn, feast on his decaying flesh.[15]

Frankenstein's Creature, then, emerges at the intersection of two forms of generation: one organic and one technological (or proto-industrial). Indeed his monstrosity derives from the conjunction of these two modes. The lasting effect of Frankenstein's Creature is not merely the horror of his hyperbolic organic nature (the exaggeration of his skeletal and muscular development, the animality of his form, the too-evident signs of bodily decay), nor a simple fear of new technology, but an anxiety about attempts to engineer the former by means of the latter. In particular, the universally negative reactions the Creature faces within the narrative reflect a cultural concern during the early decades of the nineteenth century regarding the new wave of scientific, and especially agricultural, manipulations of nature: these included experimental stock breeding to accelerate meat production, the trialling of new crops, innovations in drainage and cultivation, and artificial alterations to chemistry of the soil (Ritvo 1987: 47–8). Perhaps the most controversial technique used by such 'improvers' was that involving hybridization. By 1800, '[n]ot only horse breeders, but also pigeon fanciers, vintners, and agriculturalists were, for the first time, breeding and cross-breeding numerous animals and plants' (Nichols 1997: para. 2). Ritvo documents a simultaneous fascination and a widespread unease with these kinds of experiments (1987: 45–121; 1998: 51–130, 113–14). Amid such epistemological flux, the political and social fears of the time – pollution of the European type through miscegenation, the overthrow of class hierarchies by a proletariat disenfranchised by industrialization, challenges to patriarchal norms from proto-feminists (including Mary Shelley's mother) – became indissolubly fused with rapidly changing views of non-human animals. Anxieties about racial difference remained inseparable from the definition of the human as a species; ideas of gender, sexuality and animality could not be disassociated; and the classification and management of species continued to be undertaken in conjunction with the administration of social class (Ritvo 1987: 45–121; 1998: 27–50, 131–87).

The Pest of Future Ages

The vendetta between the scientist and Creature in Shelley's novel becomes irremediable only when Frankenstein destroys his half-completed second creature, the female demanded by the first Creature in order that he might live in the 'exchange of those sympathies necessary for my being'. Frankenstein abandons his task because of sudden foreboding about the uncontrollable agency of this female:

> I was now about to form another being, of whose dispositions I was alike ignorant; she might become ten thousand times more malignant than her mate, and delight, for its own sake, in murder and wretchedness. He had sworn to quit the neighbourhood of man and hide himself in deserts, but she had not; and she, who in all probability was to become a thinking and reasoning animal, might refuse to comply with a compact made before her creation (Shelley 1996 [1818]: 114).

His experience with the first creature has taught Victor his own ignorance of non-human agency. At first, he imagines this expressed at the level of the individual organism. But even if the female creature does prove recalcitrant at the individual level, an even more threatening kind of rebellion may be enacted by the two creatures together: that of species agency. If the two creatures do become companions,

> one of the first results of those sympathies for which the daemon thirsted would be children, and a race of devils would be propagated upon the earth who might make the very existence of the species of man a condition precarious and full of terror (114).

As McLane argues, Victor imagines that the interpersonal struggle between himself and the monster would become 'in this second experiment a world-historical contest between imagined populations – the 'whole human race' versus 'a race of devils' (2000: 103); a return to that life-and-death competition between humans and other species which technological modernity promised to end.

What Frankenstein fears, and what he seeks to prevent by aborting the female creature, is the same uncontrollable overproduction of feral life that accompanied modernity's expansionist endeavours wherever it went. Imagining 'that future ages might curse me as their pest' (Shelley 1996 [1818]: 114), Frankenstein recognizes his own potential responsibility for the creation of a new category of vermin, a species of creatures liable to reproduce exponentially like Crusoe's cats, Swift's Yahoos, the rats of Peru and Virginia or the rabbits of Australia and New Zealand, and all the other species imported into Europe's colonies as elements in the process that Crosby calls 'ecological imperialism' (1986). Frankenstein's Creature embodies this exchange of animal matter even in his individual origins: a collection of material imported from different species and different places, driven from the scene of his awakening immediately, and thereby following an itinerary that takes him further and further beyond the peripheries of the European world. Hence Victor's eventual recognition of how small and crowded European expansion has made the world, so that 'the monster who invades Geneva cannot be confined to the 'vast wilds of South America"' (McLane 2000: 106). No more than a century after the narratives of Defoe and Swift, the impact of species mobility and ferity has become so widespread that the future can be envisaged as a global laboratory overrun by its experiments.

The theme of the experiment that escapes and becomes autonomous remains the most enduring and widespread interpretation of Shelley's tale, and can be seen at work today in everything from public concerns about genetic engineering to films like *The Terminator* and *Jurassic Park* . But while this reading testifies to popular acknowledgement of the unpredictability of non-human agency, such has been the authority of science that such agency has only recently begun to be recognized in the context of the laboratory. Identifying the recalcitrance with which non-human actors play their part, Bruno Latour describes the competing experiments conducted by Pasteur and his rival, Pouchet, in which the microorganisms being studied 'change[d] camps', 'betray[ing]' the two men by proving both of the hypotheses with which they were trying to discredit each other (1987: 84). Nature, declares Latour, proves at best a 'belated, sometimes faithful and sometimes fickle ally' to the techno-sciences that depend on its apprehension (94). Anticipating this postmodern critique of scientific modernity, Shelley envisages her creature as a congeries (a 'filthy mass', to use Victor's phrase) of experimental matter, gathered together from the slaughterhouse, the dissection room and the vivisector's table, but capable of giving form, voice and action to the unpredictable and rebellious agencies that may be at work in the laboratory, and may escape from it, in spite of the scientist's confidence in his mastery over that space.

The relationship between *Gulliver's Travels* and *Frankenstein* provides an index of the shift in cultural attitudes over the century that separates them. For Swift, the new science is a significant target, but it is only one of the many absurdities he perceives in Enlightenment modernity: others include party politics, capitalist speculation, emergent consumerism, class relations, militarism and imperialism. For Mary Shelley however, the practices of science – in particular the relationship between industrial technology, laboratory-based experimentation and organic nature – have expanded to fill the main focus of her literary gaze. Nor does she interrogate these domains from a sardonic position outside them, as Swift does, for her reading, like that of her husband and peers, shows a committed (albeit amateur) investment in the scientific debates of her day. In both of these respects Shelley's closest literary descendent is H. G. Wells. However, unlike Shelley, and of course unlike Swift before her, Wells' commitment to scientific thought and practice was unambivalent. Because he combined his zealous championship of science with the strategic use of elements from the literary works of two of its more famous critics, Wells' novels demonstrate vividly the conflicted place of scientific discourse in late nineteenth-century human–animal relations.

Moreau's Island

The Island of Doctor Moreau is H. G. Wells' most direct response to *Gulliver's Travels* and *Frankenstein*, two of his favourite texts.[16] Like Gulliver, Walton and Frankenstein, Wells' narrator, Edward Prendick, is a man of science who goes voyaging and finds himself marooned in an extreme location. His antagonist, Doctor Moreau, isolates himself from everyday social congress to conduct radical experiments upon animals, like Frankenstein and the virtuosi of Lagado. The flayed dog that flees from Moreau's clinic, causing a scandal that forces him out of England, recalls both the grotesque laboratory escapee whose actions drive Victor from his native town, and the canine vivisection witnessed by Gulliver at the Grand Academy. Of course the main debt to Shelley is the 'house of pain' where Moreau tortures the living flesh of animals to create his own rational creature – a direct imitation of Frankenstein's 'workshop of filthy creation' in which he uses vivisection and dissection to achieve the same aim. And the main debt to its Swiftian precursor occurs at the conclusion of *Moreau*, where, just as Gulliver upon returning home cannot bear the animalistic propensities of English Yahoos, Prendick is haunted by the notion that he and the citizens of London are no more than 'Beast People, animals half-wrought into the outward image of human souls'(Wells 1996 [1896]: 204–6).

Humanizing Brutes, Brutalizing Humans

Indeed, *Moreau* turns upon a very Swiftian chiasmus: the portrayal of people so brutal, and animals so hominoid, that the hierarchical opposition between 'man and beast' disintegrates as it is reversed, reinstated and reversed again. Typically however, Wells reconfigures this trope using terms drawn from science, specifically the late nineteenth-century fascination with comparative anatomy and the possibilities of physiological mutation. Marooned on Moreau's remote Pacific island, Prendick encounters strange beings and concludes that the doctor is modifying humans into animal forms for 'some hideous experiment' (Wells 1996 [1896]: 109). 'They were men', he accuses Moreau, 'whom you have infected with some bestial taint' (126). Correcting him, however, Moreau replies that the reverse is true: *'non sunt homines, sunt animalia qui nos habemus . . .* vivisected. A humanising process', he informs Prendick, in bad 'Schoolboy Latin' designed to escape the understanding of the surrounding creatures, while at the same time suggesting a parody of the jargon by which nineteenth-century medical science and natural history sought to rarefy and universalize their arts (127). As Carrie Rohman puts it, 'Moreau's vivisections, which humanize animals, vividly register the inverse fear that humans already have animal qualities' (2005: 125). By the end of the novel, once Prendick can no longer tell (physiologically) anthropomorphized animals apart from (metaphorically) zoomorphized humans, deconstruction of the distinction 'beast' and 'folk' is complete.

The Swiftian tone persists most obviously in relation to Prendick's own repeated misprisions. For all his repugnance at the beast-figures he encounters, events and his own reactions keep displaying Prendick's own animality to the reader, for example when he awakens and attempts to get up but finds that his hammock, 'anticipating my intention, twisted round and deposited me upon all-fours on the floor' (Wells 1996 [1896]: 106). This slip echoes a moment in the preceding chapter when, during his unauthorized tour of the island, Prendick observes several of the inhabitants drop briefly from two legs to go 'on all-fours like a beast'. Adoption of this posture, even for a moment, even by accident, gives a 'transitory gleam of . . . true animalism' (96, 99). Similarly, like Gulliver adopting the disposition of the peoples he visits, Prendick remarks that although at first he is struck by 'the disproportion between the legs of these creatures and the length of their bodies', soon 'my eye became habituated to their forms, and at last I even fell in with their persuasion that my own long thighs were ungainly' (151). Before long Prendick has trouble recalling how the island's inhabitants differ from human types seen in England (154).

Nonetheless, he works hard to maintain a sense of his intellectual and cultural difference from those he encounters – all the more so once he concedes their anatomical similarity. Wells' satirical intent is most evident in his narrator's encounter with the figure he refers to as the Ape-Man or the Monkey-Man. Their initial meeting recalls strikingly Gulliver's encounter with his first Yahoo. The 'simian creature' moves back and forth between trees and the ground, chatters in a way that Prendick has trouble understanding and registers a variety of expressions in quick succession. Each of the traits that distinguish the human from the animal – or fail to do so – is surveyed in turn: hands, feet, tools, clothes (Wells 1996 [1896]: 112–13).

Like Gulliver's first Yahoo, and like Frankenstein's newly arisen Creature when he first approaches his progenitor, the Ape-Man makes gestures that are open to misinterpretation. Gazing at Prendick's hands, he extends his own, and counts 'One, Two, Three, Four, Five – eh?' This gesture, which Prendick mistakes for a greeting, is actually a recognition of taxonomic proximity, since 'a great proportion of [the] Beast People had malformed hands, lacking sometimes even three digits' (112). Like the Brobdingnagian monkey, or the Yahoos, or Frankenstein's Creature, the Ape-Man recognizes an affinity which the human (at least temporarily) denies. Nor does this affinity derive from the fact that, as Prendick later discovers, the Ape-Man was Moreau's first success, his Adam, after whose creation he 'rested from work for some days' (144). For although Prendick does 'not feel the same repugnance towards this creature that I had experienced in my encounters with the other Beast Men', and considers him 'as much of a man as Montgomery's attendant – for he could talk' (112), he fails to recognize what is apparent to the Ape-Man: that the basis of their kinship is neither a common humanity, nor Moreau's experimentation, but their shared taxonomic position as primates. Determinedly missing this point, Prendick assigns the Ape-Man the same place on the human–animal continuum occupied by Crusoe's Poll. 'I tried him with some other questions, but his chattering prompt responses were, as often as not, quite at cross-purposes with my question. Some few were appropriate, others quite parrot-like' (113). On the other hand, Prendick's own response to the Ape-Man's first attempt at communication – he repeats the digit-counting performance in turn, because he misunderstands it as a greeting – suggests that *he* is the one at cross-purposes with the other's question; he is the one engaging, parrot-like, in mimicry.

No wonder Prendick later takes issue with Moreau's reduction of the human-simian distinction to a simple anatomical feature: 'the great difference between man and monkey is in the larynx, he said, in the incapacity to frame delicately different sound-symbols by which thought could be sustained' (Wells 1996 [1896]: 136–7). Prendick's determination to maintain his sense of difference from the Ape-Man, in conjunction with the latter's evident sense of their affinity, echoes Gulliver's seizure by the Brobdingnagian monkey and his molestation by the Yahoo female, insofar as all these stories express in satirical form the human fear of taxonomic capture, through recognition, by an apishness that the animal recognizes in the human. Like these other primate primatologists, the Ape-Man calls human uniqueness into question by assuming 'on the strength of his five digits, that he was my equal' (195). At the same time, his rapid acquisition of new vocabulary and concepts comprises a mockery of certain intellectual pretensions and traditions:

> [h]e had an idea, I believe, that to gabble about names that meant nothing was the proper use of speech. He called it 'big thinks', to distinguish it from 'little thinks' – the sane everyday interests of life. If

ever I made a remark he did not understand, he would praise it very
much, ask me to say it again, learn it by heart, and go off repeating it,
with a word wrong here or there, to all the milder of the Beast People
. . . I invented some very curious 'big thinks' for his especial use. I
think now that he was the silliest creature I ever met; he had developed in the most wonderful way the distinctive silliness of man without
losing one jot of the natural folly of a monkey (196).

Wells here ridicules the unthinking repetition of dogma as a substitute for
intellectual innovation. This type of 'silliness' is satirized also in the Beast
Folk's chanting of the 'Law', and the parroted phrase 'Are we not men?',
by which their animal desires are held in check (117). Similarly, upon his
return to London, Prendick perceives that the preacher in his chapel
'gibbered Big Thinks even as the Ape Man had done' (206), while by
contrast Prendick finds solace in 'experiments in chemistry' and the 'study
of astronomy' – that is, in the kind of intellectual striving that allows access
to 'whatever is more than animal in us' (207). Here, despite Wells' satirical
debt to Swift, his very different intentions become clear. As I argued in
Chapter 1, a primary target of *Gulliver's Travels* is the notion of inhumanity, that form of brutality which is peculiar to humans and worse than that
of brutes themselves, and which is displayed in advanced form by scientific experimentalism. By contrast, Wells' target is the uncritical repetition
of conventional truisms, a 'distinctive silliness of man' whose adoption
makes the Ape-Man 'the silliest creature I ever met'; this human failing
makes him dumber than any mere dumb animal could ever be. And from
this vice, according to Wells, scientific experimentalism provides the only
hope of salvation.

It would be unwise to identify Wells' own position simplistically with
either of the novel's protagonists, as Leon Stover does by unequivocally
equating Wells' scientism with that of Moreau (1996), or as those readers
do who take the novel as an invitation to share Prendick's horror of vivisection (Hutton 1972 [1896]). Wells retains the influence of *Gulliver's
Travels* strongly enough to critique both positions by taking them to their
satirical extremes, engendering a dialectic between Prendick's position
and Moreau's.[17] Yet the novel's satirical dimensions produce a rather
more corrosive representation of science than its author probably anticipated. The power of human–animal satire, in the hands of Swift and
Wells, is that it does not stop at using animals to symbolize human failings;
it also challenges the human–animal hierarchy fundamental to modernity,
and commits itself in a far-reaching way to the proposition that humans
are animals, and that humanity is largely defined by denial of this proposition. For Swift this attitude serves his critical agenda and his broader
misanthropy, whereas for Wells it bears out a scientific truth. Even more
radically, this mode of satire – although this is seldom its primary aim, and
may even undercut the intentions of its author – cannot help but interrogate the human–animal practices that are its vehicles: agriculture, pet-

keeping, hunting, natural history, vivisection. For this reason, such satire is a dangerous beast, likely to bite the hand that unleashes it – or as Swift says of the Houyhnhnms, liable to kick backwards (2002 [1726]: 247). In Wells' case, this means that the very epistemology he seeks to reinforce by satirical means becomes subject to mockery along with all other kinds of 'big thinks'. Hence Moreau's story, like that of Frankenstein, is most commonly understood as a gruesome parable of scientific hubris (Turney 1998: 56–9).[18] To recover the novel's genuine commitment to the idea of scientific improvement, it is necessary to move from a focus on its satirical tendencies to analysis of its immersion in the biological debates and practices of its time.

Hunter and Hunted

Although neither Moreau nor Prendick should be taken as a straightforward embodiment of Wells' own ideological position, it is Moreau's view of human nature that prevails. The narrative emphatically supports his conviction that the human is nothing other than a species of animal, and no more than a transitory stage in a particular evolutionary process. Human animality, understood in primarily biological (rather than satirical) terms, is foregrounded from the outset. In the opening chapter, Prendick's close encounter with human cannibalism in the dinghy of the *Lady Vain* marks out human nature as 'fundamentally physical, instinctual, and even aggressive' (Rohman 2005: 122) – a view consistent with the late-nineteenth-century evolutionist portrayal of organic life in general (Wells 1996 [1896]: 63–4). The account of Prendick's subsequent rescue by the *Ipecacuanha* reinforces these associations (Rohman 2005: 123), for example when he is given a restorative drink that 'tasted like blood, and made me feel much stronger', when he hears a noise overhead, 'a snarling growl and the voice of a human being together', or later, when Montgomery brings him some boiled mutton, and he is 'so excited by the appetising smell of it, that I forgot the noise of the beast forthwith' (Wells 1996 [1896]: 65, 66, 67). Throughout this narrative, human and animal voices and appetites intertwine: the marks of the 'brute' – a word Prendick applies indiscriminately to animals and humans aboard the vessel (71–2) – are inscribed upon the narrator as well as on those he observes.

These rhetorical inferences of human–animal indivisibility are soon overtaken by something rather more spectacular, namely the actual hybridity of Moreau's Beast Folk. Prendick's first view of M'ling, Montgomery's companion, foreshadows the intermixture of human and bestial forms: '[t]he facial part projected, forming something dimly suggestive of a muzzle, and the huge half-open mouth showed as big white teeth as I had ever seen in a human mouth' (Wells 1996 [1896]: 69). In turn, Prendick's response to M'ling is itself animalistic. The 'animal swiftness' with which M'ling turns is matched by Prendick's reflex, described to Montgomery later as 'a nasty little sensation, a tightening of my muscles, when he comes near me' (92) – in other words the involuntary, 'instinctual' reaction of one animal to another. Similarly, the 'curious glow of excitement' on M'ling's face suggests his beast-like alertness, but also recalls Prendick's own excitement two pages earlier at the smell of mutton.

The narrator's experience of his own animality dominates the middle section of Wells' novel, which comprises three hunts. The first is Prendick's pursuit by the Leopard Man, the second his flight from Moreau, Montgomery and their accompanying dogs and Beast-Men, and the third Prendick's own participation, along with Moreau and his entourage, in the chase to catch and punish the fugitive Leopard Man. As long as he is the Leopard Man's quarry, Prendick experiences the prey beast's heightened sensory alertness – 'I saw nothing, and nevertheless my sense of another presence grew steadily' – and awareness of the vulnerability of his own animal flesh: 'I listened rigid, and heard nothing but the creep of the blood in my ears' (Wells 1996 [1896]: 101, 102). When pursued by Moreau, on the other hand, Prendick imagines himself as a potential subject for vivisection, a 'hospital rabbit' (110), and his subsequent flight focuses on his tortured body, subjected to natural trials that parallel the agonies of the laboratory: he struggles through thorny plants that leave him with 'a torn ear and bleeding face', and crosses a scalding stream that has 'a thin sulphurous scum drifting upon its coiling water' (111, 123, 124). Even after he is cornered by Moreau, Prendick's faith in the human–animal distinction is not restored by the doctor's explanation that the Beast-Men are animals humanized by vivisection. He cannot dismiss intimations of the humanity of these creatures, nor the powerful sense of his own beastliness. Instead, his perception of his own nature and that of his conspecifics changes from that of prey or experimental animal to that of predator when he joins 'Moreau and Montgomery and all their bestial rabble' (125) in the hunt for the rogue Leopard Man. At no time does he make any conscious decision to accompany them in this 'Comus rout' (109); rather, he presents himself as caught up in the ferocious 'excitement' of the pack: '[t]he whole crowd seemed to swing round . . . and I, too, was swung round by the magnetism of the moment. In another second I was running, one of a tumultuous shouting crowd, in pursuit of the escaping Leopard Man' (164).

Prendick catches up with the Leopard Man first – perhaps implausibly, yet from a literary point of view inevitably. In pursuing the embodiment of a human-animality he has fled from earlier, 'the man' (as the chapter titles refer to Prendick, indicating his allegorical function) confronts his own beastliness. 'It may seem a strange contradiction in me', he says, 'but now, seeing the creature there in a perfectly animal attitude, with the light gleaming in its eyes, and its imperfectly human face distorted with terror, I realised again the fact of its humanity' (Wells 1996 [1896]: 166). What Prendick identifies with here – what provides the grounds for his shared 'humanity' with his quarry – is in fact the Leopard Man's bestial glance and posture. As Carrie Rohman puts it:

[t]his epiphanic moment produces a surprising inversion of the traditional humanist subject position, which abjects and represses animality.
In profound contrast to that abjection, Prendick's vision privileges
animality as an *a priori*, necessary, and constitutive element of the
human. Prendick's vision insists that the Leopard Man's animality is
actually his most human quality (2005: 131).

Recognition of this shared human-animality – an impeccable insight
from the scientific point of view espoused by Wells – produces in Prendick a
rather anti-scientific reaction; that is, an overwhelming compassion.
Having recently feared for his own fate at the hands of the vivisectors, he
sympathizes with the Leopard Man's situation, aware that capture will
expose him once more to 'the horrible tortures of the enclosure. Abruptly I
slipped out my revolver, aimed between its terror-struck eyes, and fired'
(Wells 1996 [1896]: 166).

Prendick's sympathy with a specifically human animality now broadens
to include all the Beast People, as he becomes persuaded that, apart from
'the grotesqueness of the forms, I had here before me the whole balance of
human life in miniature, the whole interplay of instinct, reason, and fate in
its simplest form' (Wells 1996 [1896]: 167). In Swift's hands, this perception
would be satire; for Wells it is science. As Stover points out, the notion of
the human animal as wracked, and indeed defined, by an 'internal struggle'
is expanded upon by Wells in a piece of science journalism published in the
same year as *Moreau*, where he defines 'civilised man' as a combination of
'(1) an inherited factor, the natural man, who is the product of natural
selection, the culminating ape', and '(2) an acquired factor, the artificial
man, the highly plastic creature of tradition, suggestion, and reasoned
thought' (Wells [1896], in Philmus and Hughes 1975: 217). Wells goes on to
answer, in no uncertain terms, the radical questions raised by the satirical
elements in his novel (something Swift, of course, would never do), by
advocating the 'careful and systematic manufacture of the artificial factor in
man'. On this point the avowed ideology of the author comes nearest to
that of his protagonist. For both Wells and Moreau, the human may be an
animal, but it is the only beast capable of 'artificial' self-development.

In this regard, *Moreau* concisely repeats a central paradox of modern
biological thought and practice. On one hand, the nineteenth-century life
sciences continued the modern project of abolishing any absolute biological
distinction between humankind and other types of organism. Studies in
comparative physiology and anatomy reduced humans to purely physical
forms, acted upon by material forces and sensations, while zoology – following Charles Darwin – recast *Homo sapiens* as a temporary category, just one
stage in a long evolutionary process that included non-human ancestry and
envisaged the possibility of non-human descendants. On the other hand, the
scientific paradigm reinstated an epistemological abyss between humans and
all other organisms, by means of its conviction that only humans were
capable of transcending the objective world through empirical investigation

and abstract reflection. This contradiction shapes the conclusion to *Moreau*. After his sojourn on the island Prendick feels that, like all his species, he is 'not a reasonable creature' at all, 'but only an animal tormented with some strange disorder in its brain, that sent to wander alone, like a sheep stricken with the gid'. Seeking escape from this perception he devotes his days 'to reading and to experiments in chemistry, and . . . many of the clear nights in the study of astronomy'. Only the transcendent perspective offered by the practices of science can offer reassurance of a lingering human difference from the 'mere' animal: 'it must be, I think, in the vast and eternal laws of matter . . . that whatever is more than animal within us must find its solace and its hope' (Wells 1996 [1896]: 203–7). This sums up the Wellsian paradox of human nature. As an animal, 'man' is subject to the laws of matter; but as the only animal capable of scientifically reflecting upon and experimenting with these laws, 'man' may stretch his plastic animality to become more than he is now. For Wells this belief was not mere theory but a practical necessity upon which the social and biological future of the human species depended.

Man-Making

'The publication of Charles Darwin's *On the Origin of Species* in 1859 is usually considered to mark the beginning of a new era in the study of life', writes Harriet Ritvo. 'Certainly, for those who were persuaded by it, Darwin's theory of evolution by natural selection . . . eliminated the unbridgeable gulf that divided reasoning human being from irrational brute', and thereby 'dethroned . . . humankind almost implicitly' (1987: 39).[19] H. G. Wells could hardly have shown himself more persuaded by Darwin's representation of *Homo sapiens* as one animal species competing among others. But recognizing the abolition of humankind's ontological seclusion from the rest of the organic world is not the same as relinquishing the human claim to power over nature (including its own nature). Actually, for Wells, accepting the former 'dethronement' made it all the more imperative to maintain human supremacy by means of intellectually-informed manipulation of the material world. Insisting that both biological and cultural aspects of human existence – that is, the 'inherited factor, the natural man' and 'the acquired factor, the artificial man' – obey the laws of evolution, Wells locates the artificial factor as the human species' (sole) evolutionary advantage. As such, human culture and technology must operate according to the same principles that govern inherited adaptations in other animals, by serving the competition for supremacy in the great experiment of natural selection.

Moreau's artificial moulding of non-human species into hominoid forms represents a literal application of this version of Darwinian theory. Wells locates the fictional Noble's Isle near the Galapagos, made famous by Darwin as Nature's own laboratory for experiments in evolutionary mutation (Stover, in Wells 1996 [1896]: 84 note 30). The project that Moreau describes to Prendick compresses into a decade the Darwinian descent of man, recasting it as an ascent that reflects Wells' ideological predilections:

> I began with a sheep, and killed it after a day and a half by a slip of the scalpel; I took another sheep . . . It looked quite human to me when I had finished it; but . . . it remembered me, and was terrified beyond imagination; and it had no more than the wits of a sheep. The more I looked at it the clumsier it seemed, until at last I put the monster out of its misery. These animals without courage, these fear-haunted, pain-driven things, without a spark of pugnacious energy to face torment – they are no good for man-making.
>
> Then I took a gorilla I had; and upon that, working with infinite care, and mastering difficulty after difficulty, I made my first man . . . With him it was chiefly the brain that needed moulding; much had to be added, much changed. I thought him a fair specimen of the negroid type when I had done him . . . I taught him the rudiments of English, gave him ideas of counting, even made the thing read the alphabet. But at that he was slow – though I've met with idiots slower . . . When his scars were quite healed, and he was no longer anything but painful and stiff, and able to converse a little, I took him yonder and intro-duced him to the Kanakas as an interesting stowaway.
>
> They were horribly afraid of him at first . . . but his ways seemed so mild, and he was so abject, that after a time they received him and took his education in hand. He was quick to learn, very imitative and adap-tive, and built himself a hovel rather better, it seemed to me, than their own shanties. There was one among the boys, a bit of a missionary, and he taught the thing to read, or at least to pick out letters, and gave him some rudimentary ideas of morality (Wells 1996 [1896]: 142–5).

Darwin's account of human evolution from quadruped mammal to ape to upright hominid is here combined with a theory of racial development. The modified gorilla (recalling the apelike ancestors assigned to *Homo sapiens* by Darwin) provides a measure for the allocation to various human types of different stages of evolutionary advancement: he is 'a fair speci-men of the negroid type', intellectually slow but quicker on the uptake than some human 'idiots'. Naturally at home among the Kanakas the Doctor has brought to the island as servants, he becomes their student in moral education but their superior in the manual and mental skills required for building.

The diverse types created by Moreau reflect a familiar racist taxonomy of bestial comparisons. The 'black' faces of M'ling and the Ape-Man; the 'elfin' countenances of the turbaned boatman, wrapped up like people 'in the East'; the Satyr Man's 'ovine . . . expression – like the coarser Hebrew type': these represent respectively the primitivist, orientalist and anti-semitic stereotypes that dominated nineteenth-century race theory (Wells 1996 [1896]: 69–70, 82–3, 157). Wells' mobilization of these stereotypes foreshadows the difference that Darwinian thought would make to nine-teenth- and twentieth-century theories of both class and racial difference. Application of the principles of natural selection to human populations, for example in the 'science' of eugenics proposed by Darwin's cousin Francis Galton, would result in the segregationism practised in South Africa and the USA, or at the most brutal end of the scale, the state-sponsored geno-cide promulgated in Nazi Germany (Hawkins 1997: 82–103; 216–48). But a more widespread, insidious and durable application of social Darwinism occurred under those colonial administrations which aimed to regulate the social and reproductive lives of native peoples in ways that eased their assimilation into the supposedly superior stock represented by European settlers.[20] This latter paradigm comes closest to Wells' utopian vision for the future. He anticipates a 'great synthesis', in which 'all these old isolations, these obsolescent particularisms' of nationality, race, language and market will be broken down by 'the forces of mechanical and scientific develop-ment' (1902: 246).[21] The result would be a 'world state' ruled by the 'men of the New Republic', under whose scientifically devised social codes 'there will recommence a process of physical and mental improvement in mankind' (1902: 307).

From the Wellsian point of view, Moreau's experiments in artificial muta-tion are therefore not only defensible but responsible. Wells' own objections to Moreau, insofar as they can be divined, would relate less to his work itself, than to the fact the Doctor pursues his ambitions in egotistical soli-tude (like Frankenstein before him), and thus in contradistinction to the spirit of 'scientific socialism' that Wells espoused, whose direction he commended to the hands of an elite collective, 'an informal, unselfish, unauthorised body' of scientific workers, a 'conscious apparatus of educa-tion and moral suggestion . . . shaping the minds and acts and destinies of men' (Wells [1897], in Philmus and Hughes 1975: 228). Moreau's social negligence is compounded by his failure to provide for his new species a proper programme of education and discipline: again like Frankenstein, he abandons his creatures, permitting the resurgence of their animal instincts and beastly flesh.

The result of Moreau's neglect encapsulates what Wells perceived to be the most significant threat facing humankind: the possibility of human evolutionary stagnation, or worse, degeneration. In articles written at the same time as his early scientific romances, Wells sought to raise public and scientific awareness of this danger. In these he refuted a general misunder-standing regarding Darwinian theory, namely that evolution is always progressive and 'will continue with increasing velocity under the supervi-sion of its extreme expression – man'. On the contrary, the antithesis is just as possible, if not more likely – namely 'degradation'. 'There is', he wrote, 'no guarantee in scientific knowledge of man's permanence or permanent ascendancy' (Wells [1891], in Philmus and Hughes 1975: 158, 168). Elsewhere he emphasized the evolutionary disadvantages of *Homo sapiens*. Humankind 'breeds later and more sparingly than any other creature' – for example the 'fecund rabbit', the 'swarming microscopic organisms of the pond', or bacteria – which decreases our species' opportunities for the production of competitive mutations. Meanwhile the modern social order courts degradation inasmuch as it suspends the principles of natural selection, by 'its careful preservation of all the human lives that are born to it – the halt, the blind, the deaf and dumb, the ferocious, the atavistic', which are permitted to 'grow to maturity and pair under such complex and artificial circumstances that even a determinate Sexual Selection can scarcely be operating' (Wells [1896], in Philmus and Hughes 1975: 214).

In objecting to the complacent notion that human supremacy was the inevitable outcome of evolution – an assumption that elsewhere he labelled 'Bio-Optimism' or 'Excelsior Biology' (Wells [1895], in Philmus and Hughes 1975: 206–10) – Wells echoes the *fin de siècle* pessimism of many of his contemporaries. A year before *Moreau* was published, Hungarian doctor and journalist Max Nordeau described what he called a 'Dusk of Nations', whose symptoms he diagnosed using a model of organic debilitation (2000 [1895]: 13–15). 'Degeneracy', Nordeau wrote, 'betrays itself among men in certain physical characteristics', such as 'unequal development of the two halves of the face and cranium . . . imperfection in the development of the external ear . . . squint-eyes, hare lips, irregularities in the form and position of the teeth . . . webbed or supernumerary fingers' (15–16). These are the physical traits that Prendick observes everywhere among the Beast Folk and which, after the death of Moreau, become exaggerated as they 'descend' from their humanoid states: 'their foreheads fell away and their faces projected', '[t]hey held things more clumsily', 'hair began to spread over the exposed limbs', 'they walked erect with an increasing difficulty' (Wells 1996 [1896]: 196–7). Yet Prendick is less dismayed by the reversion of the Beast People to their original species forms – which indeed might be taken as a gratifying re-establishment of the human–animal boundary – than by their continued manifestation of two alarming features. The first occurs because in each of his subjects 'Moreau had blended this animal with that; one perhaps was ursine chiefly, another feline chiefly, another bovine chiefly, but each was tainted with other creatures'. Hence they do not decline into 'ordinary bears, wolves, tigers, oxen, swine, and apes', but retain 'something strange . . . a kind of generalised animalism appearing through the specific dispositions'. The second source of continuing uneasiness are those 'dwindling shreds of the humanity' which 'still startled me every now and then, a momentary recrudescence of speech perhaps, an unexpected dexterity of the forefeet, a pitiful attempt to walk erect'. Most uncannily of all, Prendick realizes that he too undergoes 'strange changes': his clothes hang on him 'as yellow rags, through whose rents glowed the tanned skin'; his hair grows long and matted, and his 'eyes have a strange brightness, a swift alertness of movement' (Wells 1996 [1896]: 198). Prendick's degeneration into something resembling the goat-man Alexander Selkirk, and the 'decline' of Moreau's Beast Folk into a creeping, trans-specific animalism are two manifestations of the same frightening power: that of a dynamic, contagious, protean, more-than-human vitality.

Pain-Driven Things

In the novel's crucial Chapter 14, Moreau's explanation to Prendick of his career repeats, at times almost verbatim, arguments that Wells was simultaneously advancing for serious public consideration in his journalism. In his essay on 'Human Evolution', for example, Wells described 'what we call Morality' as 'the padding of suggested emotional habits necessary to keep the round Paleolithic savage in the square hole of the civilised state. And Sin', he added, 'is the conflict of the two factors – as I have tried to convey in my *Island of Dr Moreau*' (Wells [1896], in Philmus and Hughes 1975: 217). This theory – compatible with the way Freud was developing his psychoanalytic paradigm at around the same time – is advanced by Moreau, who describes 'moral education' as 'an artificial modification and perversion of instinct; pugnacity is trained into courageous self-sacrifice, and suppressed sexuality into religious emotion' (Wells 1996 [1896]: 136–7). The examples given here of biological instincts remade by morality – pugnacity and sexuality – will continue to be advanced as the most essential of human traits by social Darwinists, sociobiologists and evolutionary psychologists throughout the twentieth century and beyond. They also, of course, suggest the ideological emphasis on competitive struggle that aligns such theories with capitalism.

Moreau's description of his experimental progress from sheep to gorilla, cited above, implies a biological hierarchy based on aggression. The sheep is 'no good for man-making' because it has already been modified by domestication, leaving it 'without courage', 'fear-haunted, pain-driven' and lacking the necessary 'spark of pugnacious energy' (Wells 1996 [1896]: 142). It is for this reason that his current experimental subject is a predator, a puma. Where Darwinism introduces an arboreal structure to replace the older, hierarchical model of relationships among species, the Chain of Being (Ritvo 1998: 28–30), Moreau reinvests natural history with power relations, fusing the structure of evolutionary competition with the structure of the food chain. Associating supremacy with ferocity, this world view places *Homo sapiens* necessarily in the predator category, determinedly answering the question posed by the virtuosi of Brobdingnag about how humans feed. As Peter Kemp argues, carnivorousness is repeatedly associated with humanity in Wells' fiction (Kemp 1982: 12–15, 20–22). The traveller in *The Time Machine*, returning from a society based on the cannibalistic exploitation of one human class by another, immediately demands that his friends save him some mutton: 'starving for a bit of meat', he refuses to tell his story 'until I get some peptone into my arteries' (Wells 2001 [1895]: 71, 73). In *Moreau*, Prendick's hunger for mutton after he is rescued by the *Ipecacuanha* is also identified with maintenance of a (specifically masculinist) form of humanity: '[h]unger and a lack of blood-corpuscles take all the manhood from a man' (Wells 1996 [1896]: 79). Sheep, then, are good for man-feeding but no good for man-making.

A more ambiguous relation to meat-eating is embodied by Montgomery. Moreau's assistant displays several of the physical and emotional signs associated with evolutionary degradation, prefiguring the degenerative symptoms that will be manifested by the Beast Folk near the end of the story: he has 'a dropping nether lip' and 'watery grey eyes, oddly void of expression'; he speaks 'with a slobbering articulation' and 'the ghost of a lisp' (Wells 1996 [1896]: 65–6). He also manifests the jittery emotionalism which some *fin-de-siècle* theorists identified with degeneracy (Nordeau 2000 [1895]: 16–17), for example when he shows 'ill-concealed irritation' and an 'odd want of nerve' at the sounds emanating from Moreau's laboratory (Wells 1996 [1896]: 93). Nevertheless, Montgomery is an inveterate carnivore. Indeed his liability to degeneration is shown by his inability to discipline his appetite for flesh. Irresponsibly, he imports and releases a cage of rabbits, instructing them to '[i]ncrease and multiply' to make up for 'a certain lack of meat' on the island (85). It is the presence of these animals that tempts the scarcely-repressed predatory instincts of the Beast Folk: the first confirmation of the Leopard-Man's reversion is the discovery of one of Montgomery's rabbits 'rent to pieces, many of the ribs stripped white, and the backbone indisputably gnawed' (159). Montgomery confesses that he has taught M'ling how to cook rabbit, and has seen him licking his hands. 'I wish, Montgomery', says Moreau disdainfully, 'you had kept your taste for meat in hand . . . We may find ourselves in a mess yet through it' (160–1). The same failure to discipline his appetites characterizes Montgomery's degeneration after the Doctor's death. He gets drunk with some of Moreau's hybrids, and ends up 'howling' and 'yelping' with them on the beach: '[y]ou've made a beast of yourself', Prendick tells him primly, '[t]o the Beasts you may go' (181–2).

Montgomery thus exemplifies the consequences of failure to maintain the balance between animal instinct and cultural mores – between what Wells considers the 'inherited factor' and the 'acquired factor'. The same dialectic is satirically conveyed by means of the 'The Law' that the Beast Folk chant: '[n]ot to go on all-Fours . . . Not to suck up Drink . . . Not to eat Flesh or Fish . . . Not to claw Bark of Trees . . . Not to chase other Men; *that* is the Law. Are we not Men?' (Wells 1996 [1896]: 117). As the 'grey Sayer of the Law' explains to Prendick, the ceremonial iteration of these prohibitions is required to keep in check the appetites which each Beast-Person has inherited from his or her native animal body (or bodies):

> [s]ome want to follow things that move, to watch and slink and wait and spring, to kill and bite, bite deep and rich, sucking the blood . . . Some go clawing trees, some go scratching at the graves of the dead; some go fighting with foreheads or feet or claws; some bite suddenly, none giving occasion (121).

Predatory hunger is therefore at the same time a signifier of human superiority to other animals, as occupiers of the top rung of the food chain, and an opportunity for humans to extend their evolutionary advantage by the development of those artificial controls over the appetites which enable flexibility, delay of gratification, forethought and conscious choice-making. In this respect the taste for meat, and its management, is essential to human being, or rather, to that specific form of animality which defines the human as such. This 'carnivorous virility' repeats at the physical level the function that science fulfils for Wells at the epistemological level.[22] It identifies the irreducible animality of the human, while at the same time allowing the willed transcendence of animal nature which is demanded by the savage competitiveness of that nature, and transacted via modern agricultural, scientific and industrial practices. For if meat-eating stands for 'man's' animal nature, it also functions as a paradigm of the requirement for him to discipline and educate his beastly, organic self.

The same is true, according to both Wells and Moreau, of pain, which also exemplifies animal materiality, and so provides the human animal with an opportunity to transcend and mould the limitations of fleshly, instinctual beastliness. Again, Moreau's contrast between the sheep and gorilla as potential subjects for man-making is salutary. The sheep is too 'pain-driven' to provide a suitable substrate from which to mould a human disposition. Moreau argues that transcendence of pain constitutes an evolutionary advance from animal to human, and thence from human to something higher. 'This store men and women set on pleasure and pain, Prendick, is the mark of the beast upon them, the mark of the beast from which they came!' (Wells 1996 [1896]: 140–1). This theory repeats Wells' own speculations, advanced two years earlier in an essay entitled 'The Province of Pain', where he wrote that '[p]ain is simply our intrinsic medical adviser to warn us and stimulate us'; hence 'with men, the more intelligent they become . . . the less they will need the goad to keep them out of danger' ([1894], in Philmus and Hughes 1975: 195–7). Moreau's vivisectionist procedures, then, are the artificially-assisted acceleration of this evolutionary process. He even implies that the pain inflicted by non-anaesthetized surgeries constitutes a kind of purgatorial rite which those animals capable of a human-like transcendence of their fleshly torments will survive. Only by immersing his subjects in the 'bath of burning pain' can he 'burn out all the animal' and 'make a rational creature' (Wells 1996 [1896]: 146–7).

A Man with a Scalpel

The provocative effect of these speculations about human and animal pain cannot be overestimated, especially in the context of the bitter anti-vivisection debates of the late nineteenth century. Moreau's career echoes many elements of this controversy. He embodies 'the figure of the archvivisector', a popular stereotype rendered easily recognizable by some high-profile trials of physiologists charged with cruelty (Ritvo 1987: 159) and by a number of anti-vivisection novels published at this time. For example Wilkie Collins' *Heart and Science* (1883) featured the sadistic Doctor Benjulia, whose 'place in popular consciousness' foreshadowed both 'Dr Moreau and the popular belief in 1888 that Jack the Ripper was a vivisecting surgeon of London University who had extended his research from dogs to prostitutes' (Lansbury 1985: 130, 141). But behind all these figures stood the 'shadowy foreign presence' of Claude Bernard, 'the foremost physiologist of the nineteenth century' and the most influential proponent of vivisection as the royal road to advancement in human medicine (153, 155). Bernard's *Handbook for the Physiological Laboratory* (1873), the standard text for such research, was the major influence on Wells' first published book, *A Text-Book of Biology* (1893). However, Bernard was less known in England for his scientific achievements than for a furious public scandal arising from an account, published in the *Morning Post* in 1875, of the treatment of dogs in his laboratory (Lansbury 1985: 171). Similarly, Moreau's exile is the result of an exposé by a journalist who posed as his laboratory assistant, and whose 'gruesome pamphlet became notorious' because of 'a shocking accident – if it was an accident . . . [o]n the day of its publication, a wretched dog, flayed and otherwise mutilated, escaped from Moreau's house' (Wells 1996 [1896]: 89).

At the time Bernard wrote and practised, physiology was working hard to achieve respectability by shaking off its earlier, more lurid associations, including the grotesquery of public spectacle (exemplified by Astley Cooper's 1801 dissection of an elephant before an appreciative crowd), and the reliance upon 'resurrectionists' (grave-robbers) who had provided cadavers for research and teaching in the years before the Anatomy Act of 1832 gave surgeons access to bodies from prisons and workhouses (Lansbury 1985; Marshall 1995: 71; Liggins 2000). Yet these were, of course, the very kinds of horrific associations repeatedly evoked by antivivisection campaigners and novelists alike. By taking Bernard's attitude and rhetoric out of the secluded space of the professional laboratory, and combining it with a literary tradition of scientific critique, Wells' novel makes both Moreau and his real-life model seem like true legatees of Frankenstein's febrile obsessiveness, and of the intellectual frenzy that pervades the Grand Academy of Projectors in Lagado. Hence, just as Bernard famously attested that '[t]he physiologist is no ordinary man', but 'a scientist, possessed and absorbed by the scientific idea that he pursues', Moreau refers to the 'strange, colourless delight' of the 'intellectual desires' experienced by the scientific investigator. And where Bernard wrote that the scientist does not even 'hear the cries of animals' or 'see their flowing blood[;] he sees nothing but his idea, and is aware of nothing but an organism that conceals from him the problem he is seeking to resolve', Moreau tells Prendick '[t]he thing before you is no longer an animal, a fellow-creature, but a problem'; hence he has 'gone on, not heeding anything but the question I was pursuing' (Bernard 1957 [1865]: 132; Wells 1996 [1896]: 141–2).[23]

Yet undermining physiological research and providing ammunition for the anti-vivisectionist cause would not have been Wells' aim, judging from his non-fiction contributions to the debate, where his position seems closest to that of Bernard and, indeed, Moreau.[24] 'In spite of the activity of the Society for the Prevention of Cruelty to Animals in our midst, and of the zealous enemies of the British Institute of Preventive Medicine', he wrote sarcastically, there can be no 'absolute proof' that animals feel pain. 'No scientific observer has, as yet, crept into the animal mind; no reminiscences of metempsychosis come to the aid of the humane' (Wells [1894], in Philmus and Hughes 1975: 194). These comments implicitly link an over-abundance of humane sensibility to degeneration, to the metamorphosis of human into mere beast.[25] The same is true of the representation of vivisection in *Moreau*. Although the novel gives extraordinarily vivid expression to the cries of the animals from Moreau's 'House of Pain', there is also ample evidence to associate Prendick's and Montgomery's sympathetic reactions with degeneracy.[26] Although both are supposedly men of science – Montgomery has studied biology at University College, and Prendick under Huxley (Wells 1996 [1896]: 66–7, 84) – each manifests an 'odd want of nerve' at the cries emerging from Moreau's operating room (93). Sympathetic identification with the Beast Folk brings animalization for Montgomery, who has 'a sneaking kindness for some of these metamorphosed brutes, a vicious sympathy with some of their ways' (152–3). Here the meaning of 'kindness' slips from compassionate sympathy to kinship, as though the former inevitably produces a degraded or 'vicious' form of the latter. Yet Prendick is also compromised by his reaction to Moreau's experiments. 'It was as if all the pain in the world had found a voice', he writes; '[t]he world was a confusion, blurred with drifting black and red phantasms, until I was out of earshot of the house' (94). This description recalls Max Nordeau's diagnosis of the degenerate, who is inclined to weep 'copiously without adequate occasion' and assume 'a condition of mental weakness and despondency, which, according to the circumstances of his life, assumes the form of pessimism, a vague fear of all men, and of the entire phenomenon of the universe, or self-abhorrence' (2000 [1895]: 16). The same cosmic pessimism characterizes the reactions of both Prendick and Montgomery after the death of Moreau. 'This silly ass of a world', says Montgomery, 'What a muddle it all is!', before sinking into a drunken and beastly 'bank holiday' (179), while of course Prendick upon his return to London is overcome by nothing other than a vague fear of all men.

In pathologizing the effects of emotional sympathy *The Island of Doctor Moreau* exemplifies two powerful cultural effects characteristic of modernity in the late nineteenth century and first part of the twentieth. The first is the radical separation of epistemological authority from emotional response, best represented by the scientific requirement for disengagement with affect in the pursuit of empirical objectivity. The second is the discrediting of the Enlightenment and Romantic valorization of sympathy and sentiment, which will henceforth be banished to the undervalued domains of popular and feminine culture. For the decades that closed the nineteenth century and began the twentieth saw the conclusive defeat of the anti-vivisection movement and the triumph of scientific authority (Lansbury 1985: 152–3, 64–5, 188). Indeed, the first decisive indications of how this battle would turn out occurred simultaneously with the publication of *Moreau*, but in America rather than England. The culmination of the anti-vivisection movement across the Atlantic occurred with the campaign by the Washington Humane Society to pass the McMillan Bill, aiming to restrict vivisection. Two factors combined to defeat this bill, and would in time succeed in banishing anti-vivisectionism to a radical social fringe. First, American physiologists organized 'a phalanx of . . . medical and scientific bodies' to testify against the bill, crushing their opponents under 'a landslide of scientific authority' (Turner 1980: 114). Second, the development of the diphtheria antitoxin in 1894, and its dissemination over the following years, was seized on by scientists as proof of the necessity of vivisection, and the acceptance of this argument produced a decisive improvement in public support for experimental physiology: '[i]n 1894 McMillan's bill might have stood a chance; by 1896 it was doomed' (115). As Turner puts it, '[a]nti-vivisection proved to be one of the last convulsive shudders in the arduous effort of digesting science into a culture previously dominated by literary and religious modes of thought'. With the legislative defeat of the anti-vivisection movements around the turn of the century, 'the dominion of science was secure' (120).

Ironically, despite Wells' own disdain for anti-vivisectionism, *Moreau* is now most likely to be read as a dire warning about the risks of arrogant scientific experimentation. There are a number of reasons for this. One is that the genre to which the novel belongs, that of science fiction horror, has tended to be disdained by cultural and scientific elites but embraced within the realm of the popular, within which neither the scientific nor the modernist scorn for 'sentiment' has much authority. In addition, it seems clear that the legacies of *Gulliver* and (especially) *Frankenstein* have proven too powerful for Wells. Swift and Shelley have, as it were, ghost-written his novel, giving it a tone that agrees more with their reservations about scientific experimentalism than with Wells' advocacy of it. At the same time, Wells' ideological motivation is also compromised by his narrative skill: he succeeds too well in imagining the fictional embodiments of otherwise abstract scientific principles. It is one thing to write theoretically about the transcendence of pain; quite another to show that principle put to work by a man with a scalpel.

One more feature of nineteenth- and early twentieth-century modernity has also contributed to this reading of *Moreau*: a shift in the meaning and function of monstrosity. The growing authority of the life sciences resulted in the discrediting of many traditional hybrids (unicorns, mermaids, sea monsters and so on) while 'actual' monstrosities – humans and animals born with physical characteristics inconsistent with current norms – were identified, described and contained by the taxonomic systems developed by teratologists (Ritvo 1998: 131–87). At the same time, however, as fast as science disproved the existence of various mythical monsters, new monsters reared their heads in the popular imagination, this time spawned by anxieties about science itself. Wells may have intended Moreau's experiments to embody the perceived threat of evolutionary decline, but for the majority of his readers they are more liable to evoke anxieties about technoscientific culture itself, and in particular the revolution in agricultural practices, from selective breeding to laboratory-based genetic modification. Darwin himself associated increased incidence of monstrosity in both animals and humans with over-breeding (Ritvo 1998: 141), while a mid-nineteenth-century agricultural writer all but anticipated the plot of *Moreau* in suggesting that experiments in hybridizing domestic animals had 'fulfilled the threat of Caliban and "peopled the isle with monsters"' (cited in Ritvo 1998: 133).

The Coming Beast

Prendick's experience is the realization of Frankenstein's nightmare about the possible consequences of his own experiments: beyond the confines of the laboratory, monstrous creatures multiply in a faraway location, their individual and collective agency accumulating to threaten the very existence of European humanity. The most rebellious laboratory specimen of all is the Puma Woman, Moreau's last experimental subject and the cause of his own death. Like the flayed dog, the Puma Woman emerges from the 'House of Pain' showing the vivid physical signs of her torment: 'an awful face . . . not human, not animal, but hellish, brown, seamed with red branching scars, red drops starting out upon it, and the lidless eyes ablaze' (Wells 1996 [1896]: 171). In a reversal of Moreau's experiments she mutilates the body of her tormenter, leaving the hand that administered the surgery 'almost severed at the wrist', and battering in the Doctor's head with the same bonds he used to keep her restrained during surgery (178).

As the female counterpart of the novel's other main rebel, the Leopard-Man, and a literary descendant of the monstrous spouse Frankenstein stopped himself completing, the Puma Woman evokes the conventional association between femininity and feral animal agency.[27] Whereas Moreau admits a general tendency amongst the Beast People to revert, so that '[a]s soon as my hand is taken from them the beast begins to creep back, begins to assert itself again' (Wells 1996 [1896]: 146–7), following his death, it is Prendick who associates this rogue carnality with femaleness:

> [s]ome of them – the pioneers, I noticed with some surprise, were all females – began to disregard the injunction of decency – deliberately for the most part. Others even attempted public outrages upon the institution of monogamy. The tradition of the Law was clearly losing its force. I cannot pursue this disagreeable subject (197).

The 'disagreeable subject' that Prendick's prudishness forbids him from detailing is the same feral reproductive energy and fecundity that Frankenstein foresaw in his female creature, and indeed that Gulliver shrank from during his encounter with his Yahoo admirer.

The capacity of non-human species for promiscuous reproduction, unrestrained by social inhibitions, was one of the main threats that Wells identified to human domination. Far from guaranteeing the permanent primacy of the slow-maturing, slow-breeding *Homo sapiens*, he suggested that instead 'Nature is, in unsuspected obscurity, equipping some now humble creature with wider possibilities of appetite, endurance, or destruction, to rise in the fullness of time and sweep *homo* away into the darkness from which his universe arose' (Wells [1891], in Philmus and Hughes 1975: 166–8). And the best evolutionary advantage of this 'Coming Beast', as he ominously labelled it, would be its fertility:

> [t]he true heirs of the future are the small, fecund, and precocious creatures; those obscure, innumerable plastic species that die in myriads and yet do not diminish, that change this way or that as the pressure of necessity guides . . . No doubt man is lord of the whole earth of today, but the lordship of the future is another matter . . . No doubt he is the heir of all the ages, but the herring, the frog, the Aphis, or the rabbit, it may be, is the residuary legatee (Wells [1894], in Philmus and Hughes 1975: 131).

This, famously, is the scenario played out in *The War of the Worlds*, which emphasizes the unexpectedness of the Coming Beast. In that novel, both humans and Martians in turn prove catastrophically vulnerable to species they had not accounted for: the former nearly wiped out by the Martians themselves, and the latter by the 'small, fecund . . . obscure, innumerable . . . myriads' of terrestrial bacteria.

In *Moreau*, the animal species that offers the most potent condensation of scientific and popular anxieties about animal resistance is thus not the puma, leopard, ape, nor indeed any of the hybrids the Doctor creates; it is the rabbit. From the point of view of modern instrumentalism, of course, the fecundity of rabbits makes them a most renewable and plastic resource. Hence in *Moreau* they feature as potential laboratory subjects, meals and pets. Montgomery introduces them as a self-reproducing meat supply, while Prendick's description of the 'little pink animals' created by Moreau imagines their possible marketability as less destructive substitutes for the pet rabbit in 'gentleman's parks' (Wells 1996 [1896]: 156). On the other hand, their fulfilment of these roles makes rabbits symbols of the reversibility of human–animal power, and of the unpredictability, versatility and reproducibility of animal agency. Even the little pink rabbit-substitutes spit, scratch and kick when Prendick captures them. Meanwhile, of course, it is the multiplying presence of Montgomery's meat-source that inspires the Leopard Man's apostasy.

The use of the rabbit to exemplify the fragility of human dominion is explicit in Wells' essay on 'Human Evolution', in which an extended passage demonstrates how the 'fecund rabbit . . . throws the factors of human stagnation . . . into effective contrast'. Estimating average offspring, lifespan, and mating cycles of rabbits, Wells reckons the responsiveness of this species to the demands of natural selection to be so prolific that it is 'almost out of comparison with that of the human animal', which has since 'the age of polished stone . . . undergone as much modification as the rabbit (under rapidly changing circumstances) would experience in fifty years' (Wells [1896], in Philmus and Hughes 1975: 212–13). According to this radical subversion of the conventional narrative of modernity, it is non-human animal nature that appears as the ultimate benefactor of 'rapidly changing circumstances', rather than human beings. Nor was this mere fantasy. By the time Wells was writing, the tiny rabbit populations first introduced to Australia and New Zealand in the mid-nineteenth century had swelled to such proportions that they seriously threatened the economic viability of the empire's farm colonies. Moreover the unpredictable effects of colonial experiments in acclimatization were continuing to multiply. During the 1890s mustelids were introduced to control rabbits in New Zealand, only to achieve plague proportions themselves and become the most significant threat to native fauna (Druett 1983: 150–77).

There is another way in which Wells uses the rabbit as an embodiment of anxiety about scientific practices. In an echo of the waking nightmares suffered by Frankenstein, in which 'a multitude of filthy animals' inflict on him 'incessant torture' (Shelley 1996 [1818]: 101), Prendick imagines himself becoming subject to Moreau's experimental practices, 'locked in . . . as ready as a hospital rabbit for my fate' (Wells 1996 [1896]: 110). This reversed vivisection paranoia is anticipated in an earlier chapter, when upon being thanked by Prendick for rescuing him from the dinghy of the *Lady Vain*, Montgomery comments dismissively, 'I injected and fed you much as I might have collected a specimen' (75). These moments recall the pen-and-ink sketch of a rabbit dissecting a man that Wells drew in a copy of his first published book, the *Text-Book of Biology* (1893) – 'virtually a dissection manual' – given to his wife-to-be Catherine Robbins (Parrinder 1995: 50). Such recurrent images of the vivisector vivisected signal a perception by Wells that science and its practices should entail continual awareness of the animality of the human, its vulnerability to the same biological principles and the same fates that govern other animals. The same awareness lies behind the humanoid Eloi in *The Time Machine*, who live as 'fatted cattle' to be bred and harvested by the technologically ingenious Morlocks, and the Martians in *War of the Worlds*, who collect their human fodder in huge baskets, later drawing out their blood through pipettes in order to inject it into their own bodies. As the narrator of the latter novel comments, '[t]he bare idea of this is no doubt horribly repulsive to us, but . . . we should remember how repulsive our carnivorous habits would seem to an intelligent rabbit' (Wells 2003 [1898]: 144).

Creeping Things

The scientific romances and journalism of H. G. Wells are expressions of a culture poised between a declining Enlightenment and Romantic sensibility of humane sympathy, and an ascendant scientific positivism. The shift in authority from the former to the latter prepares the ground for both Freudian psychoanalysis and modernism, according to which animality will be internalized as a savage, primal aspect of the human psyche (to be either repressed, or accessed via art and therapy), while animals themselves are mustered into the domains of science, industry and commodity culture, or into the diminishing wild.

Nevertheless Wells recognizes the ways in which the endeavours of modernity may be surprised and thwarted by non-human animality in general, and by animals in particular, both at the level of the species and of individual organisms. '[T]here is still something in everything I do that defeats me', Moreau admits reluctantly; 'something that I cannot touch, somewhere – I cannot determine where – in the seat of the emotions. Cravings, instincts, desires that harm humanity, a strange hidden reservoir to burst suddenly and inundate the whole being of the creature' (Wells 1996 [1896]: 146). When he first makes his Beast Folk they seem 'indisputable human beings', but afterwards, '[f]irst one animal trait, then another, creeps to the surface and stares out at me' (146–7). This creeping animality, which remains beyond the reach of Moreau's scientific manipulations, manifesting both 'in the seat of the emotions' and in the 'stubborn beast flesh [that] grows, day by day, back again' (145), achieves its most extreme embodiment outside the main narrative of the novel.

Moreau refers to 'a thing' – even he recoils from describing it in detail – created by him as 'purely an experiment', but which went on a killing rampage around the island after getting loose 'by accident' (as the flayed dog did back in London, and as the Puma Woman will before long). This creature, which 'wasn't finished', 'a limbless thing with a horrible face that writhed along the ground in a serpentine fashion', 'immensely strong and in infuriating pain' (145), embodies the most potent and threatening aspect of non-human life as it was conceived by Wells and other post Darwinian thinkers: its capacity for endless experimentation and changes, its plasticity, fecundity and precocity.

The same preoccupation is represented by the 'putrefactive and disease bacteria' that defeat the Martians in *War of the Worlds*, after all human attempts at resistance have failed – a triumph ironically foreshadowed in the opening sentence of that novel, in which Martian scrutiny of the earth is compared to 'a man with a microscope' examining 'the transient creatures that swarm and multiply in a drop of water' (Wells 2003 [1898]: 181–2, 41). The double dethronement of human power and privilege, first by Martians and then by bacteria, harks back to the destabilizing effect of microscopic and telescopic technologies in *Gulliver's Travels*. Elias Canetti has coined the phrase 'Lilliput effect', to describe the experience of 'a single large individual seeing himself in opposition to a numberless host of tiny aggressors', a perception exemplified by antipathy towards 'vermin'. 'Whether these are mosquitoes or lice, locusts or ants, they have always occupied men's imaginations. Their threat lies in the fact that they appear in great crowds and very suddenly' (1962: 419–20). To this list we might add Crusoe's cats, Gulliver's Brobdingnagian wasps and rats, the 'multitude of filthy animals' imagined by Frankenstein, and Montgomery's rabbits. The same anxiety is invoked by Wells again in 'The Empire of the Ants', a story about a species of rapidly mutating insects who have learnt to work in an organized hierarchy, manufacture weaponry out of poison crystals, and are carnivorous (for Wells, a sure sign of evolutionary pugnacity) (1927 [1905]; Parrinder 1995: 75–6). At the end of the story it is forecast that 'they will finally dispossess man over the whole of tropical South America', be 'halfway down the Amazon' by 1920, and reach Europe by '1950 or '60 at the latest' (108).

According to Canetti the Lilliput effect becomes most intense when it accompanies the evocation of germinal animality; when the very cells of the body 'are attacked by hosts of bacteria and other minute creatures which settle among them and which, being alive, are always active in their own way' (1962: 418–19). Wells was fascinated by this notion, pointing out in an early piece of journalism that even so-called individual humans are merely collocations of other living agencies. He gives the example of phagocytes, amoeboid cells that 'wander through the body, here engorging bacteria, and there crowding at an inflamed spot or absorbing an obsolete structure', which seem to display 'far more initiative and freedom than a factory hand in the body politic' (Wells [1892], in Philmus and Hughes 1975: 192). Concomitantly, he suggests that 'the gregarious assembly of cattle, in the social intercourse of rooks and wolves, and men also', should be considered 'the faint beginnings of a further synthesis, into the herd, the pack, the flock, or the party', wondering '[h]ow far may we speculate in the future of further developments of the cooperative principle?' (191). Answering his own question, he goes on to argue that the ability to recognize and operate according to this collective mode of agency is another of the human's animal inheritances which must be turned to evolutionary advantage, in a combination of Darwinian and Socialist principles, so that '[t]he village commune of the future will be an organism' (191–2; see also Kemp 1982: 3–4). For all its fervour, this does not rank among Wells' more accurate prophecies. On the contrary, among the overwhelmingly capitalist societies of nineteenth- and twentieth-century modernity, it was precisely this association – between animality and a networked agency capable of outperforming the individualistic intentionality privileged by post-Enlightenment humanism – that came to represent the residual threat posed by a non-human nature otherwise perceived as under the sway of human sovereignty. Nowhere in literature is this threat more potently embodied than in *Moby-Dick*, which provides the focus for my next chapter.

3   Rendering the Whale

The Breaching

Moby-Dick emerged at a point of crucial historical transition in several areas of American life. The first half of the nineteenth century witnessed a heightened confidence in the globalization of the American economy following the war of 1812. However, near the middle of the century, this economic triumphalism was accompanied by political crisis: 1850 and 1851, during which Melville was writing his novel, were the years of the doomed 'compromise' that attempted to reconcile opponents and proponents of the slave economy. The mid-nineteenth century thus represents a tenuous balance between a pugnacious American imperialism – exemplified by the Mexican War and the accompanying ideology of manifest destiny – and the menace of civil discord made all the more inevitable by that expansionist drive.

The oceans, especially the Pacific, provided a space in which these contending currents met and mingled, and the whaling vessel became a setting for the enactment of tensions produced by globalizing commerce (Niemeyer 1999). It provided, in the form of oil and spermaceti, the fuel and lubricant without which the industrial revolution could not have occurred at such a pace (Roman 2006: 66). *Moby-Dick*'s narrator rhapsodizes about the contributions made to America's economy and the dissemination of its values and influence by the vast whaling fleet which, at the apogee of the industry, spanned the planet.[1] At the same time, the tensions aboard the *Pequod*, which are also condensed into the malignant figure of the White Whale, embody contemporary strains and threats produced by industrialization at both the natural and the cultural levels. As Cesare Casarino has argued, the 'factory floor' of the whaling vessel was the setting for a playing out of the vicissitudes of globalizing industry: the epochal shift from mercantile to industrial capitalism, an ensuing redefinition of the relationship between labour and capital, and the unpredictable effects of intimate and extended interaction amongst a radically 'international, multiethnic, multilingual and especially multiracial labor force' (2002: 5, 74–5). In 1851, moreover, the catastrophic fate of the *Pequod*, suggesting the transience and fragility of these economic and social transactions, uncannily anticipated the collapse of the sperm whale fishery as well. For the middle of the century was also a turning point for whaling: during these years 'Californian fever' began to take labour away from the centres of the industry, which were further undermined by the financial crisis of 1857 and the concurrent flight of investment capital; the obsolescence of spermaceti and whale oil was assured by a cleaner, cheaper and more easily accessible alternative once petroleum began to flow from Pennsylvanian oil wells in 1859, and the Civil War, during which whaling vessels proved easy targets, completed the decline. Meanwhile it became increasingly hard to deny, in the second half of the century, that over-exploitation of cetacean species had made voyages longer, more expensive and less remunerative – and thus, in the end, financially non-viable.[2]

That animals, dead or alive, should figure at the centre of these historical and economic shifts is no surprise. *Moby-Dick*, and the mid-century whaling culture it represents, represent a period in which industrialization was energetically at work, producing – along with urbanization, alteration in the economic status of women, redefinition of labour structures and environmental degradation – a radically new relationship between humans and other animals. Industrial techniques were absolving farmers from close proximity to their livestock; assembly-line specialization of tasks was beginning, alienating workers from the material being processed; geographical and psychological gaps were widening between an increasingly urbanized human populace and most other species. Meanwhile, natural history and social science alike were rewriting authoritative perceptions about relationships between human societies and the natural world; in the mid-nineteenth century this entailed a transition from Christian to evolutionary notions of the 'chain of being', which – as discussed in the previous chapter – simultaneously broke down received divisions between the human and the animal and installed new ones (Wilson 2000).

The whaleman stood with one foot on either side of these many faultlines. He was praised as a harbinger of American values, and vilified for his immoral influence over the 'innocent savages' of the Pacific (Hart 1995 [1834]; Cheever 1991 [1850]). He was both a romantic adventurer into wild space and a prototype of the industrial labourer, farmer and meat-processor (Reynolds 2002 [1839]). His day's work alternated between highly dangerous encounters with the vast materiality of the living animal, and the reduction of that gigantic life to a collection of partial and dead resources, a commodity to be measured by the barrel, reified by the factory ship's technological procedures and its specialization of labour (Browne 1968 [1846]). No wonder that *Moby-Dick*, like its sources, oscillates so vigorously between apparently opposed attitudes to the whale: wonder and contempt, mundane nonchalance and transcendent awe, humanized fellow-feeling and the calculus of market value and profit.

Trying-Out

The narrative, form and thematics of *Moby-Dick* are all driven by the question: what do whales mean? Critical replies to this have mostly concentrated upon reading cetaceans as a screen for the projection of human meanings, but attended only incidentally to what else they might mean, or how they might mean otherwise – that is, the ways in which whales trouble or escape human representation. Even John Simons, who decries the reduction of animals to mere repositories for symbolic values, repeats this interpretive tendency in his own discussion of *Moby-Dick*, reading it as a 'sustained exploration of the symbolism of the non-human', in which '[t]he non-human becomes a vehicle, albeit a marvellous one, for the human to express his or her humanity' (2002: 113–15). No doubt the novel's repeated and extravagant indulgence in allegorization has helped to prevent critics from seeing the traces left by the animal upon the text.

Most certainly, compelling accounts of the novel have been generated in this way, one of the most important being Alan Heimert's '*Moby-Dick* and American Political Symbolism', which in 1963 delineated an allegorical relationship between the text and mid-nineteenth century America that has influenced most subsequent readings. Heimert identified the *Pequod*, the White Whale, and the various human characters with the key players in the doomed 'compromise' of 1850 and 1851 – the years of the novel's composition – which attempted to assuage tension between pro- and anti-slavery interests and thus avert the Civil War (Heimert 1963). Subsequent political readings, while drawing upon Heimert, have modified and ambiguated his strict allegorical correlations. Michael Rogin's *Subversive Genealogy* (1985), for example, accepts the associations between the novel and the slave and capitalist economies of mid-nineteenth-century America, but examines these in a more three-dimensional way. Others also offer more nuanced accounts of details of Heimert's structure: Staud (1992) concentrates on Melville's use of the name *Pequod* as coded recognition of the dispossession of indigenous Americans; Niemeyer (1999) focuses upon the quest narrative as an interrogation of the expansionist doctrine of Manifest Destiny; and Casarino reads the whaling ship as a 'crucial laboratory for that crisis that goes by the name of modernity' (2002: 1). By their nature, these political readings, while offering vital insights into the novel's relation to its context, omit consideration of the material impact of non-human animals, and of the vexed question of their potential for agency. In this way, a vital motivating factor in the text and its sources remains unrecognized.

It might be expected that a more recent critical development, that of eco-criticism, would attend to this dimension. Although it mainly emerged during the 1970s in response to perceptions of a global environmental crisis, this way of reading the novel was anticipated in 1947, when poet Charles Olson called the *Pequod* a 'precision instrument', describing the factory ship as 'one of the most successful machines Americans had perfected up to that time' (1947: 12, 23). It was extended by Leo Marx in

1964, when he used the novel to exemplify the dialectic between industrial technology and nature – the 'machine' and the 'garden' (1964: 277–319). Following these cues, an alternative set of allegorical correlations to those proposed by Heimert were advanced, their basic structure indicated by the title of Stephen Ausband's article, 'The Whale and the Machine', from 1975. Here, Ahab's relation to his crew embodies the mechanistic and dehumanizing social relations created by industrialization, and his drive to subjugate the natural world is aligned with the railroad – as the technological instrument of the westward expansion of America – and the concomitant dispossession of indigenous Americans and destruction of animal species and habitats (Ausband 1975). Similarly, a decade later, Richard Wixon calls the novel 'an allegory in which . . . the white whale may represent the beautiful and frightening power of nature, and the destruction of the *Pequod* and Ahab's death may be an apocalyptic prophesy for the future of the United States' (1986). In a more recent eco-critical reading, Elizabeth Schultz moves beyond this binary opposition between whale and machine, suggesting instead that Melville breaks down the 'dualism between nature and culture' when he 'simultaneously compares whales to natural forms and to human technological inventions'. For Schultz, this movement constitutes a 'dynamic environmental vision' that evokes the possibility of a non-dualistic, non-destructive relationship between human technology and the natural world (2000: 111–12).

Yet the same assumptions that motivate ecocriticism's interest in the non-human can inhibit its ability to read what the animal means. Even in Schultz's account, there remains something problematic about the ease with which affinities can be found in the novel with present-day environmentalism – for example when the final sinking of the *Pequod* is envisaged as 'anticipating the desire, if not the design, of twentieth-century environmental activists for the annihilation of forces antagonistic towards marine conservation' (2000: 110). Such projections either ignore or misconstrue the way the materiality of the animal impacts upon its nineteenth-century context, and in effect, re-allegorize the whale, which resumes its function as a blank slate for the inscription of human meanings and values. Instead of embodying the American nation in 1850, the whale now represents nature as conceived according to the late-twentieth-century environmentalist principle of biodiversity. What continues to evade these critics is the historical specificity of the novel's fixation upon the possibility that the whale possesses an active independent agency, a resistance to human projects and projections.

Only one study has addressed head-on this obsession with the White Whale's apparent intentionality. Robert Zoellner's book *The Salt-Sea Mastodon*, published in 1973, describes *Moby-Dick* as a sustained competition between two versions of the whale: on one hand, Ahab's 'transcendental' version of Moby Dick as a calculating, deliberative, rational and malign agent; and on the other, the 'naturalistic' view of the whale, as represented by Ishmael's gradually-emerging conviction that the whale is 'only' an animal, to which such attributes cannot be ascribed (Zoellner, 1973: 146–65).

Zoellner insists that the second view gains ascendancy over the first, insofar as the whale's actions prove, upon careful reading, to be dictated solely by instinct, and thus evince the animal's obedience to the dictates of nature, understood according to a deterministic Darwinian model. Moby Dick initially becomes aggressive only because the *Pequod* disrupts his insistent leeward trajectory – which, drawing upon Ishmael's earlier remarks about the regularity of whale migrations, Zoellner attributes to the 'instinctual', 'compulsive' and 'inexorable primal impulse' to find the seasonal feeding grounds of the Pacific. The destruction of the *Pequod*'s boats on the second day ensues from 'undirected', 'unfocused', 'random' reactions to the attacks initiated by the crew: 'Moby Dick does not *choose* . . . does not *decide* . . . does not *follow* any apparent plan of action' (1973: 247–66). In arguing that the novel strips from the whale all symbolic attributions in order to reveal a 'naturalistic' picture, Zoellner inevitably imposes his own theoretical assumptions, which are again those of environmentalism (1973: 266). Even while critiquing the severance between human and nature imposed by modernity, he reinstates the dichotomy by insisting upon the animal's blind enslavement to instinct, and so conversely defining a notion of conscious intelligence that preserves agency for humans alone.

The failure of Melville's criticism to account satisfactorily for the implications of animal agency in *Moby-Dick* derives, I suggest, from the lack of a methodological vocabulary within which such a possibility might be articulated, and the lack of a critical context within which it might be taken seriously. How is non-human agency to be understood in Melville's novel? How to think about what the whale means? Addressing these questions requires, along with a more nuanced theory of agency itself, a thoroughgoing historicization of both the novel and the structures of feeling it reflects.

The Flurry

> About the 'whaling voyage' – I am half way in the work . . . It will be a strange sort of book, tho', I fear; blubber is blubber you know; tho' you may get oil out of it, the poetry runs as hard as sap from a frozen maple tree; – & to cook the thing up, one must needs throw in a little fancy, which from the nature of the thing, must be ungainly as the gambols of the whales themselves (Melville 1960: 108).

This first reference to *Moby Dick*, in a letter written by Melville in May 1850, explicitly parallels his determination to impose meaning on the 'gambols' of the whales with the industrial processes that render them into a consumable product. Melville favoured this comparison, elsewhere describing the book in its final drafts as being 'in his flurry' – the whaleman's term for the death-throes of the animal after harpooning – and adding, 'I'm going to take him by his jaw, however, before long, and finish him up in some fashion or other' (129).

In figuratively associating his artistic rendering of the animal with its industrial rendering for oil, Melville displays an attitude very different from the popular sentiment in present-day Western societies, which regard any cetacean as a peculiarly 'charismatic' animal. In post-industrial cultures today – with some obvious exceptions – whales are protected collectively because the rarity of some species vividly embodies the fragility of ecological biodiversity. And individual cetacean lives are valued because their mammalian characteristics, along with their purported intelligence and benignity, invite in humans a sense of kinship all the more distinctive because it coexists with other features that embody a radical otherness: their sometimes colossal proportions; their morphological similarity to an utterly different order of creatures; their occupation of an 'alien world' in the oceans. Sympathy for whales has spread well beyond the countercultures of environmentalism and animal rights.

Moby-Dick was written at a time when such attitudes were conspicuously absent. Yet the few critics who take seriously the animality of Melville's whales nevertheless tend to read into this nineteenth-century work a late-twentieth-century structure of feeling – namely, that same compassionate awe which attends contemporary environmentalist attitudes toward cetaceans. This is most often linked to critics' readings of the novel's penchant for both anthropomorphism and identification with the whale, which becomes interpreted as evidence for Melville's attack on the nineteenth-century reduction of nature to a passive resource to be exploited at will by human industrial capitalism. For Zoellner, the perception by Ishmael that 'Leviathan is, like man, a placental mammal' leads to a 'growing feeling of *fraternal congenerity* regarding the whale' (1973: 185). Similarly, Schultz argues that by humanizing the whales' 'emotions and behavior' Melville appeals to the 'nineteenth- (and I may add, twentieth-) century reader's feelings' suggesting 'an intrinsic and irresistible interdependency among diverse species of life' (2000: 100).

These readings are not necessarily false, but they are misleading insofar as neither critic attends adequately to Ishmael's investment in the industrial processing of the animal, to which the novel assigns an importance equal to, or greater than, these moments of humanized compassion. Both Zoellner and Schultz also overestimate the novel's anxiety about species extinction. Amongst the writers concerned with whaling prior to 1850, only one concluded that fears about the decline of whale populations were well-founded (Cheever 1991 [1850]: 108, 155). The consensus among the rest was most authoritatively voiced by Charles Wilkes, reporting on the United States Exploring Expedition which he commanded during the 1830s and 1840s: '[a]n opinion has, indeed, gained ground within a few years, that the whales are diminishing in numbers; but this surmise, as far as I have learned from the numerous inquiries, does not appear to be well founded' (Wilkes 1845: vol. V, 493).[3] It was only decades after Melville wrote his novel that this view was comprehensively debunked, following the sudden collapse of the sperm-whale fishery (Macy 1972 [1880]: 217; Starbuck 1989

[1882]: 96, 113). Hence, Ishmael voices the dominant opinion of his time when, in a chapter that clearly draws upon Wilkes, he asserts that 'we account the whale immortal in his species, however perishable in his individuality' (Melville 2002 [1851]: 354).

In order to avoid anachronistically misunderstanding the novel's 'humanization' of the whale, its frequent anthropomorphic and sympathetic evocations need to be examined in their proper historical context. Without doubt, the first killing of a whale by the *Pequod* crew is graphically portrayed:

> [a]nd now abating in his flurry, the whale once more rolled out into view; surging from side to side; spasmodically dilating and contracting his spout-hole, with sharp, cracking, agonized respirations. At last, gush after gush of clotted red gore, as if it had been the purple lees of red wine, shot into the frighted air, and falling back again, ran dripping down his motionless flanks into the sea. His heart had burst! (2002 [1851]: 233).

Zoellner argues that at this moment 'Ishmael feels *with* the whale rather than *against* the whale', registering a compassionate impulse that inaugurates 'the redemptive process he must undergo' in achieving a better understanding of nature (1973: 169–70). Shultz echoes this view: 'this whale is not merely a statistic or a resource; Melville transforms it, especially through his touching concluding sentence, into a suffering, feeling being' (2000: 105). However this moment, like so many in the novel, draws directly upon previous non-fictional accounts of whaling. The most likely source for this scene is Thomas Beale's *Natural History of the Sperm Whale*, which describes a whale as '[m]ad with the agony' produced by repeated lancing, adding that at times 'his pain appears more than he can bear':

> [t]he fatal lance is at length given – the blood gushes from the nostril of the unfortunate animal in a thick black stream, which stains the clear blue water of the ocean to a considerable distance around the scene of the affray. In its struggles the blood from the nostril is frequently thrown upon the men in the boats, who glory in its show! . . . And the mighty recontre is finished by the gigantic animal rolling over on his side, and floating an inanimate mass on the surface of the crystal deep, – a victim to the tyranny and selfishness, as well as a wonderful proof of the great power of the *mind* of man (1973 [1839]: 165–7; italics in original).

It can hardly be claimed that Beale's evocation of the whale's suffering – no less emphatic than Melville's – aims to critique whaling, since his entire volume constitutes a vigorous apologia for the industry. Rather, Beale affects a kind of sublime pathos – seeing the animal as 'a victim to the tyranny and selfishness . . . of man' – in order to augment the epic and heroic connotations of whaling, which is thereby elevated beyond its vulgar status as mere commerce, and comes instead to encode the supremacy of the human over the natural world: 'wonderful proof of the great power of the *mind* of man'. This rhetorical strategy and the ideology it serves pervade all Melville's sources.[4] And the same (to current sensibilities) incongruous combination – of an intense, anthropomorphic identification with the animal and an equal valorization of its killer – characterized the representation of nineteenth-century big-game hunting, where it was deployed to celebrate imperial power (Ritvo 1987: 266, 278). In Melville and his sources, then, a descriptive emphasis on the gruesomeness of the whale's death serves to demonstrate not concern for the suffering of the animal, but romanticized admiration for the dangers faced by whale-men, as heroic crusaders in an industry crucial to national and global prosperity.

The next moment of sympathy that Shultz and Zoellner identify in *Moby-Dick* is the killing of an aged and crippled sperm whale. To be sure, Melville repeatedly invokes 'pity' in describing this animal's laborious attempts at escape:

> [i]t was a terrific, most pitiable and maddening sight. The whale was now going head out, and sending his spout before him in a continual tormented jet; while his one poor fin beat his side in an agony of fright…. [H]e had no voice, save that choking respiration through his spiracle, and this made the sight of him unspeakably pitiable; while still, in his amazing bulk, portcullis jaw, and omnipotent tail, there was enough to appal the stoutest man who so pitied (2002 [1851]: 279–80).

For Zoellner, this whale symbolizes 'the universal suffering which can – or should – draw all sentient beings together in brotherhood' (1973: 174). Shultz also points out how Melville lingers over the pitiful death of this animal, 'investing this whale with distinction and dignity. Melville adds the rhetoric of sentiment to that of sensationalism to intensify his reader's sorrow for the whale's death' (2000: 105):

> from the points which the whale's eyes had once occupied, now protruded blind bulbs, horribly pitiable to see. But pity there was none. For all his old age, and his one arm, and his blind eyes, he must die the death and be murdered, in order to light the gay bridals and other merry-makings of men, and also to illuminate the solemn churches that preach unconditional inoffensiveness by all to all. Still rolling in his blood, at last he partially disclosed a strangely discoloured bunch or protuberance, the size of a bushel, low down on the flank.
> 'A nice spot', cried Flask; 'just let me prick him there once'.
> 'Avast!' cried Starbuck, 'there's no need of that!'
> But humane Starbuck was too late. At the instant of the dart an ulcerous jet shot from this cruel wound, and goaded by it into more than sufferable anguish, the whale now spouting thick blood, with swift

fury blindly darted at the craft, bespattering them and their glorying crews all over with showers of gore, capsizing Flask's boat and marring the bows. It was his death stroke (Melville 2002 [1851]: 282).

As Howard Vincent argues, this incident draws on Beale and Browne (1949: 268–7). And as Zoellner and Schultz suggest, Melville deliberately concentrates various elements from his sources to highlight the vulnerability of this particular whale: the animal's age and general infirmity, his missing fin, his evident terror, and particularly, his blindness and the painful ulcer on his side. But other elements in the passage – ignored by the critics – complicate whatever sympathy might have been effected in Melville's mid-nineteenth-century reader. In conformity with his usual discursive technique, Melville vividly juxtaposes a number of competing attitudes.

Obviously, the image of the crew 'glorying' in the gore of their prey, taken directly from Beale's romanticization of the hunt, suffers from its unflattering association with the ignoble pleasure Flask takes in delivering an especially cruel blow to an aged, crippled, blind and dying animal. And as Schultz points out, this unedifying brutality undercuts the chapter immediately following, entitled 'The Honor and Glory of Whaling' (Melville 2002 [1851]: 284–6; Schultz 2000: 106). On the other hand, anti-cruelty doctrines – beginning to be advanced in the name of religion at the time Melville was writing (Turner 1980: 29–34, 45) – are thoroughly satirized, shown to be oblivious to their own participation in an industrial economy that depends upon the slaughter of whales: the spermaceti and oil that motivate the hunting of this animal will 'illuminate the solemn churches that preach unconditional inoffensiveness by all to all'. The simultaneous deployment of contradictory sensibilities typifies Melville's *oeuvre*. In this case, along with religious hypocrisy (one of his favoured targets), he challenges two opposing kinds of romanticism: that which heroicizes an activity driven by motives that are nothing other than economic, and that which criticizes the butchery perpetrated by working men while turning a blind eye to its own consumption of the products of their labour. Sentimentalism and anthropomorphism are shown to be at work on both sides, amongst both opponents and proponents of whaling.

The emergent humane sensibility, however, is not entirely absent from Melville's sources. In Browne's *Etchings*, one of the author's shipmates recounts a vivid dream in which he became a whale, and endured the process of slaughtering, dissection and trying-out:

> I've come to the conclusion it's a solemn warnin' against the catchin' of whales. *Whales has feelin's as well as any body. They don't like to be stuck in the gizzards, and hauled alongside, and cut in, and tried out in them 'ere boilers no more than I do;* and if I live to get away from this bloody old blubber hunter, you won't see me in no such un-Christian business while my name's Barzy M'F–– (1968 [1846]: 201, italics and ellipsis in original).

This passage is informative regarding the likely response of Melville's contemporaries towards sympathetic identification with whales. Throughout Browne's narrative, Barzy is a figure of affectionate humour, and this dream typifies his general naïveté. It also implies the extravagant imaginative faculty routinely attributed to whalemen – evidenced elsewhere in the same volume by the extended fantasy, resulting from fever and inebriation, of a character called John Tabor, involving a whaleback ride around the globe (1968 [1846]: 170–82).

Henry Cheever, who alone among Melville's sources condemns the industry outright, repeats Barzy's words verbatim as the views of 'an old whaleman', but fails to note that they derive from a dream and are treated humorously in their original context. He adds that such sentiments 'may seem foolish', and goes on to demonstrate the deeper source of his concerns about whaling: namely, the 'immorality' of whalemen, and in particular their failure to keep the Sabbath at sea (1991 [1850]: 125–7). Of course, in their origins, movements to protect animals from cruelty were most often accompanied by the impulse to control human elements disruptive of eighteenth- and nineteenth-century class structures.[5] In the same way, in both Cheever and Browne, concern for cruelty to animals serves their demands for improved regulation of whaling culture, at a time when mariners were often seen as renegades, divorced as they were for long periods from the supposedly civilizing influence of home (Marr 2001). Melville's scepticism about the discourse against cruelty to animals therefore fits his distaste for missionary evangelism, and his sympathy for social outsiders.

Nevertheless, Cheever goes further than any other contemporary writer in producing an assessment – although a heavily qualified one – of the propriety of animal exploitation. His conclusion is to recommend the principle expressed by William Cowper in 'The Task': '[i]f man's convenience, health, / Or safety interfere, his rights and claims / Are paramount, and must extinguish theirs' (1784, cited in Cheever 1991 [1850]: 115).[6] This rational approach, deriving from the calculated, measured Enlightenment humanism I have discussed earlier in relation to Defoe, undertakes to calibrate sympathy for animals against the interests of humans. But all others who wrote about the industry, if they did not exclude such considerations altogether, would have considered 'profit' and 'commerce' necessary additions to Cowper's enumeration of human investments that outweigh the 'rights and claims' of animals. As pre-eminent British whaleman William Scoresby wrote about the hunting of females and calves in the Arctic,

> [t]here is something extremely painful in the destruction of a whale, when thus evincing a degree of affectionate regard for its offspring, that would do honor to the superior intelligence of human beings; yet the object of the adventure, the value of the prize, the joy of the capture, cannot be sacrificed to feelings of compassion (1823: I, 475).

How precisely do these contrasting demands – that of commerce, and that of compassion for non-human animals – shape Melville's 'humanization' of the whale in *Moby-Dick*? The clearest answer is provided by the character of Starbuck, whose attempt to stop Flask's tormenting of the infirm whale during the incident cited above comes closest to representing the parameters of the mid-nineteenth-century discourse about animal suffering. The aversion to cruelty displayed by 'humane Starbuck' is both practical and economically rational – since Flask's sadism endangers the crew as it counterproductively agitates the tormented animal – and it mirrors his distaste for unprofitable heroism: 'in him courage was not a sentiment; but a thing simply useful to him . . . For, thought Starbuck, I am here in this critical ocean to kill whales for my living, and not to be killed by them for theirs' (Melville 2002 [1851]: 102–3). In the same way, he objects to Ahab's metaphysical quest because it distracts from the commercial objective of the voyage: '[h]ow many barrels will thy vengeance yield thee even if thou gettest it, Captain Ahab?' (139).

Starbuck's calculating materialism features significantly during an extraordinary moment at the novel's centre. During the pursuit of a vast school of whales, a boat is caught in the middle of the circling whales, surrounded by fearless cetacean young:

> these smaller whales – now and then visiting our becalmed boat from the margin of the lake – evinced a wondrous fearlessness and confidence . . . Like household dogs they came snuffling round us, right up to our gunwhales, and touching them; till it almost seemed that some spell had suddenly domesticated them. Queequeg patted their foreheads; Starbuck scratched their backs with his lance; but fearful of the consequences, for the time refrained from darting it (Melville 2002 [1851]: 302).

For ecocritics this moment provides a consciousness-altering experience of inter-species communion: 'once you have so touched Leviathan, you can never again return to the excoriated sterilities of the Ahabian world-view' (Zoellner 1973: 181). And Schultz agrees, arguing that here Melville 'confirms the cetacean-human kinship and his commitment to persuade his readers of humanity's implication in cetacean suffering and destruction' (2000: 102). However, considering the mid-nineteenth-century utilitarian view of compassion for non-humans, as embodied by Starbuck, I suggest that the key qualification in Melville's evocation of this moment is that the lance remains harmless only 'for the time', and because Starbuck is 'fearful of the consequences' of provoking hundreds of nearby protective adult whales. The text leaves no doubt that, given different circumstances, these 'household dogs' would immediately transform from pets into prey.

Moreover, Melville's humanized cetaceans can just as rapidly become cattle to be harvested. This is apparent even in the most racially anthropomorphic identification of human with whale. From their becalmed whaleboat, the three whalemen glimpse sperm whale mothers nursing their young, who are explicitly compared with human infants at the breast. The novel goes on to describe a newborn calf, and the amazement of the observers at seeing the

> long coils of the umbilical cord of Madame Leviathan, by which the young cub seemed still tethered to its dam. Not seldom in the rapid vicissitudes of the chase, this natural line, with the maternal end loose, becomes entangled with the hempen one, so that the cub is thereby trapped (Melville 2002 [1851]: 303).

To which Melville adds a footnote:

> [w]hen by chance these precious parts in a nursing whale are cut by the hunter's lance, the mother's pouring milk and blood rivallingly discolor the sea for rods. The milk is very sweet and rich; it has been tasted by men; it might do well with strawberries (303, note 7).

For Schultz, this 'sequence of astonishing imagistic juxtapositions' represents 'a confirmation of cetacean and human kinship, sexual and social' (2000: 104). Taking into account the mid-nineteenth-century structures of feeling described above, however, this passage appears more like an ironic intensification of the antagonistic demands of sympathy and commerce – and hence another instance of that uneasy ambivalence which characterizes Melville's portrayal of the relation between humans and whales. In particular, the suggestion that whale-milk 'might do well with strawberries' reintroduces to this nursery idyll the implications of other industrial uses of animals, for it implies the association, not infrequent in Melville's sources, between whale-hunting and the farming of cattle.[7] In short, the attitude to whales evinced here might best be compared with the conceit, common enough today, that sentimentalizes newborn lambs or calves, while at the same time accepting with equanimity that both are products or by-products of the industrial farming of meat and dairy commodities. This parallel is reinforced if we consider that Melville's contemporaries describe the slaughter of whale calves as a standard technique to bring their mothers alongside for the kill (Reynolds 2002 [1839]: 558).

Flensing

To citizens of Western post-industrial societies at the start of the twenty-first century, whales are familiar, even in their charismatic and radical otherness. As icons they are ubiquitous, from movie screens to coffee-table books to bumper stickers; we can access intimate details of their physiology and ethology via wildlife documentaries, nature magazines and websites; we can watch them perform in marine parks, visit them in the ocean on whale-watching voyages, swim with them as eco-tourists, and be lulled to sleep by CDs of their songs.

For the vast majority of nineteenth-century readers, by contrast, the whale was known in a very different way. As a commodity, its fats and oils and other bodily products were intimately familiar, indeed omnipresent. And as a biblical, mythical and literary representation it was also easily recognizable. On the other hand, as a living being the whale was a much more remote entity, indeed radically unknowable to the majority of people. *Moby-Dick* anticipates its readers' non-apprehension of the living whale by emphasizing its resistance to human signifying systems. In chapters dedicated to the whale's representation in science, art and philosophy, Ishmael satirizes its conceptual processing. Interwoven with these, chapters detailing the technicalities of the whaling industry examine the processing of the whale as a commodity. Ultimately, Ishmael concludes that neither the conceptual nor the commercial process gives access to the whale itself.

Ishmael begins with the field of knowledge that claims greatest authority, that of natural history. But his chapter on 'Cetology' mocks the incapacity of Linnaean taxonomy to contain the whale – such an enterprise attempts the 'classification of the constituents of a chaos' (Melville 2002 [1851]: 115). Eschewing the taxonomist's reliance upon anatomical structure, Ishmael advances instead a principle of organization according to 'volume', cataloguing cetacean species into folio, octavo and duodecimo editions, and into books and chapters. Transposing the bulk materiality of whales into paper and ink, this parody highlights the artifice, the degree of cultural mediation, involved in human systems of knowledge about the non-human world. Like Ishmael's attempt, such epistemologies comprise no more than 'the draught of a draught' (125). Tracing from Linnaeus onwards the debate about whether the whale belongs to the class of mammals or that of fish, Ishmael concludes: '[t]o be short, then, a whale is a *spouting fish with a horizontal tail*. There you have him' (117) – in so doing, preferring the industrial understanding of the whale to the pretended authority of science.[8] Similarly, using 'the popular fishermen's names for all these fish, for generally they are the best' (121), Ishmael's descriptions pay less attention to the physiology of each species and more to its commercial utility: the quantity of spermaceti, oil, baleen and ambergris it yields.

As the novel progresses, Ishmael continues to register his dissatisfaction with the conceptual rendering of the whale by various cultural media. 'As yet', he insists, 'the sperm whale, scientific or poetic, lives not complete in any literature' (Melville 2002 [1851]: 116). Nor do the efforts of artists get any closer. Criticizing the 'curious imaginary portraits' and 'pictorial delusions' that have dominated both popular and scientific cetacean iconography, Ishmael concludes that the sperm whale must remain 'unpainted to the last' (214–21). Instead, he promises a word-portrait which claims authority from the material realities of commerce: 'I shall ere long paint to you as well as one can without canvas, something like the true form of the whale as he actually appears to the eye of the whaleman when in his own absolute body the whale is moored alongside the whale-ship so that he can be fairly stepped upon there' (214–15). A detailed description of this second way of rendering the cetacean then commences, which sidelines scientific abstractions by anatomizing the material presence of the whale in the United States economy: as a resource to be harvested, cut up, rendered down; as a fuel to light the cities of mid-nineteenth-century America, and a lubricant for its industrial machinery; as an ingredient in the perfume and a support for the clothing worn by its citizens. *Moby-Dick* thereby provides 'the technic of an industry analyzed, scrupulously described' (Olson 1947: 24), a commodity history that 'bring[s] back to visibility, behind some product so familiar as to be a precondition for everyday life, the forgotten process by which it has first been wrenched out of natural life, then worked or manufactured into a marketable good' (Brodhead 1986: 6).

Of course, conceptual and commodity processing prove inseparable: the reduction of the animal to a product generates meaning as well as revenue. So the chapters on the hunting, flensing and trying-out of the whale give rise to further mock-philosophizing, always ambiguously: 'the mystic-marked whale remains undecipherable'; the gestures made by its tail are as incomprehensible as 'Free-Mason signs and symbols', its skin is cross-hatched by 'hieroglyphics'; its head recalls the Sphinx and its hump a pyramid (Melville 2002 [1851]: 155, 246, 248, 274–5, 296). Just as it eludes the nets of scientific taxonomy, and the canvases and other media used in attempts to capture its likeness artistically, the whale cannot be rendered by enumerating its various parts in their cut and commodified forms: '[d]issect him how I may, then, I but go skin deep; I know him not, and never will' (296). Such dissection brings the observer no closer to the whale's reality than the scientific pictures criticized earlier, which because they were 'taken from the stranded fish . . . are about as correct as a drawing of a wrecked ship, with broken back, would correctly represent the noble animal itself in all its undashed pride of hull and spars' (217). Considering this, Ishmael concludes with exasperation that

> there is no earthly way of finding out precisely what the whale really looks like. And the only mode in which you can derive even a tolerable idea of his living contour, is by going a whaling yourself; but by so doing, you run no small risk of being eternally stove and sunk by him (218).

The hunt, then, comes closest to apprehending the reality of the whale for two reasons. First, only the whaler (prior to the advent of underwater marine biology and whale-watching) meets the whale in its own element:

> [t]he living whale, in his full majesty and significance, is only to be seen at sea in unfathomable waters; and afloat the vast bulk of him is out of sight . . . and out of that element it is a thing eternally impossible for mortal man to hoist him bodily into the air, so as to preserve all his mighty swells and undulations (217).

Second, the hunt alone confronts the human with that dimension of the whale which escapes or defeats all other modes of cultural mediation, scientific, artistic or economic: the animal's agency, its embodied resistance to human plans, as signified by the risk of 'being eternally stove and sunk by him'. For Ishmael, then, the real whale is the fighting whale – '[w]herefore', as he wryly concludes, 'it seems to me you had best not be too fastidious in your curiosity touching this Leviathan' (218). Wherefore, also, the fascination of Moby Dick, at the same time the most mythologized of creatures, and the most closely associated with actual fighting whales encountered during the first half of the nineteenth century.

Well before his appearance in the flesh, Moby Dick swims into view as an embodiment of all the stories about fighting whales circulating in the first half of the nineteenth century:

> [y]et as of late the Sperm Whale fishery had been marked by various and not unfrequent instances of great ferocity, cunning, and malice in the monster attacked; therefore it was, that those who by accident ignorantly gave battle to Moby Dick . . . were content to ascribe the peculiar terror he bred, more, as it were, to the perils of the Sperm Whale fishery at large, than to the individual cause (Melville 2002 [1851]: 152).

The extraordinary mystique that the novel attributes to its eponymous creation – which includes both 'the unearthly conceit that Moby Dick was ubiquitous; that he had actually been encountered in opposite latitudes at one and the same instant in time' (154) and the idea that he was 'immortal (for immortality is but ubiquity in time)' (155) – derives from the White Whale's function as an accumulation of anxieties arising from the many contemporary anecdotes about fighting whales, which offered the most prodigious display of resistance imaginable on the part of an animal to human intentions. Ishmael insists that this, beyond any other factor, produces the aura that attaches to Moby Dick:

> [n]or was it his unwonted magnitude, nor his remarkable hue, nor yet his deformed lower jaw, that so much invested the whale with natural terror, as that unexampled, intelligent malignity which, according to specific accounts, he had over and over again evinced in his assaults. More than all, his treacherous retreats struck more of dismay than perhaps aught else . . . such seemed the White Whale's infernal aforethought of ferocity, that every dismembering or death that he caused, was not wholly regarded as having been inflicted by an unintelligent agent (155–6).

The double negative in the final clause here (*not ... un*intelligent) indicates the exceptionally problematic nature, in the context of nineteenth-century industrial whaling, of suggesting that an animal could demonstrate 'intelligent malignity', 'aforethought' or any other commonly-understood attribute of agency. Notably, despite the extensive evidence that Ishmael goes on to offer in support of this contentious claim, when Moby Dick eventually appears, the inference that his actions entail such a capacity remains surrounded by qualification: '*as if* perceiving this stratagem, Moby Dick, with that malicious intelligence *ascribed to him*'; '[a]s *if* to strike a quick terror into them, by this time being the first assailant himself'; '*as if* satisfied that his work for that time was done'; '*as if* bent upon escaping'; '[h]e *seemed* . . . now only intent upon pursuing his own straight path' (410, 416, 417, 423, italics added; Zoellner 1973: 151–2). And so, by the time Moby Dick makes his attack upon the *Pequod*, the novel has so thoroughly flensed the whale of its surrounding layers of human meaning, and so carefully qualified its own rhetoric about the animal's actions, that its final ascription to Moby Dick of the anthropomorphic characteristics of '[r]etribution, swift vengeance, eternal malice' must be examined with great care (425).

The Gam

The imputation to whales of agency of any kind was among the most contested of notions for writers of the time. William Scorseby's *Journal of a Voyage to the Northern Whale Fishery* – the most influential of the whaling texts known to Melville (Vincent 1949: 132–3) – understands the cetacean, according to traditional Christian doctrine, as a passive resource for human use:

> like the rest of the lower animals, it was designed by Him who 'created great whales, and every living creature that moveth', to be subject to man; and, therefore, when attacked by him, it perishes by its simplicity. Instead of repelling his attacks, it generally dives at once to an immense depth, where, under a pressure often exceeding 200,000 tons upon its body, it becomes so exhausted, that, on its return to the surface of the sea, it becomes an easy prey (Scoresby 1823: 134–5).[9]

Scoresby insists that this response derives from an 'instinctive faculty generally possessed by the lower animals, and employed for the purpose of self-preservation', although in this case, by an ironic twist of the divine plan, it actually makes the animal more accessible to human enterprise.

The same concept of instinct, which denies the whale's lack of purposive or effective agency, will prove adaptable both to an emerging evolutionary natural history, and to a capitalist attitude that sees nature as a resource. Both ideologies prefer to understand the whale's response to human intervention – even when it proves destructive – as an unconscious reflex. In *Moby-Dick*, Starbuck represents the confluence of these belief systems. Observing that Ahab's obsessive quest for one particular whale 'will not fetch thee much in our Nantucket market', the first mate adds: '[v]engeance on a dumb brute! . . . that simply smote thee from blindest instinct! Madness! To be enraged with a dumb thing, Captain Ahab, seems blasphemous' (Melville 2002 [1851]: 139). By contrast, Ahab locates in the whale an inhuman, and non-divine, agency – 'some unknown but still reasoning thing puts forth the mouldings of its features from behind the unreasoning mask' (140) – a perception that challenges the three inter-twined meta-narratives of the time: a still-potent Christian theology, a dominant and expanding industrial capitalism, and an emergent evol-utionary science. Certainly, many of Melville's sources agree that no significant agency should be attributed to the sperm whale. Melville draws his scientific assertions about the exceptional ferocity of that species from the natural history of Thomas Beale (Melville 2002 [1851]: 153–4), who, as Vincent points out, actually cites these sources to debunk them (1949: 166), concluding (in a passage ignored by Melville) that sperm whales are actually 'remarkably timid', and that they habitually demonstrate 'extreme activity in avoiding their foes'. Their considerable destructive power manifests only unintentionally: 'they rarely turn upon their cruel adversaries, for although men and boats are frequently destroyed in these rencontres, they are more the effect of accident during violent contortions and struggles to escape, than from any wilful attack' (Beale 1973 [1839]: 5).

Another of the novel's sources, Frederick Bennett, upholds this ortho-doxy, but he accounts for instances of apparent aggression in more telling manner:

> [s]perm whales are naturally timid, and disposed to fly from the remotest appearance of danger: and although many instances occur amongst them of a bold and mischievous disposition, which leads them, when molested, to attack and destroy both boats and men, yet such traits rather belong to the individual, than to the general charac-ter, and may be compared to the aberrations from a mild to a vicious temper, occasionally displayed among oxen, horses, deer, and other *herbivora* (Bennett 1840: II, 176–7).

In order to deal with widespread material evidence of 'a bold and mischievous disposition' amongst sperm whales, this passage transforms the species back into a passive resource by comparing it, with marked inappropriateness, to herbivores and the most docile of domesticated animals. This rhetorical contortion proves necessary because Bennett remains disinclined to attribute a natural or characteristic agency to the whale – a disposition nevertheless starkly demonstrated by many inci-dents recounted in the earlier narrative sections of his text. Along with summaries of the most infamous attacks on ships, and of the more notori-ous 'rogue' whales, Bennett includes first-hand anecdotes in which boats encounter 'a mischievous, or "fighting" whale of the most dangerous character', which 'instead of flying from his enemies . . . rather sought to attack them'. Elsewhere he asserts that upon attack, female sperm whales 'will often endeavor to assist each other', and that 'it is generally believed, by whalers, that Cachalots will bite a line intentionally, and for the purpose of liberating their companions'. Later, comparing the Right Whale with the Sperm Whale, he remarks that the latter 'more frequently displays a disposition' to act

> offensively, and in a manner at once so artful, bold, and mischievous, as to lead to its being regarded as the most dangerous to attack of all the known species of the whale-tribe . . . Actuated by a feeling of revenge, by anxiety to escape its pursuers, or goaded to desperation by the weapons rankling in its body, it then acts with a deliberate design to do mischief; and but too frequently succeeds.

Here, Bennett emphasizes precisely those aspects of agency shown by the sperm whale which caused contemporary writers such anxiety, and which provide the main source of the uncanny terror surrounding Moby Dick: the tendency to make 'wilful, deliberate, and even judicious attempts' against human pursuers (1840: I, 177–8, 205, 265–6; II, 213–20).

Like all scientific, philosophical and economic constructions, then, the characterization of the whale as a passive resource – represented by Scoresby, Beale and (when in his natural-historical mode) Bennett – cannot exclude the emergence of material instances that contest its authority. And as usual, these are sponsored most avidly by those outside the fields of epistemological authority that claim objective judgement – in this case, the whalemen themselves. By the time Melville was a crew member aboard the *Acushnet* in the 1840s, a multitude of such tales were circulating during the 'gams' or meetings between whaleships at sea. Some fighting whales were known as repeat offenders, sufficiently infamous to receive names. Even Beale repeats accounts of Timor Jack, 'the hero of many strange stories', who was slain only after several boats combined to distract him, and of New Zealand Tom, who in 1804 stove nine boats before breakfast – although Beale is careful to declare such stories 'much exaggerated accounts of real occurrences' (1973 [1839]: 183; Bennett 1840: II, 220). Melville refers to these rogue whales, and some others, in 'The Affadavit' (2002 [1851]: 171), but he omits the most notorious, who was also the most direct model for his own creation.

This animal, who like Moby Dick could be identified by his vast size and albino hue, was made famous beyond whaling culture by Jeremiah Reynolds' 1839 piece in the *Knickerbocker* entitled 'Mocha Dick, or, The White Whale of the Pacific' (2002 [1839]). From his first appearance near the island of Mocha in 1810, stories proliferated about this whale's inclination to destroy whaleboats. Reynolds claims his version comes directly from the man who eventually killed this beast, but decades later an article in the *Detroit Free Press* detailed further stories about Mocha Dick, contradicting the claim that Reynolds' informant had finished him off. According to this later account, the original white whale initiated successful attacks on whaleboats encountering him two months apart in 1840, destroyed two boats the following year, and in 1842 carried out an unprovoked raid on a lumber coaster in the Sea of Japan, afterwards defeating several boats from three different ships that cooperated in attempting to subdue him (Freeman 1926: 189–95). Mocha Dick, more than any other documented animal, therefore embodies all the characteristics of the fighting whale legend that fascinated whalemen and the public alike: an initiation of hostilities, a determination to protect or avenge other members of his kind, and even the ubiquity in time and space that Melville ascribes to his own creation.

However, to give the climax of *Moby-Dick* its particular impact, Melville draws not only upon Mocha Dick as the pre-eminent 'repeat offender' amongst fighting whales, but also upon another animal whose notoriety rested upon a single incident – albeit one that captured even more sensationally the attention of popular and scientific writing about the whaling industry alike: the anonymous sperm whale who sank the *Essex* in 1820. In this case, Melville identifies the non-fictional genealogy for his fictional creation within the novel itself. After discussing famous fighting whales, Ishmael adds:

> the special point I here seek can be established upon testimony entirely independent of my own. That point is this: The Sperm Whale is in some cases sufficiently powerful, knowing, and judiciously malicious, as with direct aforethought to stave in, utterly destroy, and sink a large ship; and what is more, the Sperm Whale *has* done it.
>
> First: In the year 1820 the ship Essex, Captain Pollard, of Nantucket, was cruising in the Pacific Ocean. One day she saw spouts, lowered her boats, and gave chase to a shoal of sperm whales. Ere long, several of the whales were wounded; when, suddenly, a very large whale escaping from the boats, issued from the shoal, and bore directly down upon the ship. Dashing his forehead against her hull, he so stove her in, that in less than 'ten minutes' she settled down and fell over. Not a surviving plank of her has been seen since . . . I have seen Owen Chase, who was a chief mate of the Essex at the time of the tragedy; I have read his plain and faithful narrative... (Melville 2002 [1851]: 173 italics in original).

Melville met the *Essex*'s ex-chief mate, by now a captain, during his own brief experience whaling in the Pacific, and as his annotated copy of Chase's narrative shows, he paid very keen attention to this story while writing his novel. Moreover, his footnote to the passage above identifies in Chase's account precisely those elements of deliberate agency which, as I have shown, proved at once so problematic and so fascinating to contemporary writers. Describing his thoughts after the incident, huddled in one of two salvaged whaleboats with his crew, Chase asserts that the incident directly contradicts the orthodox understanding (represented by Scoresby and Beale) of the sperm whale's nature, as 'an animal never before suspected of premeditated violence and proverbial for its insensibility and inoffensiveness'. Instead, Chase concludes with reluctance, in a passage cited verbatim by Melville, 'that it was anything but chance which directed [the whale's] operations'. The repetition and direction of its attacks 'were calculated to do us the most injury'; the animal's 'aspect was most horrible and such as indicated resentment and fury . . . as if fired with revenge'. Consequently, Chase feels certain in concluding that the *Essex* had been subject to a 'decided, calculating mischief on the part of the whale' (Chase 2000 [1821]: 33–5; cited in Melville 2002 [1851]: 173, note 9).

The peculiarly shocking nature of this event is borne out by the fact that every whaling writer after 1820 knew and repeated the story. What made it different from other narratives of aggressive whales? Later in his narrative, Chase describes an unprovoked attack on one of the surviving boats by a 'killer fish' (or Orca) and further on, a similar experience with an exceptionally large shark, but these incidents, while potentially life-threatening, inspired none of the horror that he felt in response to the whale's attack on the ship (2000 [1821]: 62–3, 130). The difference was two-fold. First, the *Essex* whale carried out the first documented successful attack by a whale on a ship, rather than just a boat. And second, in order to do so, it appeared to demonstrate an extensive and undeniable capacity for cause-and-effect calculation in identifying the ship as the source of its persecution rather than just the boats, and in repeatedly executing a method of attack most likely to damage the vessel.

By doing so, this animal struck head-on at the capitalist fantasy of mastery over nature exercised through technology, as embodied by the factory ship. Describing the *Essex* crew's immediate reaction, Chase comments:

> [t]he shock to our feelings was such as I am sure none can have an adequate conception of that were not there. The misfortune befell us at a moment when we least dreamt of any accident. From the pleasing anticipations we had formed of realizing the certain profits of our labour, we were dejected by a sudden, most mysterious, and overwhelming calamity (2000 [1821]: 23–4).

The shock attending this incident results largely from the challenge the whale's apparent agency poses to the complacent pursuit of profits via the labour of industrial capitalism. This becomes clearer if Chase's comments are contrasted with the rhapsodic confidence with which Jeremiah Reynolds concludes his tale about the *defeat* of Melville's other primary model for his white whale, Mocha Dick. Reynolds remarks that, making allowance of 'natural embellishment', his narrative offers a 'fair specimen' of the whaleman's life:

> [c]ould we comprehend, at a glance, the mighty surface of the Indian or Pacific seas, what a picture would open upon us of unparalleled industry and daring enterprise! . . . These characteristics are not the growth of forced exertion; they are incompatible with it. They are the

natural result of the ardor of a free people; of a spirit of fearless independence, generated by free institutions (2002 [1839]: 564–5).

The epic defeat of Mocha Dick offers, to Reynolds, an advertisement for the whaling fishery as a paragon of industrial capitalism, staffed by heroic workers and managed by entrepreneurial captains. The *Essex* story, in sharp contrast, can only mean something far less reassuring to proponents of this branch of American industry.

'Scarcely a whaleman . . . but can tell some story of the attacking of boats by these monsters', wrote Alexander Starbuck, reviewing the whale fishery three decades after the publication of Melville's novel, adding, '[h]ow many instances of the destruction of ships by whales the catalogue of "missing" vessels may furnish can never be known' (1989 [1882]: 122). In the metropolitan centres, however, away from the realities of the industry, such accounts were received with scepticism and mockery.[10] Perhaps this is one reason for the failure of *Moby-Dick* during Melville's lifetime, and for the dedicated allegorizing of the story by critics during and after the Melville revival of the twentieth century. Considering the religious, economic and scientific investments in maintaining both an absolute confidence in the invincibility of human enterprise, and an impermeable division between human and animal based on the former's allegedly unique capacity for calculated intention, it is easy to see why recognition of animal agency fell into a disrepute from which it is only just recovering.

Whale-Lines

Regarding the evidence of cetacean agency, nineteenth-century writers are left with two options. They may deny such a capacity to the non-human, attributing its apparent manifestation to the operation of instinct on the part of the animal, or to hyperbole on the part of the whalemen. Alternatively they may register the possibility that agency is not the sole prerogative of the human – a position they can only represent according to anthropomorphic claims that whales have behaved 'judiciously' or with 'malice aforethought', or that they have planned and executed 'vengeance'.

But how else could the agency of the animal be conveyed? It is my contention that, as a result of Melville's compulsive juxtaposition of competing ideologies, and his exorbitant elaboration of their central motifs, *Moby-Dick* fractures the orthodox nineteenth-century model of agency into a profusion of agentive effects. This radical redefinition of the relation between human and animal proved illegible to his contemporaries, and to twentieth-century critics, insofar as both retained their investment in a humanist valorization of coherence and singularity. The current dissolution of modernity offers a context and a vocabulary within which alternative assemblages involving non-human causes and effects can be retrieved from their captivation within humanist ideology.

The novel's ethnography of the commercial processing of the whale derives from Browne's *Etchings of a Whaling Cruise*, which similarly describes the tools of the whaleman's trade, and the anatomy of the whale (1968 [1846]: 51–8). But in Melville, these chapters perform an additional narrative function: each introduces to the reader one implement, or one part of the whale's body, which will prove crucial in the climactic confrontation. Entering like characters in theatre whose personality profiles contribute to the drama, these anatomies and artefacts function as what Bruno Latour calls 'quasi-objects, quasi-subjects' (1993: 89). Ahab's blade, for example, which he cools in the blood of his harpooners, becomes a 'malignant iron [that] scorchingly devoured the baptismal blood' (Melville 2002 [1851]: 372), thereby assuming the same malign intentionality attributed to Moby Dick himself. Earlier, the chapter on 'The Line' introduces another non-human agency that proves crucial in the final scenes:

> [t]hus the whale-line folds the whole boat in its complicated coils, twisting and writhing around it in almost every direction . . . Perhaps a very little thought will now enable you to account for those repeated whaling disasters – some few of which are casually chronicled – of this man or that man being taken out of the boat by the line, and lost . . . But why say more? All men live enveloped in whale-lines (228–9).

What seems a characteristic piece of allegorical moralizing – turning the whale-line into a symbol of the human condition – actually foreshadows the precise manner of Ahab's death. Hence, rather than preserve agency for Ahab or Moby Dick, the novel multiplies the kinds of human and non-human agency that will interact in the final moments of the narrative.

Of course, the most visible and threatening manifestation of the potential for non-human agency remains the body of the whale. But the chapters anatomizing the sperm whale complicate further the agentive effects ascribed to the animal. In 'The Battering-Ram' Ishmael emphasizes various features of the whale's forehead – the impregnability of the case of spermaceti, encompassed by thick blubber – that will effect the destruction of the *Pequod*. But the kind of agency embodied, its exact location, is less than simple:

> [n]ow, mark. Unerringly impelling this dead, impregnable, uninjurable wall . . . there swims behind it all a mass of tremendous life . . . and all obedient to one volition, as the smallest insect. So that when I shall hereafter detail to you all the specialities and concentrations of potency everywhere lurking in this expansive monster; when I shall show you some of his more inconsiderable braining feats; I trust you will have renounced all ignorant incredulity (Melville 2002 [1851]: 268).

If this passage seems to conceive of the animal's agency as a singular 'volition' or intentionality located in the brain, to which the whole 'mass of
tremendous life' owes obedience, the chapters following complicate this
suggestion, detailing instead a profusion of 'specialities and concentrations
of potency' lurking in different parts of 'this expansive monster'. 'The Nut',
for example, warns against estimates of the whale's 'braining feats' based on
the volume of its cerebral cavity, which may seem small in proportion to its
body (at least in comparison to the relative sizes of brain and body in a
human). Instead, given the resemblance of the spinal vertebrae to 'a strung
necklace of dwarfed skulls', Ishmael envisages a kind of brainpower
operant along the whale's entire body:

> phrenologists have omitted an important thing in not pushing their
> investigations from the cerebellum through the spinal canal . . . viewed
> in this light, the wonderful comparative smallness of his brain proper is
> more than compensated by the wonderful comparative magnitude of
> his spinal cord (276).

Consequently, Ishmael notes that the Sperm Whale's hump, which 'rises
over one of the larger vertebrae', must be considered 'the organ of firmness
or indomitableness in the Sperm Whale. And that the great monster is
indomitable, you will yet have reason to know'. As in the chapters on cetology, Melville deploys a mock expertise to undercut the authority of scientific knowledge, and thereby dislocates the humanist association between
will and brainpower, speculating that the body of the whale might mobilize
kinds of agency beyond the ken of anthropocentric concepts of rational
intention.

At the end of the spine Ishmael locates a further source of potency when,
in another anticipatory phrase, he remarks that the tail is used as 'a mace in
battle' (Melville 2002 [1851]: 294).

> But as if this vast local power in the tendinous tail were not enough,
> the whole bulk of the leviathan is knit over with a warp and woof of
> muscular fibres and filaments, which passing on either side of the loins
> and running down into the flukes, insensibly blend with them, and
> largely contribute to their might; so that in the tail the confluent meas-
> ureless force of the whole whale seem concentrated to a point (294).

The tail, like the head, can function as a localized site for the concentration of a network of force and volition, of muscular power and nervous
communication – but these capacities, instead of being confined to a single
organ or subject to a centrally organized will, are distributed in a fluent
and complex way throughout the animal. And so it proves: during the
three-day contest concluding the novel, the whale's head, tail, jaws and
flanks all at various moments effect the defeat of *Pequod*'s boats, crew and
captain (416–17).

The final confrontations between the whale, the *Pequod* and Ahab thus occur as intersections between different forms of agency. Moby Dick notices the ship as he wheels to face Ahab's boat: 'catching sight of the nearing black hull of the ship; seemingly seeing in it the source of all his persecutions; bethinking it – it may be – a larger and nobler foe; of a sudden, he bore down upon its advancing prow' (Melville 2002 [1851]: 424). Here, a contradiction exists between the anthropomorphic suggestion that the whale perceives the ship as 'a nobler foe', and the alternative interpretation that the attack results from his blindness to Ahab's approach, a possibility foreshadowed by Ishmael when he describes the position of the sperm whale's eyes on either side of its head, such that 'he can never see an object which is exactly ahead', a fact 'to be remembered by the reader in some subsequent scenes' (262; Zoellner 1973: 264–5). The same ambivalence – about whether intentional volition or contingency better explains the animal's actions – characterizes Moby Dick's advance on the *Pequod*:

> [f]rom the ship's bows, nearly all the seamen now hung inactive; hammers, bits of plank, lances, and harpoons, mechanically retained in their hands, just as they had darted from their various employments; all their enchanted eyes intent upon the whale, which from side to side strangely vibrating his predestinating head, sent a broad band of overspreading semi-circular foam before him as he rushed. Retribution, swift vengeance, eternal malice were in his whole aspect, and spite of all that mortal man could do, the solid white buttress of his forehead smote the ship's starboard bow, till men and timbers reeled (425).

Describing this moment, Melville abandons the perspective of Ishmael, who is not on the *Pequod*, occupying instead that of the crew aboard the ship. Suspended like automatons, their tools hanging 'mechanically', the seamen embody the paralysis of the mode of agency central to modernity – located in the human, expressed by the manipulation of technology in action upon a passive nature – as they wait for a quite different kind of cause to take effect. From their 'enchanted' viewpoint, though, the nature of the whale's agency remains utterly ambiguous. Certainly, the animal's 'whole aspect' demonstrates those anthropomorphic qualities which Ahab, and some of Melville's sources, have projected on to the rogue whale: '[r]etribution, swift vengeance, eternal malice'. On the other hand, the specific element within the network of agencies enlivening the whale's body that proves critical at this point is the 'battering-ram', and a fluctuation of narrative focus between the animal's 'whole aspect' and his 'solid . . . forehead' reflects the tension between bodily network and anatomical location by which the novel earlier complicated the representation of non-human agency. Moreover the phrase 'predestinating head' hints that this part of the animal's anatomy, rather than expressing agency in its own right, behaves as an agent *on behalf of* some effect or outcome decided in advance – which again contradicts the crew's ascription to the whale of a singular humanized intentionality. Even at the moment of maximum impact, then, agentive power remains dispersed, undecidable and unpredictable.

Similarly, in the struggles between Ahab and Moby Dick preceding their mutual disappearance from the novel, multiple vectors of agency intersect. Throughout the narrative, although it appears to be Ahab's will that drives the other characters and the action, this most vivid manifestation of humanist intentionality is undercut by the captain's repeated diagnosis as a 'monomaniac' – a condition understood in the mid-nineteenth-century precisely as loss of agency, possession by another power, inability to control one's own actions (Rogin 1985: 118).[11] And when, seeking to regain the initiative, Ahab deploys his weapons against the animal, trying to reduce it to mere quarry, the results are never what he intends. The first time his harpoon finds its mark, the whale 'spasmodically roll[s] his nigh flank against the boat' so that three oarsmen, 'who foreknew not the precise instant of the dart, and were therefore unprepared for its effects' are flung out of the boat (Melville 2002 [1851]: 424). Here, and in narrating his next attempt, the novel's language removes agency from Ahab and bestows it upon those instruments by which he seeks to enforce a masterful separation between human and animal, but which function only to connect them more closely:

> [t]he harpoon was darted; the stricken whale flew forward; with igniting velocity the line ran through the groove; – ran foul. Ahab stooped to clear it; he did clear it; but the flying turn caught him round the neck, and voicelessly . . . he was shot out of the boat, ere the crew knew he was gone (426).

Modernity would identify three categories at work here – the human, the animal and the artifactual – to which it would assign different orders of being, and it would attribute agency only to the first. But by previously introducing each of the agentive elements involved, chapter by chapter, the novel has set the scene for their interfusion. The animal acts, Ahab acts, the tools act: the sharpness of the harpoon causes the whale to fly forward; the whale's acceleration causes the line – personified a couple of pages earlier as 'treacherous' (424) – to catch Ahab around the neck. Various actors, animal, human and technological, cooperate and disappear in a moment, bound together in a manner apposite to the intertwined network of agencies that motivates the novel's action.

This interpretation relies upon the same deliberate permeation of the Enlightenment dichotomy between nature and society that characterizes the work of Latour, along with such formations as actor network theory, which re-conceive agency as 'distributed much more widely, perhaps unpredictably, across many different kinds of things associated with (what are conventionally taken as) rather different orders of reality (the natural, the cultural, the discursive, the economic, the psychological)' (Philo and Wilbert 2000: 16). Agentive networks of this kind are collective because they attach us to one another, because they circulate in our hands and define our social bond by their very circulation. They are discursive, however; they are narrated, historical, passionate, and peopled with actants of autonomous forms. They are unstable and hazardous, existential, and never forget Being (Latour 1993: 89).

The climax of *Moby-Dick* engages various of the elements involved in what Latour calls 'collectives', which mobilize both 'bodies and souls, property and law, gods and ancestors, powers and beliefs, beasts and fictional beings' (106–7). Each of these linked pairs, which modernity seeks to separate into discrete ontological categories, are in the novel divided and subdivided into a skein of sometimes competing and sometimes cooperating pulsions, forces and volitions: the animal's forehead, skull, spine, flanks and tail; the human's commercial instinct and passion for mastery; Ahab's will to kill the whale and to be killed by it; technology's power to penetrate the animal and to entrap the human; the natural body and the textual corpus of the nineteenth-century leviathan.

Schooling[12]

The networked form of agency that occurs at the climax of *Moby-Dick* catches Ahab bending because he has tried throughout the narrative to fuse all the actants within his sphere of influence – that is, aboard the *Pequod* – into his own singular, monomaniac intentionality. To do so, he has drawn on the rhetorical and material power of industrial technology, imagining his relation to the crew in mechanical terms – 'my one cogged circle fits into all their various wheels, and they revolve' (Melville 2002 [1851]: 143) – and even fantasized about the construction of a mechanical automaton completely obedient to his command (359). Ahab's desire to subject non-human nature to the iron will of the industrial disposition is reflected throughout the novel – most obviously in the extended descriptions of the technologies by which whales are processed into oil to power factories, but also in the various rhetorical figures that translate 'natural' phenomena into human artefacts or technologies. Hence, for example, the whale's regularity of locomotion is compared with 'the mighty iron Leviathan of the modern railway' (414). Similarly, Jeremiah Reynolds likens the breathing of Mocha Dick to the action of a steam-engine (2002 [1839]: 551). This comparison can also work in reverse, as when Reynolds describes a ship with its try-works in operation:

> there are few objects in themselves more picturesque or beautiful, than a whaleship, seen from a distance of three or four miles, on a pleasant evening, in the midst of the great Pacific. As she moves gracefully over the water, rising and falling on the gentle undulations peculiar to this sea; her sails glowing in the quivering light of the fires that flash from below, and a thick volume of smoke ascending from

her midst, and curling away in dark masses upon the wind; it requires little effort of the fancy, to imagine one's self gazing upon a floating volcano (550).

Reynolds' fervour reflects an emerging cultural attitude whereby advances in industrial technology, because they seemed to be associated with an apparent 'worldwide surge' in 'democratic egalitarianism', were 'used to figure an unprecedented release of human energy in science, politics, and everyday life' (Marx 1964: 191). It is this widespread excitement about steam-engines, railroads, factories and new cities that allows Reynolds to use the Romantic lyricism associated with natural sublimity in the service of the very process, that of globalizing industry, against which literary Romanticism defined itself in the first place. In this respect, the wonders of nature are subsumed by, and put in the service of, the miracle of industrial capitalism.

However, *Moby-Dick* documents a conflict between two opposing structures of feeling produced by industrialization. On one hand the novel reflects the wonderment produced by marvels like the locomotives and steamships; on the other, it anticipates the eclipse of that wonder by realization of the ways in which industrial capitalism would reduce human and non-human life to exploitable labour and raw materials. Both attitudes are expressed by rhetorical figures that swap human attributes and non-human ones, and which are inseparable from the material exchanges that occur all the time between so-called society and so-called nature.

For Latour, exchanges between society and nature have always functioned as 'the unthinkable, the unconscious' upon which depended the very establishment of 'the modern constitution' (1993: 37) – that is, the ideology of progressivist humanism that emerged in the European Enlightenment and was operating at full cultural, economic and political strength by the time Melville wrote. Latour argues that seventeenth-century political and scientific theory inaugurated a false dichotomy between the realms of nature and society, assigning humans and non-humans to separate ontological planes, upon which were predicated the most authoritative epistemologies of modernity: liberal democracy, capitalism and empirical science (32). To understand modernity, and in particular its insistent compartmentalization of knowledge, therefore requires analysis of what Latour calls 'translation': the continuous process of exchange and transfer between non-human and human domains, recognition of which is foreclosed by the modern constitution (10–11). Such translations occur materially, conceptually and representationally: they are simultaneously 'real, quite real', and at the same time 'discursive' and 'narrated' (1993: 89). They give the lie to the modern constitution, which 'explained everything, but only by leaving out what was in the middle' – that is to say, 'hybrids, monsters – what Donna Haraway calls "cyborgs" and "tricksters" . . . whose explanation it abandons' (47; citing Haraway 1991).

Melville's whales become sites for precisely this kind of translation. At certain moments they act as screens for the projection of models for human society; at others they are called upon to shape that society, or are shaped by it. Hence, for example, the 'fighting' whale, against whom Ahab pits himself so compulsively, occurs not as a mere opposition to industry, or a symbol of its challenges, but as a live, active commingling of the worlds of human industry and cetacean ecology. Summing up his expedition's global survey of marine life, ocean currents, whale distribution and the activities of the whale fishery, US commander Charles Wilkes suggested that whales had, as a result of saturation whaling, 'indeed become wilder, or as some of the whalers express it, "more scary", and in consequence, not so easy to capture' (1845: vol. V, 493). Melville expands on this inference, noting that whereas

> in former years (the latter part of the last century, say) these Leviathans, in small pods, were encountered much oftener than at present . . . those whales, influenced by some views to safety, now swim the seas in immense caravans, so that to a large degree the scattered solitaries, yokes, and pods, and schools of other days are now aggregated into vast but widely separated, unfrequent armies (Melville 2002 [1851]: 353).

Ishmael here repeats his hypothesis that, 'owing to the unwearied activity with which of late they have been hunted over all four oceans', sperm whales 'are now frequently met with in extensive herds . . . as if numerous nations of them had sworn solemn league and covenant for mutual assistance and protection' (298). Melville identifies a material instance of the interchange between culture and nature, whereby the behaviour and social structure of cetaceans is reshaped in response to human economic and industrial enterprise. At the same time, *Moby-Dick* ascribes to sperm whales – insistently, as Melville repeats the notion three times in different chapters – a capacity to learn and to pass on that learning which cannot be reduced to instinct, a form of 'behavioral transmission that doesn't rest on genetics' (de Waal 2001, 214) – or in other words, a culture.[13] Animal agency – individual and collective – is not just a counter to human enterprise but a product of it.

Of course, positivist science – of the twentieth century, but also of Melville's time – would scorn Ishmael's ascription to whales of structures deriving from human society and politics: armies, armadas, nationals, leagues, covenants. For Latour, the prohibition on anthropomorphism is a regulatory mechanism, put in place by the modern constitution to maintain a strict separation between human and non-human ontologies by dismissing comparisons between humans and animals as poetic license, popular sentimental error, or unscientific indulgence (1993: 136–8). Such anthropomorphic conceits were routine in eighteenth-century natural history. The Linnaean system, 'as propounded in late-eighteenth-century England', divided what it called the 'Vegetable Kingdom' into 'Tribes' and 'Nations', allocating obviously sociological characteristics to its subdivisions within the latter class: grasses were described as 'plebeians', lilies as 'patricians', mosses as 'servants', flags as 'slaves' and so on (Thomas 1984: 66). Rhetoric of this kind represented a vestige of the pre-Enlightenment analogical paradigm for understanding the relation between human beings and the natural world, whereby the macrocosm reflected the divinely ordained structure of human life, and *vice versa*. However the increasingly dominant scientific demarcation between nature and society meant that such comparisons fell into disrepute during the nineteenth century. Naturalist Hartley Coleridge wrote in 1835 that '[t]he real habits of animals . . . should be carefully observed and they should not be described as performing human actions to which their natural actions have no imaginable analogy or resemblance' (cited in Thomas 1984: 68). Nevertheless, the interfusion of humans and nature, as it was foreclosed from consideration by the natural and social sciences, remained or returned in a variety of other forms.[14] The ascription to animals of symbolic meanings significant to the human world remained 'an article of faith for many Victorian country folk, [although] it no longer had the support of intellectuals'; moreover, '[e]ven as the older view was driven out by the scientists, it began to creep back in the form of the pathetic fallacy of the Romantic poets and travellers, for whom nature served as a mirror to their own moods and emotions' (Thomas 1984: 91). *Moby-Dick*, of course, deploys precisely these popular and Romantic translations between nature and society both extensively and vividly.

More recently, the evocation and analysis of anthropomorphic effects has come to be seen as an opportunity for resisting, critiquing or investigating the operation of scientific epistemology, and of modernity itself (Crist 1999). Certainly, in *Moby-Dick* such metaphors at times demonstrate the kinds of material and practical interfusion occurring between the human and non-human realms. As Latour puts it, '[t]he expression "anthropomorphic" considerably underestimates our humanity', which is actually woven together from 'alliances and exchanges' between many kinds of 'morphism', including 'technomorphisms, zoomorphisms, phusimorphisms, ideomorphisms, theomorphisms, sociomorphisms, psychomorphisms' (Latour 1993: 137).[15] Thus, for example, Captain Ahab, for all his mechanistic rhetoric, incorporates into his own body the substance of the animal he hunts – his 'ivory leg had at sea been fashioned from the polished bone of the sperm whale's jaw' (Melville 2002 [1851]: 109) – as well as fusing it with the factory ship he commands, fitting his prosthetic leg into an auger hole in the deck (109). Like Haraway's cyborg, Ahab's body – human, animal and technological – occupies more than one of the ontological realms into which modernity sought to divide the real. And his monomaniac determination to pursue the White Whale arises from this same inter-implication of domains. It was after the amputation of his leg during his first encounter with Moby Dick, Ishmael hears, that Ahab's 'torn body and gashed soul bled into one another, and so interfusing made him mad' (156). The wound inflicted by Moby Dick provides the site of a maddening interfusion between soul and body, human and nature, man and whale, grafted together bone to bone, leg to jaw. Ahab's subsequent career will be motivated by this point of translation: the incommensurable contradiction produced by the human's material dependence on the body of the animal, combined with the simultaneous exclusion of the animal from the cultural definition of what it is to be a human.

Taken together, the anthropomorphic humanizing of the whale and the zoomorphic animalizing of the human indicate the volume and impact of the traffic between the so-called social and natural domains. And these exchanges are nowhere more apparent than in *Moby-Dick*'s portrait of gender organization, both human and cetacean. Women are, of course, all but absent from *Moby-Dick*, but femininity is not. On the contrary, the novel exemplifies an historically specific modification of gender codes, effected through complex transfers between nature and culture. Mid-nineteenth-century masculinity and femininity and the zoology of sexual difference are used to define each other, and to naturalize the resulting gender ideology. These gender transactions are effected by a complex interplay between human and non-human.

Most obviously, Melville describes in 'The Grand Armada' – during the moment when Ishmael gazes into the profound centre of the sperm whale's social organization – precisely that gendered separation into supposedly complementary spheres of activity that was concurrently at work in American society, 'as if the cows and calves had been purposely locked up in this innermost fold':

> [b]ut far beneath this wondrous world upon the surface, another and still stranger world met our eyes as we gazed over the side. For, suspended in those watery vaults, floated the forms of the nursing mothers of the whales, and those that by their enormous girth seemed shortly to become mothers. The lake, as I have hinted, was to a considerable depth exceedingly transparent; and as human infants while suckling will calmly and fixedly gaze away from the breast . . . even so did the young of these whales seem looking up towards us, but not at us, as if we were but a bit of Gulf-weed in their new-born sight. Floating on their sides, the mothers also seemed quietly eyeing us (Melville 2002 [1851]: 302–3).

The rhetoric of calm, transparency and immediacy pervading this passage seems to guarantee its verisimilitude: here, of all the descriptions of whales offered by the novel, it appears to promise the reader a clear view of the intimate natural life of the animal, devoid of literary or symbolic coloration.

Of course this is far from being the case. As Vincent has argued, the passage draws closely upon descriptions of nursing whales in Melville's favoured sources (Vincent 1949: 304–5).[16] Furthermore, the comparison with human infants hints at a simultaneous co-construction of the natural history of the whale and the social life of nineteenth-century Americans. As Ann Douglas points out, the economic and cultural position of women in the American north-east underwent a profound change during the first half of the nineteenth century. Industrial manufacture replaced the female domestic labour that had been economically vital during the so-called 'Age of Homespun' at the end of the eighteenth century, with a consequent loss in 'self-reliance and social responsibility' for women. Education for young girls, instead of teaching them to be home-workers, now trained them to spend their husbands' incomes, and their manual involvement in the material economy was substituted with an exorbitant cult of maternity: '[p]raise of motherhood could bolster and promote the middle-class woman's biological function as tantamount, if not superior, to her lost economic productivity' (Douglas 1998: 51–9, 74). The central nursery idyll of 'The Grand Armada' evidently and vividly partakes of this apotheosis of human motherhood, while at the same time, typically, Melville implies that these whales, even the mothers and newborn offspring, are simply resources waiting to be harvested – as in the footnote to this passage, discussed earlier, which envisages the 'precious parts in a nursing whale . . . cut by the hunter's lance' so that 'the mother's pouring milk and blood rivallingly discolor the sea for rods' (Melville 2002 [1851]: 303 note 7). This (by now familiar) juxtaposition of an emotional humanization of the whale and a brutal recognition of its consumption comes very close to an admission of the price paid by both the animal and the human female for their place within industrial capitalism.

All the same, Douglas overestimates the author's intentional commitment to the politics of gender equality when she concludes that Melville 'consistently produced a literature of inclusiveness. What his society would not allow him to conceive – sexual equality, a non-oppressive economic system, an honest culture – he also included by making his work a recognition of the price of their loss' (1998: 329). However she does point out one important moment at which the novel does not ignore its own exclusion of women (304–5). The last extended exchange between Ahab and Starbuck prior to the meeting with Moby Dick – the closest Ahab comes to turning back from his destructive course – involves the Captain's recognition of the damage produced by the economic separation between the genders: 'for forty years has Ahab forsaken the peaceful land, for forty years to make war on the horrors of the deep! . . . away, whole oceans away, from that young girl-wife I wedded past fifty, and sailed for Cape Horn the next day, leaving but one dent in my marriage pillow' (Melville 2002 [1851]: 405–6). But despite Starbuck's appeal to his affection for home and family, Ahab cannot turn back: 'what cozening, hidden lord and master, and cruel, remorseless emperor commands me; that against all natural lovings and longings, I so keep pushing, and crowding, and jamming myself on all the time . . . ?' (406). The novel implies a psychological or ontological answer to this question, but Ahab's monomaniac drive, frequently represented in reference to industrial technology – '[t]he path to my fixed purpose is laid with iron rails, whereon my soul is grooved to run' (143) – can equally be read as a metaphysical by-product of the industrial economy's impact upon the gender organization of mid-nineteenth-century America, a mythopoeic sublimation of an economically motivated separation of men and women into widely demarcated economic zones.

Ahab's idyll, and his relentless pursuit of the whale, therefore represent the strictest possible adherence to the gendered spheres of activity organized by an industrializing economy, which required a strengthening of the opposition between an aggressive, courageous and active masculinity, and a tender, nurturing and passive femininity – complementary gender dispositions consonant with, respectively, the competitive and acquisitive arena of capitalist enterprise, and the accompanying sanctum of the privatized nuclear family. Moreover, the novel illustrates how these attributes came to be located in nature. Just as a contemporary cult of American motherhood informs Ishmael's paean to the whale nursery in 'The Grand Armada', the subsequent chapter discovers in bull whales the 'naturally' opposing virtues of masculinity: '[i]n cavalier attendance upon the school of females, you invariably see a male of full grown magnitude, but not old; who, upon any alarm, evinces his gallantry by falling in the rear and covering the flight of his ladies' (Melville 2002 [1851]: 305). The chapter goes on to distinguish between these 'harem' schools, comprising mostly females guarded by a single male, and the 'schools composing none but young and vigorous males':

> while those female whales are characteristically timid, the young males, or forty-barrel-bulls, as they call them, are by far the most pugnacious of all the Leviathans, and proverbially the most dangerous to encounter; excepting those wondrous greyheaded, grizzled whales, sometimes met . . .
>
> Like a mob of young collegians, [the young males] are full of fight, fun and wickedness, tumbling round the world at . . . a reckless, rollicking rate . . . They soon relinquish this turbulence though, and when about three fourths grown, break up, and separately go about in quest of settlements, that is, harems.
>
> Another point of difference between the male and female schools is still more characteristic of the sexes. Say you strike a Forty-barrel bull – poor devil! all his comrades quit him. But strike a member of the harem school, and her companions swim around her with every token of concern, sometimes lingering so near her and so long, as themselves to fall a prey (307).

In this passage human sociological practice and natural-historical observation are engaged in a mutual authorization that irons out all contradictions. So, for instance, the inconsistency between the purported timidity of the females and their refusal to escape when their companions are struck is explained by an appeal to a femininity – animal and human – that finds its highest calling in maternity, which requires a deferential but intractable 'concern' for the well-being of others at the expense of the self. And the incongruent combination of pugnacity and cowardice in the character of young males is processed into coherence by a notion of masculinity that manifests in youth as a reckless but selfish aggressivity, and in maturity by a courageous protection of the weaker members of the social order. In short, an entire sociology and psychology of gender, class, educational and social development – perfectly evolved to suit the economics of industrial capitalism – is being advanced by means of its interfusion with cetacean ethology.

Evidently, only heroicization of the male leviathan could properly elevate his human antagonists to epic heights, thereby glorifying the whaling industry and the expansionist industrial capitalism it represented. Hence, only the male rogue whales were ever made famous as individuals by being given names: New Zealand Tom, Mocha Dick, Timor Jack, Don Miguel. That captains responded to the encounter with such animals as a contest of masculinities is attested by the example of John DeBlois, who described his nemesis, which had already destroyed several boats and would eventually sink his ship, as a '[n]oble fellow', and admitted that the increasing danger of the situation only strengthened his resolve 'to secure this "fighting whale" . . . My blood was up, and I was fully determined to have that whale, cost what it might' (in Sawtell 1962: 72). In the same manner, Jeremiah Reynolds immortalized Mocha Dick as a 'renowned monster, who had come off victorious in a hundred fights with his pursuers', and his vanquisher as an embodiment of the free, unpretentious, everyday heroism of the worker under capitalism, 'of a spirit of fearless independence, generated by free institutions' (2002 [1839]: 565).

Nevertheless, the kinds of self-contradiction that betray the work of gender construction emerge even in this apologia for virile capitalist endeavour, because in Reynolds' narrative, the fight with Mocha Dick actually occurs after, and in relation to, an attack upon the whaleboat initiated by a female sperm whale (2002 [1839]: 558). To be sure, this animal attacks only after her calf has been killed by the whalers, which helps to assimilate this evidence of feminine courage and aggression into the category of maternal care. On the other hand, Reynolds makes equally clear that Mocha Dick's attacks were always motivated by a desire to extract 'vengeance' for the slaughter of his companion whales, so the only remaining trait that identifies the bull whale as a more willing, ferocious and effective fighter than the cow is his greater size. Similar contradictions appear in the natural historical accounts upon which Melville drew, where again they show the ideological complicity between natural history and human sociology. Most striking of all is the level of confusion in *Moby-Dick*'s source texts about whether the male or the female sperm whale was most liable to become 'mischievous'. Beale and Bennett, for example, agree that the nurturing tendencies of the females incline them to remain by the side of their wounded companions, while the young males swiftly abandon their fellows (Beale 1973 [1839]: 53; Bennett 1840: I, 177–8). Moreover Bennett explicitly discounts the suggestion, advanced by Melville, that the most formidable opponents of the whalers were old solitary bulls, asserting instead that '[a]n old female, and a half-grown male, are considered the most troublesome to encounter, from their active and combative temper' (1840: I, 206). In fact, first-hand accounts by nineteenth-century whaling writers of female fighting whales are not hard to find.[17] They are simply easy to overlook, for they are ascribed a far lower degree of significance than the epic battles with their larger male counterparts – precisely because the gender politics of nineteenth-century human family life and the complementary economics of industrial capitalism coded as masculine the most prodigious of non-human challenges to human enterprise.

As Melville was aware, America's much-vaunted ideal of democracy depended upon the exclusion of large sectors of the adult population. Its reliance upon the labour and lives of women, and their disenfranchisement, shapes *Moby-Dick* in striking ways. These and other elements of the democratic unconscious are thrown into sharp relief when *Moby-Dick* is put alongside Melville's most important fictional source: Joseph Hart's Nantucket whaling story *Miriam Coffin*. Hart's novel struggles explicitly with the problematic role of women in the industrial economy. *Miriam Coffin* parallels the narrative about the voyages of two vessels, the *Grampus* and the *Leviathan*, with a plot that centres upon the activities of the eponymous character, who, while her husband is at sea, enters into the masculine sphere of entrepreneurial capitalism with considerable virtuosity. However, Miriam's business skills, which include speculation on credit rather than existing assets, the undercutting of competitors, and the fostering of business confidence through conspicuous consumption – tactics that might inspire admiration in today's money market – bring disaster in Hart's novel, and are roundly condemned by her husband on his return: '[g]et thee gone to thy kitchen, where it is fitting thou should'st preside . . . and do thou never meddle with men's affairs more!' (1995 [1834]: 317). Melville, however, represses the possibility of female economic and cultural agency altogether by utterly excluding women characters from his novel. Moreover, his apotheosis of Moby Dick again assists in this transaction, because Ahab's nemesis is so profoundly masculinized.

Just as it displays overtly this paranoia about the economic agency of women, *Miriam Coffin* is explicit about other anxieties that pervade Melville's novel in coded forms. Another striking difference between the two novels is that Hart shows no concern about the possibility of animal agency: a ship is indeed sunk by a whale, but only accidentally, as it thrashes about in its flurry. Instead, the dramatic tension of *Miriam Coffin* depends upon the malign intentions and actions of human 'savages', embodied initially by the murderous Indian Quibby, and later by the aggressive islanders who attack the ship in the Pacific (Hart 1995 [1834]: 155–62, 282–8, 300). Replacing these evil or bellicose primitives with the erotically primordial but acquiescent noble savages Queequeg, Tashtego and Daggoo, and replacing an accidentally destructive whale with the intentionally vengeful Moby Dick, Melville transfers onto the animal the threat posed to modern America by its economic dependence upon various disenfranchised human elements. The White

Whale – which, as Ishmael tells the reader, 'swam before [Ahab] as the mono-maniac incarnation of all those malicious agencies which some deep men feel eating in them' (Melville 2002 [1851]: 156) – thus provides a screen for contemporary anxieties about American industry's economic exploitation of all those who were not white men.[18]

The *Pequod* thus embodies an industry that consumes humans as it consumes animals – two processes that the text understands by interfusing them. Naming the ship after an indigenous people decimated and dispos-sessed by the settler forbears of its white crew (Staud 1992), comparing the whalebone included in the vessel's construction to the wearing of ivory trophies by 'any barbaric Ethiopian emperor', calling it a 'cannibal of a craft, tricking herself forth in the chased bones of her enemies' – the novel uses the *Pequod*'s ingestion of Native American, African and Pacific associa-tions to characterize its devouring of the animal, and *vice versa* (Melville 2002 [1851]: 70). Read in this light, the last resort to anthropomorphism in describing the whale assumes another significance. The '[r]etribution, swift vengeance, eternal malice' ascribed to Moby Dick as he bears down finally upon the *Pequod* derive simultaneously from industrial capitalism's anxiety about non-human agency, and from a more occult sense of those human debts which America in 1851 could scarcely admit, let alone address. These half-recognized interconnections will recur vividly half a century later, when the material and metaphysical dimensions of *Moby-Dick*'s portrait of human–animal relations under industrial modernity are split off from each other and taken up, respectively, by Upton Sinclair and the modernists.

4   Modernism and the Hunt
for Redemption

As Moby Dick sounds for the last time, taking with him Ahab and the *Pequod*, he embodies a plunge in the cultural authority of Romanticism, and especially its characteristic evocations of animality. The struggle between the White Whale and his antagonist exemplifies (despite Melville's pervasive irony) the apogee of the Romantic encounter between human and animal: in the remaining decades of the nineteenth century the Romantic aesthetic and structure of feeling were gradually devalued. This occurred, as I have argued in Chapter 2, because of the growing influence of positivist science and industrial capitalism, which denigrated emotionally laden relationships between humans and animals as immature and unrealistic, and confined them to the socially disempowered spheres of feminine domesticity, maternity and child-rearing.

During the first half of the twentieth century, the movement known as modernism brought about a parallel discrediting of sympathetic and sentimental engagement with animals in the aesthetic sphere. Rejecting the complacencies of Victorian modernity, the modernists aimed also to dispense with – or in some ways, reform – the legacy of the last great literary revolution, Romanticism, which they felt had been tamed by intervening generations. The wildness of Romanticism had been domesticated; its sublime potency reduced to mawkishness; it was time for art to break loose, go feral and return to a revitalizing savagery. As this rhetoric suggests, the modernist break with the past entailed, and in many ways depended upon, a revaluation of human–animal relationships. In place of the sympathetic disposition that characterized many nineteenth-century narratives, modernism offered primal engagements between humans and savage beasts – the jungle, the hunt, the tooth-and-nail contest – or else it showed the perversion of these vital, primitive relationships into acts of degraded cruelty towards animals in domestic settings. As I will show in this chapter, modernists like Lawrence and Hemingway, in privileging the hunt, display a simultaneous fascination and frustration with *Moby-Dick*. They are drawn to, and they draw upon, the intense savagery of Ahab's pursuit of the White Whale, while seeking to discard what they perceive to be the cloying sentimental detritus surrounding it.

Like the aesthetic programmes against which it reacted, modernism of course arose out of particular economic, social and especially technological conditions. In particular, the modernist taste for the rhetoric of the hunt is best understood in relation to the accelerating industrialization of human–animal relations. This can be shown by attending first to a novel that represents not only a grim, urban, landlocked revision of *Moby-Dick*, but also a transition between the evolutionist socialism of H. G. Wells and the mythopoeic psychologism of the modernists: Upton Sinclair's *The Jungle* (1906).

The Disassembly Line

The first decade of the twentieth century – the same years that saw the defeat of the anti-vivisection movements in Britain and the United States – produced, in Sinclair's novel, the most excoriating of challenges to the treatment of animals under industrial modernity. Sent by a socialist newspaper to research the Chicago meat-packing industry in 1904, Sinclair chose to present his findings in novelistic form. The resulting exposé cut local meat consumption by half, caused an international scandal, persuaded President Roosevelt to launch an investigation into the meat-packing industry, and impelled the federal government to pass its first comprehensive Pure Food and Drug laws (De Grave 2003: ii-iii).

Sinclair's protagonists, Lithuanian immigrants Jurgis and Ona Rudkos and their relatives, are drawn to America by the hope of personal and familial betterment, the central dream of modernity. Hence, initially, they perceive even the buildings and endlessly smoking chimneys of the meat-packing plant in heroic colours: to them 'it seemed a dream of wonder, with its tale of human energy, of things being done, of employment for thousands upon thousands of men, of opportunity and freedom, of life and love and joy' (Sinclair 1906: 33–4). Recalling the rhetoric of wonder that pervades the descriptions of industrial whaling by Reynolds, Beale and (albeit ironically) Melville, the new immigrants' first perceptions of Packingtown repeat the captivation of the American popular imagination by industrial technology half a century earlier. Next day, visiting the plant in operation, Jurgis observes the workers operating the 'disassembly line' system upon which the meat-packing industry relies for its unprecedented scale of production, whereby 'some eight or ten million live creatures turned into food every year' (38):

> [t]hey had chains which they fastened about the leg of the nearest hog, and the other end of the chain they hooked into one of the rings upon the wheel. So, as the wheel turned, a hog was suddenly jerked off his feet and borne aloft . . . once started upon that journey, the hog never came back; at the top of the wheel he was shunted off upon a trolley, and went sailing down the room. And meantime another was swung up, and then another, and another, until there was a double line of them, each dangling by a foot and kicking in frenzy – and squealing . . .

> Meantime . . . the men upon the floor were going about their work . . . one by one they hooked up the hogs, and one by one with a swift stroke they slit their throats. There was a long line of hogs, with squeals and lifeblood ebbing away together; until at last each started again, and vanished with a splash into a huge vat of boiling water. It was all so very businesslike that one watched it fascinated (40).

Sinclair evokes here the logical end point of Crusoe's enclosures, or the instrumentalist attitude to organic life embodied by the virtuosi of Lagado and their descendants, Frankenstein and Moreau. The meatpackers have perfected an extreme form of instrumentalist reductionism: a 'porkmaking by machinery, porkmaking by applied mathematics', whereby animals and humans both become quotients in the algebra of capitalist production (40).

So the animal is disassembled and repackaged as a range of products, some cuts for ham, others for pork and bacon, entrails for sausage casings, grease to make soap and lard. Similarly the processes are broken down and distributed and the worker thereby reduced to a fraction of his or her capabilities. 'It was all highly specialized labor', writes Sinclair, 'each man having his task': the 'splitters' do 'not a thing all day except chop hogs down the middle', the 'cleaver men' chop the carcass into quarters, the 'knocker' with his sledge hammer kills the steer, the 'butcher' bleeds it, the 'headsman' severs its head, the 'floorsman' makes the initial cut in the hide, others rip the skin before 'half a dozen more in swift succession' examine it, roll it up and take it away (Sinclair 1906: 40–4).

The Jungle extrapolates the consequences of the industrial mode of rendering the animal, an updated model of the prototype described by Melville aboard the *Pequod*. However, advanced industrial production, by segmenting the transformation of nature into a sequence of simplified tasks, removes the residual pre-industrial elements that allowed Melville to heroicize whaling culture. The whaleman's intimate engagement with the non-human world is replaced with urban alienation, his camaraderie with desperate competition for a place in the line, his skill and knowledge with manual repetition, his courageous acceptance of danger with the certainty of injury. The resistant forms of non-human agency embodied by the White Whale are similarly transformed to suit the industry. Watching the 'continuous' stream of hogs 'pressing on' up the steep chutes that lead into the building from the pens outside, Jurgis learns that 'the hogs went up by the power of their own legs, and then their weight carried them back through all the processes necessary to make them into pork' (Sinclair 1906: 38). The animals' own animate energy, their fear-induced muscular exertion and their strenuous desire to escape the confinement of the pens, takes them through the first stage of the process, after which the force of gravity on their struggling bodies combines with human labour and mechanical propulsion to power the rest of the system.

Yet even amid this mechanistic system a kind of feral agency erupts at times: indeed the logic of mathematical efficiency itself – the formula that equates increased pace with greater productivity – can result in chaos: '[s]ometimes, in the haste of speeding-up, they would dump one of the animals out on the floor before it was fully stunned, and it would get upon its feet and run amuck'. The repeated and predictable sequence is temporarily disrupted: the steer runs 'blind and frantic'; the men dash for safety, 'slipping here and there on the floor', and risk 'running upon a knife' since almost all carry them; finally the floor boss rushes up with a rifle and begins 'blazing away' (Sinclair 1906: 134). Here again the fates of the human and non-human elements of the system are conjoined: the desperate unpredictability of the animal matches that of the workers, and all are equally vulnerable to the butcher's knife and the boss's gun.

Four decades before Sinclair's novel, Karl Marx identified the association between alienated worker, exploited animal and mechanized production when he described how manufacture 'converts the labourer into a crippled monstrosity, by forcing his detail dexterity at the expense of a world of productive capabilities and instincts; just as in the States of La Plata they butcher a whole beast for the sake of his hide or his tallow' (1906 [1867]: I.IV.XIV, 38). The Frankensteinian experiment of advanced capitalist production, Marx notes, 'makes man a mere fragment of his own body' and a 'mere appendage of the capitalist's workshop', a disembodied limb readily replaceable from the mass of available labour, which therefore can be used, and used up, like the tallow or hides from an animal, or like the mechanical components of a motor. 'All the year round they had been serving as cogs in the great packing machine', writes Sinclair, 'and now was the time for the . . . replacing of damaged parts' (1906: 92).

This production system, which renders down human and non-human organic life and then reassembles its elements into a perpetual-motion human-beast-machine, would become the quintessential engine and emblem of modernity for the first half of the twentieth century. As Carol Adams points out, Henry Ford derived his plan for the assembly line, which he famously applied to automobile manufacture and which then spread throughout the manufacturing sector, 'from the overhead trolley that the Chicago packers use in dressing beef' (Adams 1990: 53; citing Ford and Crowther 2000 [1922]: 81). But of course culturally speaking, the technique had been centuries in the making. Citing Michel Foucault's *Discipline and Punish* (1977), Annabelle Sabloff contends that 'the machine metaphor, with its fragmenting of projects, bodies, tasks, time, and space, was actually active well before the industrial revolution', and that 'its enacted presence in clerical, military, educative, and other domains' in due course 'helped shape human compliance to the industrial revolution's factory model' (2001: 98–9).[1] In fact, as I have argued in Chapter 2, the machine metaphor first found its expression and application in the study of non-human animals by proponents of the new science, followers of Descartes and Bacon, in the seventeenth and eighteenth centuries. Typically, modernity initially develops the theory and trials its practice in relation to animals – in this case, the reduction of living bodies to a manipulable congeries of physical movements and materials – before applying the results to human labour and the manufacture of commodities. As John Berger puts it, '[n]early all modern techniques of social conditioning were first established with animal experiments' (1980: 11–12).

It is therefore both historically and culturally appropriate that throughout his novel Sinclair shows human workers suffering fates identical to those of the animals they process. Hearing 'stories about the breaking down of men, there in the stockyards of Chicago' (1906: 23), the initially strong Jurgis laughs, but during winter he starts to recognize that the industry 'squeeze[s]' its workers 'tighter and tighter, speeding them up and grinding them to pieces and sending for new ones' (78). This equation between the fate of the worker and that of the animal goes beyond the merely figurative, for each is subject to unremitting disintegration and replacement in material terms as well. Describing conditions of the killing beds, Sinclair declares it 'a wonder that there were not more men slaughtered than cattle' (1906: 94–5). 'Let a man so much as scrape his finger pushing a truck in the pickle rooms' and 'all the joints in his fingers might be eaten by the acid, one by one'; the hands of the wool-plucker go 'to pieces even sooner', their fingers eaten off by the acid used to loosen the wool; anyone working at the stamping machines is bound sooner or later to 'forget himself and have a part of his hand chopped off'. The man who works as a butcher, floorsman, beefboner or trimmer injures himself so often that his thumb is reduced to 'a mere lump of flesh against which the man pressed the knife to hold it', while his nails are torn away by pulling hides. The beef-lugger, like a beast of burden, is crippled by carrying 'two-hundred-pound quarters into the refrigerator-cars' all day. Finally there are the workers in the cooking rooms, who sometimes fall into the floor-level vats of boiling tallow, 'and when they were fished out, there was never enough of them left to be worth exhibiting'; indeed 'sometimes they would be overlooked for days, till all but the bones of them had gone out to the world as Durham's Pure Leaf Lard!' (115–16).

Sinclair blends the fate of human workers with that of meat animals, as Marian Scholtmeijer points out, in order to demonstrate the radical dehumanization suffered by the worker under industrial capitalism (1993: 153). However, elsewhere he has recourse to another kind of animal comparison: he alludes to wild animality as an index of the regressive state into which competition casts both workers and capitalists. Jurgis Rudkos, as he gains awareness of the exploitation of his family by the capitalists, experiences the city as a 'wild-beast tangle' where 'human beings writhed and fought and fell upon each other like wolves in a pit' (195). Such conceits appear to be consistent with the tendency in Marxist thought to regard the animal dimension of human being 'as some sort of biological residue, a thing left over from humanity's past' which must be transcended through the 'transformation of nature in production by means of human labour' (Noske 1997: 73). Hence, in the Marxist account, technological inventiveness is not the cause of exploitation in itself; indeed if control of industry were seized by the working class, 'the human-nature relationship could be a rational one benefiting all humankind' (77). Like Marx and Wells, Sinclair's socialists envisage their cause in evolutionary terms, according to which social cooperation and technological innovation act as advantageous adaptations in a 'struggle for existence' wherein 'the strong overcame the weak, and in turn were overcome by the strongest', unless they could 'save themselves by combination – which was a new and higher kind of strength' (Sinclair 1906: 387). Jurgis listens with fascination to Dr Schliemann, a socialist proponent of 'the new science of agriculture' practised 'under the direction of expert agricultural chemists', who envisages a prosperous garden-state of 'made soils and intensive culture' producing 'ten or twelve crops in a season, and two hundred tons of vegetables upon a single acre', along with 'apples and oranges picked by machinery, cows milked by electricity' – all under the direction of and for the benefit of the people (406).

Capitalism, by contrast, because it reduces social relations to raw individualism and competition, cannot bring about advancement, but produces instead a regression epitomized by the debased jungle of the city, whose inhabitants are either exploited as prey and beasts of burden or forced into an atavistic and 'predaceous' animality of their own (Sinclair 1906: 387). Certainly this habitat brutalizes Jurgis, who attacks the boss who has sexually exploited Ona, sinking his teeth into the cheek of his 'prey' (179), tearing away flesh in his teeth before lapsing into lethargy 'like a wild beast that has glutted itself' (181). When he seeks solace with a prostitute we hear that 'the wild beast rose up within him and screamed, as it has screamed in the Jungle from the dawn of time' (259). Later he loses the only agency granted by this atavistic animality, the capacity for ferocious violence, becoming instead 'like a wounded animal in the forest . . . forced to compete with his enemies upon unequal terms' (268), 'as literally crippled as any wild animal which has lost its claws' (333).

Accounting for this imagery, Scholtmeijer asserts that animality *per se* is coded negatively in *The Jungle*. Sinclair's 'use of the beast metaphor is loose in the extreme', she asserts, but whether applied to 'sexual passion', 'insanity', 'pent-up rage in the prison, or mindless obeisance in the stockyard', it always indicates 'degeneration of one sort or another' (1993: 152). However, I suggest a distinction is actually at work in Sinclair's representation of animality – the same distinction between domestic animal and wild predator that was apparent in Defoe, whereby the former is given (measured) respect and even sympathy as a product of human enterprise, while the latter is demonized as representative of the potential for degeneration. In Sinclair's novel there are at least two moments at which the plight experienced by industrially farmed animals comes into sharp focus. Although brief, these moments are carefully placed at the beginning and end of Jurgis' career in the meatpacking industry, in a way that provides an interpretative frame for the events between.

Despite his awe at the power and energy of the packing plant during his first visit, Jurgis cannot help 'thinking of the hogs; they were so innocent, they came so very trustingly; and they were so very human in their protests'. Each one is 'a separate creature', with 'an individuality of his own, a will of his own, a hope and a heart's desire', yet each is subject to a 'horrid Fate' that suddenly 'swooped upon him, and . . . seized him by the leg . . . cut his throat and watched him gasp out his life'. 'Dieve – but I'm glad I'm not a hog!' he mutters (Sinclair 1906: 40–1). It would be easy to dismiss this as glib sentimentalism or tongue-in-cheek anthropomorphism, except that Sinclair returns to it near the end of the novel, in a way that gives it the status of a conclusion to be drawn from Jurgis' experiences. After working in many different parts of the plant, then losing his job, becoming a vagrant, going to prison and eventually becoming converted to socialism, Jurgis suddenly recalls how,

> when he had first come to Packingtown, he had stood and watched the hog-killing, and thought how cruel and savage it was, and come away congratulating himself that he was not a hog; now his new acquaintance showed him that a hog was just what he had been – one of the packers' hogs. What they wanted from a hog was all the profits that could be got out of him; and that was what they wanted from the workingman, and also that was what they wanted from the public. What the hog thought of it, and what he suffered, were not considered (374–5).

By focusing on the suffering body as the site for sympathetic identification between exploited worker and exploited animal, Sinclair – contrary to Scholtmeijer's judgement that *The Jungle* is entirely lacking of 'sensitivity to the animal's plight', or any trace of 'narrative allegiance with the animal' (1993: 150–1) – actually draws on the legacy of nineteenth-century animal advocacy. In some ways, therefore, *The Jungle* envisages the liberation of farmed animals as a proper dimension of social justice: once the workers have wrested control of the means of production from 'the Great Butcher' (Sinclair 1906: 375) – the Beef Trust that runs Packingtown, 'the Spirit of Capitalism made flesh' – the exploitation of animals will wither away. 'So long as we have wage slavery', Jurgis' new mentors explain to him, 'it matters not in the least how debasing and repulsive a task may be, it is easy to find people to perform it. But just as soon as labor is set free, then the price of such work will begin to rise'. Under socialism, then, 'year by year the cost of slaughterhouse products will increase; until eventually those who want to eat meat will have to do their own killing – and how long do you think the custom would survive then . . . ?' (406–7).

Nevertheless, in its time, despite the public outcry it provoked, *The Jungle* had little or no positive impact on the exploitative conditions it describes. The most frequently cited outcome of the exposé, the Pure Food and Drug Laws of 1906, dealt only with 'the adulteration of edible products, not with the inhumane treatment of the workers who process the products' (De Grave 2003: xii) – nor, of course, with that of the animals who provide them.[2] 'I aimed at the public's heart', commented Sinclair ruefully, 'and by accident I hit it in the stomach' (cited in De Grave 2003: i). The official response, by treating the furor as a public health issue rather than a concern about human and animal exploitation, further removed the latter from visibility.

The screening from public view of the mass slaughter of animals is one element of Berger's claim that animals 'disappear' under industrial capitalism (1980: 24). Sinclair's novel suggests this occurs less by means of absolute secrecy, and more as a kind of complicity between the industry's techniques of managed visibility and the public will-to-ignorance. 'They make a great feature of showing strangers through the packing plants, for it is a good advertisement', Jurgis is told, but 'the visitors did not see any more than the packers wanted them to' (Sinclair 1906: 39). Tours are on offer, but anything that contradicts the ideology of modernity as human advancement – for instance the radical exploitation of workers and unsanitary treatment of food products – is screened from public view. Meanwhile the disassembly-line slaughter of animals is made visible, but presented as a spectacle that epitomizes the ineluctable acceleration towards greater efficiency and human benefit. Watching the movement of the overhead trolley, hooking up beast after beast, the observers too are swept away (albeit only figuratively) by the very energy and irresistibility of progress itself: 'it was a thing as tremendous as the universe – the laws and ways of its working no more than the universe to be questioned or understood'. To an observer like Jurgis, to speak 'skeptically' about the system seems like 'profanity'; the only proper attitude is 'to take a thing like this as he found it', to regard 'its wonderful activities' as 'a blessing to be grateful for, as one was grateful for the sunshine and the rain' (47). Again, Jurgis' attitude repeats that of mid-nineteenth-century Americans in the face of industrial technologies like the locomotive, which according to Leo Marx was perceived as 'at once a testament to the will of man rising over natural obstacles' and at the same time 'confined by its iron rails to a pre-determined path', suggestive of 'a new sort of fate' (1964: 191). The animals' deaths are presented to the public eye according to that genre of realism which purports to offer unmediated access to the inevitable, the irresistible, the way-things-must-be. They are real deaths, and really seen, but presented in a way that demands from the viewers a response that is also *realistic* – as that term is understood by capitalist and scientific modernity; that is, as a pragmatic recognition that certain kinds of suffering or deprivation are unavoidable and must be accepted in the pursuit of progress or profit.

So it is that Sinclair's novel brings the exploited animal of industrial agriculture into view, but in a way that makes it disappear all the more thoroughly, as the result of two different tendencies in bourgeois modernity. The first derives from that 'middle-class desire not to be able to see cruelty' which Erica Fudge identifies as the motivation for much of the animal welfare activism of the nineteenth century (2002b: 12). The second reason that animals tend to vanish despite Sinclair's attempt to represent them is the evolutionary progressivism that his novel shares with Marx, Engels and

Wells. To the extent that animality (both human and non-human) is conceived as an underlying, primitive, potentially violent and regressive substrate requiring refinement or transcendence, scientific and technological 'improvement' of animal nature will be readily accepted.

A Savage Enough Pilgrimage

As discussed in Chapter 2, the impact of Darwinian evolutionary theory on the cultural terrain of modernity proved to be erratic, partial and sometimes contradictory. Its potentially revolutionary undermining of beliefs about human supremacy were mostly inhibited (or ignored) due to the widespread interpretation of evolutionism as another of modernity's narratives about progress towards an ever-more advanced human state. Accordingly the notion of animality remained aligned with savagery and degeneracy. For my purposes, the term *therio-primitivism* provides a useful, if ungainly, shorthand for this specifically modern conjunction between animality and pre- or non-modern forms of humanity. Wells, Sinclair, Marx and Engels all demonstrate the negative version of therio-primitivism, whereby animality is conceived as a state out of which the human must be forged, or from which it must travel, using as its tool or vehicle the innovations of science – technology, industry, biology and medicine or dialectical materialism. However at the turn of the twentieth century a more ambivalent form of evolutionary therio-primitivism was simultaneously shaping two other thought-experiments: psychoanalysis and modernism.

Sigmund Freud explicitly associated primitivism with the unconscious or 'primary process' of the human mind, for example in 'Totem and Taboo' (1915), where he compares the form of 'savage' societies with the early 'stages of an individual's libidinal development' (1985: 148). Moreover for Freud, primitivism was also inextricably tied up with animality. He drew on the notion of 'instinct' to describe the drives, impulses and reactions characteristic of the unconscious, and used Darwinian evolutionary theory to explain the development of 'civilized' means to manage these (Freud 1985: 185–6; Lippit 2000: 96–100). For example in the case history of the 'Wolf Man' Freud refers to 'the far-reaching *instinctive* [*instinktiv*] knowledge of animals' as a way of explaining the 'hardly definable knowledge, something, as it were, preparatory to an understanding' which is at work in the child who witnesses 'the primal scene' (1988 [1918]: 363–4, italics in original; cited in Norris 1985: 119). And in *The Interpretation of Dreams* he cites a proverb – 'What do geese dream of? Of Maize' – and remarks that '[t]he whole theory that dreams are wish-fulfilments is contained in these two phrases' (Freud 1976: 212).[3] Later in the same text he states that in the dream-work 'wild beasts are used to represent the libido, a force dreaded by the ego and combated by means of repression' (1976: 536). Perhaps the most striking aspect of Freud's therio-primitivism, however, is the way it expresses the fate of animals under modernity. During the nineteenth and twentieth centuries, as wild animals were hunted, eradicated, displaced or deprived of their habitats on an unprecedented scale, they reappeared – just as the contents of the unconscious reappear, according to Freud – in horror stories, wish fulfilment fantasies, jokes and art (Berger 1980; Lippit 2000). Meanwhile livestock species, as Sinclair's novel demonstrates, were processed in new ways that removed knowledge of their lives and deaths from public consciousness, just as in Freudian theory the psyche forecloses recognition of unconscious fears, desires and transgressions. Hence the psychoanalytic understanding of civilization – as the advancement of techniques for the repression of the (animalistic) unconscious – precisely transposes into psychological terms the material and cultural marginalization of animality under modernity.

Given the pervasive influence of the therio-primitivist paradigm in the first part of the twentieth century, it is no surprise to find that it operates at the heart of literary modernism – albeit usually in reversed form. The accepted account of modernism is that the movement arose as a challenge to the received verities of Victorian and Edwardian modernity, and gained its greatest momentum as a result of the First World War. Belief in the supreme humaneness of European civility, social advancement through technological innovation, and the imperialist narrative of progress was severely compromised by a conflict in which the metropolitan powers exterminated a generation of each other's citizens using the most advanced technologies yet produced – poison gas, tanks, flame-throwers, machine guns, battleships and bi-planes. Disgusted by the inventive brutality of modern 'civilization', the modernists were propelled into its conventional opposite: primitivism.

In fact, this destination had been mapped out in advance of the war by the growing influence of psychoanalysis and by the impact of Sir James Frazer's monumental work of anthropology, *The Golden Bough*, which suggested that the authentic energy of any culture comes from its buried foundations in ancient myth and ritual. In the same month the war began, a number of artists declared their subscription to the fundamental apothegm of the Vorticist Manifesto – 'The Art-Instinct is Always Primitive' – as proclaimed in Wyndham Lewis' magazine *Blast* (Matthews 2004: 93). In reclaiming the cultural qualities denigrated by the strident progressivism of Victorian modernity, then, modernist writers and artists did not seek to eliminate the received dichotomy between civilization and primitivism; rather they embraced it, but by reversing its values. Accepting the conventional association of non-Western cultures – especially those indigenous to Africa, the Americas, Australia and the Pacific – with savagery, simplicity, instinct, libido and appetite, modernists declared that the role of art was to cut through the corrupt impedimenta of civilization and reconnect with an authentic human-ness defined by its primitive connection to nature. The negative therio-primitivism of socialist theory – the anxiety about regression to savage animality manifested in Wells and Sinclair – was inverted to produce a redemptive therio-primitivism. Animality, at its most wild and untamed, was not the enemy of humanity, but its possible, perhaps its only, salvation.[4]

Margot Norris describes this as the 'biocentric' aspect of modernism, which treats 'the animal (including the human as animal)' and 'Nature, the realm of the biological', as 'a plenum'. A revaluation of the relative merits of wild animality and modern humanity follows from this premise. '[T]he animal's desire is direct and appropriative' and its 'natural power is sufficient for its kind', while humans' desire is 'mediated' and their biological power 'supplemented by signifiers and symbols'; 'the animal is autotelic', it 'lives for itself in the fullness of its being' and 'surrenders to biological fate and evolutionary destiny', whereas 'cultural man' is 'driven by his *manque-à-être*' and his disregard for 'the physicality of what is' (1985: 4). For Norris, biocentrism is traceable to Darwin – not the reading of Darwin that had been assimilated to nineteenth-century progressivism, but the Darwin who represents a 'break with eighteenth-century rationalism'. Rejecting Descartes' 'model of nature as a machine', this radical Darwinism 'put in its place innumerable, dispersed, trivial organic forces operating unconsciously and irrationally, on an ad hoc basis, subject to chance, over time'. By means of this revolutionary insight, 'in the very bloom of the Industrial Revolution, the machine and the rational intelligence that designs it become philosophically inimical to the burgeoning vitality of Nature and of living things' (6–7). The organicist challenge to the authority of technology and industry is one of the features that distinguishes modernist therio-primitivism from the Marxist critique of capitalism or the narratives of Wells and Sinclair. Vilification of the machine gains particular force following World War One, not just because of the scale of the carnage resulting from military-industrial technology, but because the conflict was itself an expression of the worldwide competition between the European industrial powers for raw materials to feed their rapidly growing infrastructures.

Norris argues that the paradigmatic biocentric novelist is D. H. Lawrence, and indeed the contrast between a repressive instrumentalism and a vibrant organicism is everywhere in his work – epitomized by protagonists like Ursula Brangwen in *The Rainbow*, for example, who begins the study of biology at university but comes to the conclusion that scientific thought perpetuates the mechanistic misrepresentation of life. 'I don't see why we should attribute some special mystery to life', remarks her professor, Dr Frankstone, who has apparently failed to learn from the mistakes of her near-namesake: 'life consists in a complexity of physical and chemical activities' (Lawrence 1981 [1915]: 390). In contrast Ursula, examining a unicellular organism under magnification, finds that 'in her mind the world gleamed strangely, with an intense light, like the nucleus of the creature under the microscope'; 'an intensely-gleaming light of knowledge' that she cannot understand but knows is 'not limited mechanical energy' (383–4).[5] Throughout the novel Ursula perceives the degradation of the English landscape under industrialization. The colliery is the equivalent of Sinclair's Packingtown, a 'monstrous mechanism that held all matter, living or dead, in its service', which she initially desires to 'smash' but eventually resolves to escape (308). Having done so – or so she imagines – via her affair with Skrebensky, whom she thinks of as a 'wild beast' who has 'escaped from the show . . . straight back into its jungle', Ursula goes about with 'her eyes dilated and shining like the eyes of a wild animal', contemptuously dismissing the rest of the populace as a 'subdued beast in sheep's clothing', a 'primeval darkness falsified to a social mechanism' (389–90).

Lawrence's critique of machinic culture expressed itself, inevitably, as a virulent anti-militarism during the war years. This led him into a period of itinerant voluntary exile which lasted, with the exception of brief visits back to England, until his death in 1930. 'It has been a savage enough pilgrimage these last four years', he wrote in 1923 to John Middleton Murry, identifying a major motivation in his choice of destinations. His flight took him to a series of places – Italy, Ceylon, New South Wales, New Mexico, and Mexico – which he perceived as likely locations of the authenticity with which supposedly primitive peoples inhabited the world. In both *The Plumed Serpent* and *St Mawr*, the two novels Lawrence was working on during his travels to Mexico and New Mexico, such authenticity depends upon re-accessing primal forms of human–animal relation. The latter novel centres upon Lou Witt, another of Lawrence's biocentric heroines, who becomes captivated by the stallion St Mawr and persuades her husband Rico to buy him. Ostensibly a domesticated animal, St Mawr nonetheless emanates a savage energy, 'that air of tense, alert quietness which betrays an animal that can be dangerous' (Lawrence 1925: 16). St Mawr refuses to accede to the tasks assigned by humans. Raised for stud purposes, he refuses to 'answer', and nor can he be used as a coach-horse: 'there's no putting him between the shafts. He won't stand it' (18). Moreover the rumours of two 'accidents' cling to him: his former owner's son's 'skull smashed in' against a tree branch, and a groom fatally crushed against the side of a stall (18–19). Much of the novel is concerned with Lou's attempt to understand the 'uncanny threat' and the 'non-human question' posed by St Mawr (20) – which proves to have everything to do with the conflict between modern and primitive forms of connection to animality.

Lawrence ascribes to horses a primordial and mythical aura, presumably (in accordance with the requirements of therio-primitivism) to offset their status as domesticated animals. 'With their strangely naked equine heads, and something of a snake in their way of looking round, and lifting their sensitive, dangerous muzzles', they seem to move 'in a prehistorical twilight', evoking 'another world, an older, heavily potent world' in which 'the horse was swift and fierce and supreme, undominated and unsurpassed' (1925: 26). St Mawr remains a recalcitrant element in the field of calculable and predictable outcomes dictated by civilized modernity. He is a non-human agent with his own questions, intentions, and memories: '[t]hey gave him a beating once or twice . . . and he doesn't forget' (26). This memory of equine indomitability becomes reactivated during a ride in the country that Lou undertakes with Rico and his effete friends, Flora Manby, her sister Elsie and the latter's husband, Frederick Edwards. Seeing a dead adder that has been stoned to death earlier in the day, St Mawr shies 'as if a bomb had gone off' – a simile that links needless human violence against wild nature with the mechanized destructiveness of modernity (79, 82). When Rico attempts 'viciously' to reassert control the horse rears and falls backwards onto him, and when Edwards intervenes he is kicked in the face (80). As the horse rises of his own volition, he again evokes a prehistoric beast: 'St Mawr gave a great curve like a fish, spread his forefeet on the earth and reared his head', remaining in this position, 'almost like some terrible lizard, for several moments' (80).

Following this incident Lou struggles to comprehend the stallion's recalcitrant agency. 'Was there something mean and treacherous in St Mawr's spirit?', she wonders; '[i]f so, then have him shot'. 'It would be a satisfaction, and a vindication of human rights' to destroy the horse if his repeated acts of rebellion comprise nothing more than 'the slavish malevolence of a domesticated creature . . . taking his slavish vengeance, then dropping back into subservience' (Lawrence 1925: 87). But when she visits St Mawr after the disastrous outing, Lou senses in him something more than this, namely the wild, untamable agency of 'real freedom', the 'intensely self-disciplined, poised . . . tension of self-defence, self-preservation, and self-assertion' that marks 'the wild thing's courage to maintain itself alone and living in the midst of a diverse universe'. Although he is 'feeling somewhat subdued' there remains 'something obstinate and uncanny' in the horse that 'made him not relent' (87–9). St Mawr refuses to revert to the subservience that would mark his rebellious tendency as the mere treachery of the domesticated beast. Instead, Lou feels 'a great animal sadness' emanating from him, 'the woe of human unworthiness. The race of men judged in the consciousness of the animals they have subdued, and there found unworthy, ignoble' (89–90). The source of St Mawr's hostility and his grief, and the nature of the challenge that he poses, is thus identified as the loss of the primitive relation of ferocious 'nobility' that once pertained between human and horse. Once 'it had been a fulfilment for him to serve the brave, reckless, perhaps cruel men of the past, who had a flickering, rising flame of nobility in them', but now this flame was 'dead, guttering out' in a 'light of exhaustion and *laissez-faire*' (90). In this psychosocial history, the horse comprises the therio-primitive creature *par excellence*. Neither unattainably wild nor slavishly domestic, the horse of antiquity is valued for the courage, strength and animus that it displayed, but also recognized and called forth in its rider. What St Mawr resists is the modern degradation, epitomized by industrial modernity, of this primordial bond. Since 'Man' now 'invents motor-cars and other machines, automobile and locomotive', writes Lawrence, '[t]he horse is superannuated, for man. But alas', he adds, 'man is even more superannuated, for the horse' (90).

St Mawr's rebellion also confirms Lou's suspicion that her husband belongs to an over-refined class of men. Rico is identified, as Norris points out, with the 'metaphorics of mechanized and remote-control violence' – the deadliness of militarist modernity – in contrast to the 'spontaneous, autotelic power of wild animals' (1985: 183): 'Rico's anger was wound up tight at the bottom of him, like a steel spring that kept his works going, while he himself was "charming", like a bomb-clock with Sevres paintings or Dresden figures on the outside' (Lawrence 1925: 33). On the other hand Rico manifests the slavish, ignoble anger that Lawrence associates with an utterly domesticated beast. He is like 'a horse that might go nasty any moment', but in contrast to St Mawr's bold hostility, when Rico gets angry 'his upper lip lift[s] from his teeth, like a dog that is going to bite. Yet he daren't quite bite' (15). In this, he stands for all the men of Lou's genera-tion: 'the animal in them has gone perverse, or cringing, or humble, or domesticated, like dogs. I don't know one single man who is a proud living animal' (61).

True 'nobility' resides in the pre-industrial, pre-modern intimacy between primitive man and primitive animal. St Mawr strikes Lou as 'the first noble thing I have ever seen', and her mother agrees that amongst the English aristocracy she has not seen 'any *man* that could compare with him' (Lawrence 1925: 31 italics in original). In fact, the Welsh component of the horse's name signifies 'high rank', and the only human who consistently understands him is Lewis, the Welsh groom. As a Celt, Lewis is described both as a 'little aboriginal' and at the same time as '[l]ike an animal' himself: in one peculiar scene Mrs Witt insists on grooming the groom, cutting his hair while Lewis looks 'stealthily round, like a creature in a trap' (25, 56, 58). Later she will listen enthralled to his assertion that 'if you cut a tree down without asking pardon, trees will hurt you some time in your life', that '[t]he world has its own life, the sky has a life of its own', and that '[m]any things twitch and twitter within the sky, and many things happen beyond us' (124). In contrast to the domesticated masculinity of Rico and Frederick Edwards, Lewis represents an indigenous, therio-primitive and animistic virility. So does his friend Phoenix, the half-Mexican, half-Navajo servant of Mrs Witt. Having suffered shellshock in the war, Phoenix is in flight (like Lawrence) from the mechanized nightmare of modernity, and undergoes his own 'savage pilgrimage' back to health via the mediation of St Mawr. In Phoenix's eyes London is 'a sort of dark mirage', beyond which he perceives 'the pale deserts of Arizona' where 'a horse-shape loom[s] large and portentous . . . like some pre-historic beast'. And he rides 'as if he and the horse were all one piece' (27).

Primeval riders at one with their steeds; modern brutes thrown from their mounts; horses falling backwards onto men or kicking out at their faces: *St Mawr* conducts a sustained modernist manipulation of the tradi-tional conceit of the horse and rider as an emblem for the human mind harnessing and directing the body's animal passions. As I discussed in Chapter 1, this conventional trope is reversed in the fourth voyage of *Gulliver's Travels*, in which rational, ascetic equines corral and yoke savage hominids. Lawrence reconfigures the emblem in a different way. Humanity is 'no longer its own master', but is 'like a horse, ridden by a stranger, smooth-faced, evil rider', by the 'pseudo-handsome ghoul' of 'ideal mankind'. The rider here represents abstract, instrumentalist inhumanity disguised as humane virtue, '[m]asquerading as the ideal, in order to poison the real', dedicated to 'multiply[ing] itself million upon million, rear[ing] up city upon city' while '[a]t the same time secretly, viciously, potently undermin[ing] the natural creation' (Lawrence 1925: 84–5). Hence, although Lawrence's human-equine reversal differs markedly from Swift's, it nevertheless targets the same quality that Swift covertly satirizes in the Houyhnhnms.[6] The cast of thought that in the eighteenth-century context could plan the complete elimination of a 'pest' population, now armed with the technology of twentieth-century industrialism, assumes the power to overtake the entire world, while on the other hand industrial '[p]roduction must be heaped upon production' until 'the accumulation of mere existence is swollen to a horror' (85). Like Swift, too, Lawrence focuses on the threat of castration as an exemplification of modernity's preference for utility, calculability and mastery over engagement with the unpredictable vitality of living flesh. This solution to feral animality, which the Houyhnhnms learn from Gulliver and plan to apply to the Yahoos, is suggested as a way of subjugating St Mawr without destroying him (105). For Lou, such 'humanitarianism' is a 'mean', 'barren', 'eunuch cruelty', a metonym for '[o]ur whole eunuch civilisation, nasty-minded as eunuchs are, with their kind of sneaking, sterilising cruelty' (107).

For Lawrence, the only means of escape from the modern double-bind of organic sterility and industrial productivity is offered by re-engagement with the vital stuff of life, as emblematized by the primal union between human and beast. As his use of the figure of the horse-rider suggests, this reconciliation can occur literally or metaphorically, that is, either as an actual symbiosis between the ferocious nobility of humans and non-human animals, or as a reconfiguration of the relationship between human-ness and animality within the human sensibility. Aware of the risk that this might be taken as a naïve, reactionary regressivism, Lawrence has Lou specify the difference between her idea of a 'pure animal man' and a mere 'cave man'. The latter is not 'a real human animal at all' but merely 'a brute, a degenerate', whereas the former 'would be as lovely as a deer or a leopard, burning like a flame fed straight from underneath . . . He'd be all the animals in turn, instead of one, fixed, automatic thing, which he is now, grinding on the nerves' (1925: 61). The undesirable alternatives against which the 'pure animal man' is defined – crude atavism on one hand and mechanistic lifelessness on the other – are presented as conditions of stagnation, in contrast to the protean, hybrid vitality that Lawrence finds at work in authentically primitive (rather than basely degenerate) societies.[7] Hence, for example, his praise for Etruscan art, which represents the human being as 'a bull or a ram, a lion or a deer, according to his different aspects and potencies', in whose veins merged different animal currents, 'the blood of the wings of birds and the venom of serpents' (Lawrence 1992 [1932]: 122–3).

St Mawr is unashamedly didactic in its diagnosis of the modern malaise, and its treatment. 'What's to be done?' the narrative asks, replying, '[t]ry to hold fast to the living thing, which destroys as it goes, but remains sweet'

(Lawrence 1925: 85–6). Despite the directness of this moral imperative, however, the novel fails to take its own advice – fails to hold fast to its own remarkably vital evocation of the 'living thing', St Mawr – so that the horse slips unnoticed out of the narrative, leaving only an abstraction. This is inevitable, given that Lawrence's real interest is in animality conceived as an ideal and protean state, a kind of therio-anthropomorphic flux within which any particular animal could only be a temporary stand-in. After Rico's accident, Lou and her mother return to America, taking St Mawr with them to save him from death and castration. Thereafter both Lou and the novelist lose interest in the horse. Transported to American ranch culture, the stallion ceases to embody the 'wild, natural thing' he represented in England. He seems 'pleased with [the] rough handling' by the Texan ranch-man, and immediately accedes to the function he refused to fulfil at home, that of stud animal. The reader last sees St Mawr following 'at the heels of the boss' long-legged black Texan mare, almost slavishly' (154). Leaving both the horse and Lewis behind, Lou travels around the south-west states with Phoenix. Far from industrious cattle-raising Texas she happens upon a 'little tumble-down ranch' in New Mexico, called Las Chivas, 'man's last effort towards the wild heart of the Rockies' (165), where she stays because it provides access to the same quality she once saw in St Mawr: 'something wild, that will hurt me sometimes', a 'wild spirit' that 'saves me from cheapness' (185–6).

For all its insistence on the urgency of a renewed intimacy between humanity and animality – either hostile or symbiotic – modernist therio-primitivism thus repeats the modern transformation of the animal into an abstraction. Where industrial modernity reduces animals to a collection of raw materials or a sequence of processes, the modernist aesthetic sublimates them into essence. As a consequence, actual animals always prove inadequate. So it is that once he ceases to embody the 'wild, natural thing' St Mawr disappears from the story that bears his name – the last time he is mentioned is Lou's realization that '[e]ven the illusion of the beautiful St Mawr was gone' (161) – to be replaced by another representation of therio-primitive redemption, Las Chivas. Clearly, then, a particular animal can only ever provide a temporary signifier of the redemptive power of vital 'animality'. In his Tanner Lectures at Princeton University in 1997–8, J. M. Coetzee advanced exactly this critique of therio-primitivism (although he did not call it that) via the persona of fictional novelist Elizabeth Costello. Addressing an audience on the topic of 'The Animals and the Poets', Costello identifies Lawrence as one of a line of writers who 'celebrate the primitive and repudiate the Western bias toward abstract thought' and who do so by seeking to recover an attentiveness to animals 'that our faraway ancestors possessed and we have lost' (Coetzee 2003: 97). However she goes on to argue that 'despite the vividness and earthiness' of such writing there 'remains something Platonic about it'. This is because, even as it seems to offer the 'record of an engagement' with a particular animal, what actually concerns primitivist writing is animality in general. Hence, for example, when the modernist poet Ted Hughes writes a poem about *a* jaguar, he is really concerned with '*the* jaguar', with 'jaguarness embodied in this jaguar'. Just as later on, when he writes his marvellous poems about salmon, they are about salmon as transitory occupants of the salmon-life, the salmon-biography' (96, 98 italics in original). To see the consequences of this trans-figuration of actual animals into representatives of an essential animality, we might turn to another writer mentioned by Elizabeth Costello as emblematic of this tradition.

Chicago, Pamplona, the Serengeti, the Gulf Stream

Modernist therio-primitivism has no more notorious a representative than Ernest Hemingway: today his work reads like a caricature of this version of human–animal relations. Everywhere, Hemingway's writing is impelled by the conviction that the human can step out of the empty artifice of modern living and into truth – that is, an authentic and immediate rela-tion to the vital essence of existence – by means of the struggle to the death between human and beast. By his own account, Hemingway learnt to write 'commencing with the simplest things, and one of the simplest things of all and the most fundamental is violent death'. However, 'now that the wars were over', the only place to witness this was 'in the bull ring' (Hemingway 1932: 10). And so he went to Spain and wrote his first successful novel, *The Sun Also Rises*, about bullfighting. Hemingway's is the crudest form of redemptive therio-primitivism. Particular modes of repeated animal killing – in particular the bullfight, big-game hunting and fishing – are conceived as re-enactments of primal rituals, regenerative links to the anthropological and ontological foundations of human being. This project is paralleled at the aesthetic level by Hemingway's famously laconic style, which purports to return literary form to a simple vitalism appropriate to its primordial content. Accordingly the reader is told, during the climactic bullfight in *The Sun Also Rises*, that the technique of the *torero* Romero 'gave real emotion, because he kept the absolute purity of line in his movements and always quietly and calmly let the horns pass him close each time' (Hemingway 1962 [1926]: 167). Real emotion and purity of line are the highest values in Hem-ingway's aesthetic, and the enactment (in literature or in life) of the violent death of an animal is a means to realize these artistic goals. Hence bullfighting, when performed properly, is not merely a physical contest but a 'tragedy' and a form of 'sculpture' (Hemingway 1968: 116–17; 1932: 97, 197). Most emphatically, it requires abrogation of any concern for the an-imal's welfare, a factor consistent with the modernist contempt for Victorian sentimentalism. Having learned what can be done with the bull 'as an artist-ic property' Hemingway feels 'no more sympathy for him than for a canvas or the marble a sculptor cuts' (97).

As well as epitomizing the relationship between Hemingway's aesthetic and his view of human–animal relations, the bullfight demonstrates most clearly the contrasts between Hemingway's therio-primitivism and

Lawrence's. *The Plumed Serpent* – published by Lawrence in the same year as *The Sun Also Rises* – begins with an extended description of a bullfight, in which the confrontation between man and animal represents the opposite of what it means for Hemingway. For Lawrence the bullfight is an artificial colonial imposition, imported from Europe like the fighting bulls themselves (1987 [1926]: 7). To his protagonist Kate, there is in the bullfight 'no glamour, no charm'. The toreadors are 'grotesque and effeminate-looking fellows in tight, ornate clothes', whose performances show them to be '[j]ust about as gallant as assistants in a butcher's shop' (14). In both novels the fights begin, according to custom, with the carefully arranged goring to death of a number of horses. In *Death in the Afternoon* Hemingway expends some effort arguing that this part of the ritual is not to be taken seriously, but is merely the 'comedy' that precedes the 'tragedy' of the fight between man and bull (1932: 9–13). Accordingly in *The Sun Also Rises* Brett demonstrates what an 'extraordinary wench' she is by observing the horses' evisceration with avidity rather than dismay (1962 [1926]: 165). In *The Plumed Serpent*, though, when the blindfolded horse is disembowelled by a bull, Kate is told '[n]ow, Miss Leslie, you are seeing *Life!*', but all she feels is disgust: '[h]uman cowardice and beastliness, a smell of blood, a nauseous whiff of bursten bowels!' (Lawrence 1987 [1926]: 16 italics in original). Another contrast is apparent in the two novelists' portrayal of the relationship between masculinity and the bullfight. During Hemingway's fight, Robert Cohn's nausea at the sight of the horses' suffering marks him as a neuter – Mike compares him with a steer (1962 [1926]: 165, 141) – whereas in Lawrence's narrative it is the toreadors who look 'like eunuchs' (1987 [1926]: 14).

A comparison between these two writers shows the range of possible attitudes and meanings – as well as the internal contradictions – associated with the modernist deployment of therio-primitivism. For example, as in the case of Lawrence, Hemingway's writing was animated by an ongoing 'savage pilgrimage' to a series of locations defined by their difference from metropolitan modernity. Born into a middle-class household in a suburb of Chicago, the global capital of industrial animal production, Hemingway soon fled to those arenas in which he felt he could encounter life at its most authentic: the bullrings of Spain, the cock-fighting circles of Cuba, the marlin-fishing grounds of the Gulf Stream, and the big-game trails of the Serengeti. Meanwhile, in his fiction, Hemingway 'located the significant life-restorative gestures of his characters in a renunciation of enclosure and controlling citified resources' (Gajdusek 2001: 94). In contrast to Lawrence, though, Hemingway's search for the authentic human experience he disdained to find in urban modernity took him not away from war but into it: as a youth he attempted to fight in the First World War, and subsequently, famously, involved himself in the Spanish Civil War. Of course guns remained for Hemingway a crucial means to experience truth – if not in war, then in hunting – but in other ways he appears to share Lawrence's rejection of the accoutrements of technological modernity. In his safari book, *The Green Hills of Africa*, and in his journalism, Hemingway associates automobiles with a shallow, easy and inauthentic form of hunting (1998 [1935]: 12, 46; 1968: 181). He also shares Lawrence's privileging of the relationship between 'primitive' peoples and non-human nature, but he deploys this trope, once again, in a more blatant and less nuanced manner. By the 1940s it had become commonplace to describe Hemingway as a 'primitive' who created 'Indian-like heroes who survive in a world of hostile forces by acts of propitiation and ritual', while the writer himself frequently repeated his claim to have Cheyenne blood (Love 2003: 120). More than anything, however, he felt his redemptive relation to the primitive was expressed and reinforced by hunting. '[A]ll the country in the world is the same country and all hunters are the same people', he writes, boasting also of the kind of capacity that identifies him directly with pre-modern hunters, indeed with animals themselves: 'hunting at home I have several times smelled elk in the rutting season before I have seen them and I can smell clearly where an old bull has lain in the forest' (Hemingway 1998 [1935]: 73, 178). Where Lawrence proposes a metaphysical appropriation of the supposed virtues of primitive peoples, Hemingway claims to be a primitive himself, and thus to possess these virtues innately. On the other hand, while Lawrence's view of native cultures is often condescending, Hemingway's dealings with actual native peoples are colonialist in the most vulgar and retrograde sense. In *Green Hills* he treats his tracker M'Cola with casual disdain. The Kenyan might be useful for his local knowledge, but he can by no means be trusted with a loaded gun behind one's back, and he tends to be sulky when reprimanded for failing to keep the 'Bwana's' gun clean (61: 146–7).

An equally telling comparison between Lawrence's and Hemingway's therio-primitivism can be drawn in relation to their representation of animals themselves. For all his aversion to rhetorical flourishes that render artificial an otherwise 'true' experience or 'real' emotion, at crucial moments Hemingway, like Lawrence, does transform his animals into mythopoeic monsters. A rhinoceros he shoots in Kenya resembles a Ceratopsian dinosaur, lying 'long-hulked, heavy-sided, prehistoric-looking', armoured with a 'hide like vulcanized rubber', and so ancient that there is 'moss growing on the base of his horn' (Hemingway 1998 [1935]: 61). A bull faced by a *torero* 'seemed like some great prehistorical animal, absolutely deadly and absolutely vicious' (Hemingway 1968: 114). For Lawrence, on the other hand, the bullfight has the opposite effect, destroying the mythic glamour of the animal and reducing it to a dumb beast: although previously Kate has 'always been afraid of bulls, fear tempered with reverence of the great Mithraic beast', the sight of the animal running '[b]lindly and stupidly' at the *muleta* makes her see it as merely idiotic (1987 [1926]: 17).

The difference between these two writers therefore lies not in their mode of representation of animals: both deploy the techniques of modernist therio-primitivism. Where they diverge is in their view of how human–animal relations, and the cultural practices through which these are mediated, might allow human access to the redemptive authenticity that animality represents. In Hemingway, animal and human become one through the mediation of the instrument the human uses to capture or kill the animal. *Torero* and bull are united by the sword as the death-blow is delivered: 'Romero's left hand dropped the muleta over the bull's muzzle to blind him, his left shoulder went forward between the horns as the sword went in, and for just an instant he and the bull were one' (Hemingway 1962 [1926]: 218). And describing another of his favoured modes of encountering wild animality, Hemingway identifies the 'great pleasure' of big-game fishing as the experience of engagement with 'the unknown wild suddenness of a great fish', with the animal's 'life and death which he lives for you in an hour while your strength is harnessed to his'. This moment of communion depends on 'conquering this thing which rules the sea it lives in', on the fisherman's ability 'to feel that fish in his rod, to feel that power and that great rush, to be a connected part of it and then to dominate it and master it and bring that fish to gaff' (1968: 188–9, 257). Here, then, is the formula for Hemingway's therio-primitivism: access to the revitalizing energy of the wild animal depends upon its harnessing and eventual conquest. It is not a mere identification but an appropriation, whereby the human captures and consumes the animal's vitality and purity.

Glen Love argues that Hemingway 'often turns against the earth itself in his version of primitivism, adopting an aggressive and isolated individualism that wars against those natural manifestations he reveres' (2003: 121). And indeed, his most highly charged moments of therio-primitivism are pervaded by a crude masculine competitiveness. In *Green Hills* Hemingway's pride in killing the 'prehistoric-looking' rhino suffers instant deflation when he discovers that his friend Karl has shot one so large that it makes his 'look ridiculous'; later he gets a prize bull kudu, only to find that the one shot by Karl has 'the biggest, widest, longest-curling, heaviest, most unbelievable pair of kudu horns in the world. Suddenly, poisoned with envy, I did not want to see mine again; never, never' (1998 [1935]: 64–5, 204–5). Nor is the reader supposed to dismiss this as petty rivalry; nothing could be less trivial to a big-game hunter than the impressiveness of his trophies. For Hemingway, sport is as serious as – indeed, in its purest forms, practically synonymous with – artistic creativity. He conceives both as practices that access and channel the most authentic forms of human experience. 'We have very primitive emotions', Ernest's mentor Jackson 'Pop' Phillips tells him. 'It's impossible not to be competitive. Spoils everything, though' (206). By tying his therio-primitive art into sporting contests, Hemingway repeats the ideology of nineteenth-century capitalism, which defined competitive individualism as the fundamental law of both human and non-human nature. It is perhaps for this reason that Hemingway's therio-primitivism prospered in the twentieth century, while Lawrence's did not. Trophy-hunting, shooting safaris, big-game fishing and bullfighting remain popular pastimes, commodified forms of identification with a supposedly primal human essence that owe something of their glamour and appeal to the stature of Hemingway and his celebrity. As Norris puts it, 'the entire safari cult of competition and trophies, celebration and largesse, photography and taxidermy, externalizes the experience for consumption by social consciousness' (1985: 198).

These pastimes have been dignified by at least one professional philosopher, José Ortega y Gasset, whose *Meditations on Hunting* has become sacred writ for the metaphysically inclined sportsman. The key elements of Ortega's essay correspond precisely to Hemingway's attitude. It emphasizes hunting as a 'tactile drama', a 'tragedy' that connects the human to his origins, insofar as *'man's being consisted first in being a hunter'* (Ortega y Gasset 1972 [1947]: 19, 118; italics in original). It portrays hunting as an act of counter-modernity. Because the sporting hunter by definition abjures the advantages that technological modernity might bring (except of course the gun) in order to give the animal a chance of survival, hunting remains definitively and regeneratively atavistic: 'by hunting man succeeds, in effect, in annihilating all historical evolution, in separating himself from the present, and in renewing the primitive situation' (135). Blood sports thus offer the only real way to connect modern citizens redemptively to their own animality. To 're-enter Nature', 'man' must 'temporarily rehabilitat[e] that part of himself which is still an animal', by 'placing himself in relation to another animal'; however 'there is no animal, pure animal, other than the wild one, and the relationship with him is the hunt' (139–40). Despite this apparently humble re-entry into animal nature, the stakes of the hunt are always the reassertion of human mastery, for hunting comprises 'a relationship between animals *which excludes an equality of vital level between the two'* (55–6; italics in original). Hence, although his relinquishing of modernity reduces the hunter to a state of animalistic primitivism, the object is to prove his superior animality – that is, his humanity – by demonstrating mastery of the quarry without the need for the assistance provided by modern civilization.

Hemingway's clearest and most mythopoeic rendering of this philosophically influential definition of the human occurs in the parable that cemented his claim to the Nobel Prize for Literature in 1954, namely *The Old Man and the Sea* (1957 [1952]). The story is also – although it is seldom read this way – a reworking of *Moby-Dick*. In *The Green Hills of Africa* Hemingway describes Meville as a writer 'who had the good fortune to find a little, in a chronicle of another man and from voyaging, of how things, actual things, can be, whales for instance, and this knowledge is wrapped in the rhetoric like plums in a pudding' (1998 [1935]: 21–2). And since he goes on to suggest that 'a new classic' has the right to 'steal from anything that it is better than' (22), it seems justifiable to see *The Old Man and the Sea* as his attempt to scrape away the indigestible, over-rich rhetoric from Melville's novel and reveal its kernel of truth. Given Hemingway's privileging of the hunter–animal relation, in *Green Hills* as elsewhere, it is no surprise that he regarded Melville's discovery of 'how things, actual things, can be' as inhering in the hunting of Moby Dick by Ahab, and in the way the harpoon unites them.

In Hemingway's novel an old Cuban fisherman, Santiago, is driven by hunger to fish further out in the Gulf Stream than is usually considered safe. A huge marlin takes his line, and an epic struggle ensues. Eventually the old man prevails, and he lashes the fish's body to the side of his skiff and turns for shore. Sharks attack the body of the fish, and although the fisherman fights them off, by the time he crawls ashore nothing is left but a huge skeleton lashed to the boat. The inspiration for the narrative can be found in a story Hemingway relates in his journalism, about an old Cuban fisherman found lost at sea with the vast skeleton of a marlin strapped to his boat after a comparable adventure (1968: 253–4). But his portrait of the relationship between man and animal is shaped by elements selected from *Moby-Dick* and reworked according to the aesthetic and philosophical predilections of modernism. Like Ahab, Santiago turns the mundane task of harvesting marine life for a living into a metaphysical quest. The grandeur of this higher pursuit is contrasted, in both novels, with the base, greedy voracity of the sharks who come to gorge themselves parasitically on the fruits of courageous human labour (Melville 2002 [1851]: 237–40; Hemingway 1957 [1952]: 99–109). As in Melville's novel, the combat between this particular man and this particular animal is predestined: Santiago knows that somewhere far off the coast swims 'my big fish' (31), just as Ahab knows he will meet Moby Dick in the Pacific. Both Ahab and Santiago are bound to their quarry unto death, and so the harpoon and line become symbolic of the human's constitutive, albeit fatal, relationship to nature. But where Ahab's final recognition of this destiny is bitter and (from Hemingway's perspective) grandiloquent – '[t]owards thee I roll, thou call-destroying but unconquering whale; to the last I grapple with thee; from hell's heart I stab at thee' (Melville 2002 [1851]: 426) – Santiago's is laconically dignified. '"Fish", he said softly, aloud, "I'll stay with you until I am dead". He'll stay with me too, I suppose, the old man thought' (Hemingway 1957 [1952]: 49). Moreover, where Ahab fails both to recognize his kinship with the animal he hunts, and to master it – the two elements central to Hemingway's version of therio-primitive redemption – Santiago succeeds on both counts, even though he may die from the exhaustion of his adventure after the novel ends. 'You are killing me, fish', he says to himself, '[b]ut you have a right to. Never have I seen a greater, or more beautiful, or a calmer or more noble thing than you, brother' (85).

Yet this apparent mutuality poses a problem for Hemingway's mythos. Although hunting or fighting the animal is the privileged means to access therio-primitive authenticity, the power of the animal to fulfil this function is lost as soon as it is killed. Hence, perhaps, Hemingway's repeated disappointment with the corpses of the animals he shoots. In *The Old Man and the Sea*, however, the problem is a symbolic one. Whereas Ahab and Moby Dick exit Melville's narrative together, both alive (albeit temporarily in Ahab's case) and bound together, Hemingway's marlin is killed well before the story ends. The problem is resolved by poetically extending the marlin's life beyond its literal death, postponing its inevitable disintegration from a living embodiment of vital energy to a mere trophy, in the form of the vast skeleton which is all that remains by the time the skiff returns to shore. So after the dead marlin is lashed to the side of his boat, the old man thinks of himself as still bound to a living animal, an equal. He wonders to himself, 'is he bringing me in or am I bringing him in?' Rather than towing him behind or carrying the fish in the skiff 'with all dignity gone', man and animal are 'sailing together lashed side by side and the old man thought, let him bring me in if it pleases him' (Hemingway 1957 [1952]: 92).

Hemingway's crucial revision of the agonism between Ahab and Moby Dick lies in transforming it from an examination of the conflict between industrial modernity and the organic world to the evocation of a savage communion between human and nature in a pre-modern setting. 'With his crude skiff and his handlines', Santiago 'is as close as one could imagine to a virtual Stone Age fisherman living in the mid-twentieth century', writes Love, and so 'intended to be both the vessel of his author's conception of primitivist natural nobility and of tragic consciousness'. Where Ahab mobilizes the rhetoric and technology of industrial modernity, Santiago deploys instead a 'keen biophilial awareness' and a 'store of skills, which seem to be the distilled accumulation of generations of tradition' (Love 2003: 127). Ahab sees Moby Dick as a 'demon', but to Santiago the great marlin is a 'brother' and a 'friend' (Hemingway 1957 [1952]: 51, 85). Ahab boasts he would 'strike the sun' if it insulted him (Melville 2002 [1851]: 140), whereas Santiago accepts with gratitude the proper limits placed on his struggle with nature: 'imagine if a man each day should have to try and kill the sun? We are born lucky, he thought' (Hemingway 1957 [1952]: 70). In place of Ahab's monomaniac oaths of vengeance and declarations of undying hatred, Santiago expresses what Hemingway perceives to be the primal goodness and respectfulness of the hunt. 'Fish', he says calmly, 'I love you and respect you every much. But I will kill you dead before this day ends' (51). In revising Melville, *The Old Man and the Sea* repeats the move characteristic of the modernist idealization of hunting: it steps out of history, and specifically out of modernity, engaging in a tragic ritual – in the form of literature, blood sport, or literature about blood sport – that regenerates the intimate affiliation between the human and animal nature.

The irony, however, is that for all his primitive wisdom, Santiago approaches his marlin not like a down-on-his-luck Cuban fisherman, but like a wealthy American sportsman. The story was conceived and written during the many hours spent by Hemingway marlin-fishing on his launch *Pilar* off the Cuban coast. Many of Santiago's characteristic attitudes are those of his creator – such as his repeated comparison between his own situation and that of Joe DiMaggio, the fisherman's son 'who does all things perfectly even with the pain of the bone spur in his heel' (Hemingway 1957 [1952]: 19, 64). Even the great marlin is perceived according to a sensibility flavoured by America's national sport. When the fish first jumps, Santiago sees that its 'sword was as long as a baseball bat' (58). Moreover, an angler fishing for his survival would surely pursue a number of smaller fish rather than hang on to a trophy quarry that is carrying him too far out; yet when Santiago hooks a second fish while being towed by the giant marlin, he cuts it free and pulls up his other baits so he can concentrate on the big game (48). Similarly, the central drama of the novel – the long struggle to the death between man and fish – derives from the techniques of sport-fishing. A fundamental aspect of competitive (as distinct from subsistence) marlin fishing is the choice of a line that is neither too strong nor too weak, which tests the angler's skill because he or she must play the fish to exhaustion without either letting it escape, or else (unsportingly) allowing it no chance of escape. Hence, in his sports journalism for *Esquire*, Hemingway writes that in marlin-fishing 'the most satisfaction is to dominate and convince the fish and bring him intact in everything but spirit to the boat' (1968: 255). But he also transfers this element, derived from the leisured, privileged context of sport-fishing, to his parable of primitive and mythic struggle, so that in *The Old Man and the Sea* the fragility of the line, which must be struggled with to the point of breaking but not beyond it, stands for a series of metaphysical *agones*: between man and beast, hunter and quarry, artist and authentic emotion. Santiago 'knew that if he could not slow the fish with a steady pressure the fish could take out all the line and break it'; instead, he thinks, 'I must convince him . . . I must never let him learn his strength nor what he could do if he made his run' (59). For all the universalizing essentialism of Santiago's adventure, it thereby remains indebted more to sportism than to a genuinely primitive relation to nature.

The Last Great Hunt

The contrast between Lawrence and Hemingway is nowhere clearer than in their divergent representation of animal agency. For Lawrence, the non-human only becomes a destructive force because of humans' attempts to dominate and repress it. The therio-primitive epiphany comes when a character recognizes that human and non-human life are mutually constituted by the pulsion of energies and potencies that go beyond anthropomorphic ideas about agency, or anthropocentric belief in mastery over nature. For Hemingway, on the other hand, animal agency is innately antagonistic, and it must be challenged, harnessed and overcome in order for authentic experience and real emotion to be realized, whether by art, ritual or blood sports.

Hence, in the context of the bullfight, Hemingway has to insist on the wildness and untamed nature of the animals, which belong to 'a strain that comes down in direct descent from the wild bulls that ranged over the Peninsula', and are kept as 'free ranging animals' until they are brought to fight (1932: 104). But in fact this is a very cultivated wildness: the animals are tumbled over, branded, and tested for bravery by *picadors*; those found wanting 'are marked for veal' (111–12). 'Genetic control', as Norris points out, 'is necessary to keep the bulls feral' (1985: 215). Moreover in this context 'bravery' is also a carefully managed concept. Hemingway measures it by the predictability of the animal's willingness to attack. 'The really brave bull welcomes the fight, accepts every invitation to fight, does not fight because he is cornered, but because he wants to' (1932: 111). Norris points out that *Death in the Afternoon* includes a discussion of 'its antithesis', a Spanish publication called *Toros Celebres*, which documents 'rebel bulls, insurrectionists, as it were, bulls willing to kill but not to play according to the rules of the *corrida*, who crash through the *barrera*, goring carpenters, policemen, and random spectators'. For Norris this volume documents 'the bull's point of view and interest' and bears witness to 'the autonomy of the animal, its use of its power for its own ends, and the uncontrollability of its aggression rather than its manipulation'. Hemingway, however, only 'mentions *Toros Celebres* in order to cancel it' (Norris 1985: 209), insisting that '[a] bull that jumps the barrera is not a brave bull. He is a cowardly bull who is simply trying to escape the ring' (Hemingway 1932: 111). Another kind of cowardice, that of the bull who 'is difficult to fight since he will not charge the picadors more than once if he receives any punishment', is synonymous with the animal's ability to learn quickly (140). But in fact any bull will learn 'so rapidly in the ring that if the bullfight drags, is badly done, or is prolonged an extra ten minutes he becomes almost unkillable by the means prescribed in the rules of the spectacle' (105–6). Hence if the *torero* cannot slay the animal within fifteen minutes, by law it must be slaughtered in the corrals, because '[i]f the bulls were allowed to increase their knowledge as the bullfighter does' by fighting repeatedly, 'they would kill all the bullfighters' (26–7). As Norris remarks, all these rules guarantee that '[t]he knowledge and science of the matador is therefore optimally pitted only against the danger inherent in the bull's body, that is, of its bulk and horns, rather than against the danger of his mentality' (1985: 212).

Hemingway's account of animal agency displays the same anxiety that was apparent in debates about cetacean agency in the nineteenth century. In the latter context, as I argued in my previous chapter, the natural historian's insistence that whales could not display anything other than instinctual, reflexive responses was pitted against the whaleman's experiences of cetacean behaviours that could not be so explained. Hemingway mobilizes the concept of animal agency as pure instinct by dismissing other modes of behaviour displayed by the bulls – a capacity to learn, a deliberate recalcitrance in the face of human manipulation, the ability to attack in a calculated rather than an impulsive fashion – as degradations of the animal's true nature. Nevertheless, some hint of the alternative possibilities of animal agency does emerge on one of the few occasions when Hemingway actually admires an animal for escaping, rather than demonstrating the mastery of the hunter. Suggestively, this occurs during a whale-hunt. In a light-hearted piece for *Esquire* in 1936, entitled 'There She Breaches! *or* Moby Dick off the Morro', he describes encountering a pod of sperm whales, and trying to harpoon one, off the Havana coast while out marlin fishing in his launch. The tale becomes a racy pastiche of Melville's epic, in which Hemingway and his friends adapt their available materials to the demands of whale-hunting rather than marlin-fishing. They decide to use their 'three-inch hurricane hawser' as a whale line, lifebelts to act as drugs, a '6.5 mannlicher' and a 'Mauser pistol' to shoot the whale, and a killing lance 'to finish him', after which they plan 'to get a rope around his flukes, make a hole in him and pump him full of air with the air mattress pump' so they can tow him into Havana (Hemingway 1968: 263). These improvised whale-hunting tools give Hemingway the perfect excuse to display an Ahab-like monomania, combined with a machismo designed to impress his Cuban friends: 'I knew the harpoon gun would never carry out the weight of the hawser and that the effective range could only be the length of the wire cable, but I knew no reason why we could not get close enough to get the harpoon in solidly' (262). He also remembers his Melville well enough to avoid Ahab's fatal mistake: 'I could feel Bolo trembling with excitement as he held the hawser above his head. "For God's sake don't get tangled in that", I said. "Throw it when I shoot and step back clear"' (265).

Their quarry, however, proves as redoubtable as his namesake. He swims along ahead of the launch 'seemingly unconcerned, but when we speeded up the engine to come up on him close enough to fire the harpoon into him he would submerge' (Hemingway 1968: 262). Hemingway and his mates manage only one good shot with the harpoon, which immediately pulls out, leaving the school to dive out of range. After the men return to shore Hemingway even repeats, intentionally or not, Ishmael's frustration at the inadequacy of human attempts to picture the whale: the photographs of the hunt turn out 'uniformly lousy' because the man who took them had 'moved the camera in excitement', allowed his lens to be soaked by a whale spout, or snapped too late, thereby achieving 'masterly shots of the holes [the whales] would leave in the water when they went down' (266). Still keen to 'get one' next time he has the chance, Hemingway resolves to 'study up' on sperm whales, like Melville's narrator, but then he concludes with an uncharacteristic admission that here is an animal that would always be beyond him: 'the more I learn about them the luckier I think we were that the harpoon pulled out. I think that a sperm whale might have made several very interesting moves before he permitted us to employ the mattress pump' (268). Only here, haunted by the ghostly reappearance of Moby Dick off the Morro, does Hemingway accept, albeit frivolously, the possibility of a non-human agency capable of moves that exceed all the advantages granted by human cultivated skill and practised, pragmatic intelligence.

For Lawrence, on the other hand, this is always what makes non-human animals compelling: their refusal to be confined by modernity's definitions of agency. In contrast to the 'cold, almost cruel curiosity of the upper will', the 'acute attention of the experimental scientist'– exemplified by Dr Frankstone in *The Rainbow* – he posits a 'ganglial' or 'vertebrate' mode of being, a 'blood-consciousness' shared by human and non-human animals alike (Lawrence 1931 [1923]: 55–6). Explaining this notion further, he asserts that

[m]an has two distinct fields of consciousness, two living minds. First, there is the physical or primary mind, a perfect and spontaneous consciousness centralising in the great plexuses and ganglia of the nervous system and in the hind brain. Secondly, there is the ideal consciousness, which we recognise as mental, located in the brain.

What we call 'instinct' in creatures such as bees, or ants, or whales, or foxes, or larks, is the sure and perfect working of the primary mind in these creatures. All the tissue of the body is all the time aware. The blood is awake: the whole blood-system of the body is a great field of primal consciousness (Lawrence 1962 [1925]: 135).

Envisaging this primary consciousness as not centred in the brain or confined to the cranial cavity, but transmitted via impulses throughout the body in the veins, the nervous system and spine, Lawrence draws upon that form of networked, dispersed volition attributed by Melville to the sperm whale. Indeed, in his own essay on *Moby-Dick*, Lawrence analyses the story he calls 'the last great hunt' in precisely these terms. He suggests that the White Whale represents 'the deepest blood-being of the white race', the last, lonely and endangered link between the modern European psyche and its savage animality, threatened with destruction by Ahab, whose mechanical monomania stands for 'the maniacal fanaticism of our white mental consciousness' (1933: 145, 160). And then he seizes on a passage ignored by almost all other critics:

> [d]ilating on the smallness of the brain of a sperm whale, Melville significantly remarks . . . 'that much of man's character will be found betokened in his backbone . . .' And of the whale, he adds: 'For, viewed in this light, the wonderful comparative smallness of his brain proper is more than compensated by the wonderful comparative magnitude of his spinal cord' (154–5; citing Melville 2002 [1851]: 276).

As I argued in the preceding chapter, this passage is crucial to the alternative, non-rationalist form of agency alluded to by Melville. And it is this same paradigm that Lawrence develops into an explicit theory of 'vertebral communication' in *Kangaroo*, the novel he was working on while writing the first version of the essay on *Moby-Dick*. In *Kangaroo* he compares the unpredictable behaviour of the working-class masses with the 'herd instinct' in non-human animals, suggesting that in both cases, communication between individual members of the collective is 'sub-mental' or 'telepathic', entailing 'a complex interplay of vibrations from the big nerve centres of the vertebral system'. When it occurs amongst humans, therefore, this phenomenon brings them closest to the condition of pack-animality; closest, indeed, to that networked form of agency which Melville embodied in his White Whale. 'The highest form' of this 'vertebral telepathy', writes Lawrence, occurs among 'the great sperm whales. Communication between these herds of roving monsters is of marvellous rapidity and perfection'. And so, when the 'preponderantly vertebral' powers of the human masses arrive at 'such a pitch of vibration' that they are transformed into 'a great, non-mental oneness . . . then, like whales which suddenly charge upon the ship which tortures them, so they burst upon the vessel of civilization' (Lawrence 1994 [1923]: 298–301).

At the end of *St Mawr* a comparable agentive effect is represented by the dishevelled ranch where Lou settles, but in this case it occurs between humans and other organisms. Overrun with the half-wild 'fire-mouth' goats that give the place its name, and with 'pack-rats, swarming' (Lawrence 1925: 167–8), Las Chivas appears as a kind of a gone-to-seed version of Crusoe's obsessively maintained enclosures. Despite the efforts of its former owners, no profit can be made, because the living environment is inimical to human mastery. 'Always, some mysterious malevolence fighting, fighting against the will of man' (169), a 'curious, subtle thing, like a mountain fever, [which] got into the blood, so that the men at the ranch, and the animals with them, had bursts of queer, violent, half-frenzied energy . . .' (169). Lou's chickens stray or are carried away and her horses are struck by lightning, while she experiences the same breakdown of language that affected Alexander Selkirk. 'When she was saying something, suddenly the next word would be gone out of her, as if a pack-rat had carried it off ' (174). Surrendering to the energy of the place, Lou abandons all attempts to wrangle the interaction between human and non-human agencies, accepting that the ranch is infused by 'something wild, that will hurt me sometimes and will wear me down sometimes', but which nevertheless 'wants me' (185–6). When asked by Mrs Witt what she expects to 'achieve' at Las Chivas, she simply replies 'I love it here . . . I was rather hoping, mother, to escape achievement' (182).

Boneyards

Hemingway, too, loved the wild – or so his admirers insist. Mary Allen compares his writing with the trophies from his big-game hunts: 'through death the respected and loved animal is preserved', she writes, so that both hunter and writer bestow 'immortality' on these 'excellent creatures' (1983: 193). Robert Fleming remarks that Hemingway 'loved animals, but he loved them as a young man of his generation loved them', learning about 'wild birds, mammals, and fish by hunting or catching them', preserving his prey as a young man through taxidermy and later 'by enclosing it in the amber of his prose' (1999: 1). Whether or not one finds persuasive the association between art and hunting, or literature and taxidermy, it seems necessary to consider the sheer scale of this appetite and its ecological consequences. Although Fleming and others insist that Hemingway was 'taught by his father to respect the animals he killed and to utilize them fully' (1999: 2), Romesburg notes that '[w]hile writing *A Farewell to Arms*, he and his wife Pauline caught six hundred trout in one month, and after finishing *For Whom the Bell Tolls*, he and his family celebrated by shooting four hundred jackrabbits' (in Fleming 1999: 140). And Hemingway himself comments that in researching *Death in the Afternoon* he watched the killing of 'over fifteen hundred bulls' (1932: 225).

The same contradictions emerge when critics try to portray Hemingway as a proto-environmentalist. Such attempts usually involve reproducing his remarks at the end of *The Green Hills of Africa*: '[a] continent ages quickly once we come. The natives live in harmony with it. But the foreigner destroys, cuts down the trees, drains the water . . . and in a short time the soil . . . starts to blow away' (1998 [1935]: 200).[8] Yet earlier in *Green Hills* Hemingway includes a rather different perspective in relation to the Gulf Stream, another of his famous haunts and the setting for *The Old Man and the Sea*. Here, the survival of the environment in the face of human history is both guaranteed and effortless: 'this Gulf Stream you are living with, knowing, learning about, and loving, has moved, as it moves, since before man', and will continue to flow 'after the Indians, after the Spaniards, after the British, after the Americans and after all the Cubans and all the systems of governments, the richness, the poverty, the martyrdom, the sacrifice and the venality and the cruelty are all gone'. By now the stream is a metaphor for the timeless processes of nature itself, within which human history comprises a merely transient pollution, like the 'high-piled scow of garbage' which spills its load of 'palm fronds, corks, bottles, and used electric light globes, seasoned with an occasional condom or a deep floating corset, the torn leaves of a student's exercise book, a well-inflated dog, the occasional rat, the no-longer-distinguished cat'. Fortunately 'the stream, with no visible flow, takes five loads of this a day when things are going well in La Habana', yet 'in ten miles along the coast it is as clear and blue and unimpressed as it was ever before the tug hauled out the scow' (108). Glen Love observes that as a symbol of nature's capacity for unconditional forgiveness and endless replenishment the Gulf Stream has aged remarkably badly. He cites Hemingway's son Gregory, who commented that '"even the sea can endure only so much", as he described the degradation of the Gulf Stream waters in more recent times' (Love 124; citing Hemingway 1976: 25). Indeed, environmental scientists are now debating the possibility that, if the Greenland ice sheet melts in response to human-induced climate change, the Gulf Stream may slow, change its direction or even shut down (Gagosian 2003).

The fate of Hemingway's Gulf Stream imagery demonstrates the scale and pace of change affecting perceptions of the non-human world as a result of modernity's decline. In its orthodox, celebratory mode, modernity sees the natural world as a great domain to be mastered, endlessly inviting and endlessly exploitable, while on the other hand critical modernity – exemplified by the works of Jonathan Swift and Mary Shelley – portrays non-human organic life as an ungovernable corrective to human arrogance. Even the modernists evoke the non-Western, non-human wild as a remote and limitless source of replenishment for a modern civilization poisoned by its own waste. It is not until the second half of the twentieth century, as I will discuss in my next chapter, that literary narratives recognize that the regenerative power of organic nature may be finite. The modernism of both Hemingway and Lawrence thus suffers from a fundamental neglect of history – or rather, a desire to escape from it into the revitalizing flux of a mythopoeically rendered vitalism. But history does not confine its influence to human society: environmentalism represents the belated recognition of this fact, while the social, cultural and material histories of animal individuals and populations have been neglected even longer. Recently, however, environmental scientists, ethologists and cultural historians have begun to produce animal histories, as one might call them to distinguish them from natural history, which deals only in organic and evolutionary narratives.

Inevitably, such animal histories have an intimate relationship with human ones. The example most relevant to Hemingway is that of big-game hunting, a lucrative international enterprise, and the most active contemporary manifestation of modernist therio-primitivism. Describing his attendance in 1999 at the Seventh Annual Convention of Safari Club International, Matthew Scully discovers the same metaphysics at work that imbue Hemingway's writing. He cites James A. Swan's *In Defense of Hunting* (1995), promoted at the convention by its celebrity speaker, General Norman Schwarzkopf. Like Hemingway and Ortega y Gasset before him, Swan insists that hunting can 'serve as a conduit to a realm of existence that transcends the temporal'; that it constitutes an 'act of love', an 'antidote' to urban 'alienation' and an opportunity to access 'a primal energy' (Scully 2002: 54–5, citing Swan 1995: 35, 144). Meanwhile the Hemingway brand of human–animal relationship continues to be exploited by tour operators – as demonstrated by the frequency with which they invoke Hemingway's name, image and works in their sales pitches.[9] For many of the hunters who attend the Safari Club convention, the ultimate vacation from modernity is to go in pursuit of the African 'big five': lion, leopard, rhinoceros, buffalo and elephant. Some go for the bull elephant alone: 'big tuskers' are on offer at 10,000 American dollars (47).

As Scully points out, what the hunters enjoy as a refreshingly atemporal and transcendent experience is an irreducibly historical and material one for the animals. Evidence is growing that elephants remember the trauma of violent death in ways that extensively distort their social behaviour. Even one of the safari operators admits to Scully that '[e]lephants are very sociable animals – when you kill the adults the younger ones become dysfunctional. Africa is full of wild, dysfunctional elephants' (2002: 87). Ethologists observing elephant populations throughout Africa (and South Asia) have documented a marked increase in the frequency and savagery of elephant attacks against humans and other animals, and have concluded that decades of hunting, poaching, culling and habitat loss have resulted in a widespread trauma at both the individual and the collective levels. Behavioural psychologist Gay Bradshaw writes that elephants 'are known for their intimate and intricate social organization', describing for example their behaviour in response to the death of kin: holding vigil for days over the body of a dead calf; returning for years to visit a deceased family member's bones; burying, holding or caressing them in apparent displays of mourning (Bradshaw 2004: 145–7; Siebert 2006). The removal of members who play key social roles – including matriarchs, mothers, 'aunties' and dominant bulls, the favoured targets of safari hunters – impacts severely on the generation deprived of their presence. Moreover, neuropsychological and behavioural studies show that witnessing the violent death of family members produces similar effects in elephants and humans: post-traumatic stress, psychological damage and dysfunctional interactions (Bradshaw *et al.* 2005). Studies of the extreme forms of aggression shown by elephants in recent years 'have determined that the perpetrators were in all cases adolescent males that had witnessed their families being shot down' (Siebert 2006). Barbara Noske describes a herd of elephants descended from survivors of a massacre in South Africa's Addo National Park in 1919, who are to this day 'mainly nocturnal' and 'reported to be among the most dangerous elephants in Africa'. These animals are 'the cultural heirs of the fear and hatred among their ancestors of our species', displaying what 'may even be interpreted as a sense of history' (1997: 111, 155).

In her novel *The White Bone* (1999), Barbara Gowdy imagines an elephantine sense of history from the inside. The novel begins with the statement that 'it is true what you've heard: they never forget. They themselves think this accounts of their size. Some go so far as to claim that under that thunderhead of flesh and those huge rolling bones they *are* memory' (1999: 1). The story centres on a family of elephants attacked by humans, and details the survivors' attempt to find safety in a violent and degraded environment. Since, to the elephants, memory is no less vivid than reality, the massacre – in which the matriarchs are shot, alongside the calves who seek their protection, and then decapitated by chainsaw – inflicts enduring psychological wounds on the remaining animals (86–90, 148). The novel also recognizes the damage to the structure of social relationships: '[t]hese are bad days . . . All the old matriarchs slaughtered or deranged and the new matriarchs too ignorant to know where the safe drinking is' (151). Gowdy's elephant protagonists speculate on the motivation for the carnage in a way that associates it with a commodified therio-primitivism. According to the elephants' mythological history, humans (or 'hindleggers') were themselves elephants before their fall into viciousness and destructiveness, and a senior bull suggests that their obsession with hunting and trophy-gathering is motivated by a perverted 'nostalgia' for this lost, primitive innocence (113).[10]

Hemingway, according to his son Patrick, 'never shot an elephant . . . He thought it wrong – he felt that elephants are our equals' (Pooley 1986: 50–1 italics in original). In his posthumously published novel *The Garden of Eden* (1986), 'upon which he worked from 1946 until his death in 1961', a central plotline concerns the protagonist's writing of a story about the killing of an elephant by his father in Africa (Love 2003: 134). Alone with his dog Kibo one moonlit night, David encounters a huge bull elephant. He runs to tell his father and the latter's African guide Juma, only to be enlisted in a hunt. As they track the elephant, David's father encourages him to display the characteristics of Hemingway-style masculinity: stoic endurance, courage and a taste for the kill. However this rite of passage becomes compromised by David's growing perception of the elephant's social and affective attributes. Juma and David's father find what they expect, which is that the elephant was returning to visit the remains of his *askari* (a term Hemingway translates as 'friend'), another bull killed by the guide some years before. 'Juma pointed out where the great elephant they were trailing had stood while he looked down at the skull and where his trunk had moved it a little way from the place it had rested' (180). 'How long do you suppose he and his friend had been together?' David asks. His father translates the question to Juma and replies, '[p]robably four or five times your life . . . He doesn't know or care really'. In response to which David thinks, 'I care' (181).

This narrative is remarkable in evoking a form of affect which literary modernism, as Hemingway practised it, conventionally despised above all else: sentimentalism, especially as associated with compassionate identification between humans and animals. Indeed the currently pejorative tenor of the word 'sentimental' – which includes connotations of artifice, puerility, triteness, melodrama and the manipulation of emotional response – owes a good deal to modernism. During the Enlightenment, as I have described in earlier chapters, sentiment achieved a high cultural value, when its cultivation was espoused in literature and philosophy as a counterpoint to the increasing authority of reason. However, a thorough-going devaluation of sentimental feeling began in the latter part of the nineteenth century, as demonstrated by the writing of H. G. Wells, largely because of the increasing authority of industrial capitalism and scientific positivism. Subsequently, the taste for sentimental narratives would be associated with the least authoritative expressions of cultural life: femininity rather than masculinity, childishness rather than maturity, fancy and whimsy rather than rationality or realism (Chapman and Hendler 1999: 3–4). Accepting, indeed embracing, the new social organization of taste and sensibility, modernism attempted to regain for art some of the cultural authority lost to science and industry by thoroughly repudiating all forms of sentimental narrative and affect: '[a]n attack on sentimentality was one of the few threads uniting the internal variety of modernisms' (Bell 2000: 160). The modernists presented sentimentalism not just as a symptom of the Victorian complacency they sought to disturb, or the mass culture from which they wished to distinguish themselves, but also an ideological ruse, an affective opiate, by which bourgeois consciousness was manipulated, flattered and politically neutralized. By contrast, modernist art undertook to challenge its audience, to shock it out of mawkish passivity and comfortable identification using techniques designed to disorient and alienate (Bell 2000: 160–6).

Inevitably, sentimental attachment to animals became a particular target of modernist suspicion. Even Lawrence, for all his evocations of intense human–animal sympathy, ensures his characters are reminded of this: in *Women in Love* Birken asserts that '[n]othing is so detestable as the maudlin attributing of human feelings and consciousness to animals', a view Ursula eventually accepts, telling herself '[h]ow stupid anthropomorphism is! . . . The universe is non-human, thank God' (1989 [1920]: 139, 264). Meanwhile, in Virginia Woolf's biography of Elizabeth Barrett Browning's spaniel Flush, the meeting between dog and mistress presents a mockery of the Victorian taste for anthropomorphic identification: '[h]eavy curls hung down on either side of Miss Barrett's face; large bright eyes shone out; a large mouth smiled. Heavy ears hung down on either side of Flush's face; his eyes, too, were large and bright: his mouth was wide' (Woolf 1933: 26). The story goes on to satirize the repression of instinctual animal life by a stifling bourgeois sentimentalism. Where Barrett Browning's poem in praise of her dog eulogizes his loyal watch beside a sickbed – '[d]ay and night unweary . . . within a curtained room' where 'no sunbeam brake the gloom' (Barrett Browning 1900 [1844]: 71) – Woolf portrays Flush strain-ing against the claustrophobic, over-furnished atmosphere. 'He could not help dancing round the room on a windy autumn day when the partridges must be scattering over the stubble', or at the sound of 'guns on the breeze' or dogs barking outside; nevertheless when Miss Barrett calls Flush back from the door, 'another feeling, urgent, contradictory, disagreeable – he did not know what to call it or why he obeyed it – restrained him'. Like any modernist beast, what Flush really wants is to go hunting, but confined to Miss Barrett's 'bedroom school' he learns instead to 'resign, to control, to suppress the most violent instincts of his nature ' (35). Although presented here in humorous form, these are of course the same attitudes towards human–animal relations that characterize the therio-primitivism of Lawrence and Hemingway. More commonly, modernists dwell on the barbarous but authentic treatment of animals that they consider typical of therio-primitivism. Thus Lawrence details the mundane cruelty to small animals observed by Kate amongst the Mexican Indian peasants (1987 [1926]: 218–19), and of course Hemingway's pugnacious anti-sentimental-ism is everywhere on display, for example in his account of the bullfight, where he insists that concern for the animals' suffering must be replaced with an entirely aesthetic assessment of the disembowelling of horses and the lancing of bulls (1932: 9–16).

How then to account for the apparent sentimentalism and anthropomor-phism of David's relation to the elephant in *The Garden of Eden*? Obviously one explanation is that, late in life, Hemingway's properly modernist attitude to human–animal relations deteriorated into maudlin regret. Indeed, the novel reflects some doubt about the aesthetic value of this narrative, empha-sizing David's struggle for authenticity. 'All morning, writing, he had been trying to remember truly how he felt and what happened on that day . . . his feeling about the elephant had been the hardest part' (174). A second explanation is that the story does not reflect Hemingway's troubled flirtation with sentimentalism at all, but is actually designed to demonstrate David's ongoing immaturity. As he finishes the narrative he thinks to himself that '[i]t was a very young boy's story' (201). David's inability to detach from the victimized animal could also signify his emasculation, in a way that echoes the disdainful allusions to Robert Cohn's sympathy for the gored horses in *The Sun Also Rises*. Yet ultimately, both David and his lover Marita seem to find the story successful, in terms of the modernist criterion of authentic affect (204).[11] A third explanation can also be advanced: as Philip Fisher has suggested in the context of nineteenth-century fiction, sentimentalism need not always be conventional in its social effects, but can instead operate as 'a politically radical technique' that 'trains and explicates new forms of feeling' (1985: 17, 18). As I will argue in the next chapter, a return of precisely this function of sentimental narrative has been occurring since the middle of the twentieth century, as the influence of high modernism has receded. It seems possible that Hemingway's unfinished novel anticipates this effect.

Certainly, when examined closely, David's narrative in *The Garden of Eden* is rather more ambiguous than the kind of sentimental anthropomorphic identification mocked by Woolf, or the 'maudlin' ascription to animals of human attributes that Lawrence's characters detest. David's initial encounter with the elephant conveys the sense of a life form that is massively other-than-human, an engagement less anthropomorphic than zoomorphic. Instead of the perception that elephants are like humans, the passage describes a shared participation by human, dog and elephant in a sensory field which also includes other elements, such as the newly-risen moon and its shadows, the breeze from the hills and the scents it carries:

> [t]hey did not hear the elephant and David did not see him until the dog turned his head and seemed to settle into David. Then the elephant's shadow covered them and he moved past making no noise at all and they smelled him in the light wind that came down from the mountain. He smelled strong but old and sour and when he was past David saw that the left tusk was so long it seemed to reach the ground.... The dog kept close behind him and when David stopped the dog pressed his muzzle into the back of his knee . . . David came close enough to see [the elephant] cut off the moon again and to smell the sour oldness . . . [W]hen David moved up toward the bulk of the elephant again he felt the wet muzzle against the hollow of his knee . . . David reached behind him and closed the dog's jaws gently with his hand and then moved slowly and unbreathing to his right . . . until he could see the elephant's head and the great ears slowly moving. The right tusk was as thick as his own thigh and it curved almost down to the ground (Hemingway 1986: 159–60).

Typically, Hemingway repeats a few simple elements – the size of the elephant's tusk, its old and sour smell, the touch of the dog's muzzle – in order to achieve a phenomenal realism. Yet the associations of these repeated details also bind the three figures together: the dog's nose and the odour of the elephant, which David also smells; the elephant's tusk and the dog's jaws, which David grasps; the elephant's tusk and David's leg, which the dog nuzzles. The three figures are united, not by vision or hearing, the two senses most privileged in modern humanist representation, but by smell and touch, modes of perception more strongly associated with animal sensation and communication. As Jeff Wallace argues (in relation to Lawrence), moments that appear to be anthropomorphic can instead arise from the recognition that 'distinctions between the human and the non-human might "leak" in more than one direction', so that anthropomorphism comes to seem 'less a "mistake" than an expanded acknowledgement of material kinship' between humans and animals, with the possibility that 'analogy can work both ways: if we are like them, they are like us; to the extent that we are animal, they are human' (2005: 135).

After David's father shoots the elephant and brings him down, he offers his son the kill shot into the animal's ear, but David refuses and Juma delivers it instead, 'angrily', because the elephant has injured him badly during the hunt. David wonders 'if the elephant had recognized [Juma] when he tried to kill him. He hoped it had. The elephant was his hero now as his father had been' (201). Even this apparent anthropomorphism actually represents a shift in David's primary identification away from humans, from his father and Juma, and toward animals, namely the elephant and the dog:

> I saw him in the moonlight and he was alone but I had Kibo. Kibo has me too. The bull wasn't doing anyone any harm and now we've tracked him to where he came to see his dead friend and now we're going to kill him. It's my fault. I betrayed him (181).

David understands the friendship between the two elephants in the context of his own reciprocated bond with Kibo, a cross-species identification so strong that he thinks that his father and Juma 'would kill me and they would kill Kibo too if we had ivory' (197–8).

Whether or not *The Garden of Eden* as a whole can be read as a revision of modernism's rejection of sentimentalism and anthropomorphism remains a matter for scholarly debate.[12] However that may be, David's story does represent another kind of challenge to the kinds of human–animal relationship privileged by Hemingway throughout most of his career, because it recognizes and foregrounds, in more than one way, those historical dimensions which are by definition excluded by therio-primitivism. The story focuses on a particular animal with a particular biography, who therefore cannot simply be another stand-in for wild animality in its transcendent and atemporal sense. Moreover, even the hunters in the story accept that sense of historicity which ethologists are now attributing to elephants: this animal is found because he can be relied upon to visit the bones of his *askari*, and he also perhaps attacks Juma in revenge for that killing. And David's story dwells insistently on the impact that human economics and history have on elephant populations. Juma and David's father are contributors to the ivory trade, and the tale hints at the possibility that elephant aggression might be the result of initial depredations by humans. David's father justifies the hunt by saying the animal was a 'murderer . . . Juma says nobody knows how many people he has killed', to which David replies, '[t]hey were all trying to kill him weren't they', and his father says, '[n]aturally . . . with that pair of tusks' (201–202).

The fate of the elephant, in fiction and out of it, provides a singular instance of the fundamental shortcoming of therio-primitivist modernism. In its distaste for modernity the therio-primitive impulse rejects the ideology of progress by stepping outside of history altogether, seeking solace or guidance in a timeless dimension where animals, human environments and the relations between them can be seen essentially, as they are, as they always have been. But history will not be transcended, and the material changes wrought upon the world by modernity cannot be evaded. Lawrence's mythic St Mawr falls back into the mundane life cycle of a thoroughbred animal: when last seen he is pursuing a thoroughbred mare, suggesting that his legacy will belong to the racetrack and so to the kind of sporting exploitation of animals that Lawrence derides elsewhere. Hemingway's apparently eternal Gulf Stream proves susceptible to historical degradation. The great whales, whose ability to evade capture lures writers as diverse as Melville, Lawrence and Hemingway into their repeated pursuit, diminish in numbers or are slowly poisoned by toxic wastes. The apparently limitless wilds of Africa are replaced with game reserves, and their extraordinary megafauna become a collection of commodities, a finite and managed resource, or a traumatized population of death-bound neurotics. Animals, even wild animals, are no more outside of history than humans are – indeed they remind us that as organic beings we, as they do, experience history in our bodies and carry the past in our flesh.

5   Animal Refugees in the Ruins of Modernity

The writers central to the first four chapters of this book, despite exhibiting otherwise conflicting attitudes towards wild non-human nature, all take for granted its expansiveness and its continued existence, whether as a challenge to human enterprise or a resource for its enrichment. Crusoe on his island experiments with the enclosure of wild space in order to make it productive, but remains surrounded by an untamed nature – represented in the framing narratives about his encounters with African lions and European wolves – that constitutes both a threat and an invitation to modernity. Swift imagines a globe that includes whole populations unknown to and ignorant of Europe. In Shelley's tale, the wildernesses of the Southern Hemisphere and the Arctic North, where the Creature feels most at home, connote the limits of European modernity. *Moby-Dick* mentions, only to dismiss, the possibility that sperm whale numbers may be diminished by human hunting. As for the modernists, both Lawrence and Hemingway envisage a wild nature – if not in industrialized England or urban America, then in Australia, Mexico, Africa or the Gulf Stream – still capable of providing inexhaustible aesthetic and spiritual replenishment.

With remarkable suddenness, this faith in the boundlessness of non-human nature loses authority in the second half of the twentieth century and is replaced by ubiquitous images of a diminished and fragile world. Recent human–animal narratives concentrate on claustrophobic and denaturalized environments, within which animal life – including that of the human animal – is captive and threatened. Often the entire planet appears as an exhausted Crusoe's Island, a prison rather than a defended enclosure, at risk from nature's depletion rather than its wild superabundance, from over-cultivation rather than lack of cultivation. Alternatively the natural world becomes a Lilliput, wherein Western modernity's appetite seems as prodigiously unsustainable, its waste discharge as voluminous, its ecological footprint as destructive as that of a gargantuan Gulliver. Or, more commonly still, writers imagine the globe as a vast scientific experiment, a worldwide workshop of filthy creation, as lethally out of control as Frankenstein's Creature.

Island, Ark and Zoo

An obvious recent example is the novel *2007* by Australian naturalist and journalist Robyn Williams. The premise of this satire is a worldwide breakdown of human–animal relations. The story opens with simultaneous acts of civil disobedience on the part of various species: forty baleen whales sink a Japanese whaling vessel, a mile-wide flock of pelicans occupies Heathrow airport, hundreds of cows invade Melbourne's Tullamarine Freeway, pythons attack a line of bulldozers poised to raze Amazon rainforest, foxes mass against a Buckinghamshire hunt (Williams 2001: 1–13). The world's pets, racehorses, farmed and zoo animals break out of their confines and, along with rebellious wild species, occupy the parks and green belts of the world's cities, which are soon densely packed with animal refugees (72–80). With global transport and communications disrupted, farming and industry compromised and business at a standstill, capitalist modernity is brought to a halt by the spontaneous agency of non-human animals.

2007 reflects a growing anxiety that the relentless expansion of modernity will inevitably create a reaction; that there is no space left for human enterprise to occupy without coming into punishing conflict with the natural world. The immediate source of this structure of feeling is the rise in environmental politics since the 1960s. As a character in Williams' novel puts it, 'all those warnings we've been pummelled with since *Silent Spring* forty-five years ago have come to be realised' (2001: 51). The allusion is to Rachel Carson's 1962 treatise on the effects of pollution. Along with the possibility of extinction by nuclear war, Carson asserts, 'the central problem of our age' is the contamination of the 'total environment' resulting from industrial-scale use of pesticides and fertilizers, testing of nuclear weaponry, and other 'new chemicals [that] come from our laboratories in an endless stream' (1962: 5–7, 8). For Carson, technological modernity constitutes 'man's war against nature' (7). In Williams' novel this perception is literalized when the human response to the animal insurrection threatens to escalate into an all-out global assault using napalm and automatic gunfire (2001: 150).

Silent Spring was followed by other influential publications, such as *The Limits to Growth*, a 1972 report that used computer modelling to predict a global crisis based on extrapolation of trends in consumption and demographics. Aiming to refocus the attention of the public from day-to-day personal concerns to 'long-term, global trends', *Limits to Growth* emphasizes the idea of a 'world system' which is 'finite', subject to 'earthly limitations', and currently in the grip of an ever-tightening 'positive feedback loop' or 'vicious circle' (Meadows *et al*. 1972: 22, 31, 86–7). The whaling industry is given as an example of 'the ultimate result of the attempt to grow forever in a limited environment' (151). At the time *Limits to Growth* appeared, the same rhetoric of environmental threat, planetary bankruptcy and refugee nature was beginning to permeate popular culture and politics. Photographs of the whole earth from space, presumably released to bolster public faith in the achievements of science, came to function as icons of the planet's smallness and fragility.[1] The first Earth Day was held on 22 April 1970, while popular singer-songwriters – Bob Dylan, Joni Mitchell, Cat Stevens – wrote plaintive elegies for a fugitive organic world. 'Look at Mother Nature on the run in the 1970s', quavered Neil Young at the start of the decade.

In 1976, William Kotzwinkle published *Doctor Rat*, a darker and more sardonic precursor of Williams' narrative, in which a rebellion by laboratory rats heralds a global animal uprising – beginning in Chicago, birthplace of both the animal disassembly line and Ernest Hemingway – amongst dogs, zoo animals, livestock, whales, elephants, apes, big cats, rhinos, and many other species. At the end of the novel entire populations of insurgent animals are wiped out by military force, while the crisis is attributed by biologists to 'an unprecedented radiation of instinctive urge toward mass movement' (Kotzwinkle 1976: 220). Thirty years later, trying to account for the flash-mobbing animals in *2007*, Williams' main character Julian Griffin tells the U.S. Vice-President that 'all these animals . . . are perceiving the same catastrophe. The obliteration of their entire habitat' (Williams 2001: 55). Later he discovers the threat is even more literal. Senator Hector Breen, with the support of the White House, has developed a plan to eliminate all vertebrate species (excluding humans) by means of a genetically engineered virus that will make them infertile. Breen proposes

> [t]hat the cost saving to humanity would be vast – most infectious diseases gone, pastoral land freed up, no crowded species jumping from over-confined, shrinking habitats to do mischief. That the future of our civilization will be based on growing the meat and organic supplies we need in suburban factories, so farm animals will be redundant. And that from now on the idea of wild things is passé. Not only will there be nowhere for them to be wild, we will soon regard anything truly feral . . . with astonishment (156–7).

The scenarios central to both *Doctor Rat* and *2007* exemplify the late twentieth- and early twenty-first-century human–animal narrative, which insistently shows the result of modernity's manipulation of the non-human world as the global destruction of 'wild nature' itself.

The same pessimism shapes Margaret Atwood's *Oryx and Crake*. The novel opens with the narrator, Snowman, an exhausted and cynical Crusoe, apparently the only human survivor of a worldwide virus, a 'castaway of sorts' who subsists on the detritus of a ruined techno-culture (Atwood 2003: 41). He recalls his life before the virus, spent in artificially maintained compounds, where a scientific elite lives on processed food and relaxes in gardens landscaped with fake rocks (199). Meanwhile the rest of the world is contracted for consumption via cyberspace. Jimmy (the young Snowman) enjoys strategy games based on world military domination, trade in historical atrocities and classic artworks, or scenarios of species extinction (77–81).

Or else he searches for online pornography such as that provided by HottTotts, a 'global sex-trotting site' which reduces the third world to a Crusovian or Swiftian theme park catering for first world appetites. One scene shows a man with several little girls like a 'gargantuan Gulliver-in-Lilliput', a 'life-sized man shipwrecked on an island of delicious midgets' (89–90). Beyond these over-exploited social spaces, a post-natural world is descending into ruin: 'the coastal aquifers turned salty and the northern permafrost melted and the vast tundra bubbled with methane, and the drought in the midcontinental plains regions went on and on, and the Asian steppes turned to sand dunes' (24).

Williams and Atwood both produce narratives of accelerated environmental degradation, portraying a world in ruins as the legacy of the modern constitution. Two decades earlier, in the dying years of the Cold War, the same postmodern critique was often associated with the proliferation of nuclear arms. For example Bernard Malamud's *God's Grace* (1982) opens with a 'thermonuclear war between the Djanks and the Druzhkies, in consequence of which they had destroyed themselves, and, madly, all other inhabitants of the earth' (Malamud 1982: 3). Calvin Cohn, another last man alive (or so he thinks), survives because he is conducting oceanographic research in a deep-sea submersible when 'nuclear havoc' strikes (8). By suggesting that the thermonuclear war causes a worldwide deluge, Malamud is able to confine his protagonist to an island and thus draw satirically upon *Robinson Crusoe* as the ur-text of modernity, while at the same time engaging with contemporary concerns about the global destruction of habitats. Failing to learn from the grim lesson of the novel's opening *mise en scène*, Cohn attempts to repeat Crusoe's single-handed achievement of modernity by taming and 'improving' a potentially hostile nature – not in this case by domesticating goats, but by humanizing and civilizing the apes who take refuge on the island with him.

Another 1980s novel, Timothy Findley's *Not Wanted on the Voyage* (1984) also portrays an apocalyptic flood, in a narrative that explicitly revises the biblical story of Noah. Findley's reflection of environmentalist anxieties about dwindling habits is vividly expressed when a patch of high ground, shrinking as the waters rise, becomes – like the city parks in *2007* and the island in *God's Grace* – 'a haven for every kind of animal refugee in every kind of condition':

> [m]arsh animals – field animals – river animals – domestic animals – every one of them out of place – moved in. Hunters and prey; hosts and parasites; a whole variety of birds and beasts and insects – all in competition for the same food – prowled through the twilight. Every berry, every succulent leaf, every frog and every mouse was being destroyed (145).

In all these novels, then, islands (and boats) feature as the grim result of modernity rather than (as in Defoe's tale) an inviting challenge to it. They provide the setting for extended narratives of habitat destruction, environmental degradation, and the displacement and extinction of animal life. In *Not Wanted on the Voyage*, certain whole species – dragons, faeries, unicorns and demons – are eliminated by their exclusion from the ark by Dr Noah Noyes. And when, following its launch on the waters, the vessel is visited by dolphins and whales, Noah orders their slaughter, perceiving them as 'Pirates from the Pit', representatives of an ongoing natural vitality independent of the dispensation provided by Yaweh, since they can survive his flood without relying on Noah's preservationist efforts (236–7). Meanwhile inside the ark the saved animals suffer in their impoverished environments: One Tusk the elephant develops a stomach ulcer due to the 'endless dark' of the bottom deck; Hippo wants to submerge but only gets 'a pailful of water every morning'; Rhino 'needs a dust wallow', but can find 'only bilge and wet manure' (226–7). For other species, such as sheep and cows, the ark is a feedlot, a vertically-integrated farm in which Noah's son Japeth regularly visits the lower decks to slaughter cattle for his father's dinner (292–3). 'We are truly captives here', thinks Noah's wife, including herself among the animals, 'and yet they have called this: *being saved*' (251).

More than anything else, in its dual nature as refuge and prison, a place of salvation and place of deprivation, the ark in *Not Wanted on the Voyage* embodies the paradox of the zoo – which is in fact another of those forms of contracted space commonly found in contemporary human–animal narratives. Findley's portrayal of conditions aboard Dr Noyes' vessel contrasts ironically with the contemporary deployment, by zoos themselves, of Noah's ark as an icon of their own mission. In recent decades zoos have portrayed themselves as contributors to global conservationism: providers of sanctuary for animals at risk in the wild, educators of the public in regard to biodiversity, facilitators of the study of rare species, and sponsors of breeding programmes for endangered populations. In his study of literary representation of zoos, however, Randy Malamud cites Valerie Martin's identification of 'the fallacy of captive breeding programmes': because '[h]abitats are shrinking by the minute', the animals raised in zoos can't be returned to the wild; 'there's just no place for them to go'. Hence, while according to their own self-promotion '[z]oos operated as arks, holding animals for the future . . . it was a future that would never really come' (Martin 1994: 287; cited in Malamud 1998: 45). Similarly, at the end of *Not Wanted on the Voyage*, there is no indication that the flood waters will recede, or that nature will recover from Yaweh's petulant gesture. Although a rainbow appears to signify that the rain has stopped and a dove returns with an olive branch suggesting the reappearance of land, Noah's wife knows these are tricks. The paper rainbow and dry olive twig are the same ones that Noah used in a theatrical production prior to the deluge (Findley 1984: 351–2 italics in original).

Randy Malamud argues that zoos, rather than simply failing in their self-proclaimed conservation of biodiversity, actually promulgate attitudes that undermine this goal. Zoos 'put animals on exhibit as "specimens" and "social groups" torn from the very fabric of their ecosystems wherein they have evolved' (Fox 1990: 153; cited in Malamud, 1998: 346 note 16). Instead of daily interactions with the innumerable features of their native habitats, and with other species, zoo animals are utterly dependent on human provision for their needs. Zoos also remove (for the most part) animals' capacity for agentive resistance to interaction with humans, and subject them to constant surveillance and control. They commodify the experience of human–animal interaction, and perpetuate the belief that humans have the right to manage the natural world in both its most general and its most intimate processes (Malamud 1998: 30–2, 35–6, 43–9, 254–8). According to Malamud, the environmentalist credentials of zoos are merely an alibi for their continuing exploitation of non-human animals by global commodity culture:

> [i]n the same way that the nineteenth-century London Zoo was designed to make visitors proud of vicarious engagement in their culture's imperial prowess, today's zoos . . . condition the public to savor its participation in the thriving Western commercial culture of the late twentieth century; its privileged charge of keeping/possessing/experiencing the zoo's exotica . . . The responsibilities that, we are told, accompany our society's consumer prosperity are strikingly similar to the responsibilities that citizens in British imperial society took upon themselves . . . Zoo visits are not primarily about having fun watching animals, according to the luminary directors at the cutting edge of today's zoos . . . but about saving the planet (91–2).

Peter Høeg's *The Woman and the Ape* (1996) centres on the ambiguous function of the zoo. The novel's protagonist, Madelene, is married to Adam Burden, who with his sister Andrea works for London Zoo, a vocation they view as an enlightened response to global environmental conditions. When Madelene doubts the practice of keeping animals in captivity, Andrea tells her what a jaguar, for example, would endure 'in the swamp forests of western Brazil': three out of five die in infancy, one in two of the remainder reach sexual maturity, one in eight succeeds in mating, and '[a]fter that they die of hunger. Or thirst. If they're not eaten by other jaguars. Or gored by wart hogs' (Høeg 1996: 80). Yet the novel also emphasizes the same point made by Randy Malamud, that zoos are the legacy of British imperial history. The Burdens live in Mombasa Manor, built by parents who made their fortune as imperialists in India and British East Africa; ushering Madelene into a shed full of hunting trophies, Adam tells her that 'his parents' object had been to shoot, collect and exhibit . . . But the world had changed, now was the time to study, present and preserve' (46).

In order to clinch his bid to become director of the London Zoo, Adam has imported from the wild a specimen of a previously unknown type of great ape, closer to humans even than chimpanzees. In the course of the novel, Madelene becomes increasingly drawn to the ape, and sceptical about the Burdens' intentions. As she fantasizes about setting the ape free, though, she realizes there is no longer any 'wild nature' to which he can return:

> [w]hat she had seen from that building at Aldgate was a city that stretched to the ends of the earth. And even though she knew that to be impossible . . . [w]hat mattered was the principle of the city – modern civilization *per se*. Madelene saw that there was no longer any end to that, it had totally enmeshed the earth. There was no longer any *outside* for the ape at her elbow. Any zoo, any game reserve, any safari park whichever was now contained within the bounds of civilization (Høeg 1996: 74 italics in original).

Madelene's vision encapsulates the postmodern perception that 'the wild', in general and at large, no longer exists, having been replaced by refuges, arks, sanctuaries, parks, reserves and zoos. The same condition is represented, albeit from the perspective of animals themselves, in *The White Bone*, Barbara Gowdy's novel about African elephants. These animals inhabit a domain pervaded by threats from human hunters and poachers of ivory, and littered with their refuse: broken machinery, traps, wire fences. The novel follows the search for the legendary Safe Place, 'a place of tranquillity and permanent green browse' beyond the reach of the hunters (Gowdy 1999: 44). As the elephants discuss their destination, however, it becomes clear that even this promised land is the product of a special dispensation from modernity. Asked whether there are no humans in the Safe Place, the old bull Torrent admits '[t]here are, but they are of a different breed entirely. Peaceful. Entranced . . . They don't covet our tusks, our feet or our flesh' (73). The calf Mud has a vision of the Safe Place as a plain that 'glints with the green of new grass' and is full of elephant cows, calves and newborns. Then the vision extends to take in a human watching harmlessly from a parked vehicle: the Safe Place is evidently a wildlife reserve (316–17).[2]

Each of the writers surveyed so far portrays a world in which animal habitats are entirely shaped by human interests, within which even 'wild' animals come and go, live or die, according to the plans of governments, multinational investors, ecology managers and eco-tourism operators. However, not all contemporary novels are so negative in their portrayal of current human–animal geographies. Like the other texts discussed above, the immensely popular *Life of Pi* by Yann Martel focuses on human–animal relations in a severely restricted setting, but from a rather different perspective. The title character recounts his survival after a ship transporting his family's zoo collection from Pondicherry to Canada sinks in the Pacific. Marooned on a lifeboat with a Bengal tiger, Pi realizes that '[i]t was not a question of him or me, but of him *and* me. We were, literally and figuratively, in the same boat. We would live – or we would die – together' (Martel 2002: 164 italics in original). By establishing a relationship with the tiger, Pi survives 227 days until the lifeboat reaches the coast of Mexico, where he stumbles ashore while the tiger disappears into nearby jungle. Pi's conviction that he stands a better chance of survival if he can keep the tiger alive – surely a rather counter-intuitive one – is accepted by the reader because it encapsulates a dominant environmentalist structure of feeling, according to which the crucial factor in safeguarding the continuation of life in general is the preservation of inter-relationships between species.[3] As another of contemporary fiction's emblematic arks or Crusovian islands, Pi's lifeboat represents the simplest form of this vital interaction, providing an allegory of biodiversity: environmentally speaking, humans and animals are 'in the same boat'.

Examined more closely, though, the environmentalist veneer of *Life of Pi* proves rather thin. This becomes apparent in the novel's representation of zoos, and its associated theory of the distinction between humans and other animals. Far from being portrayed as a place of 'deadened sensibility' (Malamud 1998: 15) or environmental deprivation, the zoological park owned by Pi's family is idealized. According to Pi it is 'huge', 'spread over numberless acres', with an incessant 'riot of flowers', where visitors sit or walk in tranquillity (Martel 2002: 12–13). His description underemphasizes the presence of cages and barriers: instead, '[s]uddenly, amidst the tall and slim trees up ahead, you notice two giraffes quietly observing you', or else the visitor finds 'two mighty Indian rhinoceros' beyond 'a low wall' (13). On one hand the zoo is compared with a luxury hotel in which the 'guests' receive 'not only lodging but full board' and 'receive a constant flow of visitors' (13); on the other it is a place where humans can immerse themselves in the wonders of nature, a 'paradise on earth' in which the young Pi becomes 'a quiet witness to the highly mannered, manifold expressions of life that grace our planet' (14–15). Pi also rehearses the argument voiced by Andrea Burden in Høeg's novel, that captive animals are protected from the vicissitudes faced by their 'free' counterparts. 'Animals in the wild', Pi asserts, 'lead lives of compulsion and necessity within an unforgiving social hierarchy in an environment where the supply of fear is high and the supply of food low and where territory must constantly be defended and parasites forever endured' (16). Hence they are, 'in practice, free neither in space nor in time, nor in their personal relations'. On the contrary,

> [a]nimals are territorial. That is the key to their minds. Only a famil-
> iar territory will allow them to fulfil the two relentless imperatives of
> the wild: the avoidance of enemies and the getting of food and water.
> A biologically sound zoo enclosure . . . is just another territory, pecu-
> liar only in its size and in its proximity to human territory. That it is so
> much smaller than what it would be in nature stands to reason.
> Territories in the wild are large not as a matter of taste but of neces-
> sity. In a zoo, we do for animals what we have done for ourselves with
> houses: we bring together in a small space what in the wild is spread
> out (17).

Pi's account of the contracted space that typifies the condition of contemporary non-human animals – that of the zoo, the island and the enclosure – makes into virtues those very features which the other novels discussed above portray as most debilitating: constriction of movement along with control by, dependence upon, and intimate proximity to, human beings.

Of course the merest knowledge of either zoos or zoology is sufficient to discredit Pi's claims, which cannot account (among other things) for the pathologically repetitive behaviour of many confined animals, the needs of migratory species whose territories are defined not by boundaries but by vastly extensive paths of travel, the distress produced by inappropriate climatic conditions, or the other incalculable effects of removing organisms from the network of relationships that comprise their native habitats. These considerations are ignored because Martel is less concerned with the fate of animals than with advancing a particular view of the human condition, which is – despite the novel's glossy postmodern style – fundamentally that of humanist modernity. In short, *Life of Pi* presents humans as innately different from and superior to animals because they possess a greater capacity for rational inventiveness, adaptability to new circumstances, and mobility.

The novel's reclamation of the values of scientific modernity is evident in the way it echoes – with admiration, unlike the other texts discussed above – Crusoe's triumph over nature. Marooned after a shipwreck on a circumscribed terrain, fearful of wild animals, Pi survives in the same way that Crusoe does – through the application of a calculating rationality: '[r]eason is the very best tool kit' (Martel 2002: 298). He begins as his forerunner did, by taking an inventory of items salvaged from the shipwreck (145–6). He rations these with mathematical precision, while at the same time putting them to ingenious new uses. He even establishes his control over nature, like the hero of the original Robinsonnade, by 'farming', albeit for water rather than milk or meat: the solar stills, with their plastic 'udders' full of fresh water, remind Pi of 'cows grazing in a field' (188). Of course the most evidently Crusovian relationship in the story is Pi's life-preserving domination of Richard Parker, the tiger, who represents all the aspects of the savage nature that Defoe's protagonist masters: he is at once Pi's wild beast enemy, his domesticated pet and his man Friday.

The technique employed by Pi to establish his dominance over the tiger combines applied rationality with the other primary modern virtue, that of mobility. Pi trains Richard Parker by provoking the tiger to intrude on his territory and then punishing him for doing so by rocking the boat back and forth. This works, he claims, because tigers are prone to seasickness, so the animal comes to associate the human's territory with nausea and avoids intruding (Martel 2002: 202–4). In other words, Pi dominates the tiger, and therefore survives, because humans are good travellers and animals are not. The credibility of this proposition depends, of course, on the reader's agreement with Pi's earlier comments about zoos, and especially the suggestion that the 'key to [animals'] minds' is their territoriality, which is understood as an innate acceptance – even or especially in 'nature' – of confinement to limited space.

However implausible this may be as a hypothesis about animals, its main purpose is to serve the novel's view of humanity. Martel is the son of diplomats whose family life included periods living in Quebec, Spain, Alaska, British Columbia, Costa Rica, France, Mexico and Ottawa. His perception of global mobility as fundamental to human nature is both a product of the history of modernity – as embodied by Crusoe and Gulliver, those inveterate globetrotters – and a reflection of the particular form taken by this disposition in late capitalism, which is most purely expressed by tourism. Pi's sensibility is, more than anything else, that of the tourist. His affection for zoos as embodiments of the wonder of nature, and his comparison of captive animals with hotel guests, suggest the superficial perspective of the transient visitor. Even the long digression on Pi's religious experiences reads like a tourist guidebook, for he collects faiths like souvenirs. In the same way, on his lifeboat tour of the Pacific, Pi's relinquishing of his native vegetarianism is presented less as a necessity than as an opening up to the omnivorous taste for difference that characterizes a truly modern, global disposition. Thus, although it poses as the simple story of a simple Indian boy, Martel's novel refuses the particularities of location and floats free of historical and geopolitical context, and in so doing offers a rhapsody to the power of the (touristic, all-consuming, privileged, globalized, Western) human spirit. This imperialistic and modern disposition, which applies to people, artefacts, environments and animals, is summed up in Pi's relation to the emblematic animal with whom he is marooned, a wild tiger captured for a zoo, given an English name, exported across the world, tamed like a circus animal and finally, irretrievably, lost to his native environment.

If tourism embodies the privileged disposition created by global consumer capitalism, its counterpoint is forced migration or detention, the displacement of populations, the internment of refugees. In a parallel sense, the underside of the zoo and wildlife park is the factory farm and the pound or animal shelter. The latter is the setting for J. M. Coetzee's novel *Disgrace*. The protagonist, David Lurie, leaves his university position after a scandal resulting from his sexual predation of a young student and is granted 'refuge on an indefinite basis' by his daughter, Lucy, who runs a boarding kennel on a rural smallholding (2000: 65). Despite his initial disdain for the dogs, Lurie finds himself identifying with them, especially those who are now surplus to the requirements of the new South Africa. In one scene Lucy finds him stretched out on the concrete floor of a cage beside Katy, an old bulldog bitch: tickling the dog behind the ears, he murmurs: '[a]bandoned, are we?' (78). Bereft of any meaningful occupation, Lurie helps out Lucy's friend Bev Shaw at her crowded animal clinic. This mostly involves euthanizing unwanted dogs. Coming from the nearby shanty-town, these animals are the organic surplus of colonial modernity, suffering from a range of ailments, 'but most of all from their own fertility' (142); their superfluity contrasts with the social function of the dogs Lucy cares for: 'Dobermanns, German Shepherds, ridgebacks, bull terriers, Rottweilers. "Watchdogs, all of them . . . [w]orking dogs"' (61). Nevertheless, both classes of dogs live or die according to their ability to serve the social pattern, the distribution of security-protected wealth and over-fertile poverty in turn-of-the-millennium South Africa. The fate of Bev Shaw's animals is associated with that of a human underclass by a literary allusion that occurs to Lurie: '[t]he dogs are brought to the clinic because they are unwanted: *because we are too menny*' (146: italics in original). The phrase comes from Thomas Hardy's *Jude the Obscure*, from the note left by Jude's eldest child when he hangs himself and his siblings, believing this sacrifice will free his parents from the increasingly difficult task of providing for them. Coetzee thus links his novel with Hardy's, which documents the process by which, as a result of nineteenth-century industrialization, the rural working class became disposable, indeed became an unwanted human surplus.

A comparison can thus be drawn between the animal shelter, as a site to which the organic residue of colonial history is consigned, and Nicholas Mirzoeff's description of the internment camp as the defining spatial technology of global late capitalism. For Mirzoeff, the function of 'the empire of camps' is 'to maintain low-waged manufacturing workers in their place in the global marketplace and reduce the social welfare costs of the advanced nations to the lowest possible point' while at the same time 'continuing to permit the instant, electronic nomadism of capital' (2002: 12). In the same way, the nomadism of animal capital – the global import and export of livestock, pet animals and zoo animals – is encapsulated by the zoological 'cargo' carried by the vessels in *Life of Pi* and *Not Wanted on the Voyage* (Martel 2002: 100; Findley 1984: 210–11), while its necessary converse is the forced disappearance of unwanted animals. In Findley's novel the latter effect is represented by the elimination of all animals forbidden a place on the ark: they perish either in the rising flood or in the great fire set by Noah as the ultimate sacrifice to his God (1984: 124–8). Findley draws on images of cattle pyres from the 1967 and 1981 outbreaks of Foot and Mouth disease in Britain, as well as anticipating media imagery from 2005 showing bonfires of live chickens in response to the avian influenza scare.[4] Such practices also manifest the attempt to control the mobility of non-human agents – in this case, viruses – while preserving the global mobility of agricultural capital. As Findley's novel suggests, the threat posed by non-human mobility may occur at the level of the individual animal (like the cat Mottyl who is smuggled aboard and breeds both kittens and sedition), the species (like the pair of demons, who take part in the uprising and are consequently thrown overboard), or at the viral or genetic level (like the rogue gene in Noah's family that produces ape-children, who are also thrown overboard).

The tension identified by Mirzoeff, created by globalization's need to maintain the nomadism of capital while restricting the movement of rogue populations, can also be shown at work by contrasting the novels of Martel and Coetzee. *Life of Pi* celebrates a touristic globetrotting sensibility, possessing worldwide visiting rights to a zoo-like world of (contentedly) imprisoned wild nature; *Disgrace* concentrates on the elimination of unwanted animals behind the 'closed and locked' doors of the animal shelter (Coetzee 2000: 142). As in Mirzoeff's account of the relation between global capital and the internment camp, these spaces cannot be understood separately. The expanding populations of unwanted animals – homeless pets, infected livestock, feral pests, or inconveniently placed wild species – are the by-products of those modes of animal consumption that define modernity: the enclosure of ever-greater areas of land for animal farming, the trade in pets, the eco-touristic taste for encounters with wild species. And thus the principle of organized containment is applied even to the populations of so-called wild species: whales, seals, elephants, wolves, bears, all are culled when their numbers begin to overflow the space allotted to them within the current geo-economic pattern. Indeed the oxymoronic phrase 'protected wild animal' sums up the tension identified by Mirzoeff, between global capitalism's demand for certain kinds of mobility and certain kinds of restriction, as they pertain to the non-human world.

Sacrificial Tables

Under modernity, all the human structures that circumscribe animal life – farms, zoological parks, slaughterhouses, fisheries, nature reserves – become sites for scientific manipulation. Hence, while like Crusoe's island they are spaces of refuge, the ship and the island in *God's Grace*, the ark in *Not Wanted on the Voyage*, London Zoo in *The Woman and the Ape*, the compounds in *Oryx and Crake*, the zoo and lifeboat in *Life of Pi*, even the animal shelter and kennels in *Disgrace*, are also Frankensteinian workshops. They are spaces created by and for the purpose of experimentation with the organic world.

Indeed the image of the entire globe as a post-natural, technologically saturated laboratory-at-large is a pervasive one in contemporary fiction. In *The Memoirs of Elizabeth Frankenstein*, which recasts Shelley's story from the perspective of Victor's bride, Theodor Roszak envisages the legacy of Frankenstein's experiment in just these terms. At the novel's conclusion Elizabeth awaits the arrival of the Creature who will kill her, and records a vision in which 'made things', the Creature's offspring, 'inherit the world' and 'devour the earth' (1995: 418). Similarly, in *2007*, Hector Breen presents his plan to eliminate animal life as the logical endpoint of modernity, the 'destiny' provided by 'the greatest, most powerful technology the world has ever seen' (Williams 2001: 219). He aims to recreate the planet as a co-ordinated productive system in the service of human needs, without pests, zoonotic diseases or livestock-produced greenhouse gases; without unscientifically 'sentimental' attachment to either domestic pets or untamed nature; without ferity or wildness of any kind (217). Such visions evoke what Horkheimer and Adorno in 1944 described as the 'totalitarian' legacy of the Enlightenment's 'dissolvent rationality', according to which animals would soon be 'completely eradicated', since, although formerly their 'irrationality' was needed as 'proof of human dignity', the triumph of techno-culture means that '[t]he earth, now rational, no longer feels the need of an aesthetic reflection' (1973: 6, 245, 251).

The common antipathy of literary fiction to techno-scientific thought and practice is best understood according to Latour's distinction between 'the sciences' and 'Science'. The former term, he suggests, refers to the multiplicity of theories and activities actually formulated and practised by scientists, which comprises a constantly changing, non-unified and non-totalizing network of propositions pertaining to 'the plurality of external realities'. The latter term, capitalized and singular, represents a reified and unified 'myth' that conceals how partial, provisional and contested the sciences actually are: 'Science' therefore gains social authority by claiming unique access to a unified Nature. Latour suggests a quasi-religious authority is arrogated by the Scientist, who assumes the prerogative to commune with the objective world of nature and to return to the subjective world of society 'like a latter-day Moses', bringing back 'the legislation of scientific laws, which are not open to question' (2004: 9–11, 249).

Bernard Malamud and Timothy Findley also associate the totalizing tendencies of Science with Judaeo-Christian monotheism. In Malamud's novel God is a detached and incompetent technocrat: in a brief exchange with Cohn he describes the latter's survival of the global devastation as a 'minuscule' but 'embarrassing' error (Malamud 1982: 3–4). Similarly, in *Not Wanted on the Voyage*, Yaweh indicates his plans to obliterate creation by speculating that 'the Great Experiment approaches its end' (Findley 1984: 89). And just like Latour's Scientist, Noah claims the prerogative of being Yaweh's spokesman and legislator, conferring with him alone before delivering edicts to his family.[5] He calls himself 'Doctor Noyes' – his wife wonders whether his title means 'experiments or divinity?' (266) – and undertakes research in his arbour, which is 'an alchemist's study, a theatre of magic and a laboratory' (18–19). Noah's procedures range from vivisection to conjuring, the latter exemplified by making a coin disappear beneath a bottle as it fills with water, which gives Yaweh the idea for the Flood in the first place (95–6). Noah's favourite subjects for biological investigation are kittens stolen from Mrs Noyes' cat Mottyl, who has been blinded in a previous experiment (18–19). Although the exact nature of this research is not revealed, Noah's interest in the rarer breeds of kitten suggests a concern with genetics (207). Later he dictates to his daughter-in-law Hannah 'his theories on *The Art of True Alchemy* or *The Anatomy of Quadrupeds*, in which he further explored the uses of zinc on the one hand, and the possibility of crossing a sheep with a goat on the other' (233).

With his theories about hybridization of both animal and mineral matter,[6] Doctor Noyes shares the abiding interest shown by the modern sciences in the creation of new products through combination. Like Frankenstein, however, he finds these alchemies sometimes produce dangerous reactions.

His imaginary immunity to the volatile flux of the interacting elements he manipulates is constantly transgressed. When he conducts a brutal gynaecological experiment on his other daughter-in-law, Emma, surgically opening her vagina with the horn of the still-living Unicorn in order that she can 'receive' her husband (264–6), this travesty of the myth of the unicorn caught by a virgin, an act of rape and forced bestiality, violates the human–animal distinction that Noah is obsessively determined to maintain. His own vulnerability to such intermixtures is also apparent when it is revealed that his son Japeth was born with an ape-like twin, whom Noah ordered destroyed at birth (162–5). Accordingly it is to Japeth that Noah assigns the task of killing another ape-child, Lotte, when Mrs Noyes contravenes Yaweh's instructions by saving her from the flood. Unaware of his own congenital proximity to such beings, Japeth 'think[s] it strange that so much fuss was being made' after he dispatches Lotte: '[a]fter all – he'd only killed an ape' (170). The satire is sharpened by the implied reference to the Christian tradition that makes Japheth the ancestor of Europeans, and by Findley's omission of the middle 'h' from his name. Furthermore, despite the old man's claims to the contrary, Findley makes clear that the simian taint in the family's bloodline comes from Noah rather than his wife. After the patriarch impregnates Hannah she also gives birth to an ape-child, who is immediately cast overboard (341–2, 349; Tiffin 2001: 36–7).

Findley's novel suggests that the metaphysics of religion and of Science (in Latour's second sense) alike are predicated on the sacrifice of living beings in the name of theoretical or theological abstraction. The death of the unicorn as a result of Noah's 'experiment' on Emma is immediately incorporated into his liturgical repertoire, a parody of the mutual reliance of Science and religion upon arcane vocabularies, accoutrements, locations and rites (Findley 1984: 271–3). The association between liturgical and experimental killing of animals has long been apparent in the use of the term 'sacrifice' to describe the death of an animal as the consequence of laboratory research.[7] As Lansbury argues, increasing use of this idiom by physiologists after 1900 reflects the transfer of authority and mystique from organized religion to professional science. 'The altar was translated into the operating table', she writes, where the researcher or surgeon presided over the mysteries of life and death (1985: 165). It is this aura of power that Findley challenges by showing the sacrificial order from the perspective of the sacrificed. Near the start of the novel Noah decides to punish his son Ham for the boy's inappropriate affection for non-human nature by insisting that he wield the knife in the sacrifice of a lamb:

> Ham took his father's place and held the lamb. He held it very tight against this diaphragm . . . He spoke to it – with his eyes closed . . .
> A shining moon-shaped wound had sprouted on his arm where the arm had pressed against the lamb – and the blood that flowed into Noah's basin was as much his son's as it was the slaughtered beast's (26–7).

Unable to refuse his father's command, Ham subverts it. By showing compassion for the lamb, by embracing and speaking to it, Ham elides the emotional distance that is supposed to separate the Scientist and priest from the objects of their rites. By cutting his own flesh with the same stroke that kills the animal, Ham turns the sacrifice back on its perpetrator. And by mingling his own blood with that of the lamb, Noah's middle son (whose name of course is a homonym for a type of meat) signifies a fundamental consubstantiality between human and animal which inverts the conventional meaning of the sacrifice (Tiffin 2005: 14).

This scene also repeats a moment that reappears throughout the narratives of Swift, Shelley and Wells: that of the vivisector vivisected. In *God's Grace*, a similar reversal is enacted. As a central part of his experiment in humanizing the apes who share his island, Calvin Cohn delivers a lesson on the meaning of sacrifice. He tells the story of Abraham and Isaac to Buz, his first chimp companion. Commanded by God to sacrifice his son as a sign of piety, Abraham is about to plunge in the knife when God intervenes. 'So Isaac's life was saved', Cohn concludes, 'and a ram caught by his horns in a thicket was substituted as the burnt offering, in that way affirming the idea of an animal in place of human sacrifice'. He draws an anthropological lesson from the story, which 'was probably a protest against the pagan sacrifice of human beings', and so an example of 'man humanizing himself'. To which Buz responds, 'Do you call murdering onimols a civilized oct?' (Malamud 1982: 73). At the end of the novel, once Buz has usurped Cohn's position as leader of the surviving primates, he orders him to be sacrificed. 'Where's this ram in the thicket?' Cohn asks 'with a bleat' as he is about to be killed, failing to understand that the metaphysical order that guaranteed human separation from and dominion over animals has been revised (222).

Coetzee's *Disgrace* also concludes with an instance of animal sacrifice. The scene is the animal shelter, where David Lurie is assisting Bev Shaw in her routine euthanasia of unwanted dogs. 'Was that the last?', she asks, and he replies that there is one more (Coetzee 2000: 220). He is referring to Driepoot, the three-legged dog who has attached himself to Lurie, frisking around the yard or snoozing at the feet of the aging, disgraced ex-academic while he sits in the sun. Despite Lurie's 'particular fondness' for this animal, and his awareness of 'a generous affection streaming out toward him from the dog', he chooses not to save the animal from the needle (214–15). Instead he opens the cage door to take Driepoot to the operating table.

> 'Come', he says, bends, opens his arms. The dog wags its crippled rear, sniffs his face, licks his cheeks, his lips, his ears. He does nothing to stop it. 'Come'.
>   Bearing him in his arms like a lamb, he re-enters the surgery. 'I thought you would save him for another week', says Bev Shaw. 'Are you giving him up?'
>   'Yes, I am giving him up' (220).

As the conclusion to Lurie's awakening to the suffering of other lives, which has been facilitated by his growing compassion for animals, this final scene is hard to read: it is both emotionally difficult and difficult to make sense of.[8] The language and gestures of sacrifice are certainly present. The description of Lurie's hold on the animal, comparable with Ham's in *Not Wanted*, also echoes a familiar idiom – 'like a lamb to the slaughter' – that links the act of euthanasia to the metaphysics of Judaeo-Christian sacrifice.[9]

By this point Coetzee's reader should be especially alert to animal figures of speech, since the novel is densely crowded with them. Earlier, Lurie has thought of himself as a snake, a butterfly, a dog, a predator intruding on a vixen's nest, a fox with a rabbit in its jaws, a viper, a 'shark among the little fishes', a 'strange beast' cornered by hunters, and of course the ultimate sacrificial animal, the scapegoat (Coetzee 2000: 2–3, 5, 9, 10, 25, 38, 53, 56, 91; Nyman 2003: 139). Yet in the context of the first part of the narrative, as expressions of Lurie's abstract, detached temperament, these figures are dead metaphors. The animals in each case are invoked only for their emblematic meaning, as Lurie has no interest in animal life itself. The turn comes after his exile from the university, a realm of ideas, to the country-side, where non-human life is an unavoidable corporeal presence. Once Lurie arrives at Lucy's home they both begin to inhabit, and so bring back to life, the kinds of dead metaphors he once used so easily. Lucy finds her father resting inside a cage with the unwanted bitch Katy: literally and metaphorically he is 'in the doghouse'. When Lucy is brutally raped, but decides to remain where she is under the patronage of her neighbour, Petrus, whom she knows to have been complicit in the attack, she responds to Lurie's objections by saying, '[y]es, I agree, it is humiliating. But perhaps that is a good point to start from again . . . at ground level. With nothing . . . No cards, no weapons, no property, no rights, no dignity'. 'Like a dog', replies her father. 'Yes', she agrees, 'like a dog' (205). By now the novel has taught the reader to accord this kind of simile a full range of meanings from the literal to the emblematic. Father and daughter are living out this identification with the animal that (among its wide range of meanings) stands for degradation and low materiality. Lurie's work for the animal shelter, disposing of the carcasses of unwanted dogs, brings home not only the full implications of his disgrace, but also the inescapability of the animal body, human and non-human, while Lucy's life, too, has become inextricably tied up with that of the dogs she looks after, most of whom were shot and killed during the attack on her home. This ethical acceptance of responsibility for the realities of deprivation contrasts with modernity's obliviousness to the material residue – whether it be a surplus of labour or of domestic animals – produced by privilege:

> [w]hen people bring a dog in they do not say straight out, 'I have brought you this dog to kill', but that is what is expected: that they will dispose of it, make it disappear, dispatch it to oblivion. What is being

asked for is, in fact, *Lösung* (German always to hand with an appropriate blank abstraction): sublimation, as alcohol is sublimed from water, leaving no residue, no aftertaste (142).

The surgery, operating table and needle, and the hospital incinerator to which Lurie delivers the corpses, provide the technological apparatus for the kind of sacrifice at work here: a secular ritual that borrows its metaphysics from the Christian Neoplatonic division between spirit and matter; an unscientific application of the paraphernalia of medicine. Here, then, is the wider application of the theologico-scientific rite of animal sacrifice: the removal of the inconvenient, unprofitable, suffering animal surplus produced by human social organization by rendering it immaterial, dispersing it into ether and smoke.

Taking these dimensions of the novel into account, there are two ways in which its final scene can be interpreted. The first would be to conclude that what Lurie is really giving up when he offers Driepoot for euthanasia is the prerogative of maintaining a privileged category of saved animals, whose existence is permitted only insofar as it is encompassed by the property rights which underlie contemporary capitalist societies. This reading is reinforced by Lurie's determined refusal of ownership: the dog 'is not "his" in any sense; he has been careful not to give it a name (though Bev Shaw refers to it as *Driepoot*)'; the affection between man and dog arises because '[a]rbitrarily, unconditionally, he has been adopted' by the animal, rather than the other way round (Coetzee 2000: 215). Giving up ownership rights to this dog in particular, in favour of relieving the suffering of unwanted dogs in general, is perhaps Lurie's version of starting again, with nothing, 'like a dog' himself: '[c]urious that a man as selfish as he should be offering himself to the service of dead dogs' (146). An alternative reading would take Lurie's sacrifice of Driepoot as a sign of his failure to step out of those metaphysics of sacrifice with which he has been struggling throughout the novel. According to this perspective, Lurie at the end of Coetzee's novel remains caught within the structure of humanism, as expressed by its characteristic treatment of non-human life, because ultimately he cannot bring himself to '*sacrifice sacrifice*' (Derrida 1991: 113; italics in original). The final reduction of Driepoot to a mere symbolic presence, a sacrificial token – 'like a lamb to the slaughter' – rather than an individual dog, repeats the earlier tendency to treat animals in the abstract or turn them into metaphors and thus surrenders to the anthropocentric metaphysics of *Lösung*.

The modern disposition that regards living things as abstractions – commodities, capital, raw material, objects of study – is also the target of Margaret Atwood's *Oryx and Crake*. In that novel, a scientifically advanced capitalism remakes the world by means of technological innovations abstracted from their material consequences. The instrumentalist cast of thought is most apparent in Jimmy's friend Crake, a scientific prodigy employed by the most prestigious of the biogenic corporations, whose pathological objectivism allows him to watch on the internet, without any apparent moral or emotional reaction, as sex tourists abuse third-world children on HottTotts, executioners behead prisoners on hedsoff.com, and frogs are crushed to death or cats torn apart by hand on animal snuff sites (82–3). The same cool detachment leads him to conclude that the human species is a biological dead end, to destroy it by means of the JUVE killer virus, and, like a latter-day Frankenstein or Moreau, to engineer a new humanity. Crake's anthropocidal virus is only one of a number of lethal, global-scale final solutions portrayed in contemporary human–animal fictions: Hector Breen's 'faunicide' in *2007*, the thermonuclear war in *God's Grace*, Yaweh's decision to drown his 'great experiment' in *Not Wanted on the Voyage*. These visions of a grand apocalypse, conceived in scientific rather than religious terms, derive from the crises of mid- and late-twentieth-century modernity, the various genocides and biocides that brought into disrepute its promise of endless advancement through technological innovation: [10] the concentration camps of the Third Reich, the Hiroshima and Nagasaki atomic bombs, the Cold War policy of mutually assured destruction, the growing evidence of environmental degradation and species extinction. Such phenomena suggest the bringing to lethal perfection of modernity's great experiment in manipulation of the biological world, an experiment anticipated in Crusoe's enclosures and Gulliver's importation and breeding of new livestock species.

The interconnections between various atomic-age technologies designed to organize human and non-human lives on a global scale are reflected in literary fiction as early as 1953, in Brigid Brophy's *Hackenfeller's Ape*. The story centres on a member of the rare (fictional) primate species of the title, who is being studied along with his mate in a zoo enclosure by Professor Darrelhyde, until the military decides to send the ape into orbit in a rocket as part of the space-race between the Soviet bloc and the Western allies. Of course from the 1940s onwards, a number of non-human primates were actually fired in the direction of outer space, and their survival rate was extremely low (Haraway 1991: 136–40). Attempting to save 'his' ape from such a fate, Darrelhyde appeals to the head of the League for the Prevention of Unkind Practices to Animals, who assures him that 'Percy is being sacrificed in a good cause' (Brophy 1953: 65), because the rocket experiments will lead to space stations allowing the allies to spy on 'the Ruskie' from space, 'like the eye of God, seeing everything he does, with his industrial areas and his centres of population wide open to us' (66). Brophy's satire thus suggests a structural link between the biological ordering of non-human animals – into lists of laboratory subjects sacrificed, taxonomic categories, reproductive statistics, habitat fields, research stations and zoological parks – and the administration of human space by the military-industrial complex. The Professor's superior, 'the Co-ordinator for Scientific Studies', suggests that as a result of the arms and space races, '[w]ar will soon be as unthinkable as hunting for one's food', because just as hunting has been replaced by the abattoir, 'open war is already being replaced by the concentration camp and the extermination chamber' (45, 52).

Here Brophy touches on the most controversial expression of a link between the wholesale exploitation of animals and the large-scale extermination of human beings: comparison between the Holocaust and the industrial farming of animals. Although this comparison is commonly used by animal rights campaigners and is consistent with the scenarios I have discussed so far, amongst the novelists discussed here, only Brophy and Coetzee address it directly, and only the latter in any detail. During his Princeton University Tanner Lectures in 1997–8, Coetzee presented two short fictions in which a novelist, Elizabeth Costello, addresses an academic audience on the topic of human–animal relations. The first of these, 'The Philosophers and the Animals', is structured by the comparison between the concentration camps and the industrial processing of animals (Coetzee 2003: 65). Not surprisingly, Costello's arguments offend some in her audience, not least a poet called Abraham Stern, who asserts that the link between 'the murdered Jews of Europe and slaughtered cattle' is 'a trick with words which I will not accept', an 'inversion' that 'insults the memory of the dead' and 'trades on the horrors of the camps in a cheap way' (94).

As this reaction demonstrates, the comparison between the Nazi concentration camps and the industrial animal farming and slaughter of animals tends to serve both the memory of the Shoah and the cause of animal advocacy poorly, insofar as it claims identity between two injustices that are, in human terms – that is in their social, cultural, economic and political causes, and in their intentions, meanings and consequences – far more different than they are alike. Yet the comparison persists,[11] perhaps arising from an imperfectly recognized sense that significant historical and technological links undoubtedly exist between its terms. 'Chicago showed us the way', states Elizabeth Costello; 'it was from the Chicago stockyards that the Nazis learned how to process bodies' (Coetzee 2003: 97). Her claim is a valid one, as Charles Patterson demonstrates. Chicago's Union Stockyards taught the rudiments of assembly-line manufacture to Henry Ford, whose influence on Hitler was considerable; while Himmler organized the death camps by drawing both on his own training in stock breeding and agricultural technologies, and on lessons drawn from American factory farming and genetic science (Patterson 2002: 57–79, 100–3). Nor did the application of industrial techniques to the internment and transport of human beings cease with the Third Reich. On the contrary, as Nicholas Mirzoeff argues, the contemporary 'empire of camps' – including the American base at Guantanamo Bay, the prisoner-of-war facilities in Iraq, and Australia's detention centres for illegal migrants – 'derives its technology from the concentration camps of the Nazi regime, the Gulag Archipelago and the Alien Internment camps of World War II' (2002: 12).

All of which explains why recent and contemporary novelists identify modernity with those technologies of spatial organization – from factory farms to concentration camps, from information systems to genetic engineering, from industrial-scale pesticides to nuclear armaments – which are designed to subject living populations, both human and non-human, to wholesale displacement, forced migration, large-scale incarceration, global surveillance, generalized control or mass extermination. The resulting portrayal of human–animal relations insistently recalls Swift's insight that rational instrumentalism can turn as easily upon humans as upon non-human animals – expressed in his case by linking British proposals to castrate or exterminate the Irish with the Houyhnhnms' plans to eliminate their own pests, the Yahoos.

Beastly Places

In much contemporary fiction, then, so-called wild nature is irremediably lost, or else subsumed into the manipulated and artificial spaces of the Crusovian enclosure or the Frankensteinian workshop. The wild beasts feared by Crusoe and revalued by the modernists are captured, domesticated, neutered; their fangs are drawn and their claws clipped. Martel's tiger becomes a circus performer (2002: 165); Atwood's scientists use wolf genes to create the ultimate guard dog (2003: 205); the ferocious bears in Findley's novel are so dispirited by captivity they lay their heads in Mrs Noyes' lap (1984: 233–4). As the history of modernity shows, however, the attempt to eradicate, regulate, commodify or otherwise manipulate wildness tends to result in ferity – the return of wildness, or an escape back to it, or its redirection into unexpected modes.

This reaction occurs with particular force in urban settings. The city has conventionally been understood as the ultimate expression of modernity's triumph over nature, purporting to replace human dependence on the organic environment with artificially constructed utilities providing unlimited food, water, shelter and warmth. It is also the space in which animals are thought to be subject to the most stringent control. Urban animals earn their place through their commodity value as pets, workers or exhibits in urban zoos, or else they are categorized as pests and so liable to extermination. Anthropologist Annabelle Sabloff asserts that during her research on perceptions of nature amongst city-dwellers, she was repeatedly told that '[u]rban life is inimical to nature'. And yet, as the points out, '[c]ities teem with animal . . . presence'. 'Family and feral dogs and cats roam every neighbourhood', while '[m]any species are attracted to the city precisely because of the cityscape itself': scavengers like rats and raccoons 'seek out household garbage cans, fast-food waste bins, and city dumps'; birds and bats colonize 'attics, wall cavities, hanging flowerpots, and high-rise ledges'; while a host of insects, earthworms, birds and reptiles 'are attracted by the hidden world of gardens tucked in behind countless houses' (2001: 5).[12]

In the same way, novelists challenge the illusion that the city is a zone free of both animals and their agency. In *Life of Pi* the title character asserts that '[i]f you took the city of Tokyo and turned it upside down and shook it, you'd be amazed at all the animals that would fall out: badgers, wolves, boa constrictors, Komodo dragons, crocodiles, ostriches, baboons, capybaras, wild boars, leopards, manatees, ruminants in untold numbers' (Martel

2002: 297). Similarly, in *The Woman and the Ape*, Andrea Burden describes to Madelene the scale of the non-human animal population of London. She enumerates the city's populations of working and pet animals, along with those in industrial farms, entertainment and laboratories, and then cites the innumerable 'animal lumpenproletariat of the city', the strays and 'semi-wild animals which strive to adapt to the city biotope', concluding that 'there is a greater incidence of animal life here than, for example Mato Grosso in the dry season. London is one of *the* largest habitats for non-human creatures on earth' (Høeg 1996: 67–8 italics in original).

Andrea cites this teeming urban animal presence to justify the further extension of modernity's project of studying and administering the organic world. For Madelene, however, the animal citizenry – especially the mode of illicit, non-human, feral inhabitation of the city practised by stray and 'semi-wild' animals – demonstrates the possibility of subverting the 'principle of the city – modern civilization *per se*'. Recognizing that the urban paradigm has 'totally enmeshed the earth', Madelene concludes that '[t]here's no such thing as *outside* now . . . If there's any freedom to be found it'll have to be on the inside' (Høeg 1996: 74–5 italics in original). Accordingly, when she escapes with the ape Erasmus, their route through London transgresses the human-organized modes of transport, following what Steve Baker describes as 'a non-human, *non-pedestrian* movement', a 'line of flight' (2000: 21, 118 italics in original).[13] Ignoring roads, pavements and tube trains, they hide in treetops, scale drainpipes and fire-escapes, and climb 'another storey to a heart-stoppingly haphazard network of flag-poles, cornices and balustrades. Then further up still, to the lowest unbroken run of rooftops in London'. By slipping into a kind of 'beastly place', a feral animal dimension excluded from anthropocentric configuration of the city, the escapees remain invisible to its human inhabitants.[14] 'No one noticed them. This progress of theirs was not just a journey through space, it also constituted a passage through the civilized consciousness' (Høeg 1996: 139–40).

The refugees eventually find sanctuary in St Francis Forest. Yet even this apparently natural location is encompassed and shaped by modernity. Originally established in the seventeenth century as 'an attempt to recreate the Garden of Eden' by the first Duke of Bedford, who conceived it as 'a horticultural machine designed to seize the awareness of the visitor and turn his thoughts to God', the forest epitomizes the combined metaphysics of Christianity and Science (Høeg 1996: 156). After many changes of ownership it is purchased by the Royal Zoological Society in 1970 and redeveloped as a game reserve, becoming the first breeding ground outside their native territories of the mountain gorilla, the Siberian tiger and the Australian penduline owl (157–8). However, throughout this history, St Francis Forest demonstrates vividly the potential recalcitrance of non-human environments, embodying Madelene's vision of freedom 'on the inside' of 'modern civilization *per se*'. Its founder is eaten by his imported lions while attempting to reproduce the Biblical scene of harmony between predator and prey (156–7). Over subsequent centuries the forest manifests such a profusion of resistances to human control – 'floods, droughts, lightning bolts, forest fires, outbreaks of Dutch elm disease, fire blight, attacks of Red Admiral caterpillars and heart-rot fungus' – that 'its owners had found it impossible to recruit workers locally'. Echoing Lawrence's description of Las Chivas in *St Mawr*, Høeg imagines the forest as a network of natural agencies 'so intractable . . . that some inexplicable form of geographical and biological anarchy appeared to reign there'. As such, St Francis Forest recalls the leviathan of medieval bestiaries, or perhaps Moby Dick: '[i]t was as though the land itself were an enormous creature, a buried whale which, when folks scratched its back, shook itself to throw them off' (157). Even the success of breeding programmes cannot be attributed to human mastery: 'St Francis Forest was one of the first research centres to have been arranged according to the modern-day acceptance of the fact that the more animals are left to themselves the better they will thrive' (158).

Høeg touches on a contentious issue within the politics of environmentalism itself. The growing authority of the environmental movement has recently been accompanied by an emerging critique of ecological managerialism – the governmental, bureaucratic and corporate response to public alarm about climate change, ecosystemic degradation, habitat loss and species extinction.[15] Such official measures are more often than not treated with suspicion by the novelists under discussion here, who portray them as reproducing – albeit in a new rhetorical guise – the same human, and especially scientific, intention to master nature that drove industrial capitalism and led to the current environmental crisis in the first place. In this way, contemporary human–animal fictions agree with sociologists of science such as Latour, who suggests that political ecology, despite claiming 'to protect nature and shelter it from mankind', most often involves humans in nature 'in a finer, more intimate fashion and with a still more invasive scientific apparatus' (2004: 20). Unflattering portraits of environmental management can be seen in Calvin Cohn's doomed attempts to manage interrelationships amongst his island's various primate species, Noah Noyes' brutal administration of his animal captives, and Andrea and Adam Burden's commitment to the scientific mission of London Zoo. Meanwhile, Coetzee's Elizabeth Costello attacks 'the ecological vision', according to which 'the salmon and the river weeds and the water insects interact in a great, complex dance with the earth and the weather'. For Costello, such a vision is complicit in the same Platonism that shaped both Cartesian modernity and modernist primitivism, since '[o]ur eye is on the creature itself, but our mind is on the system of interactions of which it is the earthly, material embodiment'. Believing that only '[w]e, the managers of the ecology . . . understand the greater dance' allows us to assume the right to 'decide how many trout may be fished or how many jaguar may be trapped' (Coetzee 2003: 98–9).

'Animals', however, 'are not believers in ecology', Costello adds (Coetzee 2003: 99) – an assertion amply borne out by the feral behaviour of both species populations and individuals. Suggesting that '[w]e had a war once against the animals', which we won 'definitively only a few hundred years ago when we invented guns', she suggests that

> there are still animals we hate. Rats, for instance. Rats haven't surren-
> dered. They fight back. They form themselves into underground units
> in our sewers. They aren't winning, but they aren't losing either. To say
> nothing of the insects and the microbia. They may beat us yet. They
> will certainly outlast us (Coetzee 2003: 104–5).[16]

Such phenomena, according to Latour, demand a new political ecology based not on certainty but on uncertainty, for which the maxim should no longer be '[l]et us protect nature!', but rather '[n]o-one knows what an environment can do' (2004: 25, 80). For him, nothing demonstrates the recalcitrance of non-human actors more than the surprises and scandals that occur in laboratory experiments, repetitions of what he calls 'the myth of Frankenstein' (193). In the same way, postmodern novelists frequently deploy 'Children of Frankenstein' scenarios that recall, implicitly or explicitly, Victor's disastrous enterprise, or his fear that creating a female creature would give rise to a worldwide plague of monsters.

An obvious instance is Atwood's *Oryx and Crake*, in which '[t]he whole world is now one vast uncontrolled experiment', where 'the doctrine of unintended consequences is in full spate' (Atwood 2003: 228). In fact, even before the wiping-out of the human population by the JUVE virus, the novel's scientifically dominated administration is vulnerable to unforeseen effects. Atwood ingeniously links a chain of accumulating ferities to real contemporary events. Snowman/Jimmy's favourite example of non-human recalcitrance is Alex the African Grey Parrot, whom he learns about in 'Classics in Animal Behavior Studies'. Alex was a real animal, whose appropriate use of English under the tutelage of researcher Irene Pepperberg challenged received ideas about human linguistic uniqueness, producing a contemporary version of Crusoe's reaction when addressed unexpectedly by Poll. Jimmy's favourite moment occurs when the smart aleck bird gets 'fed up with the blue-triangle and yellow-square exercise and [says], I'm going away now. No, Alex, you come back here! Which is the blue triangle – no, the blue triangle? But Alex [is] out the door. Five stars for Alex' (Atwood 2003: 54). This incident is based on Pepperberg's own reports and videos, which show that Alex did indeed use language with this level of appropriateness, and also refused at times to accede to the instructions of his human 'owner' (The Alex Foundation 2007). To the question of what animals mean, then, Alex replies both that he means what he says, and he does what he means to do. In *Oryx and Crake* this bird becomes a symbol of both entrapment and escape. Snowman dreams of the parrot's intentions being frustrated, of his receiving corn when he asks for an almond; then he dreams that Alex leaves him behind forever (260–1; 336).[17]

Atwood again refers to contemporary scientific reality when she describes luminescent green rabbits hopping through her post-apocalyptic landscape, descendants of specimens engineered with a gene from jellyfish to make them glow under ultraviolet light. This strain of animal – actually produced in laboratories during the 1990s – became notorious as a result of Brazilian artist Eduardo Kac's ongoing 'GFP Bunny' series (2000). In *Oryx and Crake* these rabbits interbreed with wild ones, and environmental managers respond by producing bobkittens, 'introduced as a control, once the big green rabbits had become such a prolific and persistent pest' (Atwood 2003: 95–6). Officially promoted as smaller and less aggressive than wild bobcats, the bobkittens 'soon got out of control in their turn. Small dogs went missing from backyards, babies from prams; short joggers were mauled' (163–4). The next step in Atwood's (partly) fictional history of accelerating ferity occurs when human agents – in the form of anti-corporate 'terrorists' MaddAddam – act in cooperation with non-human ones. They introduce a 'tiny parasitic wasp' to the installations where ChickieNobs – a laboratory-grown poultry product – are grown, 'carrying a modified form of chicken pox, specific to the ChickieNob and fatal to it'. Their other interventions include a 'new form of the common house mouse addicted to the insulation on electric wiring' that causes house fires, 'a new bean weevil found to be resistant to all known pesticides' that threatens the coffee industry, a 'minia-ture rodent containing elements of both porcupine and beaver' that destroys car engines, and a microbe that eats asphalt, turning 'several interstate high-ways to sand' (216). Crake locates the activists behind these genetic insurrec-tions and persuades them to join his own project.

The creation and release of the JUVE virus, which destroys the human grip on the planet and returns it to a state of absolute ferity, again echoes contemporary anxieties, in this case those relating to microorganisms. Early in the novel, in a scene drawn (like Noah's sacrificial inferno in *Not Wanted on the Voyage*) from contemporary media footage of cattle pyres in the wake of scares about agricultural epidemics, Jimmy watches the burning of 'an enormous pile of cows and sheep and pigs' infected, in another act of biological espionage, with a 'bug' that Jimmy's father describes as 'some-thing new'. 'Two can play at that game', says one of his colleagues. 'Any number can play', replies Jimmy's father (Atwood 2003: 15–19). Again, an instance of organic ferity based in reality achieves fictional escalation in Jimmy's lifetime: as the JUVE virus spreads and the human world descends into chaos, control over non-human agency slips away. Snowman lives in fear of meeting 'a crocodile, escaped from a defunct Cuban handbag farm and working its way north along the shore' (105). He also has to watch out for wild bobkittens, for wolvogs who have escaped their guard duties and become ferocious predators (108), and especially for pigoons. Created in the scientific compounds by splicing human genes into pigs, thereby producing a host with multiple organs ready for grafting into human beings, these animals frightened Jimmy when he visited their pens as a child, 'glanc[ing] up at him as if they saw him, really saw him, and might have plans for him later' (26). Now, living free, they have become danger-ous, not only because they have grown tusks – despite being engineered to be tusk-free, 'they were reverting to type now they'd gone feral, a fast-forward process considering their rapid-maturity genes' (38) – but also because they have the cognitive capacity to pursue the 'plans . . . for later' that Jimmy saw in their eyes as a child. '[B]rainy and omnivorous', with long memories and 'human neocortex tissue growing in their crafty, wicked heads', the pigoons attempt to hunt and trap Snowman using communication, cooperation, instrumental thinking and complex calculation of human behaviour. 'They have something in mind, all right', he thinks, when the pigoons lay siege to him outside a derelict building: 'they've had it planned, between the two groups . . . They were waiting for him, using the garbage bag as bait. They must have been able to tell there was something in it he'd want' (234–5, 267–71).

Atwood's narrative about the collapse of scientific modernity into feral chaos belongs at the end of a line of influence I traced in Chapter 2, which takes in *The Island of Doctor Moreau* and goes back to *Frankenstein* and *Gulliver's Travels*. *Oryx and Crake* opens with an epigraph from the latter text and is shot through with Swiftian moments (Atwood 2003: vii). Watson-Crick, where Crake works, is a latter-day Grand Academy of Lagado, known as 'Asperger's U. because of the high percentage of brilliant weirdos that strolled and hopped and lurched through its corridors. Demi-autistic, genetically speaking; single-track tunnel-vision minds, a marked degree of social ineptitude' (193). Taken to see Crake's work, Jimmy expects to see '[a] liver tree, a sausage vine. Or some sort of zucchini that grew wool' (302). And in the post-apocalyptic world, Snowman experiences a moment found in all three precursor texts, the nightmare of reverse vivisection: he vows to avoid 'tortur[ing] himself' by yearning for impossible treats that no longer exist 'as if he were some caged, wired-up lab animal, trapped into performing futile and perverse experiments on his own brain' (45).

The novel's most Frankensteinian or Moreauvian project is again an exercise in 'man-making', the engineering of a new strain of hominid, the Crakers. At first glance Crake seems to reverse the dream of his predecessors by dedicating himself to, rather than struggling against, the escape and autonomy of his non-human creations, manipulating Jimmy into releasing them after the JUVE virus has depopulated the planet. Like Frankenstein and Moreau, however, Crake is ultimately driven by a thoroughgoing scientific abstractionism, insofar as his masterpiece is designed in accordance with a radical version of two dogmas: Darwinism and its late-twentieth-century descendant, evolutionary psychology. Viewing the world as nothing but a complex interaction of biologically driven forces, Crake perceives human beings as mere 'hormone robots', albeit 'faulty ones' (Atwood 2003: 166). Convinced by this paradigm's account of the links between sexual competition, hunting and warfare, he attempts to remove these behaviours from his creatures' genetic programme. The Crakers are herbivores, and thus strangers to the competitive bloodthirstiness associated with predation. Their nutritional patterns are modelled on the proverbially harmless Leporidae (hares and rabbits), their dispositions

placid ('purified by chlorophyll'), and their communal identity so non-indi-
vidualistic that Snowman can hardly tell them apart (101, 158–9). Sexual
competition has been replaced by a ritual courtship in which the females in
oestrus show bright-blue buttocks and abdomens – 'a trick of variable
pigment filched from the baboons' (164) – and the males, in response,
display erect blue penises – 'a feature suggested to Crake by the sexual
semaphoring of crabs' (165). Thanks to Crake's zoomorphic innovations
'there's no more unrequited love these days, no more thwarted lust',
because 'it's only the blue tissue and the pheromones released by it that
stimulate the males'. Once the female selects her mates the 'sexual ardour
of the unsuccessful candidates dissipates immediately, with no hard feeling
left'. The result is '[n]o more prostitution, no sexual abuse of children, no
haggling over the price, no pimps, no sex slaves. No more rape . . . no more
property to inherit, no father-son loyalty required for war' (165).

Despite all these benefits, Atwood presents Crake's meticulous genetic
programming as another form of confinement, which locks his creatures
into a territorial and behavioural enclosure. The Crakers are stuck in their
own ark, so to speak, which is both sanctuary and prison. Twice a day the
men form a circle around their territory and urinate outwards: they are
scent-marking, an instinct given them by Crake in imitation of 'the canids
and the mustelids, and a couple of other families and species as well' (154).
To Snowman, 'the ring-of-pee boundary' recalls not protection but incarceration: it 'smells like a rarely cleaned zoo' (155). Their moat of wet earth
reproduces, in fact, the conditions under which they first came into being,
inside the Watson-Crick laboratory enclosure, a bubble-dome with an artificial blue sky, a 'projection device that simulated dawn, sunlight, evening,
night', 'a fake moon that went through its phases', and 'fake rain' (302).

Yet, for all Crake's ingenuity in designing a behavioural enclosure that
will keep his creatures safe, and keep other life-forms safe from them, by
the end of the novel there are signs that even the Crakers are about to go
feral. 'They're up to something . . . [that] Crake didn't anticipate . . . Good
on them, thinks Snowman. He likes it when Crake is proved wrong' (157).
The error made by Crake repeats that of Noah Noyes, Calvin Cohn,
Frankenstein, Moreau, Crusoe and the virtuosi of Lagado. Indeed it is the
miscalculation that Latour identifies at the heart of the modern constitution: the ascription of agency solely to the heroes of modernity, the scientists and ecology managers, and the corresponding failure to account for
the 'formidable capacity' of the objects of their manipulations to behave as
'troublemakers' and 'scandals', as 'obstacles' to mastery, as 'mediators with
whom it is necessary to reckon', as 'active agents whose potential is still
unknown' (2004: 81–2).[18]

Forest, Field and Wilderness

The attempt to represent the agency of non-human actors creates, for the
contemporary novelist, a problem of characterization. Insofar as the novel

is aligned with the ideology of bourgeois humanism, its most valued conventions – psychological realism, an emphasis on deep affect, the commitment to portraits of individual consciousnesses – are anthropocentric; that is, they are designed to allow the exploration of human (and humanist) character. To apply these techniques to a non-human protagonist is to engage in anthropomorphism. Not surprisingly, it is *Moby-Dick*, the *locus classicus* for the novelistic representation of non-human agency, which demonstrates the two favoured options for writers confronting this challenge. The first is to accept the necessity of representing non-human agents in anthropomorphic terms; the second is to find ways of describing agency at work through the interactions of a complex and widely-dispersed network of actants, both human and other-than-human. Taking Melville's cue, the writers under discussion here tend to combine these two approaches.

In *2007*, the narrative sometimes focuses upon particular non-human 'characters', for example two border collies who act as ambassadors between the animal rebels and the human authorities (Williams 2001: 85, 129–30, 242). At other times it evokes the phenomenon of networked agency. Attempting to understand how all the world's animals simultaneously decide to revolt against human domination, the scientists discuss

> examples in nature of organisms combining in unbelievable numbers but without clear leadership. Slime moulds do it. Shoals of fish do it, flocks of birds do it, changing direction as if one leader has given the order, shown the way. But there is no top creature, no actual *leader* (38–9 italics in original).

A blend of these two forms of representation – the portrayal of decision-making by individual actors, and the evocation of unpredictable networks of actants – occurs when particular animal characters act as catalysts for wider, ramifying webs of cause and effect. *Hackenfeller's Ape* exemplifies this tendency in its portrayal of Percy, the primate of the title. Via his long-standing relationship with Professor Darrelhyde, by means of the imitation for which apes are proverbial, Percy has begun to acquire some of the defining aspects of the human psyche. Possessed of a 'mental vision flicker[ing] on the verge of being human', Percy is 'an animal discontent with his monkeydom' who longs to learn human speech (Brophy 1953: 21–3). Perceiving these tendencies, the Professor resolves to save the ape from being sent into space in a military rocket. He breaks into the zoo at night with Gloria, a casual acquaintance whose help he has enlisted. Once the cage has been opened, Darrelhyde enters to address the ape, '[f]orgetting that Percy knew neither words nor reason'. His expectation that the animal will cooperate in a human way is immediately corrected: noticing the opening, Percy

> vaulted through the hatch, knocking Darrelhyde away, crossed the cage, emerged, skipped over the path – 'Stop him!' Darrelhyde shouted to Gloria when the animal had already passed her by – cleared

a fence, and then appeared, still, intent, outlined in moonlight, sitting on the crest of a sloping roof opposite (82).

Ignoring the pleas of his rescuers, Percy undertakes a feral tour of the zoo. Travelling 'exaltedly, by roof, tree and fence' – in a manner repeated by Erasmus and Madelene in *The Woman and the Ape* – he passes 'like a substantial angel across the Zoo, touching off here and there the note of each species, as if he had been a child left alone in a concert hall with the deserted instruments of a full orchestra'. He blows on two Indian Pandas and disappears before they wake up; ripples the water of the sea lion's pool but is 'a quarter of a mile away when he hear[s] the responding bark'; incites a display from a peacock who mistakes him for a peahen; provokes uproar in the Parrot House by jabbering through the keyhole, and then goes on to pursue, 'like Caliban, his wondering, half-befogged, half-enlightened way' (84–6). However, once this initial burst of action slows, Percy's 'mind grapple[s] with the idea that he had thrown away a chance. If he had trusted, he would have been in the Professor's company now'. Accordingly he searches for the way back to his cage, only to be shot dead by a zoo employee who mistakes the ape's gestures of reconciliation for an impending attack (101). Percy's behaviour while he is at large oscillates between two models of agency. One is the expression of a vivacious, unpredictable line of flight, which galvanizes the kinds of inter-species interactions that have been dulled by the imposition of barriers to movement. The second, a pseudo-humanist process of self-reflection, rational calculation of risks and advantages, and conscious decision-making – capacities half-instilled in Percy by his anthropomorphizing relationship with the Professor – leads to his death.

A somewhat different combination of anthropomorphic and zoomorphic modes of behaviour is at work in Findley's portrayal of Mottyl, Mrs Noyes' elderly cat in *Not Wanted on the Voyage*. Findley humanizes the notions of biological diversity, ecological balance and relationships amongst species. The ability of animals to read the behaviour of other species is translated into the cat's enjoyment of 'gossip' among her 'acquaintances' in the wood (Findley 1984: 42). Animals' intimate sensory knowledge of their locale is also processed into human terms: groves of catnip provide Mottyl with opportunities to get 'almost as drunk as Mrs Noyes'; areas in the wood that are nutritious, therapeutic or relatively safe are represented as 'holy places' or 'sanctuary places' (42–44). When Mottyl discovers the body of Barky the dog covered in flies 'she pray[s] for the dog – by leaving her heat-infested traces nearby'; a theri-anthropic representation of the necessary, cautious sensitivity of animals when faced by evidence of sudden illness or death (57). As the novel proceeds, the conventions of humanist agency are also destabilized, again by a constant code-switching between anthropomorphic and zoomorphic dialects, a two-way translation of (what Findley imagines to be) animal modes of experience into human ones, and back again. For example, Mottyl's actions are not deliberate decisions reached by rational calculus; instead they emerge from an internal dialogue with the 'calm,

even tones' of the '*whispers*' that she hears, the '[m]onotonic and reassuring
. . . instinctive, enigmatically perceived commands', which she attends to 'as
she did any other of her physical senses' (28 italics in original).

Once aboard the ark Mottyl provides the main outlet for ferity since, unlike the other animals, she is neither locked up nor supposed to be there at
all. According to Yaweh's decree the only two domestic cats to survive the
flood should be his own pets, Sarah and Abraham. But against Noah's
instructions Mrs Noyes smuggles aboard her own cat, already pregnant to
the tomcatting Abraham. Even before the ark is launched, then, the
principles of its ecological management have been infiltrated by the kind of
fertile non-human agent that is, according to Noah's and Yaweh's plans, not
wanted on the voyage. Moreover Mottyl's presence catalyzes the expression
of grievances among the imprisoned animals and their formation into
unprecedented alliances. When she falls to the bottom deck, the inmates
cooperate to rescue her; at Hippo's suggestion, One Tusk the elephant lifts
the cat to the deck above: '[w]e are all in this together – and we must do what
we can do' (Findley 1984: 227–9). She then sends a message 'passed from the
Unicorn to the Porcupine and from the Porcupine to the Weasel and from
the Weasel to the Vixen', creating a network of communication that will be
put to use during the 'Great Revolution of the Lower Orders' – an insurrection attempted against Noah's tyranny by the animals, Mrs Noyes, her
son Ham and his wife Lucy (231). The last-named, who is Lucifer in disguise,
also incarnates an other-than-human vitality: her hair has a 'glossy sheen'
like 'an animal's coat' (248), and while brooding on schemes for rebellion she
goes into a 'cat-trance' during which, like Mottyl herself, she listens to voices
(319–20). The revolution therefore arises from a combination of human and
other-than-human agencies. Mottyl calls Crowe, who unlatches the cages to
release the lemurs, snakes, wombats and nightjars, and then takes a message
to Emma, Japeth's ostracized wife, who removes the barricade keeping the
rebels at bay. Having gained control, the revolutionaries begin to answer the
requests of the still-captive animals: more light, special feeds, visits to the top-
deck to feel the sun (317–18, 335, 345).

Findley conceives the conflict between upper and lower orders in
markedly gendered terms. Noah's autocratic rule is promulgated in the
name of the patriarchal Yaweh, and depends on the labour of the muscular
Shem, the martial athleticism of Japeth and the acquiescent service of
daughter-in-law Hannah. In contrast the 'Revolution of the Lower Orders'
occurs by means of a network of feminine agencies embodied by Mrs
Noyes, Lucy, Mottyl, Crowe and Emma. These are figures associated with
the feral spaces beyond the religious and scientific parameters that govern
Noah's domain. When Mrs Noyes absconds from the ark to search for
Mottyl she relishes her escape into wildness:

> wandering through the fields or walking along some trackless path . . .
> she felt that civilization was falling away from her shoulders, and she
> was gratified. What a burden it had been! . . .

One morning, Mrs Noyes lifted up her skirts and – squatting in full view of the windows of an abandoned carriage – she peed. How wonderful that was! (Findley 1984: 146).

In this respect *Not Wanted on the Voyage* takes up and extends an association between recalcitrant non-human agency, feral space and femininity that stretches back to include the amorous young female Yahoo in *Gulliver's Travels*, the putatively fertile female Creature in *Frankenstein*, the puma woman in *Island of Doctor Moreau*, and D. H. Lawrence's biocentric heroines Ursula Brangwen, Kate Leslie and Lou Witt. The same identification of female characters with feral space or the vitality of non-human life occurs in almost all the novels discussed here. In *Disgrace* David Lurie finds himself 'in the wilderness' with his daughter Lucy, who tells her father that 'there is no higher life. This is the only life there is. Which we share with animals' (Coatzee 2000: 74). In *Hackenfeller's Ape*, the pickpocket Gloria agrees to help Professor Darrelhyde because her time in prison allows her to identify with the animals in their enclosures (Brophy 1953: 71, 73). In *2007* Kate Schumpeter is the first human to make contact with the leaders of the non-human rebels (Williams 2001: 114–16, 126–131, 135–7).

The same is true of at least two contemporary parodies of *Moby-Dick*. In Thomas King's *Green Grass, Running Water*, there is no great white male Moby Dick, but instead a black female whale called Moby Jane, who turns up every year to sink the *Pequod* while Ahab rages at his crew, throwing overboard anyone who dares to deny the whiteness or maleness of his epic antagonist (King 1993: 217–22). Chistopher Moore's satire *Fluke*, published ten years later, features dolphin-like cetaceans piloting 'whaleships' made from organic technology in the shape of humpbacks and spermaceti as part of a general mobilization of the organic world against humankind. Here again it is the female protagonist, the half-human, half-non-human 'alpha female' Amy, who plays the decisive role by negotiating between the two sides of the impending conflict (Moore 2003).

Of course the Frankenstein narrative lends itself especially well to the intertwining of gender and human–animal politics. In *The Memoirs of Elizabeth Frankenstein*, Elizabeth escapes the masculine-dominated world of the Frankenstein household to live for some weeks in the forest as what she calls a 'feral woman' (Roszak 1995: 279–99). Near the end of the novel she forms an intimate bond with a stranger called Adam who also lives wild, and whom she thinks of as 'half-animal' (391) – only to discover that he is, as the reader suspects, Victor's Creature. In *Oryx and Crake*, a freer adaptation of the Frankenstein narrative, two such associations also occur. Snowman invents a post-apocalyptic mythology for the Crakers in which Oryx, who may have been the young girl Crake and Jimmy saw abused on a pornography website, becomes a kind of nature-goddess. Her prestige underwrites the principle of respect for animals, the 'Children of Oryx', which is demanded by the Craker matriarchs. The second example is provided by Jimmy's mother. Initially a microbiologist working for

OrganInc, she becomes increasingly convinced that the corporation's experiments are 'immoral' and 'sacrilegious', 'interfering with the building blocks of life' (Atwood 2003: 57). Eventually she escapes from the OrganInc compound, becoming part of the global anti-corporate activist movement. In the note she leaves for Jimmy she writes '*I have taken Killer with me to liberate her, as I know she will be happier living a wild, free life in the forest*'. Killer, too, is a feral female: she is Jimmy's pet rakunk, a hybrid of skunk and raccoon. Although at the time Jimmy is outraged, thinking that as 'a tame animal, she'd be helpless on her own', years later Snowman realizes his mother was correct: 'Killer and the other liberated rakunks must have been able to cope just fine, or how else to account for the annoyingly large population of them now infesting this neck of the woods?' (61).

The Island of Doctor Yerkes

The shift in representations of human–animal relations during the twentieth century can be measured in reference to one species, the gorilla – indeed in reference to one gorilla narrative, *King Kong*. In Merian C. Cooper's 1933 original, Skull Island and its prehistoric, super-savage inhabitants are archetypes straight from the modernist therio-primitive bestiary. By 1976, in John Guillerman's remake, Kong has become an icon of the environmentalist movement. His island home is threatened by an avaricious oil executive and his fatal fall occurs from the summit of the World Trade Centre towers (Creed 2007: 72). And when Peter Jackson remakes the film again in 2005, Kong's island is portrayed as another of postmodernity's fragile, fenced-off ecosystems, 'one of the few blank spots' on the map of globalizing Western enterprise. In a mockumentary entitled *Skull Island: A Natural History*, Jackson accounts for the exceptional savagery of species on the island by explaining that its land mass and biomass have been shrinking as a result of geological activity, 'so all of the creatures who once survived on a much bigger piece of land have now been shunted into the middle as the island sinks and the coast comes in'. Skull Island is a foundering ark, threatened both by geological contraction and by the intrusion of modernity, as represented by Denham's hired ship, the *Venture*, with its cargo of exotic animals. Accordingly the giant gorilla himself – injured, exhausted, melancholic, endangered, 'the last of his kind', *Megaprimatus Kong*, whose 'extinction result[s] from a combination of nature's wrath and the weaponry of modern man' (Jackson 2006) – embodies contemporary pessimism about the future of wild animality. For Barbara Creed, the changes in Kong's characterization over seven decades derive from an equally marked alteration in perceptions of the great apes, resulting not just from the influence of environmentalist thought but more specifically from the work of primate researchers, both in the field and in laboratories (2007: 71–3). Creed's hint is worth following up with a detailed examination of the interconnections between primate-themed fictional narratives and scientific study of the great apes over the last century.

According to Donna Haraway, primatology in the first half of the twentieth century was a 'part of the system of unequal exchange of extractive colonialism' (1989: 19). Research stations were maintained in colonial territories, from which animals were also imported to stock metropolitan laboratories, zoos and museums. Haraway focuses on Carl Akeley – explorer, hunter, natural historian, taxidermist, friend of Theodore Roosevelt and founding genius of the Akeley African Hall of the American Museum of Natural History (AMNH) – as the epitome of relationships between Western humans and the great apes during this period. The AMNH display that best expresses Akeley's contribution is the Giant of Karisimbi, the 'silverback male gorilla that dominates the diorama depicting the site of Akeley's own grave in the mountainous rain forest of the Congo, today's Zaire'. 'The gorilla was the highest quarry of Akeley's life as artist, scientist, and hunter', writes Haraway, because the animal's 'similarity to man' makes it the 'ideal quarry', "the 'other", the natural self'. Hence she imagines the 1921 meeting between Akeley and this animal as a replay of Frankenstein's meeting with his alter ego on Mont Blanc (31). The Giant of Karisimbi is also Carl Akeley's King Kong, captured a decade before Carl Denham's, brought back from a savage wilderness for display in the centre of New York. And Akeley's hunt anticipates also the African safaris undertaken by Ernest Hemingway in the 1930s. There is the same competitive desire for an ideal trophy, resulting in a considerable by-catch of lesser specimens, and the same assumption of privilege towards both the non-human quarry and local human natives (Haraway 1989: 41, 53). These similarities are not surprising. Akeley's hunting and taxidermy are no less products of American modernism than *King Kong* or the works of Hemingway. Indeed, the way in which high modernism defines itself against high modernity can be seen in Akeley's faith in the nobility of his quarry, which Haraway contrasts with Paul du Chaillu's account of his killing of a gorilla in 1855, 'eight years after it was "discovered" to science', which emphasizes the animal's depravity and viciousness (Haraway 1989: 31–2). Whereas, 'in the context of colonial expansion, apes, and especially the gorilla, came to be seen as powerful personifications of wildernesses to be fought and conquered heroically by civilised man' (Corbey, in Cavalieri and Singer 1993: 131), by the 1920s this conquest was all but complete and the gorilla became a focus of modernist nostalgia for 'Nature', a 'potent symbol of innocence' that contrasted with the corruptions of civilization (Haraway 1989: 54).

Of course, modernism only achieved such force in the early twentieth century because the modernity it critiqued was still dominant. At the same time Carl Denham and Carl Akeley were exhibiting their gigantic noble beasts, living apes were being forced into the service of modernity as well. One example is described by Coetzee's Elizabeth Costello, who recounts the work of Wolfgang Köhler, conducted at a research facility run by the Prussian Academy of Sciences on Tenerife between 1912 and 1920. Aiming to study the mental capacity of apes, Köhler puts Sultan the chimpanzee into a cage without food. He hangs a bunch of bananas from the ceiling.

They are beyond the animal's reach, but the scientist has supplied three wooden boxes. Sultan has to figure out how to stack the boxes and climb up to reach the fruit. Next day Köhler makes the crates heavy by filling them with stones, so Sultan has to empty them before stacking. 'One is beginning to see how the man's mind works', remarks Costello (Coetzee 2003: 73). Then the bananas are put outside the cage, and Sultan has to use a stick to drag them closer. 'At every turn', Costello observes, 'Sultan is driven to think the less interesting thought'. Locked in isolation, deprived of regular meals, and shown food he cannot reach, Sultan is not supposed to think, '[w]hy is he starving me?' or '[w]hy do men behave like this?' Instead he is 'relentlessly propelled toward lower, practical, instrumental reason (How does one use this to get that?)' (72–3). Captured, caged, stuck on this 'island prison camp', this 'penal colony', Sultan is forced into a contraction of cognitive space as well as physical space:

> [i]n his deepest being Sultan is not interested in the banana problem. Only the experimenter's single-minded regimentation forces him to concentrate on it. The question that truly occupies him, as it occupies the rat and the cat and every other animal trapped in the hell of the laboratory or the zoo, is: Where is home, and how do I get there? (75).

Costello recounts Köhler's experiment from Sultan's perspective in order to challenge modernity's self-congratulating demonstration of its own privileged forms of thought, 'the specialism of a rather narrow self-regenerating intellectual tradition whose forte is reasoning' (69).

Costello's critique of practical reason follows the tradition of *Gulliver's Travels* and *Frankenstein*: a narrative about science, told from the perspective of the experimental subject rather than the experimenter. It also draws on the most influential literary great ape narrative of the twentieth century: Franz Kafka's 'Report to an Academy'. Costello compares Köhler's 1917 monograph *The Mentality of Apes* and Kafka's 1919 story. Both Sultan and Rotpeter, Kafka's ape narrator, are 'captured on the African mainland by hunters specializing in the ape trade, and shipped across the sea to a scientific institute' (Coetzee 2003: 72). Both are part of a global trade in organic specimens; both experience the contraction of animal spaces that expansive modernity produces. Rotpeter's captor is the father of the contemporary zoo, Carl Hagenbeck; two years later it could have been Carl Akeley; ten years later Carl Denham. But although he yearns for a 'way out', Rotpeter emphasizes that he does not mean 'freedom' in the human sense. Observing trapeze artists flying through the air during his time in Hagenbeck's circus, he realizes that the human idea of freedom means little more than 'self-controlled movement'. 'What a mockery of holy Mother Nature!', he concludes. 'Were the apes to see such a spectacle, no theater walls could stand the shock of their laughter' (Kafka 1999 [1919]: 253–4). The discipline of the trapeze artists exemplifies modernity's fantasy of mastery over space, but it is no more than a circus trick in contrast to the nexus of sensory, social and instinctual interrelationships that comprise animals' occupation of an environment.

For Rotpeter – as for Madelene and Erasmus in Høeg's novel – there is no longer any hope of attaining 'freedom', in animal terms, from modern space. 'I was pinned down. Had I been nailed down, my right to free movement would not have been lessened'. The immediate source of his confinement is not physical but epistemological; he is held captive by how humans perceive him: 'as far as Hagenbeck was concerned, the place for apes was in front of a locker – well, then, I had to stop being an ape'. Both Sultan and Rotpeter escape the corners into which modernity paints them by 'aping' – the hidden metaphor is an ironic one, since it is humans who force them into imitation – their captors. Sultan performs the kind of instrumentalist reason that Köhler looks for; Rotpeter goes further, and ends up addressing an academy of the kind that sponsored Köhler's work on Tenerife. He begins learning from the sailors on board the ship that takes him to Europe: '[i]t was so easy to imitate these people. I learned to spit in the very first days'. One man pays him particular attention because he perceives 'that we were both fighting on the same side against the nature of apes and that I had the more difficult task' (Kafka 1999 [1919]: 257). The brutal behaviours that Rotpeter takes for signs of humanity – his 'teacher' burns him with a lighted pipe when he is displeased – are not confined to the sailors, but apparent also amongst the bourgeois Europeans whose society he eventually enters:

> I read an article recently by one of the ten thousand windbags who vent themselves concerning me in the newspapers, saying: my ape nature is not yet quite under control; the proof being that when visitors come to see me, I have a predilection for taking down my trousers to show them where the shot went in. The hand which wrote that should have its fingers shot away one by one. As for me, I can take my trousers down before anyone if I like; you would find nothing but a well-groomed fur and the scar made – let me be particular in the choice of a word for this particular purpose, to avoid misunderstanding – the scar made by a wanton shot (251–2).

The urbanity of this passage, and its scorn for the hypocrisy of European civility, recalls the Houyhnhyms' mystification at Gulliver's determination to hide his body from sight, or his association of guns and explosives with enlightenment. So does Rotpeter's assessment of his present condition. Having reached 'the cultural level of an average European' he remarks coolly, '[i]n itself that might be nothing to speak of, but it is something insofar as it has helped me out of my cage and opened a special way out for me, the way of humanity' (258).

As Coetzee's comparison of Kafka and Köhler suggests, even real-life scientific encounters between humans and other primates during the twentieth century were strongly marked by a Swiftian flavour. The exchange between human perspectives and (supposedly) animal ones has shaped scientific epistemologies no less than literary ones. Haraway has shown the two-way influence between primatology and the human sciences during the twentieth century. She gives the example of Robert Yerkes, the father of American primate studies, who spent the 1920s and 30s 'building structures (laboratories, funding, students, ideas, logics of application, myths) for the study of primates as the most revealing objects for a psychobiology of human engineering'. By constructing his 'primate model' Yerkes was also 'building a powerful technology to remodel persons', including the development of scientific approaches to 'personnel management and industrial relations' by corporate and governmental interests (Haraway 1991: 65–7).

American primatology repeatedly displays this Moreauvian tendency towards 'man-making'. In 1931, Indiana psychologist Winthrop Kellogg and his wife Luella adopted a young chimpanzee, named Gua, and brought her up alongside their infant son Donald. Both were clothed, house-trained, seated on high-chairs and taught to eat from plates using cutlery. Both were regularly tested for the development of their IQs and their acquisition of language and various emotional and social capacities. Kellogg explicitly described the aim of the experiment as 'humanizing' the ape – although the expectation, of course, was that the chimpanzee's abilities would trail behind the human's. But neither aim nor expectation was met. Since humans mature slowly in comparison with other primates, the superiority of Gua over her 'brother' in co-ordination was not surprising, but her equal or better performance in comprehension and 'pre-school tests' was. Also unforeseen was the fact that Gua's initiative, ingenuity and willpower were so far in advance of Donald's that he insistently deferred to her leadership. Indeed the experiment showed every sign of reversing its designer's intentions: 'while the Kelloggs were intently "humanizing" Gua', writes Adrian Desmond, 'the little ape it seems was unwittingly "pongising" poor Donald', who began gnawing at pieces of wood and giving chimpanzee food-barks at the sight of treats. As for language acquisition, after a few 'proto-words' – the first of which was 'Gya' – Donald gave up talking in favour of gesture. Language tests diagnosed him as 'considerably retarded for his age', at which point '[t]he experiment was aborted; Donald returned to normal and Gua to a cage' (Desmond 1979: 81–2). Had the Kelloggs read Kafka they might have anticipated this effect: as Rotpeter tells the Academy, his 'first teacher was almost himself turned into an ape' by their interaction, and 'had soon to give up teaching and was taken away to a mental hospital' (Kafka 1999 [1919]: 258).

Following the Second World War, the scientific fantasy of teaching chimpanzees to speak became something of an obsession. The traumas of the mid-century – technologies of mass destruction turned against civilian populations, and the consequent crisis of faith in modernity's virtues – lent urgency to the search for the roots of human nature. Once again apes provided the perfect mirror for humanity's self-analysis, the missing link between its contemporary crisis and its animal heritage. And the most urgent areas of enquiry were the same features of scientific humanity identified by its founders, Descartes and Bacon: language, abstract thought, instrumental logic, practical reason. The first step was to investigate the differences in linguistic ability between apes and *Homo sapiens*. Keith and Cathy Hayes, inspired by the Kelloggs' effort two decades earlier, attempted in the 1950s to teach a chimpanzee to vocalize human words, but failed 'to elicit anything short of a few baby words uttered with a thick chimp brogue, even after years of laboured coaxing' (Desmond 1979: 28). Concluding that the source of chimpanzees' failure to talk was not cognitive but physical – the absence of a larynx shaped to the production of human phonemes – another couple, the Gardners, tried teaching their experimental subject American Sign Language (ASL or AMESLAN). Rapidly learning to use manual signs appropriately and dialogically, a young female chimp called Washoe became the first of many signing apes who would undermine the Cartesian axiom that the ability to use symbolic communication is unique to humans.

Washoe's breakthrough led to subsequent experiments aiming to prove, disprove, refine or complicate the Gardners' results. Her more famous successors include the wittily named Nim Chimpsky, who spent his formative years with a large human family in a house on New York's West Side; Lucy, the adoptive child of the Temerlin family at the University of Oklahoma; Sue Savage-Rumbaugh's garrulous bonobo Kanzi and H. Lyn White Miles' chatty orang-utan Chantek, both born at the Yerkes Primate Research Facility in Atlanta, Georgia; and the biggest and most famous of them all, Koko the talking gorilla, who has lived under Francine 'Penny' Patterson's care since infancy (Desmond 1979). As each of these ape pioneers crossed the cognitive division supposed to separate humans from other animals, the bar would be raised higher. Once the ASL experiments established that apes could use symbolic representation, the debate shifted to whether they could master grammar; when they showed they could manipulate syntax, scientists asked whether they could achieve 'cross-modal matching', that is, the ability to associate 'diverse perceptions of the same object' – as experiments run by Davenport and Rogers in 1971 showed they could (Desmond 112–13).

The more positivistic language researchers, moreover, relied on the peculiarly modern logic of abstraction, also embraced by zoos, which asserts that the real nature of organic life is best ascertained by isolating organisms from their natural network of living relations. Determined to minimize the white noise produced by complex social interactions amongst apes, or between apes and their adoptive human families, these scientists returned their chimpanzee subjects to solitary confinement. Both David Premack's Sarah and Duane Rumbaugh's Lana were caged to rule out contextual variables. Such experiments not only retained the logic of rationalist instrumentalism, but made their ape subjects enact it, as Köhler did with Sultan. Premack invented for Sarah 'a system involving arbitrarily shaped, brightly coloured, plastic word-symbols', designed to test her capacity for the radically abstract thinking implied by structuralist linguistics (Desmond 1979: 90; Premack 1976). Taking this approach to a new level, Duane Rumbaugh's 'LANguage Analogue' or LANA project at the Yerkes Regional Primate Research Centre instigated 'a computer-run language trainer which would ... respond automatically to the ape's request (as long it was formulated correctly) ... and generally record and analyse all exchanges and their outcomes' (Desmond 1979: 97).

Twentieth-century writers have been drawn to the satirical potential of such procedures. Brophy's *Hackenfeller's Ape* reflects early experiments in primate linguistics in portraying the monologues that Professor Darrelhyde directs towards Percy the ape through the bars of the latter's cage. Although she insists that Percy gains a strong sense of the emotional content behind the Professor's words, Brophy notes that '[i]t was an indisputable scientific fact that Percy would never be able to speak' (1953: 21) – anticipating the findings of speech-sound analyst Philip Lieberman, who in 1972, used computer simulations to show conclusively that the ape larynx, being shorter than the human one, cannot produce the sounds necessary for human speech (Desmond 1979: 29). Brophy also anticipates the Gardners' insight that apes communicate more eloquently through gesture than through vocal language. She describes Percy watching a group of men discussing his own escape: '[d]eaf to words, he went by gestures: and the sense of crisis which the men were studiedly repressing from their conversation was immediately betrayed to the animal' (Brophy 1953: 100). Of course, as well as understanding it, Percy 'speaks' the language of gesture like a native, even across the inter-species barrier. At one point, lost in despair, the Professor clings to the apes' cage with his eyes shut, 'hanging outside where Percy so often hung from the inside', when he feels 'something leathery touch his palm . . . The monkey's forefinger had been inserted, to give comfort, in his own agonised fist' (67–8).

In *God's Grace*, too, Bernard Malamud draws out the satirical implications of language experiments with apes. Discovering that the only other survivor on board the ship is a young chimpanzee, whom he names Buz, Calvin Cohn immediately yearns to communicate with him. After he tells the ape they are the only survivors of a nuclear holocaust, 'the chimp beat his chest with the fist of one pink-palmed hand, and Cohn wondered at the response; protest, mourning – both? Whatever he meant meant meaning' (Malamud 1982: 17). Thus, initially, Cohn attends eagerly to the chimp's own 'meaning'. It is Buz who trains Cohn to recognize the gesture for *thirsty*, and, after they have their first altercation, the chimpanzee sign for *reconciliation*: '[t]he ape presented his rump to Cohn, who instinctively patted it. He seemed to signal he would like to do the same for Cohn, and he presented his right buttock and was touched by the animal. Civilized, Cohn thought' (20). But soon human meaning begins to take precedence. Cohn learns that the little ape knows AMESLAN, and later discovers, upon cutting away Buz's neck cloth, 'two flattened copper wires [growing] out of the scar where a man's Adam's apple would be' which, when connected, activate a mechanical voice-box surgically implanted by Dr Bünder (64). Similarly, in 1966 David Premack and Arthur Schwartz designed 'a mechanical voice-box controlled by a joystick that the ape could operate manually', which would eventually 'be miniaturized into an electronic device strapped to its waist or wrist' (Desmond 1979: 89). Frustrated by the inadequacy of available technology, Premack abandoned this scheme, inventing in its place the colourful symbolic system used by Sarah. Buz is a parody of such attempts. His voice, which is 'metallic' and, 'reminiscent of Dr Bünder's, sound[s] like a metachimp's', blending the accent of the scientist with mechanical sound effects, creating a tone evocative not of a living animal but a conceptual abstraction (Malamud 1982: 65). This combination is represented by the 'pong-pong' that concludes Buz's sentences, which seems to allude to his place in the taxonomic category *pongidae*, but is actually produced by the copper wires vibrating together.

As soon as the wires are connected, however, Buz asserts that without Bünder's intervention he would have started speaking anyway: '[i]f he hod waited another weeg or two I would hov done it myzelf/// I was already talging on my libs but he didn't hear it/// I would hov talged oz I do now/// pong-pong'. When Cohn asks how this could have happened 'without a proper larynx', Buz replies, '[b]ecause onimals con talg/// . . . We talg among ourselves/// Maybe someday you will hear our phonemes oz we hear yours/// If you con communicade with one living onimal/// you con communicade with all his relations' (Malamud 1982: 65–6). To Buz, the human is characterized not by the ability to talk, but by the inability to listen. In surgically altering his voice box, Bünder takes away the possibility of hearing the animal's own phonemes. This exchange satirizes the anthropomorphic precepts underlying attempts to teach apes human languages, whether vocal, gestural, written or digital. Sometimes this anthropomorphism has been as explicit as the Kelloggs' attempt to humanize Gua, but even the rigorously positivist studies depend on a human paradigm of linguistic structure and abstract thought, against which the achievements of the animals are measured. For example, Rumbaugh and Gill, having hoped their experiment might allow them to 'engage Lana in conversation to learn about a variety of things from the perspective of an ape', admit that on the contrary she has never 'asked for the names of things unless they held some food or drink that she apparently wanted, never "discussed" spontaneously the attributes of things in her world' (1976: 575). They judge it unlikely that chimpanzees will ever show the capacity to exploit 'linguistic-type skills' in order to 'enhance their broad understanding of their world and how things in it work' – a point they suggest 'might reliably differentiate language utilization by the child from that ape' (575). Since they take it as axiomatic that 'language is inherent in the covert cognitive operations that provide for the comprehension of relationships, the formulation of strategies for problem solving, and other expressions of creativity' (565), Rumbaugh and Gill's conclusion disqualifies chimpanzees from precisely those abstract and instrumentalist forms of intelligence which the scientist prizes as the ultimate human possession – the kind of intelligence, in fact, that would design such an experiment in the first place. In short, Lana has failed to become a scientist herself. Of course, as Desmond points out, Rumbaugh's programme was not designed 'to encourage Lana to "broaden her horizons", since her horizon was invariably four walls and a computer' (1979: 120). It is far from clear why such an environment – in contrast to the rich social and sensory matrices of a kin-group and a jungle ecosystem – should inspire a chimpanzee to inquire 'how things work'; or how such an animal should intuit that human language might be useful for such inquiry, considering the consistency with which her human companions associate it with the awarding or withholding of food.

In fact there is plenty of evidence that even under these circumstances, the apes have plenty to say, but no one who can hear it. Surely Lana is initiating discussion of 'the attributes of things in her world' when she vainly types out 'please machine tickle Lana' after her human companions have gone home for the night (Fouts and Mills 1997: 287)? More often, these apes use other forms of communication which their observers, attentive like Dr Bünder to human language alone, cannot hear. One instance is provided by Sarah, one of Lana's forerunners. Confined to her cell according to Premack's insistence on clinical rigour, Sarah is allowed to watch movies to alleviate her boredom.

> Recently, when shown a videotape of a TV program on wild orang-utans, Sarah . . . watched with uninterrupted attention for almost 30 minutes. When a young male was captured in a net, Sarah hooted and threw pieces of paper at the screen, seemingly aimed at the animal's captors. The trainer, watching with Sarah, reached up and touched the image of the captured animal on the screen; Sarah shuddered and turned a wildly startled face to the trainer (Premack 1976: 346).

Premack cites the incident solely as evidence of the chimpanzee brain's ability to 'recognize the relation between a picture and the item pictured' (346), while Desmond describes it as an 'engaging' story which shows that, because she can 'read' two-dimensional images like a human being, 'Sarah enjoys a rousing movie' (1979: 115). Yet it would be hard to imagine a more direct challenge from a chimpanzee subject to her experimenters, or one that seems more like an attempt to 'broaden [her] understanding of [her] world and how things in it work'. Of course, Sarah is using her native language to do so: the characteristic chimpanzee combination of non-verbal vocalization, gesticulation, facial expression and meaningful action (in this case, the throwing of objects). Translated into English, the questions Sarah poses might be very similar to those Elizabeth Costello attributes to Sultan – '[w]hy do men behave like this?'; '[w]here is home, and how do I get there?' (Coetzee 2003: 72–5) – but Premack's protocols do not allow him to consider whether Sarah is alluding to her own memory of capture and, even more strikingly, identifying empathetically with the experience of another animal, indeed a member of a different species. The experimenter remains intently deaf to the unsettling possibility that Sarah may be expressing chimpanzees' antipathy – shared with both orang-utans and humans – to enforced, captive isolation from their kin.

Gombe, Karisoke, Tanjung Puting

Twentieth-century linguistic experiments certainly changed perceptions of the great apes, but an even greater impact was made by observations undertaken outside the laboratory. Most famously, beginning in 1960, three young women were sent by palaeontologist-anthropologist Louis Leakey to study great apes in remote locations: Jane Goodall to the chimpanzees of Gombe in Tanzania, Dian Fossey to the mountain gorillas of the Varunga range between Rwanda and Congo (Zaire), and Biruté Galdikas to the orang-utans of Tanjung Puting reserve in Borneo. Leakey chose young women because he imagined them to be 'without the scientific prejudices of the masculine world of modern research' (Haraway 1989: 151). Certainly, his three most famous protégées demonstrated a remarkably feral relationship to the pieties of scientific modernity. Their stories repeat the narrative of feminine engagement with wild space that is exemplified by the fictions of Findley, Roszak and Atwood.

Jane Goodall describes how, during her isolation from human contact amongst the chimpanzees of Gombe Stream, she 'longed to be able to swing through the branches like the chimps, to sleep in the treetops, lulled by the rustling of the leaves in the breeze' (1971: 56–7). Finding her clothing cumbersome in the drenching rain, she makes her daily trek to her observation point naked, while her skin hardens against the sharp grasses (60–1). Eventually the local chimps accept her 'as part of their normal, everyday landscape. A strange white ape, very unusual to be sure, but not, after all, terribly alarming' (66). And when she has a son she applies some of the rearing techniques she has observed among chimpanzee mothers: breastfeeding on demand, carrying the infant throughout her travels through the terrain, following punishment with immediate reassurance through physical contact (215) – thereby reversing the Kelloggs' attempt to humanize baby Gua.

A similar feralizing effect characterizes the careers of Leakey's other two 'ape-women'. Dian Fossey went to the Virunga range during the 1960s to study the local mountain gorillas. She named her camp Karisoke, combining the names of the nearest peaks, Mount Bisoke and Mount Karisimbi – the latter, of course, the location for Carl Akeley's shooting of his version of King Kong. Like Goodall, Fossey set about learning the gestures and vocalizations that made up the language of her ape subjects. In 1970 she was rewarded by the first friendly gorilla-to-human physical contact recorded. As is well known, her identification with the animals did not stop there. When poachers killed Digit, a young male with whom she had a special bond, Fossey instigated a public campaign against hunting of the species. After ten years of increasingly militant direct action against poachers she shared Digit's fate and was murdered at Karisoke in 1985 (Haraway 1989: 149, 263–8). The third of 'Leakey's angels', Biruté Galdikas, arrived in Indonesian Borneo in 1971 to study orang-utans. She established a research station, Camp Leakey, in Tanjung Puting Reserve. Like Goodall she cared for her infant son amongst the apes, noting – albeit with some alarm – the influence of his orang-utan playmate, Princess: '[t]heir facial expressions, sounds, and postures became very similar', she wrote, and 'he would try to follow Princess and play with her in the trees', as well as scrambling on all fours, occasionally biting people, and even picking up sign language from his orange 'sibling' (Galdikas 1980: 849). Like both her predecessors, Galdikas became a powerful spokesperson for the protection of the animals she studied. To this day Camp Leakey operates as a combined observation centre and a rehabilitation unit for orang-utan orphans.

The work of these three women has posed perhaps the most powerful challenge of recent times to the boundary erected by modernity between human and animal. One famous example is Goodall's documentation of non-human apes' manufacture and use of tools. She observed the Gombe chimpanzee David Greybeard, and others, selecting a certain kind of twig, carrying it to an area full of termite mounds, shaping it by stripping its leaves, and dipping it into holes in such a way that termites would cling to it and could be drawn out and eaten (Goodall 1971: 43–5). Recognizing the implications of this observation, Louis Leakey wrote to Goodall that '[n]ow we must redefine tool, redefine Man, or accept chimpanzees as humans' (Jane Goodall Institute 2007). In contrast to the man-making primatology of Yerkes and his heirs, the work done by Goodall and her peers has had a man-breaking or anthropoluotic effect.

In *God's Grace* Bernard Malamud draws explicitly on Goodall's work (Malamud 1982: vi). If Buz recalls the talking apes of America's primate research centres, the other chimps are based on the troop at Gombe Stream. Esau, the strongest, is portrayed 'squatting on the ground poking long straws into the mound-nests of nonexistent ants' (144) – a wry caricature of the capacity for tool use which, in its most 'advanced' form (nuclear technology) has caused the extinction of insect life. Esau's name, that of Jacob's brother in the book of Genesis, derives from a Hebrew word meaning 'complete', because the original Esau was born hairy, strong and capable (rather like a chimpanzee baby), but was tricked by his twin into giving up leadership of the house of Israel – just as in *God's Grace* the anthropomorphized Buz, with his scientific and religious metaphysics, gains the edge over Esau as the dominant male. It is no accident that the conflict between Buz and Esau has a human antecedent, for Malamud presents it as the outcome of the chimps' incorporation of human concepts and practices. In an echo of the social-engineering agenda of Yerkes, Cohn intends to forge a better humanity from his chimpanzee raw material, judging that the nuclear apocalypse occurred because '[man] never mastered his animal nature for the good of all – please excuse the word – I am an animal myself . . . he behaved too often irrationally, unreasonably, savagely, bestially' (Malamud 1982: 133–4). By teaching the chimps to master their animality, Cohn believes he can create a population 'more carefully controlled, more easily inclined to the moral life; in the larger sense more "humanly" behaved than the species of which [he is] the last survivor' (164). Despite the chimps' scepticism – Buz says 'he would rather be a chimp', while the others respond by shitting on Cohn's head, as the Yahoos did to Gulliver (18, 69–70, 101–102) – Cohn trains them to delay self-gratification for the greater good. 'Sublimation is what I advise', he tells Esau when the latter complains about the shortage of females, '[t]hat's using one's sexual energy creatively – in thought, art, or some satisfying labour' (186–7). Esau is unimpressed, but Buz proves an apt student who, frustrated in his sexual desires, asks Cohn 'to teach him algebra so he [can] go on sublimating' (172). Meanwhile the rest of the chimps, led by Esau, become increasingly resistant. Against Cohn's prohibition they begin to hunt, kill and eat young baboons (187–91, 195–8). When reprimanded, Esau tells Cohn that 'every chimp he had known "in the good old days in the highland" had hunted small baboons. It was a perfectly natural, naturally selective, thing to do. The hunt was stimulating and the flesh delicious'. Reclaiming the forms of pack agency that are his birthright, Esau challenges Cohn's anthropomorphic attempt to reshape his behaviour: '[o]f course', he adds, 'if there was a piece of sex around instead of that horseass sublimation you are trying to trick on us, we would have something to keep our thoughts going' (194). He is referring to the young female chimp Mary Madelyn, who no longer favours her male conspecifics because of Cohn's influence, which Esau says 'has made her too proud to dip her butt for friends' (153). Cohn's humanizing programme exacerbates these violent tendencies until Buz, who has developed an oedipal sexual envy of Cohn's relationship with Mary Madelyn, collaborates with the rest of the pack to force the young female back into the troop, kill her baby, and ultimately sacrifice Cohn himself.[19]

The storyline of *God's Grace* closely echoes the history of the Gombe chimpanzees. *In the Shadow of Man* was taken to portray a kind of Edenic version of natural man, but Goodall subsequently shattered this illusion, reporting infanticide, cannibalism and excessive intra-specific aggression amongst members of the Gombe troop. During her 1978 Leakey Memorial Lecture at the British Museum, Goodall 'visibly stunned her academic audience' by detailing 'a bloody spate of panicides' that had occurred after a number of chimpanzees seceded from the main troop in 1972. Premeditated and cooperative ambushes by groups of males from the main group occurred against individuals from the splinter group until it was completely destroyed (Desmond 1979: 222–3). Desmond speculates on the causes of this internecine warfare. The males who were mostly responsible for the violence, he writes, were 'impressionable adolescents or young adults' during the preceding decade, which was 'a highly abnormal time for

Gombe apes', in large part because of Goodall herself (225). In order to observe the initially shy chimpanzees, Goodall undertook regular 'banana provisioning' from 1962 onwards. This drew chimps into her camp, but also baboons. The resulting competition increased exponentially the incidence of conflicts between chimps and baboons, as Goodall, with characteristic honesty, noted herself (1971: 130, 190–1). Prior to this period, baboons and chimpanzees coexisted as an (admittedly ambivalent) interspecies community – their young playing together, adults from different species sometimes grooming each other – within which chimp predation of young baboons was the occasional exception to a more generally amenable relationship. Now, however, in the competitive atmosphere produced by Goodall's banana distribution, what Desmond calls 'pure hunting' – that is, predation of another species for food, which Goodall observed amongst the Gombe chimps from the outset – became inflected with an exaggerated aggressive dimension. The facial expressions, vocalizations and gestures of Gombe chimpanzees when killing baboons began to exhibit forms of 'brutal', 'intimidating' and 'terrorizing' display, characteristic of competitive conflict but absent from the behaviour of chimpanzees engaged in 'pure hunting'. This suggests the young males had become 'habituated to intercommunity killing, familiar with the insidious blend of violent aggression and refined hunting which targeted one's own kind and marked it for death' (Desmond 1979: 225–7). In other words, competition between the baboons and the chimpanzees escalated occasional predation into competitive attack, a style of aggressive conflict which then spilled over, during the next decade, into savage battles between factions of the chimpanzee troop itself.[20]

The ambiguity of the relationship between baboons and chimps is incorporated into *God's Grace*, where it functions in a way parallel to human racism. When Cohn reprimands the chimpanzees for saying that the baboons are 'strangers' who don't belong to their 'tribe' Esau replies: '[t]hey're monkeys and ought to look like monkeys. Instead, they look like monkeys with dog-heads, I don't go for that' (Malamud 1982: 186). What follows is an escalating sequence of conflicts that parallels events at Gombe. First Esau, acting alone, hunts and eats the baboon child Sara (189–90). Then a group of male chimps under the command of Esau ambushes two young baboons, leading to an all-out confrontation with the baboon group (195–8). Finally, the chimps (including Buz) ambush the faction of their own troop represented by Mary Madelyn, Cohn and the infant Rebekah (207–210). Malamud presents the chimpanzees' all-too-human advance towards tribal warfare as the result of interaction between their own biological and social make-up – including both the pre-existing practice of occasional baboon-hunts, and non-monogamous sexual competitiveness – and Cohn's imposition of a humanist model of civilization, as represented by the sublimation of aggression and desire. By the end of the novel the chimpanzees have embarked on the same history of violence that led to the nuclear apocalypse with which the narrative began: they are led by a charismatic, messianic patriarch, Buz, and have a culture based around warfare with the rival baboon tribe and the metaphysics of sacrifice.

Inside the Skin of Another Species

The work of Leakey's ape-women and the primate language researchers has anointed great apes as spokespeople for the non-human world, witnesses to the damage wreaked by human enterprise, prophets of dire consequences and advocates for change. The pre-eminent example is Koko, the signing gorilla, explicitly styled by Penny Patterson as the animal kingdom's primate ambassador to humankind. Koko's diary of engagements includes an online web chat for Earth Day 1998, a video-link 'lecture' delivered to At-Bristol Natural Science Museum in 2004, an 'address' to the Children's World Summit for the Environment in 2005, and a DVD presentation to the American Bar Association in 2006 (Gorilla Foundation/ Koko.org 2007).

Koko's ambassadorial role has many parallels in narrative fiction. Kafka imagined something of the kind in Rotpeter's address to an academy. In David Quinn's *Ishmael* the narrator recounts his telepathic conversations with a silverback gorilla who offers a history of human environmental depredation and an ecological philosophy for saving the world (1995). At the climax of *The Woman and the Ape*, the inauguration ceremony of the New London Regent's Park Zoological Garden is taken over by Erasmus and his kin, who deliver a warning to humanity to change its ways (Høeg 1996: 210–17). And in *God's Grace*, too, the final word is left to an ape: as the chimpanzees embark on their repetition of violent human history, the island's sole gorilla recites a Kaddish of mourning (Malamud 1982: 223). Meanwhile, in reversed form, the scenario of a 'dumb' animal speaking on behalf of its species to a 'civilized' audience occurs in Pierre Boullé's *La Planète des Singes*: astronaut Ulysee Mérou, marooned on the planet Soror, where great apes are dominant, learns their language and ends up addressing a conference of simian scientists (1966: 113–16). This inversion of the trope of animal ambassadorship of course echoes Gulliver's representations on behalf of his conspecifics to the monarch of Brobdingnag and the council of the Houyhnhnms.

Similar scenarios occur in *The Great Ape Project*, a collection of essays by an alliance of scientists and activists brought together to 'demand the extension of the community of equals to include all great apes: human beings, chimpanzees, gorillas and orang-utans', and to argue that 'certain basic moral principles' should pertain amongst this group of species, including the right to life, the protection of individual liberty and the prohibition of torture (Cavalieri and Singer 1993: 4–5). From a literary-critical point of view, the most noticeable thing about this volume is its persistent use of the trope of human–animal reversal. Drawing together the exchanges between humans and other apes enacted by twentieth-century primatology in the laboratory, the home and the field, but overruling the varied and contradictory motivations of individual primatologists, *The Great Ape Project* welds them into a single political purpose. The book thereby extends the tradition of *Gulliver's Travels*, in which Swift also used unsettling narratives of human–animal reversal to broaden the notion of political responsibility to include populations considered beyond the pale.

The opening chapter of *The Great Ape Project*, by Goodall, begins as follows:

> [s]he was too tired after their long, hot journey to set to on the delicious food, as her daughters did. She had one paralysed arm, the aftermath of a bout of polio nine years ago, and walking was something of an effort . . . her eldest, the first pangs of her hunger assuaged, glanced at the old lady, gathered food for both of them and took it to share with her mother (in Cavalieri and Singer 1993: 10).

After three such vignettes Goodall comments that '[t]hose anecdotes were recorded during our thirty-one years of observation of the chimpanzees of Gombe, in Tanzania. Yet the characters could easily be mistaken for humans'. Having secured her readers' sympathy, Goodall details the characteristics shared by the two species: over 98 per cent of our DNA; societies in which individuals 'can make a difference to the course of . . . history'; the ability to 'learn by observation and imitation' and to pass new 'inventions' on to subsequent generations; the capacity for 'sophisticated cooperation' and 'true altruism' as well as for 'complex social manipulation', brutality, territorialism and warfare (10–13). Penny Patterson's chapter begins similarly, by presenting an 'individual' for her readers' 'consideration' who 'communicates in sign language, using a vocabulary of over 1,000 words'; has 'achieved scores between 85 and 95 on the Stanford-Binet Intelligence Test'; 'demonstrates a clear self-awareness by engaging in self-directed behaviours in front of a mirror'; 'engages in imaginary play'; uses appropriately terms like 'before', 'after', 'later', and 'yesterday'; 'grieves for those she has lost'; and has 'expressed empathy for others seen only in pictures'. Of course, this person – 'and she is nothing less than a person to those who are acquainted with her' – is Koko the gorilla (Patterson and Gordon, in Cavalieri and Singer 1993: 58–9). Other contributors to the *Great Ape Project* make use of more speculative human–animal reversals. Philosopher Raymond Corbey imagines the existence of populations of 'apes far more intelligent than humans' who have governments, industry and technology, and who live alongside a smaller, endangered population of humans, regarded by the apes as 'dull, uncivilized, and indeed unapish, lower beings'. Would it be right for the apes to hunt their neighbours, 'bringing back their hands and heads as trophies', display them in circuses and zoos, or experiment on them in laboratories (Corbey, in Cavalieri and Singer 1993: 126–7)? Similar conceits are deployed by Jared Diamond, Colin MacGinn and Harlan B. Miller in their essays (in Cavalieri and Singer 1993: 88, 146–50, 230–31). And Geza Teleki, in a chapter entitled 'They Are Us', recalls 'one evening in the Gombe hills' when he observed two male chimpanzees, who upon seeing each other 'advanced as bipeds through waist-high grass to stand close together, face to face, each extending his right hand to clasp and vigorously shake the other's while softly panting, heads bobbing', after which they 'sat down nearby and we three watched the sunset enfold the park'. 'Nevermore', concludes Teleki, 'would I regard chimpanzees as "mere animals" . . . I had seen my species inside the skin of another' (in Cavalieri and Singer 1993: 297). The primary rhetorical tactic of *The Great Ape Project* thus entails locating the most valued qualities of humanist ideology – instrumental reason, aesthetic response, familial and community responsibility – inside the skin of other species.

This is what Swift does with his portrait of the genteel and enlightened Houyhnhnms, but of course he also reverses human and animal attributes in the opposite direction. Gulliver's description of the Yahoos identifies the qualities vilified by humanism as bestial – slavishness to instinct, insensibility to finer feelings, irrationality, technological incapacity – inside the skin of humans or hominid beings. An extended recent instance of this kind of reversal is provided by Will Self's *Great Apes* (1997). Self's satire centres upon Simon Dykes, a member of the upper-middle-class artistic elite in London in the late twentieth century, who one day wakes up in a world in which chimpanzees are the dominant and 'civilized' species. The novel switches between his perspective and that of chimp psychologist Zack Busner, who is called on to treat Simon after the latter has been taken to a psychiatric facility, 'seriously disturbed', possessed by the delusion that he is human, 'that the whole world was run by humans' and that 'he had gone to sleep with his human lover and when he awoke the following morning she was a chimpanzee and so was everyone else in the world' (Self 1997: 77–8). The narrative follows Simon's painstaking adaptation (or re-adaptation) to what it calls 'chimpunity'. Unlike *The Great Ape Project*, *Great Apes* has no discernible political aim: its main commitment is to follow the ape-human reversal to its rhetorical limits, in a display of satirical virtuosity. For example Self enjoys pongizing all the key milestones in modern representations of chimpanzees. In his search for the source of Simon's delusion, Busner examines 'Edward Tyson's classic anatomical study – published in 1699 – of an immature human specimen brought from Angola'; a series of 'eighteenth-century satires, pitting evolved humans against primitive apes', including both *Scriblerus* and 'Swift's Yahoos'; Linnaeus' classification of 'the human as a species of chimpanzee' to which he assigns the name '*Pongis sylvestris* or *Pongis nocturnes*'; a film called *Planet of the Humans*; scientific studies like Robert Yerkes' 1927 classic, 'titled simply *Humans*'; 'the biographies of Washoe and the other famous humans who had been taught to sign by the Fouts'; Jane Goodall's studies of 'the wild humans of Gombe', and Leakey's famous comment that '[n]ow we must redefine *tool*, redefine *chimpanzee* – or accept humans as chimps!' (vii, x–xi, 262–3, 265 273, 325).

Alongside the enjoyment of isomorphic exchanges of human and chimpanzee elements, the most sustained aspect of Self's reversal involves the substitution of fundamental Western social forms – the nuclear family and couple-based monogamy, along with associated gender, class, educational and workplace hierarchies – with a chimpanzee society determined solely by reproductive instincts and biological hierarchies. The pongid culture of *Great Apes* is based on dominance-and-submission patterns between the alpha chimp and his various subordinates. So, in a parody of Freudian transference, the breakthrough in Simon's treatment comes when he and his therapist come to blows. After a 'brief scrimmage' of biting, hitting and screeching, Simon submits to Busner and the two engage in his 'first grooming session since the breakdown' (Self 1997: 215). Self reinterprets psychoanalysis through Goodall's accounts of hierarchical negotiations amongst chimpanzees, which are often characterized by sudden outbursts of aggression followed, once a relationship has been affirmed, by grooming to re-establish social affiliation (Goodall 1971: 112–13, 122–3). 'Busner's fingers as they played upon Simon's body were tender, placatory. "You get out the fear, get out the hurt, the anger. Attack me by all means – that's very chimp, very chimp indeed"' (Self 1997: 215). Simon experiences a further 'revelation of chimpunity' when confronted by an aggressive male stranger. Feeling 'the fur at the nape of his neck stiffen and bristle – a sensation which he had never consciously experienced before', he utters 'a series of aggressive barks, while drawing himself up to his full height', before leaping 'for the lowest bough of the first plane tree' swinging himself up and continuing his retreat 'brachiating as a chimp to the canopy born' (291–2). Re-accommodation to the chimpanzee world thus depends on accepting that instincts determine social behaviour: 'Simon was taken aback – literally – by the way his body automatically understood which apes he should present to' (302).

The association of 'chimpunity' with automatic response draws on behavioural psychology, the most faithful contemporary descendant of the Cartesian beast-machine, which views animals, including humans, as engineered by evolutionary selection to respond to stimuli in certain ways. Behaviourists have often used mechanistic metaphors to describe the hormonal, neurological and other physiological systems by which the stimulus-response pattern operates: Konrad Lorenz alluded to hydraulic mutual-feedback systems, while later generations made reference to cybernetics (Haraway 1989: 140). The result, according to Scholtmeijer, is 'a fundamentally devitalized animal', which is 'thoroughly conquered' by its reduction to 'a system of behaviours to be isolated, manipulated, and tabulated' (1993: 73). This is also the theory that underlies *Life of Pi*. Martel's narrator conquers the tiger because his observation of animals in Pondicherry Zoo, and his degree in zoology, have taught him the formulae that govern their behaviour. Hence 'flight distance, which is the minimum distance at which an animal wants to keep a perceived enemy', can be expressed in mathematical figures: three hundred yards for a flamingo, thirty for a giraffe, ten for fiddler crabs, and so on (Martel 2002: 39). Combining this calculus with a theory of dominance and submission, Pi engages in a classic stimulus-response experiment, rocking the boat and blowing a whistle 'until the association in the animal's mind between the sound of the whistle and the feeling of intense, incapacitating nausea is fixed and totally unambiguous. Thereafter, the whistle alone will deal with trespassing' (205). Pi's 'super-alpha male' status is established over the feline beast-machine by behaviourist programming (43).

Great Apes portrays another form of biological determinism even more powerfully: namely, an overriding sexual instinct operating entirely in the service of reproductive and genetic considerations. The chimps regard monogamous pair-bonding as a bestial (that is, human) aberration, 'perverse because it confers no apparent genetic advantage' (Self 1997: ix). In their world, promiscuous coupling is the only socially responsible form of sexual behaviour. Observing a mass-mating of chimpanzees in Regent's Park, Busner describes it to Simon as a manifestation of 'the absolute core . . . of chimpunity itself' (293). Imagining a society entirely shaped by sexual impulse allows the achievement of Self's main satirical objective, when the reversal is itself reversed. Asked by Busner whether 'all human consortships last a lifetime', or whether the principle of '[e]xclusive mating rights' is always respected, Simon has to reply in the negative, admitting that 'the exogamous matings' occurring outside human couple relation-ships are often 'involuntary – driven even. The human impulse towards inconstancy seems as strong as the drive to consort'. Busner concludes, 'it looks to me much the same as what chimpanzees get up to "huuu"?' (294–5). Unable to explain the difference between chimpanzee and human sexual behaviour – in a conversation reminiscent of Gulliver's attempts to persuade the Houyhnhnms that he is not a Yahoo – Simon has to accept the two species are more alike than they are different. Hence, at the core of Self's novel, providing the structural fulcrum which bears the comparison between human and chimp, and which swivels satirically to produce simi-larity out of apparent opposition, is a theory of shared human–animal behaviour based on the drive to reproduce as a means to perpetuate genetic heritage.[21]

In short, Self's satire draws upon a crude version of evolutionary psychology, a paradigm whose current dominance can be traced to the 'new physical anthropology' inaugurated by Sherwood Washburn at the University of Chicago in the 1950s. Combining 'field studies of wild primates and of living human hunter-gatherers' with 'the ongoing work on African hominid and hominoid fossils', and undertaking comparative behavioural studies of primates to connect biology and anthropology, Washburn's synthesis breathed new life into the figure of 'Man the Hunter' as the embodiment of humankind's emergence from its apelike forebears (Haraway 1989: 187, 211–12). This narrative provided an apparently universal, scientifically authoritative account of what it means to be human, consistent with the ideological mood of post-war Western societies. It imag-ined a biological basis for society according to which men were abroad, cooperating and competing, inventing weapons and pursuing material gain, while women stayed at home, preparing meals and rearing children.

In the context of the Cold War, 'this Man the Hunter was liberal democracy's substitute for socialism's version of natural human cooperation... His technology and urge to travel would enable the exchange systems so critical to free world ideology' (187). Like H. G. Wells, Washburn emphasized 'plasticity', the capacity for cultural invention, as the unifying feature of the human species, thereby transcending the racial divisions of prior anthropological generations as well as reinstating the supremacy of humans over other animals. Tool-use, especially in hunting, epitomized an innate human technological and entrepreneurial genius (200, 208). Once again, Martel's *Life of Pi* provides – like a latter-day *Robinson Crusoe* – a compression of this conjectural history. The vegetarian Pi, if he is to survive, must learn to hunt with voracity and inventiveness if he is to compete successfully against his fellow-predator, Richard Parker.

Following Washburn's intervention, the 1960s and 1970s saw the popularization of narratives about the difficulties faced in contemporary environments by Man the Hunter: problems resulting from 'eruptions of his violent natural propensities in a crowded world', and the challenges of 'creating social stability and happy families in the face of modern perverse refusals to follow nature's laws' (Haraway 1989: 127). The *Planet of the Apes* films and television series can be understood in this context. Whereas Boullé's novel, which is mainly a critique of French Cartesianism, portrays Soror's pongid society as technologically advanced, rationalistic and civil in the modern sense, the American screen adaptations recast the ape world as brutal and pre-scientific, creating a Wellsian parable about atavistic inhumanity that was consistent with Washburn's hypothesis. This cruder version of evolutionary psychology was, however, sophisticated in 1975, when E. O. Wilson's *Sociobiology* announced a renewed emphasis on 'the genetic aspects of social strategies', which might be enacted by a range of participants, both female and male, dominant and non-dominant. As Haraway puts it, '[p]rimates became ideal yuppies' in this new sociobiology which, with its talk of 'energy budgets, foraging patterns, genetic investment possibilities, sexual deceit payoffs, social manuevers', tied the (supposedly biologically determined) behaviour of humans and other apes ever more closely into the *Zeitgeist* of corporate and consumer capitalism (128).

According to Annabelle Sabloff, 'the primary error' of sociobiology lies in representing 'all non-human animal behaviours [as] inherently simple: virtually completely genetically determined, without agency or flexibility, without interior complexity or emergent social organization' (2001: 32). Hence, for example, a paradigm that locates essential behaviour in the drive to reproduce genetically will reduce sexual behaviour to its most conventional form: heterosexual procreation (Birke 1994: 105–6). This is certainly the case in Self's novel, where chimpanzee sexual behaviour is overwhelmingly determined by female oestrus, and confined to vaginal intercourse. Yet feminist primatologists have shown that in fact, among primate species, both females and males initiate intercourse when the former is not in oestrus, or when she is already pregnant. Moreover, females often show preference for low-ranking males, who within a strictly evolutionary model would constitute a poor genetic investment (Noske 1997: 116–17). And of course a large variety of same-sex activities occur very commonly amongst apes of all kinds (Bagemihl 1999: 277; Balcombe 2006: 113–15).

In accordance with the sociobiological paradigm, the chimpanzees in *Great Apes* (considered apart from the social superimpositions allowed them by the satire, which are of course borrowed from human modernity) are reduced to fighting, copulating instinct-machines. It is no doubt because of Self's reductive perception of animality that, despite the dominance they enjoy in their pongid world, his chimps remain objects of ridicule, more like apes in circuses than anything. Simon's view of a family at dinner reminds him of 'chimps' tea parties at the zoo'; elsewhere he recalls the television advertisements for PG Tips tea, which featured clothed chimpanzees dubbed with comic accents (Self 1997: 111, 158, 183, 186, 238). If there is humour here it arises from derision of animality rather than from satire against humanity, from a contempt for 'the animals with their scraggy rumps, their bandy, old men's legs, their ears bracketed with field mushrooms . . . their arses in each other's muzzles, their digits in each other's fur' (183). Once Simon becomes acculturated to his new (or prior) chimpanzee identity, this repugnant animality is transferred to the humans he sees in zoos and wildlife sanctuaries. The *Homo sapiens* observed by Simon at the zoo are insentient and beastly in the crudest sense; their eyes 'utterly without the least flicker of rationality', 'their porcine muzzles . . . devoid of feeling or expression', their speech no more than 'a low, throaty roar' (249, 250). When at the end of the novel Simon and Busner travel to Africa, the 'wild' humans they see are just as witless and brutal. They visit a research station and rehabilitation centre – an amalgam of Goodall's research station at Gombe, Fossey's Karisoke and Galdikas' Camp Leakey – run by controversial primatologist Ludmilla Rauhschutz, who describes the privilege of being able to hear 'the human night chorus, possibly one of the most awesome and profound noises there is in nature'; their 'nesting vocalization' is a 'tender exhortation by the male humans to the females, saying that the night shelters are prepared and it is time for mating activity to begin' (396–7). But as Busner and Simon listen expectantly, the cries of the humans, echoing around them in the jungle, are rendered as 'Fuuuuuuckooooooffff-Fuuuuuuuckoooooofff' (396). Despite Rauhschutz's insistence that 'wild humans [are] both sentient and intelligent', when they gather for feeding time at the camp, the humans appear as 'zombie-like' as the zoo specimens, standing 'knock-kneed, slack-jawed, arms akimbo, eyes glazed' (385, 399, 400). The only one who shows any 'spunk' is a young red-haired male who empties the sugar bowl into his mouth and then begins 'to stagger around in small circles, mewling and bellowing, "Fuckoff-fuckoff-fuckoff". He fetches up by the wall of the main hut, which he proceeds to 'rhythmically bash with his hydrocepahlic brow' – at which sight Rauhschutz comments 'with frank admiration', 'Hooo' see, the force and accuracy with which he butts the wall. I think it fair to sign that he seems to have a profound comprehension of the laws of physics' (401–402).

Obviously the target of this mockery is not actual human beings, to whose behaviour these incidents bear little relation. Rather, the final chapters of Self's novel ridicule recent attempts to argue that non-human animals' capacity for thought and feeling is greater than previously allowed by positivist science. In fact, *Great Apes* concludes with a satire aimed directly against the political intervention represented by *The Great Ape Project*. Rauschutz, the radical primatologist, is a crass stereotype of the lesbian feminist: a mannish tyrant, 'obese', with a 'disturbingly flat and animal' muzzle and 'close-cropped head fur' (388), who runs her camp 'along the lines of an old colonial district commissioner' (394). Equally crude is Self's caricature of a group of Dutch chimps visiting the camp from a 'pressure group denoted "The Human Project", the aim of which was to secure limited chimpanzee rights for wild and captive humans' (393). These chimps move with delight among the gathered humans, who nevertheless remain 'totally unresponsive' to attempts at contact, 'merely garbling incoherently in their swinish way, "Fuckoff-fuckoff-fuckoff-fuckoff", over and over' (400).[22] Reading *The Great Ape Project* alongside *Great Apes* demonstrates the radically different effects that can be generated by the human–animal reversal. *The Great Ape Project* uses reversal to argue for a measure of political equity between humans and other apes. In Self's novel, on the other hand, the intention seems to be the humbling of human pretension, but the satire actually reinstates a conventional hierarchy between human and animal. In contrast to the anthropoluotic impact achieved by Swift's human–animal reversals, or those of Kafka, Brophy, Malamud and the contributors to *The Great Ape Project*, all of which loosen the restrictive definitions of both human and non-human being, Self's inversion of *Homo* and *Pan* affirms a reductive and biologically deterministic account of human being, while consigning animal being to an ultra-Cartesian insentience and insignificance.

The Place of Sympathy

Contrasting these two texts highlights another of the most contested features of contemporary human–animal narratives: the question of taste. *The Great Ape Project* expresses a sympathetic and sometimes sentimental identification with the experience of other animals; *Great Apes* relentlessly mocks any such disposition. This distinction marks a line of conflict between alternative legacies: on one hand the Enlightenment, Romantic and Victorian genealogy of inter-species sympathy, and on the other, the distaste for sentimentalism which is shared by both science and modernism. For novelists dealing with human–animal relations, the antipathy between these traditions poses a dilemma. Two exemplary, but very different, responses are demonstrated by Coetzee's *Disgrace* and Findley's *Not Wanted on the Voyage*. Coetzee evades the contemporary suspicion of human–animal

sentiment by overleaping its nineteenth- and twentieth-century manifestations and drawing instead upon the prior tradition of sympathy as a radically disconcerting disposition (Lamb 2001), while Findley embraces the
genre of sentimental narrative, but puts it to work in radical ways.

As an academic, Coetzee's David Lurie has dedicated his career to
abstract thought, the dominant intellectual tradition of modernity. When
dealing with Romanticism, he encourages his students to read
Wordsworth's lines about Mont Blanc as a meditation on '[t]he great archetypes of the mind, pure ideas' (Coetzee 2000: 21–3). Both the mountain
and the Platonism invoked here recall Shelley's critical portrait of Victor
Frankenstein. As in that case, Lurie's abstractionism licenses him to neglect
the impact of his actions on other lives and bodies. He justifies forcing
himself on Melanie Isaacs by invoking the power of Eros and the feminine
divine, or by appealing to behaviourist theory, arguing that the suppression
of his sexual instinct would make him 'hate [his] own nature', like the next-
door neighbours' dog, beaten for his amorous adventures (52, 89–90).
After his own daughter is brutally raped, the same habit of thought inhibits
Lurie's ability to understand her response. 'You keep misreading me', Lucy
tells her father; 'I don't act in terms of abstractions' (112). It is only the non-
logical, unreasoned, counter-intellectual path of disgrace that eventually
offers a corrective to the limitations imposed by abstractionism. Helping
Bev Shaw euthanize unwanted dogs, Lurie is overtaken by a form of affect
he cannot comprehend.

> He had thought he would get used to it. But that is not what happens.
> The more killing he assists in, the more jittery he gets. One Sunday
> evening, driving home in Lucy's kombi, he actually has to stop at the
> roadside to recover himself. Tears flow down his face that he cannot
> stop; his hands shake.
> He does not understand what is happening to him (142–3).

The form of sympathy that possesses Lurie, so that '[h]is whole being is
gripped by what happens in the theatre', cannot be dealt with intellectually
(143). He identifies with the bodily reactions of the dogs, who flatten their
ears and drop their tails 'as if they too feel the disgrace of dying' (143), and
even with their stiffened corpses, which he incinerates because he can't bear
to see them roughly handled by the hospital workers. Trying to analyse his
actions, Lurie can only think that '[h]e saves the honour of corpses because
there is no one else stupid enough to do it. That is what he is becoming:
stupid, daft, wrongheaded' (146). Identifying with the dumbness of dumb
animals, even dead animals, Lurie embodies a disposition that invalidates
the privilege of abstract reason as practised by university professors.

Lurie's story parallels the critique put forward in *Elizabeth Costello*: that
the rationalist tradition from Descartes to Köhler and beyond, along with
modernist primitivism and contemporary ecological managerialism, serves
our understanding of animals poorly by rendering them in Platonic terms.

Against this tendency Costello poses the sympathetic imagination, which allows humans to identify with 'any being with whom [we] share the substrate of life' (Coetzee 2003: 80). She describes the condition shared by humans and other animals as 'fullness, embodiedness', the 'heavily affective sensation . . . of being a body with limbs that have extension in space, of being alive to the world' (78). In the final chapter of this novel, which seems to take place in purgatory after Costello's death, she has to give a statement of belief to a board of judges before she can pass on. After one failed attempt, she tells the board about a population of small frogs living in the Dulgannon River in Victoria, Australia. Her account emphasizes the frogs' suspended animation in 'tombs' of hardening mud during the dry season, followed by their revivification when the rains come 'rapping, as it were, on thousands of tiny coffin lids' (216). This story is a refusal of both abstraction-ism and simple realism. Despite her rhetoric, Costello insists the tale is 'no allegory': she is not using the frogs to refer to an abstract principle, such as faith in resurrection or in the power of life. But neither is she merely attest-ing to a material reality beyond the human. Rather, she insists, it is 'because of the indifference of those little frogs to my belief . . . that I believe in them' (217). Costello's statement is a declaration of anti-anthropocentricism – she believes in a form of non-human life that 'does not bother to believe in me' (218) – and a testimony to the radical power of the sympathetic imagination. For she can imagine the being of these creatures whose existence has nothing to do with hers, a condition moreover that blurs the distinction between life and death itself. Thinking 'of the frog beneath the earth', she

> thinks of the mud eating away at the tips of those fingers, trying to absorb them, to dissolve the soft tissue till no one can tell any longer (certainly not the frog itself, lost as it is in its cold sleep of hibernation) what is earth, what is flesh. Yes, that she can believe in: the dissolution, the return to the elements; and the converse moment she can believe in too, when the first quiver of returning life runs through the body and the limbs contract, the hands flex (219–20).

If Lurie's abstractionism recalls that of Frankenstein, Costello's feeling for the Dulgannon frogs recalls the Romantic theory of organic sympathy and the Creature in whom Mary Shelley embodies it. Costello's imaginative inhabitation of the frogs' decay into earth, and the return of life from that decay, mirrors the Creature's emergence into life from the reanimated flesh of corpses, and his return to the elements at the conclusion of Shelley's novel. It is this most radical form of sympathetic identification – based on the experience of flesh amid the flesh of the world – that also leads Costello to claim that '[f]or instants at a time . . . I know what it is like to be a corpse', and to insist that such knowledge 'is not abstract . . . but embodied. For a moment we *are* that knowledge' (76–7 italics in original).[23]

Yet there remains one limitation that Coetzee imposes on his characters' sympathetic identifications with animal otherness. He works hard to prevent their slipping from sympathy into sentimentalism, as that word is currently understood – that is, he avoids any hint of clichéd, shallow, manipulative, cloying or easy forms of emotional affect. Instead he focuses on the most uncomfortable forms of sympathetic identification – with corpses, or with unloved and nameless dogs, or indeed with the corpses of anonymous dogs – and his protagonists' thoughts remain habitually bleak, sardonic and unrelenting.[24] At one point in *Disgrace*, Lurie even pauses to reassure himself that '[h]e is not, he hopes, a sentimentalist' (Coetzee 2000: 143). This dedicated anti-sentimentalism also helps explain the novel's grim ending: Lurie's decision to euthanize the affectionate dog Driepoot exemplifies Coetzee's determination to distinguish the form of sympathy that interests him from the emotional gratification commonly associated with sentimentalism.[25]

Certainly, there are few narratives more likely to be dismissed as sentimental than that of a lovable animal saved from death and given a happy home, or that of the creature whose affection brings warmth to a cold heart. Indeed more generally, as James Serpell puts it, 'the accusation of sentimentality' is typically levelled against '[p]eople who display emotional concern for animal suffering' or 'those who allow themselves to become emotionally involved with companion animals' (1996: 170). In *Not Wanted on the Voyage*, however, Timothy Findley shows no qualms about deploying, without ironic undertones, the techniques of sentimental narrative, characterization and tone. Emotional climaxes are created from events like the rescue of the blind, pregnant, aging and abandoned cat Mottyl. The animal characters talk, have names and are endowed with (apparently) anthropomorphic personality traits and (supposedly) human virtues – including levels of courtesy, restraint and cooperation that reflect unfavourably on the human protagonists. Their number includes figures from fairy tales and children's stories: unicorns, faeries, dragons. There is a clear characterological distinction between virtue and villainy, expressed in melodramatic costume dramas that draw on pantomime traditions, such as the revolution of the lower orders, including the flamboyantly transgendered Lucy, the gin-soaked Mrs Noyes, and a sack of giggling demons, against the robed, white-bearded patriarch Noah and his brutal, blue-skinned warrior son Japeth. There are also incidents of fantastic gruesomeness: infanticide, massacre, vivisection, rape and incest. Yet Findley's is a postmodern sentimentalism, wherein the kinds of popular narrative that modernism deplored – stories of human–animal tragedy and triumph, melodramatic horrors, childlike fantasies and nostalgic appeals – are re-accessed in ways that eschew the manipulated, clichéd or easy responses conventionally associated with them.

Not Wanted thus returns to the tradition of nineteenth-century radical sentimental narrative, and rejects its subsequent discrediting by modernism. According to Philip Fisher, it is typical of sentimental narrative to evoke events 'in the deep past' which have 'left irreversible damage'. Because such stories 'invite no compensation and provide no hope of redress', they offer that 'training in pure feeling and response' which is 'at the heart of sentimental politics' (1985: 108, 121). Findley, of course, revisits one of the most ancient and best-known of all narratives, and since the outcome is decided in advance, instead of offering redress for the dominion represented by Noah, the novel invites new responses to it. Hence, the revolt of the lower orders that concludes *Not Wanted* is 'a draw', with 'no decisive victory', 'defeats on both sides', and memories that hang 'like a knife between them' (Findley 1984: 348). The flood and the ark have rendered irrevocable the division between humans and other animals (Tiffin 2001: 36–7). The barricade between the lower and upper decks, although literally breached, remains in place in a different form: when Mrs Noyes brings the sheep above deck to teach them a new song – since their previous favourite, *Lamb of God*, has taken on connotations of sacrifice – she finds they no longer share a common language (345–7). Noah proclaims 'that everything that lived and breathed and moved had been delivered into [human] hands – *forever*' (351 italics in original). On the other hand, the patriarch's supremacy has been exposed as both provisional and artificial. Mottyl has survived, as have all her kittens except one. Readers' reactions to particular incidents are likely to be similarly unstable. The novel invites them to feel disturbed by the slaughter of the child Lotte, but also to grieve at the death of Crowe or the Unicorn. Indeed, any dismay felt at the repeated killing of children – Japeth's twin, Lotte, and the baby born to Hannah – cannot be separated from sympathy for non-human species, since these are all 'ape-children', emphatically both human and animal. Moreover Findley's portrayal of the ark's lower decks binds together the plight of prisoners, children, animals and slaves – the same classes that became the focus of the nineteenth century's social conscience and so of its sentimental fiction (Fisher 1985: 94–5).

As Fisher argues, for much of the last century and more, the suspicion of sentiment has enforced a counterproductive separation between literary and popular narratives, as epitomized by the modernist belief that 'art invented patterns of feeling' while popular narratives 'soothed by means of the familiar' and 'dulled the sensibilities that art made lively'. The result was a literary, artistic and scholarly ignorance of the socially transformative potential of 'popular forms' to 'mass . . . small patterns of feeling in entirely new directions' and to pioneer 'exotic configurations of experience as a necessary practice for a transformation of moral life that is approaching' (1985: 19–20). And yet, of course, outside the boundaries of high culture and scientific practice, in the everyday lives of most people, sentimental engagements with animals never lost their intensity or potential for unconventional effects. Emotional proximity between people and their companion animals, for example, remained a major generator of sympathy and sentiment from the eighteenth century onwards (Thomas 1984: 119; Serpell and Paul 1994). Sabloff discusses some of the more subversive and unpredictable effects produced by companion animal relationships: 'pets' training their 'owners' in ways the latter might not even notice; the release of certain social prohibitions, for example against nurturing behaviour amongst men; the licensing of transitory forays into the animality of human nature; and the increased awareness of animals' perceptions, sufferings and pleasures (2001: 53–84). The political function of sentimental imagery has remained similarly versatile. The iconography of the Old Brown Dog, which became the focus for the anti-vivisection battles of the turn of the twentieth century, demonstrates the potency of such representations (Lansbury 1985: 3–26). Even Disney's saccharine creations – despite Berger's claim that they merely transform animals into 'human puppets' and thereby confirm the 'pettiness of current social relations' (1980: 13) – can have the effect of destabilizing the smooth career of capitalist modernity. The film *Bambi*, surely a high-water mark of sentimental iconography, has played a formative role in the production of generations of environmentalists and animal rights activists (Cartmill 1993: 179–88). Similarly, during the mid 1990s, the image of the baby veal calf, 'a kind of "Bambi" figure', with 'big eyes and long eyelashes', motivated members of the public who were 'not regular political activists' to protest against the export of British calves to Europe (Fudge 2002a: 39). Subversive use of kitsch animal imagery is also common among animal rights activists, for example anti-vivisection protestors dressing as Mickey Mouse outside laboratories using rodent animal models (Baker 2001: 226–31). As Steve Baker puts it, '[s]entimentality *matters*', precisely because it embodies ways of living 'inexpertly with animals' (Baker 2000: 177, 179), that is, the kinds of human–animal relation undertaken by those Sabloff calls 'people without natural history', the large social majority whose interactions with animals have never been dictated by the 'grand metaphors of the modern age', whether scientific or aesthetic (Sabloff 2001: 143 italics in original).

It seems appropriate to end this study with this reminder of the severely disabling effect that regimes of taste can have on the socially transformative function of literature. The fictions of Coetzee and Findley, and many others discussed in this chapter, demonstrate an emerging determination to dismantle such regimes, in order to re-engage literary fiction with the most vital and intimate of contemporary structures of feeling. They also suggest that today, living inexpertly with animals and our own animality amidst the ruins of modernity, we are especially in need of narratives that attempt translation between the animals we are and the animals we aren't.

Notes

Introduction

1 See for example Baker (2001: 11–15) and Burt (2005).
2 Turner (1980), Crosby (1986), Ritvo (1987; 1998).
3 Various genres of animal story are excluded from my discussion as a result of my decision to focus on these four fictional paradigms – for example, those that draw on non-human characters, images and story-lines from outside the Western cultural tradition. For discussion of this genre see Arnold and Walcott (1996), Nyman (2003), and Nyman and Smith (2004).

1 The Inhuman Fictions of Swift and Defoe

1 I use the term 'Enlightenment' in the general sense to describe an intel-lectual and ideological movement, extending beyond the eighteenth century in both directions, and characterized primarily by epistemolog-ical mobility and the *'way of thinking* introduced by Descartes' and repre-sented in the English context by the writings of Bacon, Newton, Locke and others (Hulme and Jordanova 1990: 2–3).
2 The significance of these narratives can be seen in their many retellings and derivations over the last three centuries: for example the influence of *Crusoe* and *Gulliver* on children's literature and cultural production, and indeed (following Rousseau) on the cultural understanding of the child (Cunliffe 2000).
3 Halewood and Lynch (1965) and Hammond (1982) advance the view that the Houyhnhnms represent Swift's commitment to a Stoic moral ideal. The opposing position, put forward for example by Williams (1951) and Ehrenpreis (1957), is that a society based solely on reason and devoid of any theological basis seems an unlikely utopia for a churchman to advance, and that it is uncharacteristic for Swift to offer unambiguously positive views of *anything*. The current scholarly mood is represented by Aravamudan's description of Houyhnhnm society as 'statist', 'segregate[d] according to strict racial criteria' and preoccupied with 'execrable' schemes of 'total extermination' (1999: 137).
4 These complementary tropes echo the parodies of the new science produced by the Scriblerians, the literary club surrounding Pope, of

which Swift was a member. One such piece took Edward Tyson's 1699 dissection of an 'Orang-outang' (in fact a chimpanzee) as evidence of the existence of a species of highly cultivated ape philosopher-politicians, whose history can be traced back to ancient times when 'they excell'd as much in the Arts of peaceful Government' (Wiseman 1999: 229, citing Pope). Another Scriblerian satire countered the Cartesian notion of the beast-machine by describing a hydraulically powered 'man-machine' which could 'reason as well as most of your country parsons' (Pope and Arbuthnot 2002 [1714]: 64). Similarly, in *Gulliver's Travels* the giant King of Brobdingnag speculates that Gulliver 'might be a piece of Clock-work . . . contrived by some ingenious Artist' (Swift 2002 [1726]: 86).

5 As discussed by Aravamudan (1999: 137) and Rawson (2001: 151).

6 This point is made by Oakleaf (1983: 174) and Michie (2006: 68).

7 My coinage here imitates Agamben's term *anthropophorous*, which combines *anthropos* with the suffix *-phorous*, from the Greek for bearing, forming, producing. In contrast, the suffix *-luotic* comes from *luo*, meaning to loose any person (or thing) formerly tied or fastened (for example, bandages or shoes); to free from bondage or prison; to declare unlawful; to deprive of authority; to undo, break up, demolish, dissolve, divorce, destroy, overthrow, do away with, annul, subvert.

8 Here and throughout this volume I use the notion of 'instrumentalism' as defined by Val Plumwood: a mode of relationship whereby other living beings are defined as passive objects available for manipulation according to the agenda of the user (1993: 339).

9 Here and throughout, I use the notion of 'ferity' (that is, the state or quality of being feral) to indicate those forms of wildness that represent a reaction against modernity's attempts at civilization, domestication, captivation or manipulation.

10 As Helen Tiffin argues in the context of contemporary fiction (2007b: 247–8).

11 For accounts of the association between non-human animals and non-Europeans see Thomas (1984: 42–5), Hawes (1991), Lamb (2001: 154–5) and Rawson (2001).

12 Defoe spells the word 'inhumane'. The difference in connotation that now exists between the terms 'inhumane' and 'inhuman' is due to the nineteenth-century association of the term 'humane' with compassionate sympathy for the suffering of others, especially animals.

13 Defoe and his contemporaries associate cannibalism with the uniquely human capacity for inhumanity because they believe (erroneously) that no other species eats its own kind (Rawson 2001: 76–89).

14 As discussed also by Lamb (2006: 169–70).

15 For instances of this historical theory see Bernard Mandeville's *The Fable of the Bees* (1924 [1725]: II: 230), or the writers mentioned by Thomas (1984: 28).

16 See Richard Nash's *Wild Enlightenment* for a discussion of Crusoe's feral goats that parallels my own (2003: 79–92).

17 For example Shaftesbury; see also Mandeville, who disagreed that sympathy was innate but advocated it anyway (1924 [1725]: 173–81). For relevant discussion of these thinkers see Ellis (1996: 10–11) and Flynn (1990: 171–6).

18 Dwyer also makes this point (2005: 14). Friday has (at least) two notable canine heirs relevant to this study. The first is the Dog-Man in H. G. Wells' *The Island of Doctor Moreau*, the narrator's only companion and protector after the deaths of the other humans on the island, who remarks with 'the ready tact of his canine blood' that '[t]he Master's will is sweet' (1996 [1896]: 192). The second is a sheepdog called Friday, owned by nineteenth-century New Zealand folk hero Jock Mackenzie, a Scots drover credited with the opening of vast tracts of South Island high country (which now bear his name) for sheep farming (Wedde 2007: 281).

2 Gulliver, Frankenstein, Moreau

1 As Malcomson points out, however, other aspects of Gulliver's initial observation – the colour of the creatures' hair and skin, for instance – betray their humanity and hint at their European origins (2006: 53).

2 In the later editions of the *Systema Naturae*, Linnaeus produced another variant, '*Homo ferus*' which is '*tetrapus* (walks on all fours), *mutus* (without language), and *hirsutus* (covered in hair)'. This inclusion was a reference to the '*enfants sauvages*, or wolf-children' (like Peter, the wild boy described by Defoe and Swift), who according to Agamben featured in the period as 'messengers of man's inhumanity, the witnesses to his fragile identity and his lack of a face of his own' (2004: 30). Such, as I have argued in the preceding chapter, is precisely the anthropoluotic function of the brute, mute, hirsute and tetrapedal Yahoos in the fourth part of *Gulliver's Travels*.

3 For a discussion of the racial and gender implications of these two related scenes see Rawson (2001: 163–80).

4 In fact even the foremost virtuosi sometimes found total detachment impossible. Hooke himself expressed distaste for the 'cruelty' of the dog and bellows experiment, remarking to Boyle that 'I shall hardly be induced to make any further trials of this kind, because of the torture of the creature' (cited in Jardine 2000: 116). Nonetheless after two attempts at this experiment at Royal Society meetings 'were thoroughly botched by less skilled dissectionists', Hooke did take over its public performance once more (Jardine 2000: 118).

5 A century later Mary Shelley still uses the word 'projector' to describe her protagonist Frankenstein; according to Hindle the word 'scientist' did not enter common usage until much later in the nineteenth century (1990: 29).

6 In 1999, agricultural research scientists in New Zealand gave serious consideration to a project designed to develop a breed of naked sheep (Ewan-Street 1999).

7 See Thomas (1984: 59–60), Ritvo (1987: 2–3, 47–8) and Brown (2001: 224).

8 For the applications and adaptations of the Frankenstein myth see Baldick (1987) and Marcus (2002).

9 For discussion of Bacon see Fudge (1999). The resources of Solomon's house include 'enclosures of all sorts of beasts and birds; which we use . . . for dissections and trials, that thereby we may take light what may be wrought upon the body of man'. Some of these experiments have

discovered means of 'resuscitating of some that seem dead in appearance, and the like' (Bacon 1942 [1627]: 291–2).

10 For discussions of *Frankenstein* and Rousseau see Marshall (1988), O'Rourke (1989) and Hustis (2003).

11 For the reading of *Frankenstein* as a 'failure of sympathy' see Marshall (1988: 195). For the suggestion that the novel identifies a distinction between different kinds of sympathy I am indebted to Hustis (2003); a similar point is made by Rowe (2006: 146).

12 In fact Frankenstein also applies some of the least human of these terms to himself and his family, including 'insect' (Shelley 1996 [1818]: 19), 'vampire' (49), 'spectre' (117) and 'wretch' (147). The word most commonly used to describe Frankenstein's animated being, 'creature', is routinely used in the period for non-human animals and humans as well. In the novel – apart from its applications to Frankenstein's Creature or his putative female companion – this word is used of people credited with exceptional virtue, or those who experience exceptional suffering, including Frankenstein himself (14 and 15), Clerval (16), Elizabeth (20), Justine (40), the De Laceys (73) and William (96).

13 See Butler (1996: 307 note 6), Marshall (1995: 71) and Rowe (2006: 137).

14 For discussion of the interrelationships amongst Romanticism, vegetarianism and humanitarian concern for non-human animals see Oerlemans (1994), Kenyon-Jones (2001), Perkins (2003), Rowe (2006) and Chapin (2006).

15 For further discussion of Erasmus Darwin in relation to Romantic writing, and *Frankenstein*, see Nichols (1997: 2001).

16 Wells himself makes the connection with Swift and Shelley in the preface to an omnibus edition of his scientific romances (1933: ix); see also Wilt (2003: 9). For discussion of *Frankenstein*'s influence on Wells, and on *Moreau* in particular, see Baldick (1987: 153–62). For an account of the Swiftian satirical origins of *Moreau* see Philmus (1981) and Stover (in Wells 1996 [1896]: 206 note 191).

17 See Philmus and Hughes on Wells' habit of using 'oppositional thinking' to develop his position on various scientific and social issues (1975: 6–7).

18 Hence, for example, all three film versions of the novel are unequivocal in condemning Moreau's project: see Kenton (1933), Taylor (1977) and Frankenheimer (1996).

19 For the impact of Darwinism on human–animal relations see also Turner (1980: 60–78).

20 As Barri Gold points out, Moreau's regime on the island represents a vivid playing-out of colonial power relations according to these regimes of bodily and reproductive discipline (2000).

21 It is for this reason, Stover argues, that the anti-Semitic stereotypes in *Moreau* associate Jewishness with isolationism (in Wells 1996 [1896]: 152 note 135; 155–6 note 139; 157 note 142).

22 I borrow the phrase 'carnivorous virility' from Jacques Derrida, who coins it to describe an association between masculinist power and the sacrifice of the non-human, which he perceives to characterize humanist modernity (1991: 113).

23 The comparison between Moreau's rhetoric and Bernard's is made also by Turney (1998: 57–8).
24 Wells later joined the Research Defence Society, formed in 1908 in response to the anti-vivisection movement (Lansbury 1985: 19, 149).
25 At the same time as Wells was defending vivisection, however, others – for example Frances Cobbe and Henry Salt – were deploying evolutionary theory to argue the exact opposite (White 2005: 68–70).
26 My argument in this paragraph is indebted to Stover (1996).
27 Stover and Lansbury associate the Puma Woman with the female anti-vivisectionists of the time, for whom the suffering of women and of animals was strongly linked (Stover, in Wells 1996 [1896]: 171 note 159; Lansbury 1985: 90).

3 Rendering the Whale

1 Ishmael's panegyrics on the civilizing mission of American whaling (Melville 2002 [1851]: 65, 99) draw on sources such as Edmund Burke's often-cited speech in praise of the industry (see Beale 1973 [1839]: 142–3 and Hart 1995 [1834]: xxi, 4); the 'memorial' presented to Congress by representatives from Nantucket during the 1820s (Hart 1995 [1834]: xxvi–xix); the conclusion to Charles Wilkes' report on the United States Exploring Expedition of 1838–42 (1845: vol. V 484–6); and popular 'true stories' about whaling life such as the account of 'Mocha Dick' by Jeremiah Reynolds (2002 [1839]).
2 For surveys of these trends see Thomas Macy, in Obed Macy (1972 [1880]: 290ff.); Starbuck (1989 [1882]: 110–13); Casarino (2002: 82–3).
3 Wilkes' conclusion is cited with approval in Browne (1968 [1846]: 557); see also Beale (1973 [1839]: 151–2), Bennett (1840: vol. II, 178) and Olmsted (1969 [1841]: 157).
4 See also Reynolds (2002 [1839]: 558), Olmsted (1969 [1841]: 156–7) and Browne (1968 [1846]: 297).
5 For this connection see Turner (1980: 39–59), Thomas (1984: 181–3, 295), Ritvo (1987: 125–66).
6 Keith Thomas cites the same passage, as embodying the 'one single, coherent and remarkably constant attitude [that] underlay the great bulk of the preaching and pamphleteering against animal cruelty between the fifteenth and nineteenth centuries' (1984: 153).
7 For this association see Bennett (1840: vol. II, 176–7).
8 For nineteenth-century debates about the mammalian or piscine status of whales see Browne (1968 [1846]: 59) and Ritvo (1998: 49).
9 Scoresby provides an important background figure for the opening chapters of *Frankenstein* too. In that novel, Walton's apprenticeship in arctic exploration is undertaken on Greenland whaling voyages of the kind most closely associated with Scoresby, who like Walton had a keen interest both in polar magnetism and the possibility of an Arctic passage from the Atlantic to the Pacific (Fulford *et al.* 2004: 161).
10 For doubts about Chase's account of the *Essex* sinking, see Francis Olmsted's *Incidents of a Whaling Voyage* (1969 [1841]: 144–5), which Melville knew. In the year of *Moby-Dick*'s publication, a *Punch* burlesque and an American opinion piece demonstrated urban intellectual disdain for such stories: both are reproduced in Sawtell (1962: 87–94).

11 The overwhelming of Ahab's ability to make rational decisions by his obsession with pursuit of his non-human antagonist echoes Frankenstein's vengeful pursuit of the Creature, which is driven by 'mechanical impulse' (Shelley 1996 [1818]: 141). For other evidence of *Frankenstein*'s influence in *Moby-Dick* see Baldick (1987: 74–84).

12 For a more extensive discussion of the issues discussed in this section, see Armstrong (2004), of which the remainder of this chapter is an abridged version.

13 The phrase cited here is Frans de Waal's gloss on a definition of culture proposed by Kinji Imanishi, also quoted by Erica Fudge (2002a: 133). See also de Waal's brief comments on recent studies of cetacean cultural knowledge (2001: 270).

14 See for example Elaine Crist's analysis of Charles Darwin's anthropomorphisms, which she argues do not merely represent the 'metaphorical extension of language from the human to the animal case' but are intended 'as realistic representations of animal life' (1999: 49).

15 See Philo and Wilbert for relevant discussion of Latour's comments (2000: 19).

16 The sources in question are Beale (1973 [1839]: 125–6), Bennett (1840: vol. II, 179), Olmsted (1969 [1841]: 139).

17 See for example Starbuck (1989 [1882]: 126–8) and Cheever (1991 [1850]: 185–8).

18 Many studies have shown how *Moby-Dick* satirically recognizes the nation's dependence upon the labour of Native Americans, African American slaves and conscripted Pacific Islanders. See James (1953), Heimert (1963), Staud (1992), Niemeyer (1999), Marr (2001) and Casarino (2002).

4 Modernism and the Hunt for Redemption

1 Foucault concentrates on the 'mechanisation' of disciplinary force especially in Part Three of *Discipline and Punish* (1977: 135–228).

2 The radical instrumentalism portrayed by Sinclair remains at work in industrial food production today. Sabloff cites a contemporary farm management text which recommends that its reader '[f]orget the pig is an animal. Treat it just like a machine in a factory. Schedule treatments like you would lubrication. Breeding season is the first step in an assembly line. And marketing like the delivery of finished goods' (in Sabloff 2001: 91). The exploitation of both workers and animals in contemporary large-scale hog production have been recently described, in ways remarkably similar to Sinclair's novel, by Charlie LeDuff (2000) and Matthew Scully (2002: 246–8).

3 The implications of Freud's comments about animality in the context of his theory of dreams are discussed by Lippit (2000: 164) and Creed (2007: 59–63).

4 Of course redemptive animality was not the only form therio-primitivism took following Freud and modernism; some writers continued to equate the most destructive tendencies in modernity with human animality. Hence, for example, Aldous Huxley's novel *Ape and Essence* (1949) describes a nuclear apocalypse at the hands of technologically

advanced baboons. Here an irrational aggressiveness at the heart of human being is embodied by the animal: '[e]nds are ape-chosen; only the means are man's' (Huxley 1949: 32). As my next chapter will discuss, post-war primate studies forced a revaluation of this stereotypical association of apes with savagery.

5 In his letters Lawrence decries the kind of 'scientific talk' which assumes that 'everything work[s] from a mechanical basis. It is a great lie. They think a living being is a thing that can be wound up in the head, and made to go through the proper motions' (cited in Wallace 2005: 152).

6 Lawrence often uses the human-equine figure, for example in his letters, where he asserts that 'the blood, the flesh, [is] wiser than the intellect', which 'is only a bit and a bridle' (cited in Wallace 2005: 179), and in *Kangaroo*, where he describes the human being as 'an animal saddled with a mental consciousness' (Lawrence 1994 [1923]: 263). A more conventional association between horses and the passions is apparent in such moments as Ursula Brangwen's encounter with running horses after the end of her affair with Skrebensky in *The Rainbow* (Lawrence 1981 [1915]: 423–5; Asker 1996: 116–17).

7 An example of a Lawrencean character who takes the inappropriate path of regression towards 'brute' therio-primitivism is provided by Annable in *The White Peacock*, as Asker points out (1996: 108).

8 This passage is cited approvingly by Murphy and Hays (both in Fleming 1999: 45, 166).

9 See for example Hemingway Tours and Safaris, which offers tours that re-enact Papa's therio-primitivist epiphanies, including big-game fishing and hunting in Cuba and Africa and attendance at the running of the bulls in Pamplona. The company's website includes images of Hemingway and a downloadable interview with Gregorio Fuentes, boat captain of the *Pilar* and 'the real living legend of *The Old Man of the Sea*' (Hemingway Tours and Safaris 2006).

10 For a suggestive reading of anthropomorphism in Gowdy's novel see Oerlemans (2007).

11 Cary Wolfe argues that these latter interpretations result from the editing of the published text, whereas the full manuscript shows more radical possibilities entailed by the disruption of David's identification with the victimized animal (2003: 150–9).

12 Carey Voeller reads the elephant episode in *The Garden of Eden* as part of a more general tendency in Hemingway's hunting narratives to show 'textual admissions of sympathy and sorrow linger[ing] in the margins' (2005: 75).

5 Animal Refugees in the Ruins of Modernity

1 The most famous example is 'Earthrise', taken by Apollo 8 astronaut William A. Anders from the lunar orbit on 24 December 1968, described by American nature photographer Galen Rowell as 'the most influential environmental photograph ever taken' (Zimmerman 1998: 242).

2 Graham Huggan makes the same point in his extended and suggestive reading of Gowdy's novel (2004: 714–19).

3 This is, for example, the way June Dwyer reads Martel's novel (2005).

4 For discussion of the implications of such incidents see Tiffin (2007a).

5 Ashcroft, Griffiths and Tiffin emphasize the classifying and legislating dimension of Noah's role in *Not Wanted* by reading his name as 'Doctor No/Yes' (1989: 99).

6 Zinc is an element frequently used in alloys.

7 The 1994 edition of *Dorland's Illustrated Medical Dictionary* still defines 'sacrifice' as meaning 'to kill an experimental animal' (Anderson 1994: 1,479). See also Birke, Arluke and Michael (2007: 100).

8 Many readings have been offered of this novel, and especially its final scene. My own perspective owes much to Lucy Graham's discussion of sacrificial metaphysics and animal embodiedness in *Disgrace* (2002); for an approach that is in many ways complementary see also Attridge (2004: 174–91).

9 The phrase comes originally from Isaiah 53.7; in the Christian tradition it is conventionally interpreted as a reference to the self-sacrifice of the Messiah.

10 In *Silent Spring* Rachel Carson suggests that agricultural and garden chemical treatments 'should not be called "insecticides" but "biocides"' (1962: 8).

11 Indeed Patterson argues that the animal rights movement has been significantly shaped by those 'whose advocacy of animals has been influenced and in some cases shaped by the Holocaust', including survivors and children of survivors – for example Isaac Bashevis Singer, whose remark that 'for the animals it is an eternal Treblinka' gives Patterson's book its title (2002: 183).

12 For comparable challenges to the distinction between urban and natural worlds, and between the domestic and the wild, see Jennifer Wolch's article 'Zoöpolis' (1998: 125) and Barney Nelson's *The Wild and the Domestic* (2000).

13 Baker here deploys a phrase from Gilles Deleuze and Felix Guattari, '*une ligne de fuite*', which can be rendered in English either as 'line of flight' or 'line of escape', and which indicates an unexpected, radical and tangential escape from conventional systems of control (Baker 2000: 117–19).

14 Chris Philo and Chris Wilbert coin the term 'beastly place' to describe what occurs when non-human species transgress the 'animal spaces' by which human societies seek to order them (2000).

15 See for example Merchant (1980: 217–30), Scholtmeijer (1993: 296–7) and Sabloff (2001: 146).

16 Costello's examples of recalcitrant non-human agents include the very animal, the rat, most commonly forced into service as the 'hero of science' in laboratory experiments (Burt 2004).

17 Snowman's dream of Alex's final departure may come true. African Grey parrots have become so popular as pets, because of their strong capacity to express themselves in human terms, that 'trade in the birds is driving them to extinction in an increasing part of their range' (McCarthy 2006).

18 I am grateful to Mandala White for drawing Latour's book, and especially this passage from it, to my attention.

19 Buz also recalls Sugito, Biruté Galdikas' favourite adoptive orang-utan child at Camp Leakey, who at the age of seven began drowning his orphan 'siblings', which Galdikas considers 'the dreadful consequences of inadvertently raising an orang-utan as a human being', since the oedipalized Sugito 'was acting out his jealousy of the infants who had seemingly replaced him in my affection' (1980: 832).

20 The chimpanzees of Gombe have been subject to more powerful human-made pressures than those produced by Goodall's inadvertent exacerbation of competition for food. Towards the end of *In the Shadow of Man* Goodall laments the hunting and sale of chimpanzees for meat, 'the spread of agriculture and forestry', and the transmission of human diseases to chimps as a result of the growing proximity between the two species (1971: 228–9). Three decades later Gombe Reserve, an area no larger than thirty square kilometres, is an island of green in a landscape otherwise entirely deforested to provide farmland, firewood and shelter for the people of the nearby villages and camps full of refugees from civil wars in Burundi and Congo.

21 Finding the core of both chimpunity and humanity to be constituted by aggressive and sexual instincts, Self's novel echoes, respectively, the negative therio-primitivism of Aldous Huxley's *Ape and Essence* (1949) and the bawdy racism of John Collier's *His Monkey Wife* (1930). Annamarie Jagose's 1998 novel *Lulu* represents the same legacy. Based on the story of Lucy Temerlin (Fouts and Mills 1997: 145–55), it depicts the oedipal relationship between husband-and-wife researchers and a young chimp taken into their home for linguistic and psychological research.

22 Steve Baker argues that Self is not 'entirely hostile' towards the political aims of movements like the Great Ape Project, suggesting the real target of this 'uncomfortable episode' is 'the stupidity of unthinking identification' between humans and other animals in the hope of 'merely *wishing away*' the dividing line between species (2000: 161–2 italics in original). While this pinpoints the source of Self's derision, I would add that his novel underestimates the epistemological basis of the Great Ape Project, while remaining blind to its own reductive dissolution of the chimp–human barrier through reliance on sociobiological essentialism.

23 As Lamb argues, Costello struggles to find words with which to express the extra-linguistic 'case of metamorphosis that arises from unlimited sympathy with animals' (2006: 177).

24 Graham Huggan, in an otherwise insightful reading of Coetzee, demonstrates the tendency to confuse sympathy and sentiment when he comments that Elizabeth Costello is 'sentimental to a fault' (2004: 712).

25 See Oerlemans for a comparable reading (2007).

References

Adams, C. J. (1990) *The Sexual Politics of Meat*, New York: Continuum.

Agamben, G. (2004) *The Open: Man and Animal*, trans. K. Attrell, Stanford: Stanford University Press.

The Alex Foundation (2007) 'The Alex Foundation', online at www.alex-foundation.org/index2.htm

Allen, M. (1983) *Animals in American Literature*, Urbana, Ill.: University of Illinois Press.

Anderson, D. M. E. A. (ed.) (1994) *Dorland's Illustrated Medical Dictionary*, Philadelphia: W.B. Sanders.

Aravamudan, S. (1999) *Tropicopolitans: Colonialism and Agency, 1688–1804*, Durham, NC: Duke University Press.

Arluke, A. and Sanders, C. (1996) *Regarding Animals*, Philadelphia: Temple University Press.

Armstrong, P. (2004) '"Leviathan is a Skein of Networks": Translating Nature and Culture in *Moby-Dick*', *ELH* 71: 1,039–63.

Arnold, A. J. and Walcott, D. (1996) *Monsters, Tricksters, and Sacred Cows: Animal Tales and American Identities*, Charlottesville: University Press of Virginia.

Ashcroft, B., Griffiths, G. and Tiffin, H. (1989) *The Empire Writes Back: Theory and Practice in Post-Colonial Literatures*, 2nd ed., London: Routledge.

Asker, D. B. D. (1996) *The Modern Bestiary: Animals in English Fiction, 1880–1945*, Lewiston, NY: Edwin Mellen Press.

Attridge, D. (2004) *J. M. Coetzee and the Ethics of Reading*, Chicago: University of Chicago Press.

Atwood, M. (2003) *Oryx and Crake*, London: Bloomsbury.

Ausband, S. C. (1975) 'The Whale and the Machine: An Approach to *Moby-Dick*', *American Literature*, 47, 2: 197–211.

Bacon, F. (1942 [1627]) 'New Atlantis', in *Essays and New Atlantis*, Toronto: D. Van Nostrand.

Bagemihl, B. (1999) *Biological Exuberance: Animal Homosexuality and Natural Diversity*, New York: St Martin's Press.

Baker, S. (2000) *The Postmodern Animal*, London: Reaktion.

——— (2001) *Picturing the Beast: Animals, Identity, and Representation*, Urbana, Ill.: University of Illinois Press.

Balcombe, J. (2006) *Pleasurable Kingdom: Animals and the Nature of Feeling Good*, London: Macmillan.

Baldick, C. (1987) *In Frankenstein's Shadow: Myth, Monstrosity, and Nineteenth-Century Writing*, Oxford: Clarendon Press.

Barker-Benfield, G. J. (1992) *The Culture of Sensibility*, Chicago: University of Chicago Press.

Barrett Browning, E. (1900 [1844]) 'To Flush, My Dog', in *The Complete Works of Elizabeth Barrett Browning*, New York: Thomas Y. Crowell.

Bate, J. (2000) *The Song of the Earth*, London: Picador.

Beale, T. (1973 [1839]) *The Natural History of the Sperm Whale*, London: Holland Press.

Bell, M. (2000) *Sentimentalism, Ethics and the Culture of Feeling*, Houndmills: Palgrave.

Bennett, F. D. (1840) *Narrative of a Whaling Voyage Round the Globe*, London: R. Bentley.

Berger, J. (1980) 'Why Look at Animals?' *About Looking*, New York: Random House.

Bernard, C. (1957 [1865]) *An Introduction to the Study of Experimental Medicine*, trans. H. C. Green, New York: Dover Publications.

Birke, L. (1994) *Feminism, Animals and Science: The Naming of the Shrew*, Buckingham: Open University Press.

Birke, L., Arluke, A. and Michael, M. (2007) *The Sacrifice: How Scientific Experiments Transform Animals and People*, West Lafayette, Indiana: Purdue University Press.

Boullé, P. (1966) *Monkey Planet (La Planète des Singes)*, trans. X. Fielding, Harmondsworth: Penguin.

Bradshaw, G. (2004) 'Not by Bread Alone: Symbolic Loss, Trauma, and Recovery in Elephant Communities', *Society and Animals*, 12, 2: 143–58.

Bradshaw, G., *et al.* (2005) 'Elephant Breakdown', *Nature*, 433, 7,028: 807.

Brodhead, R. H. (1986) 'Trying All Things: An Introduction to *Moby-Dick*', in R. H. Brodhead (ed.), *New Essays on Moby-Dick*, Cambridge: Cambridge University Press.

Brophy, B. (1953) *Hackenfeller's Ape*, London: Rupert Hart-Davis.

Brown, L. (2001) *Fables of Modernity: Literature and Culture in the English Eighteenth Century*, Ithaca: Cornell University Press.

Browne, J. R. (1968 [1846]) *Etchings of a Whaling Cruise*, Cambridge, MA: Belknap Press.

Burt, J. (2002) *Animals in Film*, London: Reaktion.

—— (2004) *Rat*, London: Reaktion.

—— (2005) 'A Close Reading of John Berger's "Why Look at Animals?"', *Worldviews*, 9: 203–18.

Butler, M. (1996) '*Frankenstein* and Radical Science', in J. P. Hunter (ed.), *Frankenstein*, New York: Norton.

Caldwell, J. (1999) 'Sympathy and Science in *Frankenstein*', in A. Hadfield *et al.* (ed.). *The Ethics in Literature*, Basingstoke: Macmillan.

Canetti, E. (1962) *Crowds and Power*, New York: Viking Press.

Carson, R. (1962) *Silent Spring*, Boston: Houghton Mifflin.

Cartmill, M. (1993) *A View to a Death in the Morning: Hunting and Nature Through History*, Cambridge, MA: Harvard University Press.

Casarino, C. (2002) *Modernity at Sea: Melville, Marx, Conrad in Crisis*, Minneapolis: University of Minnesota Press.

Cavalieri, P. and Singer, P. (eds) (1993) *The Great Ape Project: Equality Beyond Humanity*, New York: St Martin's Press.

Chapin, L. (2006) 'Shelley's Great Chain of Being: From "Blind Worms" to "New Fledged Eagles"', in F. Palmeri (ed.), *Humans and Other Animals in Eighteenth-Century British Culture*, Aldershot: Ashgate.

Chapman, M. and Hendler, G. (1999) 'Introduction', in M. Chapman and G. Hendler (eds), *Sentimental Men: Masculinity and the Politics of Affect in American Culture*, Berkeley: University of California Press.

Chase, O. (2000 [1821]) *The Wreck of the Whaleship Essex*, London: Review.

Cheever, H. T. (1991 [1850]) *The Whale and His Captors*, Fairfield, Wash.: Ye Galleon Press.

Clark, N. (1999) 'Wild Life: Ferality and the Frontier with Chaos', in K. Neumann *et al.* (eds), *Quicksands: Foundational Histories in Australia and Aotearoa New Zealand*, Sydney: University of New South Wales Press.

Coetzee, J. M. (2000) *Disgrace*, London: Vintage.

―――― (2003) *Elizabeth Costello*, Sydney: Knopf.

Collier, J. (1930) *His Monkey Wife, or, Married to a Chimp*, London: P. Davies.

Crane, R. S. (1962) 'The Houyhnhnms, the Yahoos, and the History of Ideas', in J. A. Mazzeo (ed.), *Reason and the Imagination: Studies in the History of Ideas, 1600–1800*, New York: Columbia University Press.

Creed, B. (2007) 'What Do Animals Dream Of? Or *King Kong* as Darwinian Screen Animal', in L. Simmons and P. Armstrong (eds), *Knowing Animals*, Leiden and Boston: Brill.

Crist, E. (1999) *Images of Animals: Anthropomorphism and the Animal Mind*, Philadelphia: Temple University Press.

Crosby, A. W. (1986) *Ecological Imperialism: The Biological Expansion of Europe, 900–1900*, Cambridge: Cambridge University Press.

Cunliffe, M. (2000) 'Reading *Gulliver's Travels* as a Child and as an Adult', in G. Weiner (ed.), *Readings on Gulliver's Travels*, San Diego: Greenhaven.

Darwin, E. (1978 [1803]) *The Golden Age; the Temple of Nature, or, the Origin of Society*, New York and London: Garland.

De Grave, K. (2003) 'Introduction', in U. Sinclair, *The Jungle*, Tucson, AZ: See Sharp Press.

Defoe, D. (1705) 'Advice from the Scandal Club', in *Defoe's Review, 1704–13*, 2, 10 (27 March).

―――― (1951 [1713]) 'Of Divinity in Trade', in W. L. Payne (ed.), *The Best of Defoe's Review*, New York: Columbia University Press.

―――― (1969 [1727]) *The Compleat English Tradesman*, New York: Augustus M. Kelley.

―――― (1994 [1719]) *Robinson Crusoe*, New York: Norton.

Derrida, J. (1991) 'Eating Well, or, the Calculation of the Subject: An Interview with Jacques Derrida', trans. E. Cadava and A. Tomiche, in E. Cadava *et al.* (eds), *Who Comes after the Subject?*, New York: Routledge.

—— (2002) 'The Animal That Therefore I Am (More to Follow)', trans. T.D. Wills, *Critical Inquiry*, 28, 4: 369–418.

Descartes, R. (1960 [1637]) *Discourse on Method*, trans. A. Wollaston, Harmondsworth: Penguin.

Desmond, A. J. (1979) *The Ape's Reflexion*, New York: The Dial Press.

de Waal, F. (1996) *Good Natured: The Origins of Right and Wrong in Humans and Other Animals*, Cambridge, MA: Harvard University Press.

—— (2001) *The Ape and the Sushi Master*, London: Penguin.

Douglas, A. (1998) *The Feminization of American Culture*, New York: Noonday.

Druett, J. (1983) *Exotic Intruders: The Introduction of Plants and Animals into New Zealand*, Auckland: Heinemann.

Dwyer, J. (2005) 'Yann Martel's *Life of Pi* and the Evolution of the Shipwreck Narrative', *Modern Language Studies*, 35, 2: 9–21.

Ehrenpreis, I. (1957) 'The Origins of *Gulliver's Travels*', *PMLA*, 72, 5: 880–99.

Ellis, M. (1996) *The Politics of Sensibility*, Cambridge: Cambridge University Press.

Ewan-Street, I. (1999) 'NZ Scientists Working on GE Sheep-without-Wool', New Zealand Green Party, online at www.greens.org.nz/searchdocs/PR4127.html

Findley, T. (1984) *Not Wanted on the Voyage*, New York: Viking.

Fisher, P. (1985) *Hard Facts: Setting and Form in the American Novel*, Oxford: Oxford University Press.

Fleming, R. E. (1999) (ed.), *Hemingway and the Natural World*, Moscow, Idaho: University of Idaho Press.

Flint, C. (1998) 'Speaking Objects: The Circulation of Stories in Eighteenth-Century Prose Fiction', *PMLA*, 113, 2: 212–26.

Flynn, C. H. (1990) *The Body in Swift and Defoe*, Cambridge: Cambridge University Press.

Ford, H. and Crowther, S. (2000 [1922]) *My Life and Work*, New York: Doubleday, Page & Company.

Foucault, M. (1977) *Discipline and Punish*, trans. A. Sheridan, London: Penguin.

Fouts, R. and Mills, S. T. (1997) *Next of Kin*, New York: William Morrow.

Fox, C. (1995) 'How to Prepare a Noble Savage: The Spectacle of Human Science', in C. Fox *et al.* (eds), *Inventing Human Science*, Berkeley: University of California Press.

Fox, M. (1990) *Inhumane Society*, New York: St. Martin's Press.

Frankenheimer, J. (dir.) (1996) *The Island of Dr Moreau*, USA: New Line.

Freeman, J. (1926) *Herman Melville*, Edinburgh: Macmillan.

Freud, S. (1976) *The Interpretation of Dreams*, London and New York: Penguin.

—— (1985) *The Origins of Religion*, London and New York: Penguin.

Fudge, E. (1999) 'Calling Creatures by Their True Names: Bacon, the New Science and the Beast in Man', in E. Fudge *et al.* (eds), *At the Borders of the Human: Beasts, Bodies and Natural Philosophy in the Early Modern Period*, Basingstoke: Macmillan.

—— (2002a) *Animal*, London: Reaktion.

—— (2002b) 'A Left-Handed Blow: Writing the History of Animals', in N. Rothfels (ed.), *Representing Animals*, Bloomington: Indiana University Press.

Fulford, T., Lee, D. and Kitson, P. J. (2004) *Literature, Science and Exploration in the Romantic Era*, Cambridge, UK and New York: Cambridge University Press.

Gagosian, R. B. (2003) 'Abrupt Climate Change: Should We Be Worried?', online at www.whoi.edu/cms/files/dfino/2006/1/Abruptclimatechange_7229.pdf

Gajdusek, R. (2001) 'The Hemingway of Cuba and Bimini and His Later Relationship to Nature', *North Dakota Quarterly*, 68, 2–3: 91–108.

Galdikas, B. (1980) 'Living with Orangutans', *National Geographic* 157, 6: 830–53.

Gold, B. J. (2000) 'Reproducing Empire: Moreau and Others', *Nineteenth Century Studies*, 14: 173–98.

Goodall, J. (1971) *In the Shadow of Man*, London: Collins.

—— (1986) *The Chimpanzees of Gombe*, Cambridge, MA and London: Belknap.

Gorilla Foundation/Koko.Org (2007) 'Events', online at www.koko.org/news/Events/

Gowdy, B. (1999) *The White Bone*, New York: Metropolitan Books.

Graham, L. (2002) '"Yes, I am Giving him Up": Sacrificial Responsibility and Likeness with Dogs in J.M. Coetzee's Recent Fiction', *Scrutiny 2*, 7, 1: 4–15.

Halewood, W. H. and Lynch, M. (1965) 'Houyhnhnm Est Animal Rationale', *Journal of the History of Ideas,* 26: 273–81.

Hammond, E. R. (1982) 'Nature-Reason-Justice in *Utopia* and *Gulliver's Travels*', *Studies in English Literature, 1500–1900*, 22, 3: 445–68.

Hansen, M. (1997) '"Not Thus, after All, Would Life Be Given": Technesis, Technology and the Parody of Romantic Poetics in *Frankenstein*', *Studies in Romanticism*, 36, 4: 575–609.

Haraway, D. (1989) *Primate Visions: Gender, Race and Nature in the World of Modern Science*, New York and London: Routledge.

—— (1991) *Simians, Cyborgs and Women: The Reinvention of Nature*, London and New York: Routledge.

Haraway, D. and Goodeve, T.N. (2000) *How Like a Leaf*, New York: Routledge.

Hart, J. C. (1995 [1834]) *Miriam Coffin, or, the Whale Fishermen*, Nantucket: Mill Hill Press.

Hawes, C. (1991) 'Three Times Round the Globe: Gulliver and Colonial Discourse', *Cultural Critique*, 18, 187–214.

Hawkins, M. (1997) *Social Darwinism in European and American Thought, 1860–1945*, Cambridge: Cambridge University Press.

Heimert, A. (1963) '*Moby-Dick* and American Political Symbolism', *American Quarterly*, 15: 498–534.

Hemingway, E. (1932) *Death in the Afternoon*, London: Jonathan Cape.

—— (1957 [1952]) *The Old Man and the Sea*, London: Jonathan Cape.

—— (1962 [1926]) *Three Novels of Ernest Hemingway*, New York: Scribner's.

—— (1968) *By-Line: Ernest Hemingway; Selected Articles and Dispatches of Four Decades*, London: Collins.

—— (1986) *The Garden of Eden*, New York: Scribner's.

—— (1998 [1935]) *The Green Hills of Africa*, New York: Scribner's.

Hemingway, G. H. (1976) *Papa: A Personal Memoir*, Boston: Houghton Mifflin.

Hemingway Tours and Safaris (2006) 'Hemingway Tours and Safaris', online at www.hemingwaytoursandsafaris.com/index.html

Hindle, M. (1990) 'Vital Matters: Mary Shelley's *Frankenstein* and Romantic Science', *Critical Survey*, 2, 1: 29–35.

Hodgart, M. (2000) 'Swift's Satire of English Politics', in G. Weiner (ed.), *Readings on Gulliver's Travels*, San Diego: Greenhaven Press.

Høeg, P. (1996) *The Woman and the Ape*, trans. B. Haveland, London: Harvill Press.

Horkheimer, M. and Adorno, T. W. (1973) *Dialectic of Enlightenment*, trans. J. Cumming, London: Allen Lane.

Huggan, G. (2004) '"Greening" Post-Colonialism: Ecocritical Perspectives', *Modern Fiction Studies* 50, 3: 701–33.

Hulme, P. and Jordanova, L. (eds) (1990) *The Enlightenment and Its Shadows*, London and New York: Routledge.

Hustis, H. (2003) 'Responsible Creativity and the "Modernity" of Mary Shelley's Prometheus', *Studies in English Literature, 1500–1900*, 43, 4: 845–58.

Hutton, R. H. (1972 [1896]) 'The Island of Doctor Moreau', in P. Parrinder (ed.), *H. G. Wells: The Critical Heritage*, London and Boston: Routledge and Kegan Paul.

Huxley, A. (1949) *Ape and Essence*, London: Chatto & Windus.

Jackson, P. (2006) (dir.) *Skull Island: A Natural History*, USA: Universal Studios.

Jaffe, L. (2005) '*Gulliver's Travels*, by Jonathan Swift: Chronology', online at www.jaffebros.com/lee/gulliver/chron.html#notes

Jagose, A. (1998) *Lulu: A Romance*, Wellington: Victoria University Press.

James, C. L. R. (1953) *Mariners, Renegades and Castaways: The Story of Herman Melville and the World We Live In*, New York: C. L. R. James.

Jane Goodall Institute (2007) 'Chimpanzee Central', online at www.jane-goodall.org/chimp_central/chimpanzees/gombe/tool.asp

Jardine, L. (2000) *Ingenious Pursuits: Building the Scientific Revolution*, London: Abacus.

Kac, E. (2000) 'GFP Bunny', online at www.ekac.org/gfpbunny.html

Kafka, F. (1999 [1919]) 'A Report to an Academy', trans. W. Muir and E. Muir, in N. N. Glatzer (ed.), *The Complete Stories*, New York: Vintage.

Kemp, P. (1982) *H.G. Wells and the Culminating Ape*, Houndmills, Basingstoke: Macmillan.

Kenton, E. C. (dir.) (1933) *The Island of Lost Souls*, USA: Paramount.

Kenyon-Jones, C. (2001) *Kindred Brutes: Animals in Romantic-Period Writing*, Aldershot: Ashgate.

King, T. (1993) *Green Grass, Running Water*, New York: Bantam.

Kotzwinkle, W. (1976) *Doctor Rat*, New York: Knopf.

Lamb, J. (2001) 'Modern Metamorphoses and Disgraceful Tales: Eighteenth-Century Fictional "It-Narratives"', *Critical Inquiry*, 28, 1: 133–66.

—— (2006) 'Gulliver and the Lives of Animals', in F. Palmeri (ed.), *Humans and Other Animals in Eighteenth-Century British Culture*, Aldershot: Ashgate.

Lansbury, C. (1985) *The Old Brown Dog: Women, Workers, and Vivisection in Edwardian England*, Madison: University of Wisconsin Press.

Latour, B. (1987) *Science in Action*, Cambridge, MA: Harvard University Press.

—— (1993) *We Have Never Been Modern*, trans. C. Porter, Cambridge, MA: Harvard University Press.

—— (2004) *Politics of Nature: How to Bring the Sciences into Democracy*, trans. C. Porter, Cambridge, MA: Harvard University Press.

Lawrence, D.H. (1925) *St Mawr; Together with the Princess*, London: Martin Secker.

—— (1931 [1923]) *Fantasia of the Unconscious*, London: Martin Secker.

—— (1933) *Studies in Classic American Literature*, London: Heinemann.

—— (1962 [1925]) *The Symbolic Meaning: The Uncollected Versions of Studies in Classic American Literature*, Arundel: Centaur Press.

—— (1981 [1915]) *The Rainbow*, London: Folio Society.

—— (1987 [1926]) *The Plumed Serpent (Quetzalcoatl)*, Cambridge: Cambridge University Press.

—— (1989 [1920]) *Women in Love*, Cambridge: Cambridge University Press.

—— (1992 [1932]) *Sketches of Etruscan Places and Other Italian Essays*, Cambridge: Cambridge University Press.

—— (1994 [1923]) *Kangaroo*, Cambridge: Cambridge University Press.

LeDuff, C. (2000) 'At the Slaughterhouse, Some Things Never Die', *New York Times*, 16 June: A1.

Lévi-Strauss, C. (1963) *Totemism*, trans. R. Needham, Boston: Beacon.

Liggins, E. (2000) 'The Medical Gaze and the Female Corpse: Looking at Bodies in Mary Shelley's *Frankenstein*', *Studies in the Novel*, 32, 2: 129–146.

Lippit, A. M. (2000) *Electric Animal: Towards a Rhetoric of Wildlife*, Minneapolis: University of Minnesota Press.

Locke, J. (1997 [1689]) 'An Essay Concerning Human Understanding', in J. W. Yolton (ed.), *The Works of John Locke*, London: Routledge.

Love, G. A. (2003) *Practical Ecocriticism*, Charlottesville: University of Virginia Press.

Macy, O. (1972 [1880]) *The History of Nantucket*, Clifton: Augustus M. Kelley.

Malamud, B. (1982) *God's Grace*, London: Chatto & Windus.

Malamud, R. (1998) *Reading Zoos: Representations of Animals and Captivity*, New York: New York University Press.

Malcomson, C. (2006) 'Gulliver's Travels and Studies of Skin Colour in the Royal Society', in F. Palmeri (ed.), *Humans and Other Animals in Eighteenth-Century British Culture*, Aldershot: Ashgate.

Mandeville, B. (1924 [1725]) *The Fable of the Bees: Or, Private Virtues, Publick Benefits*, Oxford: Clarendon Press.

Marcus, S. (2002) 'Frankenstein: Myths of Scientific and Medical Knowledge and Stories of Human Relations', *Southern Review*, 38, 1: 188–201.

Marr, T. (2001) 'Melville's Ethnic Conscriptions', *Leviathan*, 3, 1: 5–29.

Marshall, D. (1988) *The Surprising Effects of Sympathy: Marivaux, Diderot, Rousseau, and Mary Shelley*, Chicago: University of Chicago Press.

Marshall, T. (1995) *Murdering to Dissect: Grave-Robbing, Frankenstein and the Anatomy Literature*, Manchester: Manchester University Press.

Martel, Y. (2002) *Life of Pi*, Edinburgh: Canongate.

Martin, V. (1994) *The Great Divorce*, New York: N. A. Talese.

Marx, K. (1906 [1867]) *Capital: A Critique of Political Economy*, trans. S. Moore and E. Aveling, Chicago: Charles H. Kerr Company.

Marx, L. (1964) *The Machine in the Garden: Technology and the Pastoral Ideal in America*, New York: Oxford University Press.

Marzec, R. P. (2002) 'Enclosures, Colonization, and the Robinson Crusoe Syndrome: A Genealogy of Land in a Global Context', *Boundary 2*, 29, 2: 129–56.

Matthews, S. (2004) *Modernism*, London and New York: Arnold.

McCarthy, M. (2006) '"Pretty Polly" Parrot under Threat of Extinction', *Independent*, 6 July.

McInelly, B. C. (2003) 'Expanding Empires, Expanding Selves: Colonialism, the Novel, and Robinson Crusoe', *Studies in the Novel*, 35, 1: 1–21.

McLane, M. N. (2000) *Romanticism and the Human Sciences: Poetry, Population, and the Discourse of the Species*, Cambridge: Cambridge University Press.

Meadows, D. H. *et al.* (1972) *The Limits to Growth*, New York: Universe Books.

Melville, H. (1960) *The Letters of Herman Melville*, New Haven: Yale University Press.

—— (2002 [1851]) *Moby-Dick*, New York: Norton.

Merchant, C. (1980) *The Death of Nature: Women, Ecology, and the Scientific Revolution*, San Francisco: Harper & Row.

Michie, A. (2006) 'Gulliver the Houyahoo: Swift, Locke and the Ethics of Excessive Individualism', in F. Palmeri (ed.), *Humans and Other Animals in Eighteenth-Century British Culture*, Aldershot: Ashgate.

Mirzoeff, N. (2002) 'The Empire of Camps', *Afterimage*, 30, 2: 11–12.

Montag, W. (2000) 'The "Workshop of Filthy Creation": A Marxist Reading of *Frankenstein*', in J. M. Smith (ed.), *Frankenstein*, Boston: St Martin's Press.

Moore, C. (2003) *Fluke; or, I Know Why the Winged Whale Sings*, New York: William Morrow.

Morton, J. and Smith, N. (1999) 'Planting Indigenous Species: A Subversion of Australian Eco-Nationalism', in K. Neumann *et al.* (eds), *Quicksands: Foundational Histories in Australia and Aotearoa New Zealand*, Sydney: University of New South Wales Press.

Nash, R. (2003) *Wild Enlightenment: The Borders of Human Identity in the Eighteenth Century*, Charlottesville: University of Virginia Press.

Nelson, B. (2000) *The Wild and the Domestic: Animal Representation, Ecocriticism, and Western American Literature*, Reno: University of Nevada Press.

Nichols, A. (1997) 'The Anxiety of Species: Toward a Romantic Natural History', online at http: //users.dickinson.edu/~nicholsa/Romnat/anxiety.htm

—— (2001) 'The Loves of Plants and Animals: Romantic Science and the Pleasures of Nature', in James McKusick (ed.) *Romantic Circles Praxis Series, November 2001: Romanticism and Ecology*, online at www.rc.umd.edu/praxis/ecology/nichols/nichols.html

Nicolson, M. (1956) *Science and Imagination*, Ithaca, NY: Great Seal Books.

Niemeyer, M. (1999) 'Manifest Destiny and Melville's *Moby-Dick*', *Q/W/E/R/T/Y*, 9: 301–11.

Nordeau, M. (2000 [1895]) 'Degeneration: A Chapter in Darwinism', in S. Ledger and R. Luckhurst (eds), *The Fin De Siècle: A Reader in Cultural History, C. 1880–1900*, Oxford: Oxford University Press.

Norris, M. (1985) *Beasts of the Modern Imagination: Darwin, Nietzsche, Kafka, Ernst, and Lawrence*, Baltimore: Johns Hopkins University Press.

Noske, B. (1997) *Beyond Boundaries: Humans and Animals*, Montreal, New York and London: Black Rose Books.

Novak, M. E. (1972) 'The Wild Man Comes to Tea', in E. Dudley and M. E. Novak (eds), *The Wild Man Within*, Pittsburgh: University of Pittsburgh Press.

—— (1974) 'Imaginary Islands and Real Beasts: The Imaginative Genesis of *Robinson Crusoe*', *Tennessee Studies in Literature*, 19, 57–78.

Nyman, J. (2003) *Postcolonial Animal Tale from Kipling to Coetzee*, New Delhi: Atlantic Publishers and Distributors.

Nyman, J. and Smith, C. (eds) (2004) *Animal Magic: Essays on Animals in the American Imagination*, Joensuu, Finland: Faculty of Humanities, University of Joensuu.

Oakleaf, D. (1983) '*Trompe l'Oeil*: Gulliver and the Distortions of the Observing Eye', *University of Toronto Quarterly*, 53, 1: 166–80.

Oerlemans, O. D. (1994) '"The Meanest Thing That Feels": Anthropomorphizing Animals in Romanticism', *Mosaic*, 27, 1: 1–32.

—— (2007) 'A Defense of Anthropomorphism: Comparing Coetzee and Gowdy', *Mosaic*, 40, 1: 181–96.

Olmsted, F. A. (1969 [1841]) *Incidents of a Whaling Voyage*, Rutland, VT: Charles E. Tuttle & Co.

Olson, C. (1947) *Call Me Ishmael*, New York: Grove.

O'Rourke, J. (1989) '"Nothing More Unnatural": Mary Shelley's Revision of Rousseau', *ELH*, 56, 3: 543–69.

Ortega y Gasset, J. (1972 [1947]) *Meditations on Hunting*, trans. H. B. Wescott, New York: Charles Scribner's Sons.

Parrinder, P. (1995) *Shadows of the Future: H. G. Wells, Science Fiction, and Prophecy*, Syracuse, NY: Syracuse University Press.

Patey, D. L. (1991) 'Swift's Satire on "Science" and the Structure of *Gulliver's Travels*', *ELH*, 58: 809–39.

Patterson, C. (2002) *Eternal Treblinka: The Holocaust and Our Treatment of Animals*, New York: Lantern.

Perkins, D. (2003) *Romanticism and Animal Rights*, Cambridge, UK and New York: Cambridge University Press.

Phiddian, R. (1998) 'A Hopeless Project: Gulliver inside the Language of Science in Book III', *Eighteenth Century Life*, 22, 1: 50–62.

Philmus, R. M. (1981) 'The Satirical Ambivalence of *The Island of Doctor Moreau*', *Science Fiction Studies*, 8, 2–11.

Philmus, R. M. and Hughes, D. Y. (eds) (1975) *H. G. Wells: Early Writings in Science and Science Fiction*, Berkeley: University of California Press.

Philo, C. and Wilbert, C. (eds) (2000) *Animal Spaces, Beastly Places: New Geographies of Human–Animal Relations*, London and New York: Routledge.

Plumwood, V. (1993) *Feminism and the Mastery of Nature*, London: Routledge.

Pooley, E. (1986) 'Papa's New Baby, How Scribner's Crafted a New Hemingway Novel', *New York Magazine*, 28 April: 50–59.

Pope, A. and Arbuthnot, J. (2002 [1714]) *Memoirs of the Extraordinary Life, Works and Discoveries of Martinus Scriblerus*, London: Hesperus.

Pratt, M. L. (1992) *Imperial Eyes: Travel Writing and Transculturation*, London: Routledge.

Premack, D. (1976) *Intelligence in Ape and Man*, New York: L. Erlbaum Associates.

Quinn, D. (1995) *Ishmael*, New York: Bantam.

Rawson, C. (2001) *God, Gulliver, and Genocide: Barbarism and the European Imagination, 1492–1945*, Oxford: Oxford University Press.

Reynolds, J. N. (2002 [1839]) 'Mocha-Dick; or, the White Whale of the Pacific', in H. Parker and H. Hayford (eds), *Moby Dick*, New York: Norton.

Ritvo, H. (1987) *The Animal Estate: The English and Other Creatures in the Victorian Age*, Cambridge, MA: Harvard University Press.

—— (1998) *The Platypus and the Mermaid, and Other Figments of the Classifying Imagination*, Cambridge, MA: Harvard University Press.

Rogers, W. (1994 [1712]) 'From *A Cruising Voyage around the World*', in M. Shinagel (ed.), *Robinson Crusoe*, New York: Norton.

Rogin, M. P. (1985) *Subversive Genealogy: The Politics and Art of Herman Melville*, New York: Knopf.

Rohman, C. (2005) 'Burning out the Animal: The Failure of Enlightenment Purification in H. G. Wells's *The Island of Dr. Moreau*', in M. S. Pollock and C. Rainwater (eds), *Figuring Animals*, New York: Palgrave.

Roman, J. (2006) *Whale*, London: Reaktion.

Roszak, T. (1995) *The Memoirs of Elizabeth Frankenstein*, New York: Random House.

Rowe, S. (2006) '"Listen to Me": *Frankenstein* as an Appeal to Mercy and Justice, on Behalf of the Persecuted Animals', in F. Palmeri (ed.), *Humans and Other Animals in Eighteenth-Century British Culture*, Aldershot: Ashgate.

Rowse, A. L. (2000) 'The Enthusiastic Reception of *Gulliver's Travels*', in G. Weiner (ed.), *Readings on Gulliver's Travels*, San Diego: Greenhaven Press.

Rumbaugh, D. M. & Gill, T. V. (1976) 'The Mastery of Language-Type Skills by the Chimpanzee (Pan)', *Annals of the New York Academy of Science*, 280: 574–5.

Sabloff, A. (2001) *Reordering the Natural World: Humans and Animals in the City*, Toronto: University of Toronto Press.

St Clair, W. (2000) 'The Impact of *Frankenstein*', in B. T. Bennett and S. Curran (eds), *Mary Shelley in Her Times*, Baltimore, MD: Johns Hopkins University Press.

Sawtell, C. C. (1962) *The Ship Ann Alexander of New Bedford, 1805–1851*, Mystic, Conn.: Marine Historical Association.

Scholtmeijer, M. L. (1993) *Animal Victims in Modern Fiction*, Toronto: University of Toronto Press.

Schultz, E. (2000) 'Melville's Environmental Vision in *Moby-Dick*', *Interdisciplinary Studies in Literature and Environment*, 7, 1: 97–113.

Scoresby, W. (1823) *Journal of a Voyage to the Northern Whale-Fishery*, Edinburgh: Archibald Constable and Co.

Scully, M. (2002) *Dominion*, New York: St Martin's Press.

Self, W. (1997) *Great Apes*, New York: Grove Press.

Serpell, J. (1996) *In the Company of Animals: A Study of Human–Animal Relationships*, Cambridge: Cambridge University Press.

Serpell, J. and Paul, E. (1994) 'Pets and the Development of Positive Attitudes to Animals', in A. Manning and J. Serpell (eds), *Animals and Human Society*, London and New York: Routledge.

Shelley, M. (1996 [1818]) *Frankenstein*, New York: Norton.

—— (1996 [1831]) 'Introduction to *Frankenstein*, Third Edition (1831)', in J. P. Hunter (ed.), *Frankenstein*, New York: Norton.

Shugg, W. (1968) 'The Cartesian Beast-Machine in English Literature (1663–1750)', *Journal of the History of Ideas*, 29, 2: 279–92.

Siebert, C. (2006) 'An Elephant Crackup?' *New York Times Magazine*, 8 October.

Simons, J. (2002) *Animal Rights and the Politics of Literary Representation*, Houndmills: Palgrave.

Sinclair, U. (1906) *The Jungle*, London: T. Werner Laurie Ltd.

Sloan, P. (1995) 'The Gaze of Natural History', in C. Fox *et al.* (eds), *Inventing Human Science: Eighteenth Century Domains*, Berkeley: University of California Press.

Souhami, D. (2001) *Selkirk's Island*, London: Weidenfield & Nicolson.

Sprat, T. (1959 [1667]) *History of the Royal Society*, London: Routledge & Kegan Paul.

Starbuck, A. (1989 [1882]) *History of the American Whale Fishery*, Secaucus, NJ: Castle.

Staud, J. (1992) '"What's in a Name?": The *Pequod* and Melville's Heretical Politics', *ESQ*, 48, 4: 339–59.

Steele, R. (1994 [1713]) 'Alexander Selkirk', in M. Shinagel (ed.), *Robinson Crusoe*, New York: Norton.

Stover, L. E. (1996) 'Editor's Introduction', in *H. G. Wells: The Island of Doctor Moreau*, Jefferson, NC: McFarland & Company.

Swan, J. A. (1995) *In Defense of Hunting*, San Francisco: Harper.

Swift, J. (1969 [1729]) *A Modest Proposal*, Columbus, Ohio: C. E. Merrill Pub. Co.

—— (2002 [1726]) *Gulliver's Travels*, New York: Norton.

Taylor, D. (dir.) (1977) *The Island of Doctor Moreau*, Cinema 77: AIP.

Thomas, K. (1984) *Man and the Natural World: Changing Attitudes in England 1500–1800*, Harmondsworth: Penguin.

Tiffin, H. (2001) 'Unjust Relations: Animals, the Species Boundary and Post Colonialism', in G. Ratcliffe and G. Turcotte (eds), *Compr(om)ising Post/Colonialism(s): Challenging Narratives and Practices*, Sydney: Dangaroo.

—— (2005) 'Re-Imagining Communities', unpublished paper, Queen's University, Kingston, Canada.

—— (2007a) 'Foot in Mouth: Animals, Disease, and the Cannibal Complex', *Mosaic*, 40, 1: 11–26.

—— (2007b) 'Pigs, People and Pigoons', in L. Simmons and P. Armstrong (eds), *Knowing Animals*, Leiden and Boston: Brill.

Turner, J. (1980) *Reckoning with the Beast: Animals, Pain, and Humanity in the Victorian Mind*, Baltimore: Johns Hopkins University Press.

Turney, J. (1998) *Frankenstein's Footsteps: Science, Genetics and Popular Culture*, New Haven: Yale University Press.

Vincent, H. P. (1949) *The Trying-out of Moby-Dick*, Cambridge, MA: Riverside Press.

Voeller, C. (2005) '"He Only Looked Sad the Same Way I Felt": The Textual Confessions of Hemingway's Hunters', *The Hemingway Review*, 25, 1: 63–76.

Wagner, P. (1995) *Reading Iconotexts: From Swift to the French Revolution*, London: Reaktion.

Wallace, J. (2005) *D. H. Lawrence, Science, and the Posthuman*, Basingstoke, England: Palgrave Macmillan.

Watt, I. P. (1972) *The Rise of the Novel: Studies in Defoe, Richardson and Fielding*, Harmondsworth: Penguin.

Wedde, I. (2007) 'Walking the Dog', in L. Simmons and P. Armstrong (eds), *Knowing Animals*, Leiden and Boston: Brill.

Weiner, G. (2000) 'Jonathan Swift: A Biography', in G. Weiner (ed.), *Readings on Gulliver's Travels*, San Diego: Greenhaven Press.

Wells, H. G. (1902) *Anticipations of the Reaction of Mechanical and Scientific Progress Upon Human Life and Thought*, London: Methuen & Co.

—— (1927 [1905]) 'The Empire of the Ants', *The Complete Short Stories*, London: Ernest Benn.

—— (1933) 'Preface', in H.G. Wells (ed.), *The Scientific Romances of H.G. Wells*, London: Victor Gollancz.

—— (1996 [1896]) *The Island of Doctor Moreau*, Jefferson, NC: McFarland & Company.

—— (2001 [1895]) *The Time Machine*, Peterborough, Ont.: Broadview.

—— (2003 [1898]) *The War of the Worlds*, Peterborough, Ont.: Broadview.

White, P. S. (2005) 'The Experimental Animal in Victorian Britain', in L. Daston and G. Mitman (eds), *Thinking with Animals*, New York: Columbia University Press.

Wilkes, C. (1845) *Narrative of the United States Exploring Expedition During the Years 1838, 1839, 1840, 1841, 1842*, Philadelphia: Lea & Blanchard.

Williams, K. M. (1951) 'Gulliver's Voyage to the Houyhnhnms', *ELH*, 18, 4: 275–86.

Williams, R. (1977) *Marxism and Literature*, Oxford: Oxford University Press.

Williams, R. (2001) *2007*, Sydney: Hodder.

Wilson, E. (2000) 'Melville, Darwin, and the Great Chain of Being: Herman Melville's Influence on Charles Darwin's Theory of Evolution', *Studies in American Fiction*, 28, 2: 131–50.

Wilt, J. (2003) 'Introduction', in J. Wilt (ed.), *Making Humans: Mary Shelley, Frankenstein; H. G. Wells, the Island of Doctor Moreau*, Boston: Houghton Mifflin.

Wintle, S. (1994) 'If Houyhnhnms Were Horses: Thinking with Animals in Book IV of *Gulliver's Travels*', *The Critical Review*, 34: 3–21.

Wiseman, S. (1999) 'Monstrous Perfectability: Ape-Human Transformations in Hobbes, Bulwer, Tyson', in E. Fudge *et al.* (eds), *At the Borders of the Human*, Basingstoke: Macmillan.

Wixon, R. L. (1986) 'Herman Melville: Critic of America and Harbinger of Ecological Crisis', in P. A. Carlson (ed.), *Literature and the Lore of the Sea*, Amsterdam: Rodopi.

Wolch, J. (1998) 'Zoöpolis', in J. Wolch and J. Emel (eds), *Animal Geographies*, London and New York: Verso.

Wolfe, C. (2003) *Animal Rites: American Culture, the Discourse of Species and Posthumanist Theory*, Chicago: University of Chicago Press.

Woolf, V. (1933) *Flush: A Biography*, London: Hogarth.

Young, N. (1970) 'After the Goldrush', Reprise Records.

Zimmerman, R. (1998) *Genesis: The Story of Apollo 8*, New York: Four Walls Eight Windows.

Zoellner, R. (1973) *The Salt-Sea Mastodon: A Reading of Moby-Dick*, Berkeley: University of California Press.

Index

Abernathy, John 71, 73
abstractionism 9–10, 24–5, 56–8, 61,
    66, 83–4, 91, 147–50, 159, 183,
    185–6, 191, 194, 205–7, 211,
    221–2
acclimatization societies 30, 96
Actor Network Theory 123; *see also*
    agency, networks of; Latour,
    Bruno
Adams, Carol 137
Adorno, Theodore 64, 181–2
Agamben, Giorgio 6, 55–6, 68, 228n2
agency, 2– 3, 6, 17, 32, 35–6, 38, 44,
    48, 51, 75–6, 94–5, 97–8, 101–3,
    113–26, 132–3, 136, 139, 145–6,
    157–60, 171–2, 175, 189, 193–9,
    218, 233n16; networks of 16, 98,
    119–27, 159–61, 191, 196, 198,
    211
agriculture, 8, 27–30, 33, 35–6, 41,
    43, 45, 59, 74–5, 80, 90, 94, 100,
    110, 139–41, 171, 178, 180–1,
    188, 193, 234n20
Akeley, Carl, 201–2, 209
Alex (parrot) 192, 233n17
allegory, 101–2, 120, 222
Allen, Mary, 161
animal advocacy movements 188,
    233n11
animal shelter 179–81
animality, 2, 5–6, 10–11, 13, 15–16,
    20–2, 25, 27, 32–3, 55–6, 70,
    74–5, 78, 81–4, 87, 90, 96–8,
    104, 134, 138–9, 142–5, 148–54,
    160, 168, 200, 211, 219, 225
animals: as machines 7, 8, 11, 17–18,
    33–34, 50, 55, 57, 136–7, 144,

190, 207, 216–19, 227n4;
    capacity for feelings in 18, 43,
    57, 104, 140, 214, 220; cognitive
    abilities of 17–20, 39, 40, 98,
    113, 117–21, 158–60, 163–4,
    194, 201–20; consciousness in 3,
    9, 21, 22, 82, 86, 103, 197;
    culture amongst 126, 212, 214;
    herds, packs and flocks of 16,
    82, 98, 160, 196, 211;
    intelligence in 7, 104, 113–19,
    194, 201–20; intentionality in 3,
    17, 35, 98, 102–3, 115–22, 194,
    197, 204; sense of history
    amongst 163–4, 168–9, 211–14;
    tool use amongst 55, 78, 98, 210
ant 50, 98, 160
anthropocentrism 2–3, 6, 50, 54, 121,
    157, 186, 190, 196, 222
anthropoluotic animality 11, 68, 210,
    220, 227n7, 228n2; *see also*
    anthropopophorous animality
anthropomorphism 3, 10, 12, 16,
    20–1, 35, 43–4, 104–9, 114, 119,
    122, 126–9, 133, 140, 149, 157,
    166–8, 196–7, 207, 211, 223,
    231n14; see also zoomorphism
anthropopophorous animality 6, 11,
    227n7
ape 20, 54–7, 68, 78–80, 83, 85, 87,
    95, 172–6, 180–4, 187, 190,
    196–9, 200–24, 227n4
Aravamudan, Srinavas 26, 226n3
assembly line 135–7, 141, 172
Atwood, Margaret, *Oryx and Crake*,
    172–3, 181, 186, 189, 192, 193,
    194, 195, 199–200, 209

Ausband, Stephen 102
avian influenza 180

baboon 52, 180, 189, 195, 211–13,
    231–2n2
Bacon, Sir Francis 137, 205, 226n1;
    New Atlantis, 64, 228–9n9
Baker, Steve 2, 16, 190, 225–6
Bambi 225
Barrett Browning, Elizabeth 166
Bate, Jonathan 2, 62
Beale, Thomas 105, 107, 115–17,
    131, 135
bear 9, 11, 14–15, 32, 43–4, 69, 87,
    181, 189, 220
beaver 59, 193
bee 50, 160
behavioural psychology 216–17,
    221
Bell, Michael 165
Bennett, Frederick 115–16, 131
Berger, John 1, 39, 41–2, 45, 138,
    141, 143, 225
Bernard, Claude 91–2
biocentrism 144, 145, 199
biodiversity 102, 104, 174, 177, 197
birdsong 64–5, 68, 70
Birke, Lynda 218
bloodsports 153, 156–7
Boullé, Pierre, *La Planète des Singes*
    213, 218
Bradshaw, Gay 163–4
Brodhead, Richard 112
Brophy, Brigid, *Hackenfeller's Ape*
    187–8, 196–9, 206, 220
Brown, Laura 20
Browne, J. Ross 100, 107–8, 119
buffalo 59, 163
Buffon, Louis de 35, 53
bullfight 148, 150–3, 157–8, 162, 166
Burt, Jonathan 3, 226
Butler, Marilyn 71, 72

Canetti, Elias 97–8
cannibalism 10, 15, 22–31, 81, 88,
    133, 211, 227n12
capitalism 1–2, 27, 32–3, 38–9, 42,
    46, 88, 98, 115, 119, 125, 130,
    144, 153, 179–81, 186, 218;
    commodity 5, 26, 28, 46–7, 61,

77, 97, 100, 111–12, 175, 179,
    189; industrial 99, 104, 107–8,
    110, 118, 125–6, 129–34, 137–8,
    141, 165, 171, 191; investment
    27–31, 59, 60, 77, 132, 176;
    mercantile 32–3, 99
carnivorousness 88–90, 98, 229n22
Carson, Rachel, *Silent Spring* 171
Casarino, Cesare 99, 101
castration 25, 36, 37, 47, 148–9,
    189
cat 12, 16, 34–7, 40, 44, 76, 98, 162,
    172, 180, 182, 187, 189, 197–8,
    202, 223–4
Cavalieri, Paola 201, 213–15
Chain of Being 6, 88, 100
Chantek (orang-utan), 205
Chase, Owen 117–18
Cheever, Henry 100, 104, 108
chicken 161, 180
chimpanzee 54–5, 175, 201–220,
    227n4, 234n20
Chimpsky, Nim (chimpanzee) 205
Christianity 6, 17, 100, 107–8,
    114–15, 183, 186, 190
circus 12, 43–45, 179, 189, 202
Clark, Nigel 35
clothing 5, 9, 13–15, 33, 56, 59, 78,
    112, 145, 209
Coetzee, J.M., *Disgrace* 179–86, 199,
    220–23, 225; *Elizabeth Costello*
    149–50, 188, 191–2, 201–3, 208,
    221–2, 225, 234n24
Collins, Wilkie, *Heart and Science*
    91
colonialism 2, 8, 26–38, 50–2, 59–62,
    86, 96, 151–2, 179–80, 201, 220,
    229n20
commodification 29, 39, 52, 59, 60–1,
    136, 138, 153, 164, 169, 175,
    180, 202
Corbey, Raymond 201
Cowper, William, 'The Task' 108,
    230n6
cow 5, 27, 29, 36, 60, 128, 139, 171,
    174, 176, 178, 193
Creed, Barbara 200
Crist, Elaine 127
crocodile 189, 193
Crosby, Alfred 33, 34, 76, 226

Dampier, William 5, 13
Darwin, Charles 73, 83–6, 94, 98,
    103, 142, 144, 194
Darwin, Erasmus 68, 70, 73–4
David Greybeard (chimpanzee) 210
DeBlois, John 131
De Grave 140, 141
de Waal, Frans 126
deer 115, 148
Defoe, Daniel, *Compleat English
    Tradesman* 60–1; *Review* 17, 44;
    Robinson Crusoe 4–5, 11–62, 76,
    79, 98, 108, 136, 139, 161,
    170–9, 181, 187, 189, 192, 195,
    218, 226n2; *Tour Through the
    Whole Island of Great Britain* 29
degeneracy 32, 36, 86, 89, 92, 97,
    142, 148
Deleuze, Gilles 16, 233n13
Derrida, Jacques 11, 90, 186,
    229n22
Descartes, René 6–13, 17–18, 20,
    35–9, 43, 49, 50–7, 63–4, 137,
    144, 191, 205, 216, 218, 220–1,
    226n1, 227n4
Desmond, Adrian 204–8, 211–12
Digit (gorilla) 209
dog 5, 12, 16–18, 22, 28, 35, 40–5,
    58–9, 63, 70, 77, 82, 91, 94, 97,
    109, 147, 162, 165–8, 172,
    179–80, 184–6, 189, 193, 197,
    221, 223, 225, 228n17, 228n4
domestication 5, 12, 16, 35, 37, 41–5,
    88, 94, 109, 115, 134, 139,
    145–7, 178, 189, 227n9
dominion 6, 12, 14, 22, 27, 30, 32,
    38, 44, 96, 184, 224
donkey 10, 11
Douglas, Ann 128–9
du Chaillu, Paul 201

ecocriticism 101–2, 109
elephant 59, 91, 163–9, 172, 174,
    176, 181, 198
emotion 2–3, 12, 31, 38, 40, 62–6, 79,
    88–9, 92, 129, 132, 134, 150,
    153, 157, 165, 183–7, 198, 204,
    206, 221–4
enclosure 28–30, 136, 161, 170,
    177–8, 181, 195

Enlightenment 2–3, 5, 7, 10–13,
    17–18, 23–7, 30, 37–8, 49–54,
    57, 60, 62, 66, 77, 92, 97–8, 108,
    123, 125–6, 165, 182, 220,
    226n1
environment, treatment of 2, 28,
    33–5, 72, 100–2, 161, 163,
    169–77, 181, 187, 191, 193, 195,
    198, 213, 234n20
environmentalism 102–4, 162–3,
    171–7, 191, 200, 221, 225
Essex sinking 117–19
euthanasia 179, 185–6
evolution 30–1, 73, 81–90, 94–8, 100,
    114–15, 135, 139, 141–4, 154,
    163, 216, 219, 230n25
evolutionary psychology 88, 194,
    217–18
experimentalism 6, 28, 49–50, 57,
    59–3, 69–80, 93–4, 138, 159,
    170, 181–3, 200, 202, 205–9, 214

family 12–13, 16, 18, 39, 130, 215,
    218
femininity 10, 93–5, 100, 128–34,
    165, 198–200, 209–10, 213, 217
ferity 16–17, 34–8, 44, 76, 94–5,
    134–7, 148, 157, 172, 181,
    189–200, 209, 227n9
Findley, Timothy, *Not Wanted on the
    Voyage* 173–4, 180–5, 187, 189,
    191, 193, 195, 197–9, 209,
    220–1, 223–5
firearms 16, 30–2, 38, 40, 43, 152,
    154, 203
Fisher, Philip 167, 223–4
Flynn, Carol Houlihan 26–7, 31,
    38–9
Foot and Mouth disease 180
Ford, Henry 137, 188
Fossey, Dian 209–10, 219
Foucault, Michel 137
Fouts, Roger 208, 215
fox 22, 160, 171, 185, 198
Fox, Christopher 51
Fox, Matthew 175
Frankenstein's Creature 19–20, 25,
    31, 34, 41, 45, 52, 57–8, 62–79,
    170, 181, 199, 222
Frazer, Sir James 143

Freud, Sigmund 88, 97, 142–3, 216
frog 95, 173, 187, 222
Fudge, Erica 1–2, 11, 141, 225
Fulford, Tim 63, 71
fur 13–15

Galdikas, Biruté 209–10, 219, 233n19
Galton, Francis 86
Gardener, R. Allen and Beatrice 205–6
genetic engineering 59, 76, 188, 193, 195
genocide 25, 86, 226n3
giraffe 177, 216
globalization 1–4, 8, 33, 52, 60, 99, 125, 179, 180–1, 200
goat 5, 13–16, 21–2, 28–9, 31–4, 37–45, 59, 87, 161, 173, 182, 185
Goodall, Jane 209–16, 219, 234n20
gorilla 85, 88, 90, 190, 200–1, 205, 209, 213–14
Gowdy, Barbara, *The White Bone* 164, 176
The Great Ape Project 201, 213–15, 220, 234n22
Gua (chimpanzee) 204, 207, 209

Hagenbeck, Carl 202–3
Haraway, Donna 2, 33, 125, 127, 187, 201, 204, 209–10, 216–18
Hardy, Thomas, *Jude the Obscure* 180
hare 22, 70, 194
Hart, Joseph, *Miriam Coffin* 100, 132
Hawes, Clement 10, 26, 46, 52
Heimert, Alan 101–2
Hemingway, Ernest 134, 150–72, 201; *A Farewell to Arms* 161; *Death in the Afternoon* 151, 157–8, 162, 166; *For Whom the Bell Tolls* 161; *The Garden of Eden* 164–9; *The Green Hills of Africa* 151–4, 162; *The Old Man and the Sea* 154–7, 162; *The Sun Also Rises* 150, 153, 167
hippopotamus 174, 198
Høeg, Peter, *The Woman and the Ape* 175–7, 190–1, 203, 213
Holocaust 187–8, 233n11

Hooke, Robert 58, 63, 228n4
Horkheimer, Max 64, 181–2
horse 5, 7–9, 12, 16, 20, 25, 28, 36–7, 42, 47, 54, 59, 61, 74, 115, 145–51, 161, 166–7, 232n6
Hughes, Ted 150
Hulme, Peter 7, 50, 226
humane disposition 26, 42, 69, 92, 97, 107, 109, 148, 227n10
humanism 3, 16–17, 25, 68, 71, 83, 119, 121, 123, 125, 168, 178, 186, 196–7, 212, 215, 229n22
humanity, concept of 1, 2, 6, 9–27, 32, 37, 54–5, 63, 67–70, 79–82, 87–90, 94, 97, 101, 127, 138, 142–4, 149, 154, 172, 179, 187, 203–5, 210, 213, 219
hunting 11, 16, 22, 27–8, 30, 40–2, 59, 68–9, 81, 106, 108, 134–5, 150–66, 175, 187, 194, 201, 209, 212, 218
Huxley, Aldous, *Ape and Essence* 231–2n2, 234n21
hybridity 73–83, 87, 89, 93–4, 125, 182–3, 193, 200, 224

imperialism 2, 22–9, 33, 62, 76–7, 99, 106, 143, 175, 179
individualism 13, 16, 40, 63, 98, 139, 153, 195, 196
industrialization 1, 29, 33, 42, 72, 75, 77, 97, 99, 100, 102–3, 112, 124–5, 128, 135–6, 141–2, 144, 146, 148, 151, 156, 170, 180, 188, 231n2
inhumanity 23–7, 37, 68, 70, 80, 147, 218, 227n12
insect 24, 98, 173, 189, 191–2
instinct 17, 37, 81, 83, 86, 88–9, 97, 103, 114, 119, 124, 126, 142–3, 158, 160, 166, 195, 198, 203, 215–19, 221
instrumentalism 13, 24–6, 38–9, 57, 60, 63, 69, 91, 95, 136, 144, 147–8, 159, 186, 189, 194, 202–5, 207, 215, 227n8, 231n2
internment camp 180–1, 187

Jackson, Peter 200
jaguar 150, 175, 191

Jordanova, Ludmilla 7, 50, 226
Juan Fernandez Islands 5, 13, 33–4

Kac, Eduardo 'GFP Bunny' 193
Kafka, Franz, 'Report to an Academy' 202–4, 213, 220
Kanzi (bonobo) 205
Kellogg, Winthrop and Luella 204–5, 207, 209
Kemp, Peter 88, 98
King Kong 200–1
King, Thomas, *Green Grass, Running Water* 199
Köhler, Wolfgang 201–3, 205, 221
Koko (gorilla) 205, 213, 214
Kotzwinkle, William, *Doctor Rat* 172

laboratory 49, 57, 66, 76–7, 82, 84, 89, 91, 94–5, 172, 181–3, 187, 190, 192–5, 202, 209, 213
lamb 45, 110, 183–6
Lamb, Jonathan 37–8, 46–7, 221
Lana (chimpanzee) 205–8
language 8, 12, 16–18, 20, 22, 40, 72, 79, 123, 161, 185, 192, 204–10, 213–14, 224
Lansbury, Coral 91, 93, 183, 225
Latour, Bruno 76, 120, 123–7, 18–3, 191–2, 195
Lawrence, D.H. 134, 144–5,163, 166–70, 199; *Kangaroo* 160–1, 232n6; *The Plumed Serpent* 145, 151, 166, 199; *The Rainbow* 144–5, 159, 199, 232n6; *St. Mawr* 145–9, 161, 169, 191, 199; *The Symbolic Meaning* 160; *The White Peacock* 232n7; *Women in Love* 166
Lawrence, William 71, 73
Leakey, Louis 209–10, 215
leopard 30, 31, 82, 83, 89, 95–5, 148, 163, 189
Lévi-Strauss, Claude 2
Lewis, Wyndham 143
lice 50–1, 98
Liggins, Emma 91
Lilliput effect 97–8
Limits to Growth 171
line of flight 190, 197, 233n13

Linnaeus 53, 55–6, 68, 111, 126, 215, 228n2
lion 23, 30–2, 148, 163, 170, 190
Lippit, Akira Mizuta 142–3
Locke, John 10–11, 18, 20–1, 226n1
Lorenz, Konrad 216
Love, Glen 153, 156, 162, 164
Lucy (chimpanzee) 205, 234n21

Mackenzie, Jock 228n17
Malamud, Bernard, *God's Grace* 173, 181–4, 187, 191, 195, 206–7, 210–13, 220
Malamud, Randy 174–5, 177
'Man the Hunter' hypothesis 217–18
marlin 151, 155–9
Marshall, David 63–4, 67–8, 71
Martel, Yann 179; *Life of Pi* 176–81, 189, 216–18
Martin, Valerie 174
marxist theory 1, 138, 142, 144
Marx, Karl 137, 141
Marx, Leo 101–2
Marzec, Robert 28, 29
masculinity 69, 88–90, 128–32, 147, 151, 153, 165, 198, 209, 217, 229n22
material body 6–11, 15, 20–1, 36, 40, 50, 56–8, 71, 73, 86, 90, 94, 98, 107, 111, 120–4, 127, 137, 140, 147, 155, 158, 160, 185, 203, 216, 222
McLane, Maureen 67–8, 71, 75–6
meat 13, 26, 31, 33, 60, 74, 82, 88–90, 95, 100, 110, 135, 138, 140, 172, 178, 184; meatpacking industry 135–41, 188
medicine 91–3, 186
Melville, Herman 103, 117; *Moby-Dick* 4, 98–133, 134–6, 154–6, 158–60, 169, 170, 196, 199
metamorphosis 21, 28, 92
microbes 74, 76, 95, 97–8, 192, 193
microscope 50–1, 63, 97, 144
mimicry 18–20, 56, 79, 203
Mirzoeff, Nicholas 180–1, 188
misanthropy 24, 46–7, 80
Mocha Dick (whale) 116–19, 124, 131

modernism 4, 93, 97, 133–70, 189, 191, 200–1, 220–1, 223–4, 231–2n2
modernity 1–2, 4–5, 7, 11, 19, 22, 24–38, 41, 44, 48–9, 57, 61, 64, 76–7, 80, 92–3, 96–8, 101, 103, 119, 122–7, 133–7, 141–9, 151, 154, 156, 159, 162–3, 169–73, 176, 178–9, 181, 185, 187–95, 200–4, 209–10, 219, 221, 225, 227n9, 229n22
monkey 5, 21, 45, 52, 55–6, 78–9, 80, 206, 212
monstrosity 93–4, 125
Moore, Christopher, *Fluke* 199
mouse 53, 173, 193
mustelid 96, 195

nakedness 14–15, 56, 209
natural history 30, 51–4, 68, 71, 78, 81, 88, 100, 111, 114–15, 126, 128, 131, 163, 225
nature (conceived as distinct from human society) 7, 102–3, 105, , 114, 122–30, 138–9, 143–6, 153, 156, 162–3, 170–81, 189–92
Nazism 86, 188
'New Science' 7–8, 49–54, 57, 63–4, 77, 137, 226n4
Nichols, Ashton 68, 74–5
Nicolson, Marjorie 50, 57, 59
Noah's Ark 173–4, 180–4, 191, 193, 198, 223–4
Nordeau, Max 87, 89, 92
Norris, Margot 142, 144, 154, 157–8
Noske, Barbara 138, 164, 219
Nyman, Jopi 185, 226

Olson, Charles 101, 112
orang-utan 208–10, 213, 227n4, 233n19
Ortega y Gasset, José 154, 163
ostrich 59, 189
ox 23, 26, 87, 115

parrot 5, 12, 16–21, 38–40, 44, 56, 79, 192, 197; *see also* Alex (parrot)
Patterson, Charles 188

Patterson, Penny 205, 213–14
pest 12, 34–5, 45, 76, 96, 148, 181, 189, 193; *see also* vermin
Peter the Wild Boy 23, 228n2
pet 5, 12–13, 18–19, 21, 34–35, 39, 41, 45–6, 56, 80, 95, 109, 178, 180–1, 189–90, 200, 224
Philo, Chris 3, 123
physiology 38, 62, 71, 78, 83, 91–3, 183, 216
pig 27, 29, 37, 41, 59–60, 87, 135–6, 139–40, 193, 231n2
pigeon 22, 74
Planet of the Apes 215; see also Boullé, Pierre
population control 25, 36, 37
porcupine 193, 198
postmodernity 2, 4, 76, 173, 176, 178, 192, 223
predation 16, 22,' 28, 33, 38, 82, 88–90, 139, 185, 190, 212, 218
Premack, David 205–8
primatology 200–4, 210, 213, 218, 220
primitivism 23–6, 30–1, 85, 97, 132, 134, 142–57, 164, 191, 201, 221; *see also* therio-primitivism
Princess (orang-utan) 210
psychoanalysis 88, 97, 142–3, 211, 216
puma 88, 94–5, 199, 230n27

Quinn, Daniel, *Ishmael* 213

rabbit 33, 37, 76, 82, 87, 89, 95–8, 185, 192–4
raccoon 189, 200
race 2, 55, 75, 85–6, 132–3, 212, 226n3
rat 34, 45, 60, 76, 98, 161, 172, 189, 192, 202, 233n16
rationality 1, 3–29, 36–7, 41, 50, 55–60, 67, 71, 75, 77, 79, 83–4, 88, 90, 102, 108–9, 115, 119, 121, 139, 144, 147, 159–60, 165, 178, 182, 189, 196–7, 202–5, 215, 219, 221
Rawson, Claude 10, 24–6, 31
Ray, John 18, 53–4
Reynolds, Jeremiah 100, 110, 116, 118–19, 124–5, 131, 135

rhinoceros 152–3, 163, 172, 174, 177
Ritvo, Harriet 30, 35, 43–4, 56, 74–5,
    84, 88, 90, 94, 106
Rogers, Woodes 13, 15–17, 21, 33–4
Rogin, Michael 101, 123
Rohman, Carrie 78, 81–2
Romanticism 62–6, 71, 73, 92, 97,
    125, 127, 134, 220–2
Roosevelt, Theodore 135, 201
Roszak, Theodore, *The Memoirs of
    Elizabeth Frankenstein* 181, 199,
    209
Rousseau, Jean-Jacques 63–4, 70,
    226n2
Royal Society 49–50, 52, 57–9, 228n4
RSPCA 92
Rumbaugh, Duane 205–8

Sabloff, Annabelle 137, 189, 218,
    224–5
sacrifice 183–6, 213, 224, 229n22
salmon 150, 191
Sarah (chimpanzee) 205–9
satire 8, 11, 15–16, 23, 25, 28, 36, 44,
    46, 48, 51, 57–8, 61, 78–81, 83,
    89, 107, 111, 171, 173, 183, 187,
    199, 206–7, 215, 217, 219, 220,
    226n3
Scholtmeijer, Marian 138–40, 216
Schultz, Elizabeth 102, 104, 107,
    109–10
science 2, 5–9, 27, 30, 38, 49–98,
    111–12, 115–21, 125–7, 141–2,
    144, 159, 170, 172, 178, 181–2,
    186–7, 191–4, 198, 200–6,
    209–10, 215, 218, 220, 224–5;
    empirical tradition 5, 50–7, 66,
    83, 92, 125; positivism 97, 126,
    134, 165, 205, 207, 220; *see also*
    medicine, natural history, New
    Science, physiology, taxonomy,
    zoology
Scoresby, William 108, 114, 116–17,
    230n9
Scriblerus 215, 226–7n4
Scully, Matthew 163
seal 181, 197
Self, Will, *Great Apes* 215–20
Selkirk, Alexander 5, 13, 15–17, 21,
    28, 33–4, 37, 87, 161

sentiment 12, 22, 37–8, 47, 64, 92–3,
    106–7, 110, 126, 134, 140, 150,
    165–7, 181, 220–5, 234n24
Serpell, James 223–4
sheep 23, 26–7, 29, 33, 42, 59–60,
    84–5, 88–90, 145, 148, 174, 182,
    184, 193, 224, 228n6
Shelley, Mary, *Frankenstein* 4, 57,
    61–77, 79, 81, 86, 91, 93–8,
    136–7, 144, 162, 170, 181–2,
    187, 189, 192, 194–5, 199,
    201–2, 221–2, 229n12, 230n9
Shelley, Percy 72
shoes 14–16
Shugg, Wallace 7, 18
Simons, John 3, 23, 101
Sinclair, Upton, *The Jungle* 133,
    135–42, 143, 144
Singer, Peter 213–15
skin 15, 31, 39
slaughterhouse 76, 140, 181, 187; *see
    also* meat; meatpacking industry
slavery 2, 5, 26, 30, 33, 42, 45, 101
Social Darwinism 86, 88
socialism 86, 98, 135, 139–40, 143, 218
sociobiology 88, 218, 234n22
space, organization of 3, 19, 29, 41–2,
    170, 174–81, 187–90, 195, 202,
    233n14
species extinction 104, 172, 174, 187,
    191
Starbuck, Alexander 104, 119
Steele, Richard 17
Stover, Leon 80, 83–4
structure of feeling 4, 29, 37–8, 104,
    134, 171, 177, 225
Sultan (chimpanzee) 201–2, 205, 208
Swift, Jonathan, *Gulliver's Travels*
    4–12, 15, 16, 18, 20–8, 36–9,
    44–63, 66–70, 76–83, 91–8,
    147–8, 162, 170, 173, 179, 184,
    187, 189, 194–5, 199, 202–3,
    211–17, 220, 226n2, 226n3,
    227n4, 228n1, 228n2; 'A Modest
    Proposal' 10, 27
sympathy 12, 16, 37–48, 60–70, 74–5,
    83, 92, 97, 104–10, 129, 134,
    139, 140, 150, 165–8, 18–5, 208,
    214, 220–4, 227n10, 234n23,
    234n24

taste, literary 197, 220, 225
taxonomy 34, 45, 52–7, 60, 67, 79,
    85, 93, 111–12, 187, 207
technology 7, 24–5, 27, 30–1, 51,
    71–7, 84, 94, 96, 100, 102, 118,
    122–4, 127, 129, 135, 138–44,
    148, 151, 154, 156, 171, 181,
    186–8, 199, 204, 207, 210,
    214–15, 218
Teleki, Geza 214–15
therio-primitivism 142–57, 163–69,
    200, 234n21
Thomas, Keith 2, 6–7, 13–14, 18, 28,
    37, 39, 42–3, 50–1, 54, 57, 59,
    60, 115, 126–7, 224, 230n6
Tiffin, Helen 183–4, 224, 227n10,
    233n4, 233n5
tiger 23, 87, 176–9, 189–90, 216,
    218
tourism 176, 179, 181, 232n9
turkey 26, 59
Turner, James 93, 107, 226
Tyson, Edward 18, 54–5, 215, 227n4

urbanization 1, 29, 41–5, 100, 136,
    151, 163, 170, 189–90

vegetarianism 69, 179, 194, 218
vermin 12, 34–6, 43, 50, 76, 98; *see
    also* pest
Vincent, Howard 107, 114, 128
vivisection 57–8, 60, 64, 69–70,
    76–82, 90–6, 135, 182, 184, 194,
    223, 228n4, 230n24

Wallace, Jeff 168
Washburn, Sherwood 217–18
Washoe (chimpanzee) 205, 215
wasp 39, 98, 193
Watt, Ian 32

Wells, H.G. 4, 69, 135, 139, 142, 143,
    144, 165, 184, 218; 'The Empire
    of the Ants' 98; *Island of Doctor
    Moreau* 57, 77–97, 136, 187,
    194–5, 199, 228n17; *A Text-Book
    of Biology* 91, 96; *The Time
    Machine* 88, 96; *War of the Worlds*
    95, 96
whale 4, 99–133, 134, 136, 160;
    'rogue' whale 115–17, 125, 131
whaling 99–133, 135, 136, 170, 171,
    230n1
Wilbert, Chris 3, 123
wildlife reserve 176, 181, 190
wildness 15, 134, 138, 142–3, 154,
    157, 161, 170, 172, 176–7, 181,
    189, 198, 200, 209; *see also*
    ferity
Wilkes, Charles 104, 126
Williams, Raymond 4, 171–2, 196
Williams, Robyn, *2007* 171–3, 181,
    187, 199
Wilson, E.O. 218
Wintle, Sarah 8, 47, 53
Wiseman, Susan 18, 54, 55, 227n4
wolf 32, 43–4, 87, 98, 138, 170, 181,
    189
Woolf, Virginia, *Flush: A Biography*
    166, 167
worm 70, 72, 73, 189

Yerkes, Robert 204, 210, 215
Young, Neil 172

Zoellner, Robert 102–7, 109, 114, 122
zoo 11, 171–81, 187, 190, 195–7,
    201–2, 205, 219
zoology 83, 128, 178, 216
zoomorphism 20–21, 127, 167, 195,
    197